STRANGE GODS

STRANGE GODS

A Secular History of Conversion

SUSAN JACOBY

PANTHEON BOOKS, NEW YORK

Grateful acknowledgment is made to ICS Publications for permission to reprint an excerpt from
Life in a Jewish Family by Edith Stein, translated by Josephine Koeppel, O.C.D., copyright © 1986
by Washington Province of Discalced Carmelites. Reprinted by permission of ICS Publications,
2131 Lincoln Road, N.E., Washington, D.C. 20002-1199 (www.icspublications.org).

Library of Congress Cataloging-in-Publication Data
Jacoby, Susan, [date]
Strange gods : a secular history of conversion / Susan Jacoby.
pages ; cm
Includes bibliographical references and index.
ISBN 978-0-375-42375-8 (hardcover : alk. paper). ISBN 978-1-101-87096-9 (eBook).
1. Conversion—History. I. Title.
BL639.J33 2016   204ʹ.2—dc23   2015019062

www.pantheonbooks.com

Jacket image: *The Conversion of St. Paul,* 1601, by Caravaggio.
Santa Maria del Popolo, Rome, Italy/Bridgeman Images
Jacket design by Kelly Blair

Printed in the United States of America
First Edition

2 4 6 8 9 7 5 3 1

For Rose Glennon

CONTENTS

A NOTE ON LANGUAGE

Readers will notice that I use the title "Saint," as designated by the Roman Catholic Church, only when not using it would create confusion. If, for example, I were to refer to Christopher, the patron saint of travelers in Catholic lore, and the late writer and atheist Christopher Hitchens in the same sentence (I actually cannot imagine how or why I would do that), I would apply the title "Saint" to the traveling Christopher to make it clear that Hitchens has not been posthumously canonized.

Sainthood is a specific, Roman Catholic concept, not accepted by most of the world's religions or by those who do not believe in any religion. Calling Augustine of Hippo "Saint Augustine" is a value judgment made by the Catholic Church, as is the sainthood of Edith Stein, the Jewish convert to Catholicism who entered the Discalced Carmelite Order, took the name Sister Teresa Benedicta of the Cross, was murdered at Auschwitz, and was canonized by Pope John Paul II. Readers may judge for themselves, after reading the writings of men and women like Augustine and Stein, whether they believe in saints as a special, elevated category mediating between God and humanity. In a book on the subject of religious conversion in the West, the honorific "saint" comes up more often than it normally would, because conversion itself was long considered an important step on the road to sainthood by the Catholic Church.

Throughout this book, I have used standard English transliterations of the names of important historical figures in the history of religious conversion. Garry Wills, in his brilliant short study *Augustine's Confessions,* transliterates the name of Augustine's mother, Monica, as "Monnica," but "Monica" is the more recognizable spelling.

I capitalize "God" because this is common English usage—though not when I am referring to a particular god among many, or to an individual's idea of a personal god—i.e., "My god is bigger than your god." Unlike Catholic saints, God is God with a capital "G" to most people who read and write English. Who am I to deprive Him or Her of a capital letter in the orthographic universe?

PROLOGUE

And Saul, yet breathing out threatenings and slaughter against the disciples of the Lord, went unto the high priest, And desired of him letters to Damascus and the synagogues, that if he found any of this way, whether they were men or women, he might bring them bound unto Jerusalem. And as he journeyed, he came near Damascus: and suddenly there shined round about him a light from heaven: And he fell to the earth, and heard a voice saying unto him, Saul, Saul, why persecutest thou me? . . .

And Saul arose from the earth; and when his eyes were opened, he saw no man: but they led him by the hand, and brought him into Damascus. And he was three days without sight, and neither did he eat nor drink. And there was a certain disciple at Damascus, named Ananias; and to him said the Lord in a vision, Ananias. And he said, Behold, I am here, Lord. . . .

And Ananias went his way, and entered into the house; and putting his hands on him said, Brother Saul, the Lord, even Jesus, that appeared unto thee in the way as thou camest, hath sent me, that thou mightest receive thy sight, and be filled with the Holy Ghost. And immediately there fell from his eyes as it had been scales: and he received sight forthwith, and arose, and was baptized.

—THE ACTS OF THE APOSTLES, CHAPTER 9, VERSES 1–4, 8–10, 17–18

I come from a family of religious converts, spanning three generations and more than a century on both my mother's and father's sides. My father was born in 1914 into a nonobservant Jewish family whose ancestors had immigrated to the United States from Germany in 1849 and settled in New York City. My Jacoby grandfather and grandmother did not convert to Christianity, but they did send their children to a Lutheran Sunday school in Brooklyn. Although my father and his siblings were never baptized in childhood and knew that their family was Jewish, they were taught nothing about Judaism as a religion. My father's uncle, Levi Harold Jacoby, professor of astronomy at Columbia University, and one of the few Jews (religious or nonreligious) on the faculty in the early twentieth century, married an Episcopalian and did convert, dropping his undeniably Jewish first name along the way. As an undergraduate at Columbia, he was listed as "Levi Harold" in official records, but by the time he became a member of the faculty, he was plain Harold. He was a frequent source for New York newspapers, trying to explain new scientific developments, such as Einstein's theory of relativity, to the reading public. In those articles, too, there was no trace of the Jewish first name his parents had given him.

My father and his elder brother and sister took another path in the middle of the twentieth century by marrying Irish American Catholics and converting to the Roman Catholic Church. My brother and I, as children in the Middle West in the 1950s, were told that my father had converted from the Episcopal Church—a handy falsehood possibly derived from the background of the cousins descended from Levi Harold (always referred to within my branch of the family as "the other Jacobys"). When I was growing up, I could not possibly have known that in the first half of the twentieth century, mainstream Protestantism was a much more common choice than Catholicism for American Jews wishing to conceal their origins, because Protestants occupied a higher social and economic rung than Catholics in the American class hierarchy.*

This book is titled *Strange Gods: A Secular History of Conversion* precisely because most histories and personal accounts of conversion have been written by believers in the supernatural, who understandably view changes of faith mainly in terms of their spiritual origins and significance. William James (1842–1910), in his extensive discussion of conversions in *The Varieties of Religious Experience,* presents a psychological exploration of the conversion experience that holds up well, for the most part, even though his famous lectures were delivered more than a century ago at the University of Edinburgh. The important exception is James's avoidance of external social influences on conversion. With his rare combination of medical and philosophical training, as an intellectual of the first generation exposed to both Darwin and Freud, James nevertheless viewed conversion almost entirely as an individual rather than as a social experience—and he never quite made up his own mind about what goes on in the minds of ardent converts. "Were we writing the story of the mind from the purely natural-history point of view," he acknowledged, "with no religious interest whatever, we should still have to write down man's liability to sudden and complete conversion as one of his most curious peculiarities." Then he observed, in a cagey fashion that stopped just short of contradicting his earlier statement, that such conversions often produce "an altogether new level of spiritual vitality, a relatively heroic level, in which impossible things have become possible, and new energies and endurances are shown." Through such conversions, James argued, "personality is changed, the man *is* born anew, whether or not his psychological idiosyncrasies are what give the particular shape to

---

* This story is told in greater detail in my 2000 memoir, *Half-Jew: A Daughter's Search for Her Family's Buried Past* (New York: Scribner), recently published as an eBook by Vintage Books.

his metamorphosis."* Translated from early medico-psychological language that had not yet evolved into modern psychobabble, what James seems to be saying is that a man who goes to bed believing in one god or no god at all and wakes up believing in a new form of divine truth may *be* mentally or emotionally unstable (or at least highly unusual) by ordinary standards, but the weirdness of the process can nevertheless lead to a positive personality transformation. This ambiguous attitude toward conversion reflects the inconsistencies in James's own form of religion, which involved the troublesome intellectual compromises required of a man who came of age as a liberal nineteenth-century Christian while trying to make room for a psychological explanation of emotional experience that did not fit comfortably into the realm of either faith or reason.

I would never deny that an intense emotional desire to believe in something true—to see "face to face," as Paul, Christianity's first great proselytizer, put it—motivates many conversions and plays an important role in their outcome. But so do other, more earthly needs and longings, which bear only a tangential relationship, if any, to what theologians and many philosophers (including James) call the soul, consciousness, or the spirit. All of the factors that entered into conversions in my family—the desire to improve one's class status and economic prospects, to fit in with the majority, to please a mate's family and smooth the way for a mixed marriage, to gain admission to a desired social group—tend to be left out of narratives that view conversion almost entirely as a search for truth and exclude social motivation from consideration. Skepticism about conversion, especially in post-Enlightenment societies that have long eschewed physical force in matters of religion, tends to come mainly from minorities, like Jews, in which every loss of a believer to another faith diminishes the religious strength of a small group already attenuated by historical persecution and modern secularism.

In the West, the normative conversion narrative—certainly when written by non-Jews—has basically been a pro-Christian narrative. There are exceptions, the most notable being Edward Gibbon's *The Decline and Fall of the Roman Empire,* in which he portrays the triumph of Christianity as an important factor in the erosion of Roman

* See Lecture IX, "Conversion," in *The Varieties of Religious Experience.*

power. It is a fair criticism—one made by many historians—that Gibbon is too secular (or too anti-Christian and too inclined to believe in pagan society's tolerance) in attributing as much importance as he does to one element in the slow collapse of a mighty, far-flung empire with a great many economic and social problems. Nevertheless, powerful new religious ideas certainly do have powerful social consequences—especially when the religion is welded to political power and, to a greater or lesser degree, forced on others. This certainly did happen at various points in late antiquity, in ways fueled by many of the same secular discontents and longings that lead to conversion not only in socially unstable, decaying empires but in more democratic societies undergoing rapid and unsettling social change.

•

My mother's family offered the perfect example of socially influenced conversion at a time when the United States—especially in its large cities—was experiencing immense cultural upheaval as a result of immigration. In 1919, my Lutheran grandmother, the daughter of German immigrants who settled in Chicago, converted to Catholicism when she married my Irish Catholic grandfather. This switch from one branch of Christianity to another seems unremarkable in today's America, in which approximately half of the adult population has changed religions at least once since age eighteen, but it was considerably more unusual when my grandparents married.* My grandmother was required to take months of instruction in the faith and to promise that any children would be raised as Catholics before she could be married at the altar of the parish church. Had she not converted, she and my grandfather would have had to settle for the second-class status of a wedding in the rectory. Gran took a completely pragmatic, nontheological stance toward her adopted religion. "It made your gramps's mother happy," she told me fifty years later, "and it didn't make any difference to me. After all, it's the same God whatever church you go to."

Gran had taken roughly the same stance in 1944, when my father, after asking my mother to marry him, felt obliged to reveal what he

* The statistic comes from the Pew Research Center, considered the gold standard of research on American religious practices and trends today.

still considered the shameful secret of his Jewish origins to her parents. It is undeniable that a marriage between a Christian and a Jew (secular or religious) in 1944—at a time when anti-Semitism was a far more powerful social force in the United States than it is today—would have been more of a shock to the average American family than a marriage between two different kinds of Christians. "When your dad told Gramps and me there was something about him we didn't know, my first thought was maybe he had been married before," Gran recalled. "I was so relieved when he said he was Jewish, and I told him, 'Is that all? You can always convert if you want to, and if you don't, that's fine with us too.'" My grandfather, a benevolent patriarch whose familial power was only enhanced by his lack of sternness, was equally unconcerned. He was happy because he fully accepted the stereotype that Jews don't drink, don't beat their wives, and don't ignore their financial responsibility to their families—and that they therefore make good husbands. (This conviction was based largely on Gramps's friendship with a rabbi who played poker with him but never drank a beer, whether he was winning or losing. Also, my mother had previously been married to a Catholic alcoholic—a union that was eventually annulled by the Catholic Church—so the stereotypical abstemiousness of Jewish men was a particular point in my dad's favor.) My father did not convert to Catholicism until I was seven years old, and my grandparents had nothing to do with his decision. At the time, he explained his conversion in simple terms: it would be a good thing for the family to attend Sunday Mass together, and we could all go out to breakfast afterward. Nothing to it.

My entire family's attitudes toward both religious conversion and religious belief can only be described as laissez-faire, and my upbringing at home was markedly at odds with what I was taught in Catholic school about the indisputable monopoly on truth held by the church. One might well ask why my parents, whose attitudes toward changes in religious affiliation seemed largely opportunistic to me when I was young (an opinion I never had any reason to revise as an adult), sent their children to schools that tried to imbue every child with the conviction that Catholicism was the One True Church—or, as anyone brought up Catholic in the 1950s will recall, "the only *the* Church." My mother never explained her reasons to me, although she stopped attending church in her seventies and, before she died at age ninety, told me she did not want a priest to conduct her funeral. (The willingness of my mother to jettison the religion of a lifetime is yet another family mystery, now beyond the reach of daughterly or writerly inquiry.)

•

I am certain that my lifelong interest in the phenomenon of religious conversion derives in part—a very significant part—from my childhood in a family that sent decidedly mixed messages about the importance and meaning of religious loyalty. In the Catholic universe, the model of religious conversion was of course Saul on the road to Damascus: blinded by error, a man is vouchsafed a revelation from God, falls off his horse, and awakes to the light of divine, unalterable truth. That none of the converts in my immediate family ever claimed to have been swayed by a visitation from the Almighty occurred to me when I was quite young, and my sense that something other than divine grace might be at work was undoubtedly reinforced by the experience, at age seven, of grilling my father on the Baltimore Catechism when he was preparing for his conversion. There just wasn't much spiritual mystery surrounding a conversion explained by the desire to go to Mass as a family so we could all go out together to the local pancake house for a post-sacramental breakfast. What this casual, almost flippant explanation omitted—what I did not learn until I began asking questions ten years later—was the vast importance of real and perceived anti-Semitism in my father's emotional makeup. He and his siblings had known they were Jews while they were growing up; my brother and I, raised in a suburb where few Jews lived, did not. There was so little of what later came to be known as "Jewish consciousness" in our town that it never seemed to occur to anyone that "Jacoby" was ordinarily (if you went back far enough, always) a Jewish name.

Despite its evasiveness, my father's explanation contained its own truth. His conversion was quintessentially American in its pragmatism, based on the civic assumption that choosing one's religion is as much an American right as choosing one's place of residence. As a people, we have always believed in the possibility and, in many instances, the desirability of personal reinvention. What could be more of a reinvention than living out the idea that choosing another god, or, at the very least, a radically different way of life under the aegis of the same God, amounts to being "born again"? The concept of being born again through faith in Jesus is as old as Christianity itself, but the idea of changing one's essential identity by changing faiths might have been made for, if not necessarily in, America. The modern American notion of religion as a purely personal choice, nobody else's business, thank you very much, could not be further removed from the complicated historical reality of conversion on a large scale. Conversions that change entire societies, like the shift from paganism to Christianity in the late Roman Empire or the rejection of Roman Catholicism by entire countries during the Protestant Reformation, always take place within a social context that either confers significant advantages on converts or imposes serious disabilities on those who refuse to go along to get along.

•

I am often asked if I consider the exchange of one branch of Christianity for another a "true" religious conversion. One explanation for the frequency of this question (especially from Americans) is the strange belief—albeit an understandable one in terms of the long-term theological obsession of Christianity with Judaism—that any examination of religious conversion in the West must be concerned mainly with relations between Jews and Christians. That religious conversion is a much broader historical phenomenon with broader cultural implications ought to be obvious and in no way negates the particular importance of the long, fraught encounter between Judaism and Christianity in Western civilization. In any event, I doubt that there is such a thing as a "true" conversion to or from any religion, if what is meant by "true" is a purely spiritual or intellectual process uninfluenced by external social pressures. That conversion is often experienced by the devout convert as a purely individual phenomenon, motivated not by any external forces but by divine grace, does not make it so. James, in describing the 1842 conversion of a freethinking French Jew, Alphonse Ratisbonne, to Catholicism, asserts that the conditions predisposing Ratisbonne to a conversion appeared to have been slight. Then, in the next sentence, he notes that Ratisbonne had an older brother who was himself a convert and a Catholic priest. The eminent philosopher considered this familial history unimportant because Ratisbonne had a generally anticlerical bent and was not emotionally close to his brother. One can only assume that the psychological part of James's professional consciousness must have been missing in action when he reached the conclusion that having an older brother who was not only a convert but a priest had little or nothing to do with the younger brother's conversion. James's obtuseness on this point is as laughable as the notion that the conversions in my father's family from nonobservant Jewishness to Roman Catholicism and Episcopalianism had nothing to do with their marriages to Gentiles—or that their marriages to Gentiles had nothing to do with the family's long-standing ambivalence about its Jewishness.

Indeed, religious intermarriage has always provided powerful motivation for voluntary conversions throughout the world. The nuns of my childhood had a name for conversions, like my father's and grandmother's, that were the products of such marriages—invariably dubbed "mixed marriages" with a pejorative tinge. They called a switch of faith by the non-Catholic partner a "conversion of convenience." That description did not imply the charge of treachery brought by the Spanish Inquisition against Jewish Conversos; it did imply a hierarchy of conversion, in which anyone like my grandmother, who embraced the faith to please a Catholic partner, was somehow less holy than a convert who chose Catholicism out of a spiritual ardor presumed to be uncontaminated by social forces ranging from threats of execution in the bad old days to the friendly persuasion of intermarriage in twentieth-century America. It seems to me a very traditional Catholic notion that an inconvenient change of faith—one imposing social disadvantages—is to be exalted above every other type of conversion. In its extreme form, the inconvenient conversion may lead to martyrdom, and no saints are more revered in the Catholic pantheon than those born into another faith who not only converted to the One True Church but died for their new religion.

In my grandmother's case, her conversion to Catholicism obviously had nothing to do with a desire for metaphoric or literal martyrdom and was intended mainly to facilitate her life as my grandfather's wife. Nor, as her comment about "it's the same God" indicates, did her acceptance of Catholicism have anything to do with the intense spirituality of famous converts ranging from the church father Augustine to Edith Stein, the German Jew who converted in the 1920s, became a

Carmelite nun, was gassed at Auschwitz in 1942, and was canonized by the church in 1998 as a "martyr for the faith." When Pope John Paul II used the latter phrase, he was referring to the Catholic faith. This reference was deeply offensive to both secular and religious Jews, because Stein was murdered by the Nazis not for having become a Catholic but for having been born a Jew.

.

Another important factor in many conversion-redemption stories, spanning the centuries from Augustine (again) to President George W. Bush, is the desire to overcome some personal failing. Bush, as is well known, went through a profound life change by giving up alcohol when he exchanged the antiseptic mainstream Protestantism of his Episcopal New England forebears for devout evangelical fundamentalism (a shift that would surely have horrified his ancestors).

My father's conversion to Catholicism resembled Bush's "born-again" conversion in some respects—the most important one being the presence of a strong, beloved wife who told him he had to straighten himself out or she would leave, taking the children with her. I did not learn any of this until I was an adult, when Dad told me he had known that he must give up gambling or lose his family. He believed—correctly, as it turned out—that practicing a religion would help him gain control of a compulsion that threatened to ruin him. What better religion could there be than the one already practiced by his wife and children? But—unlike many other Catholic converts I have known—my father did not interpret the doctrines of the church strictly. He once told me that the only aspect of Catholicism he found truly meaningful was Confession, with its call to repentance and its promise of forgiveness. It is certainly easy to see why the sacrament would hold special significance for a man who needed to overcome a compulsion in order to make a new start. That he was also a man who talked flippantly about his newfound Catholicism as a chance to go out for pancakes after Sunday Mass underscores the complexity and diversity of motivations for conversion on the part of many people— and often within the same person—in pluralistic societies.

.

For purposes of this book, I define genuine conversion—whatever its mixture of spiritual, intellectual, and pragmatic motives—as any change of faith that requires a substantial change in the way a person lives. It hardly matters whether the convert is a secular Jew who becomes a Catholic, or an Episcopalian who becomes a born-again Baptist, if a change of faith turns the person from a ruinous to a productive path (or, in the case of some conversions, vice versa). A conversion is any shift of belief that significantly alters the course of a life. I would not, however, draw as sharp a line between conversion and what political scientists Robert D. Putnam and David E. Campbell call "switching" in their massive study *American Grace* (2010). For Putnam and Campbell, self-described conversions are essentially meaningless if a convert reports no major change in religious beliefs or practices (such as a change in church attendance or frequency of prayer). Such Americans, they say, "are not really converts in any ordinary sense. The only thing that changed was how they described their religious identity."* This definition is too limited, because major life changes do not always take place immediately and are not always reflected in fidelity to religious rituals. To pass a more emotionally informed judgment, one would have to talk to a convert five, ten, even twenty years after the fact. Putnam and Campbell, in their skepticism about conversions that do not produce demonstrable short-term changes, are at the opposite end of the spectrum from James, who was unduly impressed by the capacity of sudden conversions to produce "an altogether new level of spiritual vitality, a relatively heroic level."

Across the ages, unwillingness to part with behavior condemned by traditional religions as sinful and by modern self-help ideology as destructive has often posed a powerful barrier to spiritually motivated conversions. Augustine, as he revealed in his *Confessions* at the end of the fourth century, was convinced for many years that the paganism and polytheism still practiced by most inhabitants of the Roman Empire were false religions and Christianity was true, but he nevertheless delayed baptism because he was unwilling to accept the restrictions that becoming a Christian would place on his sexual life. "Make me chaste, O Lord, but not yet," also meant, "Make me a Christian,

---

* Much of the data in *American Grace* comes from surveys, titled Faith Matters, conducted by the authors in 2006 and 2007.

O Lord, but not yet." That this equation between Christianity and chastity was not required by Christian doctrine at the time (except by sects eventually deemed heretical) is, and has been, a subject for psychiatrists understandably interested in the "case" of Augustine. In similar fashion, my father did not convert (or switch, if you prefer) to Catholicism until he was ready to give up the gambling that had created a crisis in his life. If Putnam and Campbell had questioned my dad in 1953, I doubt he would have reported that he prayed more frequently than he did before his conversion, or even that he went to church more regularly. (He had, in fact, been going to Mass with the family for years.) But his was a real conversion in that it was linked to a major change in destructive behavior.

·

In addition to my family history, my own atheism—which I recognized and acknowledged to myself in my early teens—has spurred my interest in not only the personal but also the larger historical implications of religious conversion. I do not define "losing" the faith of one's childhood to atheism, agnosticism, or secularism as a "reverse conversion." I dislike this commonly used phrase, because it implies that the embrace of a traditional religion, based on supernatural beliefs, represents some sort of forward motion, whereas the adoption of a secular worldview, based on evidence adduced from the natural world, amounts to some sort of regression.

By my definition, a switch from a traditional faith to atheism is the equivalent of a religious conversion only when it is coupled with surrender to a secular ideology and an organization, such as the Communist Party in the 1930s, possessing many of the characteristics of anti-evidentiary authoritarian religion. If a secular belief system brooks no evidence-based challenge, it is indeed just another religion. Primo Levi makes this point forcefully in his discussion, in *The Drowned and the Saved* (1986), of believers imprisoned in Nazi concentration camps. After Auschwitz was liberated by the Red Army, Levi—one of the few survivors in the camp infirmary—was sent to be shaved by a French barber, a Communist Party member who had also lived through the Holocaust. Levi remembers commenting on the improbability of their survival to the barber. "We were men sentenced to death and freed on the guillotine's platform, wasn't that true? He looked at me open-mouthed, then exclaimed with deep disapproval: 'Mais Joseph était là!' Joseph? It took me a few moments to realize that he referred to Stalin. He had not, he had never despaired; Stalin was his fortress, the Rock sung in the psalms."

This resemblance between orthodox religion and evidence-proof secular ideology is confirmed, ironically, in the extensive body of confessional literature by former Communists who were able to break the thrall of the Party only by converting (or returning) to a traditional but equally evidence-proof religion. It is not surprising that Roman Catholicism held a deep attraction for many who became disillusioned with the Party in the 1930s and 1940s, because the Catholic Church of that era, like the Party, provided both a structure for daily living and instructions from the top down about what to believe. (Many former Communists, it should be noted, remained philosophical secularists and did not become involved with any religion. There are no reliable data on the proportion of former Party members who turned to any traditional faith.) In the United States during the Cold War years, there may have been a tendency to exaggerate the number of fallen-away Party members who sought solace in Catholicism, in large measure because Bishop Fulton J. Sheen, the first American televangelist and best-known Catholic cleric in the nation during the 1950s, had made a specialty of converting and publicizing the conversions of prominent American Communists.

For the vast majority of atheists and secular humanists, whose rejection of belief in any deity has nothing to do with politics, the development of a nontheistic worldview does not ordinarily require significant changes in everyday life. An exception must be noted here for secularists fleeing authoritarian forms of religion defined by a myriad of prohibitions, but that would be equally true if the cult member converted to a less rigid religion. At a panel sponsored in New York City in 2010 by the secular Center for Inquiry and by All Souls Unitarian Church, dozens of students who had been raised as strict Mormons or Hasidic Jews showed up to hear speakers who had left those sects and built adult lives on another philosophical basis. The main problem of the refugees from strict faith communities was not the beliefs they had converted *to*, which included Unitarianism, Reform Judaism, and a humanism rejecting any divinity, but the rigidity of the beliefs they had converted *from*. When one is raised in a religion that issues orders about the most trivial as well as the most important activities of daily life, leaving for any other faith—much less abandoning religion altogether—is an earthquake in which the ground never stops shaking. "I came here because I wanted to talk with older people raised the way I was who've built happy lives," one young woman, born into a devout Mormon family, told me at the symposium. "Over and over when I was growing up, we were told that there was nothing but misery outside the church. I didn't know anyone who *wasn't* a Mormon. And sometimes today, when I'm having what I know is just a normal life problem that all people have, like a fight with a boyfriend or a screwup at work, I worry that it's happening because I abandoned my faith." I was reminded of her when another young woman, who became an atheist in college after being raised in a devout Muslim family, told me that many of her relatives had suggested that her "apostasy" was motivated solely by the desire to have sex, drink alcohol, and generally throw aside all Muslim restrictions prescribing modesty for women. "The truth was that, for a long time, I had no idea of how to construct a new life," she recalled. "I was a hijab-wearing atheist for quite a while, because I couldn't figure out how *I* wanted to dress. It had all been laid out for me in the past."

For atheists raised not in fundamentalist environments but in more moderately observant religious families, the diminution of belief tends to occur gradually and is characterized by an incremental rejection of dogma. Atheism rarely manifests itself either as Saul's sudden knock on the head in the Acts of the Apostles or as Augustine's tortuous spiritual passage described in his *Confessions,* often dubbed the first tell-all memoir in Western literature. The form chosen by Augustine is that of a letter (or a very long prayer) to God, but Garry Wills's description of *Confessions* as a "spiritual psychodrama" is more accurate in an emotional sense. Although an atheist raised in ordinarily rather than extraordinarily devout fashion can usually identify memorable intellectual turning points, these become clear only in retrospect and are rarely accompanied by the intense emotions (including guilt) pervading Augustine's account of conversion.

.

In my memory, doubts about the existence of a deity begin, at age seven, with a visit to a hospital to see a friend who had been stricken with polio and confined to an iron lung—a spectre that haunted both parents and children in the era before polio vaccine. I asked my mother why God would let that happen to a little boy, and she replied, with a sigh that conveyed her own lack of conviction on the subject, "I don't know. I suppose God must have a plan we don't understand." The answer did not satisfy me, and only seven years later—an eternity to a child, but a short time in a life—I would conclude that there could not possibly be an all-powerful, all-loving God. I never talked about my beliefs with anyone and had no idea that others before me had reached the same conclusion about the nonexistence of a guiding divine hand. If anything influenced me, it was a growing consciousness of the pervasiveness of pain and evil. I had read Anne Frank's diary in sixth grade, in 1956, and I could not agree with her belief that "people are really good at heart." (I underlined the phrase in the paperback that still sits on my desk and was the first book I ever bought.) But, then, I knew at age eleven what Anne did not know when she wrote those words—that, while I was safely growing inside my mother in early 1945, she and her people (my people, too, but I didn't know that) were being murdered on the continent of Europe.

When I was fourteen and understood what atheism meant, I was as little disturbed by the idea that there was no deity to ensure righteousness and justice as I had been by the much earlier realization that there was no Santa Claus. In both instances, I remember a sense of pride at having entered into a more grown-up world (although I certainly understood that the same grown-ups who had been willing to admit, "Yes, Susan, there is no Santa Claus," would not have been delighted to agree with me that there was no God). Nevertheless, I could not possibly describe this stage of my intellectual and emotional development as a conversion. My nonreligious views were part of a logical progression; as a teenager, I felt relieved that my thinking was no longer constricted by an explanation of creation, salvation, and the meaning of evil and suffering that simply did not make sense to me. As an adult, I came to regard "losing" my faith as an experience that had much in common with the end of a bad love affair: first came a certain sense of regret for the loss of a familiar presence, then relief at liberation from a relationship that had required me to behave in a fashion at odds with my deepest instincts about what constitutes a good and honorable life. Sincere religious faith is both a relationship and a love affair. That is one of the many reasons atheism is not a religion.

Another reason is the undeniable intellectual relationship between atheism and science. The most specious and most frequently cited argument against atheism is that it is "just another religion," because science is its divinity. The argument is rooted in a basic misunderstanding of the scientific method, which can only reach provisional, always challengeable conclusions based on available evidence. There is no scientific counterpart to the old Baltimore Catechism's assertion (one of the many statements my father had to memorize before his baptism) that "God always was, always will be, and always remains the same." If there is one premise every student of science must accept, it is that any conclusion, however old and cherished, is subject to being modified or overturned by new data unobtainable in earlier eras of scientific and technological capability. To the extent that atheism is grounded in science, the atheist must always be open to being proved wrong.

Nor is atheism a religion on an institutional or communal level—and religion lives, perhaps most vibrantly, on those levels, too. The noninstitutional nature of atheism—whether in its physical or spiritual dimensions—is responsible for one of its greatest disadvantages in what Americans call the religious marketplace. No secular organization fulfills the human need for community in a way that a local church does. Churches, synagogues, and mosques are physical entities, there to perform good works, such as sheltering the homeless, as well as to proselytize and pass around the collection plate. A number of prominent atheists, most notably Richard Dawkins, have set up online portals for secular charitable giving, but that is no substitute for on-the-ground institutions that make a visible and perceptible difference in people's lives.

If some people convert to a religion because of the emotional support and financial help they have received from a religious institution, that is certainly understandable. In late antiquity, when wealthy Christians began to join the Catholic Church in large numbers, helping other Christians financially was a requirement for membership—and needy pagans could certainly see that conversion might bring earthly benefits as well as heavenly rewards. Today it doesn't work that way with mainstream religions: Catholic, Protestant, and Jewish charities in the United States serve people without regard to their faith. Many aggressive proselytizing churches, however, including some right-wing evangelical and Mormon communities, reserve the lion's share of charity for their believers. Or they link charity—and not always in subtle form—to conversion strategies. An evangelical adoption service created an international furor, for example, by trying to sneak presumably orphaned Haitian children across the Dominican border, to be delivered to American evangelical Christian families for adoption, after a hurricane in 2011.

The absence of a tangible structure is the main reason atheist proselytizing bears no resemblance to the fantasies of right-wing preachers, who see a vast, efficient secular conspiracy to "reverse convert" the faithful. Even when atheists do proselytize, writing books and making speeches that hurt the feelings of believers is about as personal as it gets: no member of the American Atheists or the American Humanist Association is likely to come knocking at the door and ask you to check out the newest pamphlet debunking the existence of a deity. Atheism has no hierarchies or enforcement mechanisms, no popes or bishops or imams, no fatwas or excommunication protocols. The concept of heresy does not exist within atheism. The same can be said of secularism, which is a way of acting in the world on the atheist's conviction that human reason, not divine grace, is our best hope of improving life on earth. No figure in the history of secularism has expressed this conviction more eloquently than Robert Green Ingersoll (1833–99), known as the "Great Agnostic" and the most famous orator in the United States throughout the last quarter of the nineteenth century. "Secularism teaches us to be good here and now," Ingersoll declared. "I know nothing better than goodness. Secularism teaches us to be just here and now. It is impossible to be juster than just. . . . Secularism has no 'castles in Spain.' It has no glorified fog. It depends upon realities, upon demonstrations; and its end and aim is to make this world better every day. . . ." Like many of his Enlightenment predecessors, Ingersoll regarded the relentless pursuit of converts by proselytizing religions—and the failure of such faiths to stamp out competing truth claims even with the tools of coercive state power—as evidence of the failure of orthodox religion to stand the test of reason.

•

Religious conversion is an irresistible subject for a secularist or an atheist precisely because so much human energy, throughout recorded history, has been expended on persuading or forcing large numbers of people to replace belief in one supernatural mystery with another. Yet there is an undeniable intellectual laxity inherent in any secularist contention that Christian theocracies would have spent their money on the restoration of ancient Roman plumbing and roads had they not wasted their treasure on the Crusades and the Inquisition. This is an argument unmoored from reality (not unlike arguments over the truth of supernatural beliefs), in part because there is no evidence to suggest that the effort expended on taking the lives and property of those who ungratefully refused to accept Jesus as the Messiah or the hegemony of one form of Christianity would have otherwise been directed toward the improvement of education, sanitation, and transportation.

In the Catholic education of my youth, the role of individual converts in the history of the church's triumph was always emphasized and idealized. The conversion of one person, if he or she (usually he) was powerful enough, could and did foreshadow the conversion of millions when monotheistic faith claimed political primacy for its truth. As James Carroll argues in *Constantine's Sword* (2001), "After the death and Resurrection of Jesus, the conversion of Constantine may have been the most implication-laden event in Western history. . . . Imagine how the history we trace in this book would have unfolded had the young emperor been converted to Judaism instead. It is a nearly unthinkable turn in the story, imagined in retrospect, but in prospect such a conversion would have been no more unlikely than what happened, and to entertain the idea is to wonder how Judaism, instead of Catholicism, would have fared as the locus of political and religious dominance." According to legend (which we were taught as historical fact in parochial school), the young Constantine became a Christian, and overcame his rivals to become undisputed emperor of Rome, after he saw a flaming cross in the night sky over the Tiber River in 312, before the decisive battle with a rival at the Milvian Bridge. The era when Judaism was still a religion that attracted converts (even without proselytizing) was already ending during the period when Constantine gave state preference to Christianity, and this chapter in Jewish history has faded from the collective Western historical memory. Yet Carroll's speculation is not idle in view of the religious pluralism that still prevailed at the beginning of the fourth century. What if Constantine had seen an illuminated menorah—or a Jovian thunderbolt—instead of a cross over the Tiber? For that matter, one might extend the retrospective speculation even further, to the angry Jew on the road to Damascus, and wonder what would have happened had he awakened from his fall off the horse and heard a different message after the inquiry, "Saul, Saul, why persecutest thou me?" The voice would still belong to Yeshua, but this Yeshua would claim not to be the Messiah—an assertion considered blasphemous by Saul—but one in a long line of Jewish prophets. In his blindness after the fall, Saul might then hear the voice saying, "I am part of you, and you are part of me. The God of Abraham is our God, and a living God—ours to carry forward through time. I have come not to destroy the Law but to add to its wisdom and glory." Would Saul have written very different letters to the Romans, Corinthians, et al., had he heard the voice of Yeshua the Jew instead of the voice of the Messiah sent to save the world? Had Saul been the proselytizer for a different kind of Judaism rather than for Christianity, Constantine (and many others) might never have seen the Galilean prophet as a divinity.

Although it is impossible to know how the alternate story of a non-Christian Europe would have unfolded, we do know that, until the Enlightenment, Europe was dominated by the conviction that one religion, Christianity, was in possession of absolute truth. The problem, after Martin Luther nailed his theses to the door of the church in Wittenberg in 1517, was that Europeans no longer agreed about precisely which branch of Christianity was entitled to the monopoly on truth.* The Reformation multiplied the number of sects making absolute truth claims within Christianity, but it did not alter basic assumptions about the rights of governments to demand adherence to the religious truth of the ruler and of the majority as a legal condition of full participation in civil society. It took not only the philosophical Enlightenment but the founding of the United States of America, with a Constitution infused with the conviction that the only proper function of government in relation to religion was to protect freedom of conscience for all, to attack the roots of theocratic dominion. In the new land, the practice of a particular religion would no longer be a matter of life and death. The belief that governments, as a matter of

---

* There is some dispute among scholars about whether Luther actually did nail his theses to the church door or whether the story is just a part of Luther's legend. There is no doubt, though, that many of his contemporaries believed in the literal truth of this story.

divine right, could legitimately enforce conversion and stamp out religious heresy under pain of death was also on its way out in Europe, but Europe—consider the Jacobin violence after the French Revolution—did not then have the political and legal institutions to encourage religious pluralism peacefully. Without a real government as an example, the religious toleration of the early Enlightenment and the philosophy of the High Enlightenment in England and continental Europe would have taken even longer than it did to create real religious liberty for real people. The great paradox is that the new American nation, with its formal separation of church and state, would produce a more religious population, for a longer period, than European nations whose people had suffered under the yoke of theocratic power.

In the post-Enlightenment world, fear for one's life, liberty, and property would recede as a motive for conversion and be replaced by a wide variety of other pragmatic considerations. Depending on the social circumstances and the prevailing religious prejudices of each country, these pragmatic reasons included admission to professions barred to members of minority religions by law or by custom (the former in much of Europe, the latter in the United States); social and professional advancement by affiliating with the most prestigious religious group within a society; the shedding of telltale immigrant origins; and, as always, religious intermarriage. None of these motives, it should be emphasized, ruled out the desire to, in some spiritual sense, be "born again."

•

The models of conversion in the Western world are also models of the universal human desire for emotional experience that retains its intensity over time, and that emotional need explains the relative lack of attention to pragmatic factors in iconic stories of conversions. To understand the power of emotion in conversion experiences, one need only read Paul's epistles or Augustine. More recently, there was a huge audience for the outpourings of nineteenth-century English clerical intellectuals, such as Cardinals John Henry Newman and Henry Edward Manning, who found the meaning of life in crossing the rivulet (one could hardly call it a gulf) between a state religion that rejected papal infallibility and a former state religion that accepted the iner-

rancy of Rome. In the twentieth century, the conversions from atheism
of the English writers G. K. Chesterton and C. S. Lewis (the former to
Catholicism, the latter to Anglicanism) also had an iconic quality—
especially since both men were famous writers. The highly intellectual
and intellectualized conversion stories of English cultural figures in
the twentieth century have exerted a disproportionate influence on
American ideas (especially in the educated upper-middle class) about
changes of religious faith. The outsize interest in the spiritual journeys
of English dons is due partly to a residual Anglophilia that provides
the huge American audience for television shows like *Downton Abbey*
(and for productions of Lewis's *Chronicles of Narnia* and Chesterton's Father Brown mystery series), and partly to the fit between these
unusual writers and the American stereotype of the convert solely as
an individual touched by divine grace rather than as a product of his
time and social circumstances.

To argue that there is a critical, often overlooked social component
to most conversions is not to downplay the emotional component—
whether one believes that absolute truth is both discoverable and essential to the decent and examined life, or whether one rejects the very
idea of a truth that always was, always will be, and always remains the
same. "For now we see through a glass, darkly; but then face to face:
now I know in part; but then shall I know even as also I am known."
Who among us, however skeptical, is immune to the pull of these
words? Paul's ability to frame such fundamental longing in understandable and beautiful metaphors (with a strong assist, in English,
from the translators of the King James Bible) is one reason Christianity would probably not have unfolded as it did without him. What
could be more immense, not only for the theologian but for the lover,
the thinker, the scientist in her laboratory, than the promise of knowing perfectly and fully even as we are known?

This aspiration, at once self-obliterating and self-aggrandizing,
lies at the heart of what believers are wont to call the "true" conversion experience: it accounts for the pull of conversion stories, as told
by masters and mistresses of language, not only for those who dwell
in the mansion of faith but for those who have chosen to live in the
realm of reason and naturalism. Converts who have recorded their
spiritual transitions tend to be interesting and powerful personalities,
whether one views them from a religious perspective, as instruments

and beneficiaries of divine grace; from a psychological perspective, as case studies in the extremes human beings will go to in their search for a meaning that transcends their finite lives; or from a purely secular social perspective, as actors in dramas animated by personal-*seeming* forces that are, in reality, inseparable from larger historical trends.

It is difficult to apply any rational analysis to spiritual conversion precisely because the people who write so movingly about their changes of faith—a tiny slice of converts throughout Western history—are obviously sincere in their belief that they have, at last, found absolute, unchallengeable truth. From a secular standpoint, the monotheist who adopts another monotheistic religion is the most baffling convert of all, given that each of the three great monotheistic religions has, at one point or another, insisted that there is no meaningful life, in time or eternity, outside its boundaries. I recall the astonishment of a Jewish friend—a woman of great intellectual sophistication whose education had omitted Christian theology—when I explained the doctrine of the Trinity to her for the first time: "You mean Catholics don't believe that Jesus is just the son of God but *God Himself*!" Well, yes—and it is a rather peculiar idea when you look at it from the standpoint of someone who believes in the truth of one God, the father of all, without the participation of any other deities or quasi-deities, including a son and a holy spirit. This pill could not be swallowed even by many attracted to Christianity during the period of late antiquity and was responsible for movements suppressed by the church canon but irrepressible in their tendency to pop up in new forms, in very different social and intellectual climates, throughout the next two millennia.

It is easier to understand how a pagan, believing in many gods who embody a multitude of human characteristics, might turn to belief in a three-personed deity than it is to understand how, for example, a Jew might embrace a religion insisting that the role of the Jewish people in the divine plan must end with Jesus. It is equally mystifying to contemplate the conversion to Islam of those who, having formerly worshipped Jesus as the Messiah, are now convinced that the once-supreme Galilean was only a prophet—and a less important prophet than Muhammad. The intellectual rationales for the replacement of one absolute truth by another are as diverse as the intense personalities of those who consider religious conversion the most important experience of their lives, but at some point, they all boil down to "I was blind, but now I see." This explanation is sufficient from the standpoint of faith alone but not from the standpoint of reason.

The complex motivations for conversion in every era belie the standard Christian explanation for the victory of the followers of Jesus in the world of late Roman antiquity—that Christianity was *right* and everyone with a modicum of sense saw that. Augustine could not have been more wrong when he remarked that the chief characteristic of those defined by both the church and the state as heretics was their inability to see what was obvious to everyone else. Heresies would not have needed to be suppressed by the church-state duo in the twilight of the empire had the dissidents been so few and their arguments so weak that they were unable to sway other spiritual seekers.

•

In this book, I focus on conversion in the Western world—with forays into the Middle East as the birthplace of Judaism, Christianity, and Islam—because I am concerned primarily with places in which the three great monotheistic faiths converged (and continue to do so) with competing truth claims. The split between Roman Catholicism and Eastern Orthodox forms of Christianity, as well as the interaction among Judaism, Christianity, Islam, and various nonmonotheistic religions around the globe, is equally important but would require many more volumes than *The Decline and Fall of the Roman Empire*. I have also concentrated on times and civilizations, from the twilight of the Roman Empire to the twentieth century in the United States, when conversions have been common enough to be responsible for significant cultural change.

In thinking about both the eternal and temporal power of conversion in the history of the West, the American idea of a free "religious marketplace"—a phrase that strikes people in many other countries as comical because of its economic overtones—might be seen as the completion of a full circle beginning with the potpourri of religions tolerated by the Roman Empire. Yet the intermingling of different religious traditions in the twenty-first-century global village is never friction-free, and it is violence-free only in parts of the world that have gone through the long, contentious Enlightenment rejection of theocracy and come out on the other side. To see freedom of conscience *as a human right* as the contentious idea it still is, one need only look at instances of religious persecution and violence around the world. They offer an embarrassment of examples rich with blood—massacres in the 1990s of Bosnian Muslims by Serbian Christians; the choice of death or conversion to a particular brand of Islam now being forced on Middle Eastern Christians and on dissenting Muslims by radical Islamic terrorists; the imprisonment of atheists and freethinkers in many Muslim-majority countries; the repression of practicing Christians and Buddhists in Communist China. In much of the world, the free Enlightenment conscience is still regarded with all the affection directed at Dr. Frankenstein's creature.

Even when forced conversion is not involved, intense proselytizing by monotheistic religions asserting that they represent the only "true" faith raises problematic issues throughout the world. Mainstream Islam and many Christian churches remain aggressive proselytizers for voluntary conversion today—especially in Africa, Latin America, the Indian subcontinent, and the Far East. The new proselytizers compete not only with one another but with other historically established faiths, such as Buddhism and Hinduism. In South America, Pentecostals have made considerable inroads in historically Catholic populations.

Christianity remains a forceful and successful proselytizing religion mainly in the poorest regions of the globe. The immense personal popularity of Pope Francis, exemplified by the enthusiastic reception he received in the United States last year, has created considerable speculation that Christian conversion efforts might become more fruitful in prosperous, educated countries—at least for the Roman Catholic Church. However, the pope's tolerant tone has not led to any compromise on doctrines—especially regarding contraception, divorce, and gay marriage—that have drawn educated Catholics away from the church and discouraged conversions in most developed nations. Any reference to the ineffectiveness of proselytizing in well-educated communities elicits resentment on the part of many religious moderates as well as fundamentalists. On a panel several years ago, Reza Aslan, a liberal Muslim and the author of *Zealot: The Life and Times of Jesus of Nazareth* (2013), immediately accused me of believing that all religious people are stupid when I mentioned the connection between successful proselytizing and poorly educated societies. Aslan was confusing lack of education with stupidity. I would never suggest that that every person of faith is stupid; such an idea would be, well, stupid. Who would defend the preposterous position that every devout scholar of every religion, from time immemorial, has been a fool? But it is quite a different matter to say that the intellectually brilliant Augustine was unhealthily obsessed with original sin, or that the sophisticated Pope Francis, however appealing a figure he may be in other respects, is displaying misogyny by his reaffirmation of an all-male priesthood. I do not consider the holders of such beliefs stupid; I think they are wrong. What I do argue, and my argument is amply supported by demographic evidence, is that the less educated people are, the more likely they are to be gullible when presented with the most simplistic forms of faith—those relying on literal interpretations of "sacred" books and supernatural experiences that defy evidence. Educated religious liberals may not like it, but there is a strong correlation, everywhere in the world, between secularism and higher education, and between religious fundamentalism and low levels of education.

This is not to say that only those lacking formal education are willing to embrace literal and aggressively anti-scientific forms of faith. I happened to have a doctor's appointment on the day in 2012 when an ultra-conservative senatorial candidate from Missouri, Todd Akin, opened his mouth to suggest that women who had been subjected to "legitimate rape" had natural bodily ways of preventing themselves from becoming pregnant. The doctor said to me, "Surely he doesn't really believe that." Having interviewed many such evidence-blind believers (with and without college degrees), I assured my doctor that such people reject any medical facts—such as the inability of a woman to decide, without contraception, whether a sperm will fertilize her egg—that undermine their religio-political beliefs. How much more vulnerable to the most anti-scientific forms of religion are those with no education at all, like many in areas of Africa and Latin America where Catholicism and evangelical Pentecostalism have garnered large numbers of converts in recent years? These new converts are not stupid—or they are no more stupid than any other group of people—but they are woefully undereducated. As for Akin, who lost his senatorial race, his statements prove not that all educated believers are stupid but that some stupid people with a formal education are religious believers. And, yes, there are stupid and gullible atheists, too. The atheist Ayn Rand's philosophy of "Objectivism" is every bit as mystifying as the Holy Trinity, and I have received a fair number of e-mails from atheists who worship at that goofy altar. Those religious believers who agree with Ayn Rand's extreme free-market economics simply ignore the fact that their goddess was an atheist.

.

The idea of religious choice as a human right—for the stupid, the brilliant, and everyone in between—always depends on the degrees of separation between church and state. The Puritans who founded the theocratic Massachusetts Bay Colony were concerned about their own freedom of religion, not anyone else's. Only the availability of plentiful nearby land, which enabled Roger Williams and Anne Hutchinson to flee to Rhode Island to practice their own form of faith, saved religious dissenters in the New World from the fate of their contemporaries in theocratic Europe. (Two hundred years later, the spaciousness of America would save the Mormons from their persecutors—though it wouldn't always save non-Mormon settlers on their way to Utah from the Mormons.)

By the time of the American Revolution, the colonies were populated with divergent Protestant denominations that had been at one another's throats in the Old World, along with a minority of Catholics and an even smaller minority of Jews. The framers of the Constitution wanted a new government that neither favored nor was controlled by any religion. And so the Constitution omitted any mention of God— a deliberate oversight, much debated at state ratifying conventions, that has never ceased to be a subject of dissension in American political discourse.

The godless Constitution is arguably the main reason the United States is a more religious society today than any of the nations of Europe. The separation of church and state, the framers' original gift to their own people, also separated religious dissent from political dissent—a distinction impossible in countries with an established church. If an American didn't like the faith of his fathers, he could go off and found a new religion without any imputation of political disloyalty. In the nineteenth century, when Europe was still struggling with its ancient entanglements between church and state, Americans founded three new, aggressive proselytizing faiths—Mormonism,

Christian Science, and the Jehovah's Witnesses (although the majority of Americans disliked all of these faiths for a long time). In the twenty-first century, religious conversion is much more common in the United States than it is in the more secular developed countries of Europe and Asia—ten to twenty times more common than it is in Italy, Spain, Sweden, Norway, Denmark, Germany, or Japan. Whether the default religion is Catholicism, as in Southern Europe, or Protestantism, as in most of Northern Europe, Europeans who no longer practice the faith into which they were born generally lapse into a comfortable, socially uncontroversial secularism or atheism (a word with none of the pejorative connotations that it possesses in the United States).

The American propensity for changing religions and inventing new ones is also related to the "pursuit of happiness" encoded in our national DNA. In the United States, religious choice is yet another form of personal satisfaction open to those with many other potential sources of well-being. "Religion seems more like psychology here than anything else," says a Russian friend of mine who immigrated to the United States in the late 1990s. "It's a tool to make you feel better about yourselves." I know what she means. Nowhere else on earth is the connection between religion and secular self-help psychology as strong as it is here—though religion everywhere, at all times in human history, has always been a tool for making people feel better, or less bad, about themselves.

Only in America do we speak with approval about a religious marketplace, a sort of spiritual bazaar in which everyone is free to sample the wares, whether proffered by Western monotheist faiths, Eastern religions, or the quasi-religious self-help groups that encourage people to assert, "I'm spiritual but not religious." What this statement often means is "I want the consolations of faith without the obligations of an organized religion." In any case, the varieties of religious experience on display in the American spiritual bazaar are luxury goods, to be tried on and taken home without obliging the consumer to incur any of the costs attached to religious conversion in less tolerant societies and periods of history.

But even in America, the customer is not always right if his or her religious choice falls too far outside the norm. The generally positive American attitude toward religious conversion does not apply to minority faiths perceived as "un-American"—Catholicism and Mormonism yesterday, much of Islam today. Nevertheless, the United States has displayed a remarkable capacity, since the 1970s, for tolerance toward religions that used to be despised. My father would be surprised to know that Jew-hating is socially unacceptable now—whatever anti-Semitic views Americans might still hold privately. Atheism, however, is still viewed much more negatively by Americans (although the young are more tolerant on this score) than any religion.

"I was blind, but now I see" is surely one of the most powerful metaphors written into one of the most beautiful songs of faith in the history of Christianity. But there has always been a disturbing, unsung corollary for those who are certain that they possess absolute spiritual truth: "You are blind, and now you must see what I see." In my experience, this dualism was expressed most poignantly by a devout student at Augustana College, a Lutheran institution of higher education in Illinois. I had been invited to speak in 2005 at Augustana (one of the many old, religion-based colleges in this country that bear no resemblance to intolerant fundamentalist institutions founded in recent decades by men like Bob Jones and Jerry Falwell) about my book *Freethinkers: A History of American Secularism.* After the talk, an eighteen-year-old freshman approached me and said, "My mind tells me one thing and my soul another. I see all of the arguments you're making for the importance of complete freedom of conscience in a democracy and for not imposing your own religious views on others who think differently. But I *know* that I am in possession of the truth, and I just don't know how to reconcile that with not doing everything I can to spread the truth to others, even if you might call it an intrusion on your freedom." I sympathized with this young man, although I cannot begin to understand what it feels like to think that you *know*—he chose that word deliberately when he might have chosen to say "believe"—the truth as decreed by any god. I would not be surprised—because he would not have sought me out if he had not already begun to question the faith of his fathers—if he eventually becomes one of the millions of Americans whose religious beliefs change enough to qualify as conversions. He told me that he had already made one major change in his "life plan": after a year of college, he had decided to become a high school history teacher rather than a minister.

This student, like millions of spiritual seekers in the distant past and the present, is more than a social construct. He nevertheless offers an excellent example of the social forces—in his case, exposure to a first-rate secular as well as religious higher education—that shape and potentially change individual faith. Conversion is not merely a metaphor of rebirth but a flesh-and-blood experience that plays out on earth, not in heaven. Only on the mortal plane can we begin to understand how the "curious" conversion impulse, as James put it, has shaped not just individuals but the course of Western history—for better and for worse.

PART I

YOUNG CHRISTENDOM

AND THE FADING PAGAN GODS

1

AUGUSTINE OF HIPPO (354–430)

Beware lest any man spoil you through philosophy and vain deceit, after the tradition of men, after the rudiments of the world, and not after Christ.

—PAUL, COLOSSIANS 2:8

AUGUSTINE, a teenager studying in Carthage in the 370s, begins to ponder what he will one day consider the inevitable shortcomings of human philosophy ungrounded in the word of God. This process begins, as Augustine will later recount in his *Confessions*, when he reads Cicero's *Hortensius*, written around 45 B.C.E. The young scholar, unacquainted with either Jewish or Christian Scripture, takes away the (surely unintended) lesson from the pagan Cicero that only faith—a faith that places the supernatural above the natural—can satisfy the longing for wisdom.

"But, O Light of my heart," Augustine wrote to his god in *Confessions* (c. 397), "you know that at that time, although Paul's words were not known to me, the only thing that pleased me in Cicero's book was his advice not simply to admire one or another of the schools of philosophy, but to love wisdom itself, whatever it might be. . . . These were the words which excited me and set me burning with fire, and the only check to this blaze of enthusiasm was that they made no mention of the name of Christ."[1]

The only check? To me, this passage from *Confessions* has always sounded like the many rewritings of personal history intended to conform the past to the author's current beliefs and status in life—which in Augustine's case meant being an influential bishop of an ascendant church that would tolerate no dissent grounded in other religious or secular philosophies. By the time he writes *Confessions,* Augustine seems a trifle embarrassed about having been so impressed, as a young man, by a pagan writer. So he finds a way to absolve himself of the sin of attraction to small-"c" catholic, often secular intellectual interests by limiting Cicero to his assigned role as one step in a fourth-century boy's journey toward capital-"C" Catholicism. It is the adult Augustine who must reconcile his enthusiasm for Cicero with the absence of the name of Christ; there is no reason why this should have bothered the pagan adolescent Augustine at all. Nevertheless, no passage in the writings of the fathers of the church, or in any personal accounts of the intellectual and emotional process of conversion, explains more lucidly (albeit indirectly) why the triumph of Christianity inevitably begins with that other seeker on the road to Damascus. It is Paul, after all, not Jesus or the authors of the Gospels, who merits a mention in Augustine's explanation of how his journey toward the one true faith was set in motion by a pagan.

It is impossible to consider Augustine, the second most important convert in the theological firmament of the early Christian era, without giving Paul his due. But let us leave Saul—he was still Saul then—as he awakes from a blow on his head to hear a voice from the heavens calling him to rebirth in Christ. Saul did not have any established new religion to convert *to,* but Augustine was converting to a faith with financial and political influence, as well as a spiritual message for the inhabitants of a decaying empire. Augustine's journey from paganism to Christianity was a philosophical and spiritual struggle lasting many years, but it also exemplified the many worldly, secular influences on conversion in his and every subsequent era. These include mixed marriages; political instability that creates the perception and the reality of personal insecurity; and economic conditions that provide a space for new kinds of fortunes and the possibility of financial support for new religious institutions.

Augustine told us all about his struggle, within its social context, in *Confessions*—which turned out to be a best-seller for the ages. This was a new sort of book, even if it was a highly selective recounting of experience (like all memoirs) rather than a "tell-all" autobiography in the modern sense. Its enduring appeal, after a long break during the Middle Ages, lies not in its literary polish, intellectuality, or prayerfulness—though the memoir is infused with these qualities—but in its preoccupation with the individual's relationship to and responsibility for sin and evil. As much as Augustine's explorations constitute an individual journey—and have been received as such by generations of readers—the journey unfolds in an upwardly mobile, religiously divided family that was representative of many other people finding and shaping new ways to make a living; new forms of secular education; and new institutions of worship in a crumbling Roman civilization.

After a lengthy quest venturing into regions as wild as those of any modern religious cults, Augustine told the story of his spiritual odyssey when he was in his forties. His subsequent works, including *The City of God,* are among the theological pillars of Christianity, but *Confessions* is the only one of his books read widely by anyone but theologically minded intellectuals (or intellectual theologians). In the fourth and early fifth centuries, Christian intellectuals with both a pagan and a religious education, like the friends and mentors Augustine discusses in the book, provided the first audience for *Confessions.* That audience would probably not have existed a century earlier, because literacy—a secular prerequisite for a serious education in both paganism and Christianity—had expanded among members of the empire's bourgeois class by the time Augustine was born. The Christian intellectuals who became Augustine's first audience may have been more interested than modern readers in the theological framework of the autobiography (though they, too, must have been curious about the distinguished bishop's sex life). But *Confessions* has also been read avidly, since the Renaissance, by successive generations of humanist scholars (religious and secular); Enlightenment skeptics; nineteenth-century Romantics; psychotherapists; and legions of the prurient, whether religious believers or nonbelievers. Everyone, it seems, loves the tale of a great sinner turned into a great saint.

In my view, Augustine was neither a world-class sinner nor a saint, but his drama of sin and repentance remains a real page-turner.

•

The future church father was born in Thagaste, located in today's Algeria, into the evolving middle class of a Roman town that had existed for three centuries. His father, Patricius, was a pagan, a small landowner, and a government official whose chief virtue (as far as his son was concerned) was his willingness to sacrifice financially so that Augustine could obtain the rudiments of a classical education. His mother, Monica, was a Christian focused almost entirely on her children (especially Augustine); the only thing she seems to have shared with her husband was a determination that their brilliant son be educated. But, then, nearly everything we know about Monica comes from *Confessions,* and Augustine's relationship with his mother was so intense that it could hardly escape the scrutiny of twentieth-century psychiatrists.

Monica was a piece of work, and her work blended the necessity of feminine compromise—given the inescapable fact of male social dominance—with a canny, relentless drive to prevail in matters, especially religion, of greatest importance to her. As Augustine recounts, his mother felt that women were obliged to tolerate their husbands' infidelities, and her tolerance may have been one reason why Patricius, unlike many of his contemporaries, never beat her. She kept her eyes on the prize, which was instilling Christian belief in her son in spite of the pagan education he was receiving and, eventually, drawing Patricius into the Christian fold as well. She managed to obtain this conversion only at the end of Patricius's life, and that was the story of many such mixed couples and families in the early Christian era (including the more politically consequential saga of Helena and her son Constantine). As a child, Augustine nearly died from an intestinal disorder, but Monica did not have him baptized, as her son later explained, because if he did recover she knew that he would continue to sin after being christened—and that would place him on the road to hell. What a risk taker Monica was! Faced with the choice of making sure that her gravely ill young son went to heaven in a state of grace after baptism or giving him the chance to go on sinning until he was ready to accept Christianity on his own, she rolled the dice. "Even at that age I already believed in you," Augustine writes, "and so did . . . the whole household except for my father. But, in my heart, he did not gain the better of my mother's piety and prevent me from believing in Christ because he still disbelieved himself. *For she did all that she could to see that you, my God, should be a Father to me rather than he.*"[2] (Italics mine.)

Many religious believers have criticized psychiatrists for anachronistically superimposing Freudianism on *Confessions*. But psychiatrists, whether Freudian or not, can hardly be blamed for being struck by an account of an upbringing in which an invisible, supernatural father was constantly pitted against the natural father who was feeding, clothing, and educating his son. Augustine's dilemma, however anachronistic it may be to impose Freudian terminology on the story, is timeless. For a child, the perception of one parent as the representative of just, timeless moral values and the other as the emblem of worldly striving need have nothing to do with religion to create immense emotional turmoil. Religion, however—especially when one faith insists on an absolute truth claim—ups the ante. The soothing notion that religions may be equally good, albeit contradictory—the fallback position for many mixed couples today—was not available to Christian parents when the church was in its infancy (though it was certainly available to and accepted by pagans throughout the empire). The "one religion is as good as another" perspective was not really accepted by any Western religious denomination until well into the twentieth century, and now exists only in countries and within social and religious groups that fully accept religious pluralism and reject absolute truth claims.

·

By the late 390s, when Augustine completed *Confessions*, he had long been familiar with Jewish Scripture and immersed in early Christian writings, and his references to Paul permeate the autobiography. Saul/Paul was a much greater writer and propagandist than any of those who drew their inspiration from him—from the fathers of the church to Calvinists, as well as conservative Catholic and Protestant theologians of the nineteenth and twentieth centuries. For Augustine, the authority of the church and its sole claim to truth, despite his incorporation of classical philosophy into Christian theology, became the entire point of his turbulent search for a moral center of gravity. Had Augustine been writing even a century earlier, it seems doubtful that his conversion story would have exerted anything like the direct emotional power of Paul's epistles, written (as far as the best scholarship can determine) in the first three decades after the conventional Christian dating of the crucifixion of Jesus (around the year 33).

Peter Brown, the great scholar of late antiquity and author of the definitive twentieth-century biography of Augustine, describes *Confessions* as "a masterpiece" in which Augustine "communicates such a sense of intense personal involvement in the ideas he is handling, that we are made to forget that it is an exceptionally difficult book."[3] *Confessions* certainly is a dense and difficult book, in style as well as substance; I find it impossible to forget the difficulty and the density except when Augustine steps out of the persona of God's correspondent and reveals, intentionally or unintentionally, the complexities of his own mortal moral life. Who is to say that the prayer formula— for a kind of book that had never been written before—was anything other than a conscious or more likely subconscious disguise for the intense desire of a writer to talk about his own experience, to sing his own song? I see Augustine as a man who was as driven to talk about his personal secrets as any autobiographer who has ever lived, but his religious beliefs dictated that he frame his own story in the form of a letter to the immortal Supreme Being. What Brown judges as intense involvement with ideas might also be seen as intense tension between concealment and revelation—as well as between pride of authorship and a faith that dictated humility.

What interests us about Augustine is the prism of guilt, self-loathing, vaulting ambition, grandiosity, and sheer strangeness through which he reaches an accommodation with his ruler of the universe. He may well have exaggerated his own sinfulness (how evil, really, is it to steal a bunch of pears to impress your peers, or to have one mistress and one son out of wedlock?), but what is compelling about *Confessions* is not how his sins might be judged *sub specie aeternitatis* but how Augustine himself viewed the offenses in particular and evil in general.

Augustine's preoccupation with the question of evil—the theodicy problem that poses so many more difficulties for a monotheist than for a polytheist who believes in gods with limited power—is what keeps us all reading. The paradox of the existence of evil in a world supposedly designed and presided over by an all-powerful, all-knowing, all-good deity, has always been *the* moral question for every person of faith. Atheists do not have this problem in its theological form, because the atheist rejects the idea that any supernatural being has the power to affect human moral decisions or their consequences. But the need to keep dark impulses from overwhelming the better angels of our nature is equally urgent for all sane human beings, regardless of religious or nonreligious beliefs. For all who possess a conscience—my definition of sanity—doing right when we are strongly tempted to do wrong is a moral challenge and a moral duty that never goes away. The ubiquity and sheer difficulty of this task is the reason why heresies attempting to separate good and evil into separate universes arise repeatedly throughout religious and Christian history, and it is Augustine of Hippo's fundamental subject—regardless of whether he was really a great sinner by anyone's standards but his own.

·

Augustine himself would probably have no quarrel with anyone who considers Paul a much greater writer. I know verse after verse from Paul's epistles by heart, but I have to look up passages in *Confessions*. For an English-speaker today (at least for one old enough not to have encountered the Bible for the first time in dumbed-down recent translations), the indelible impression rendered by Paul's prose is likely attributable to the proselytizer's fabulous luck in having his words rendered into the language of Shakespeare by William Tyndale and the translators of the King James Bible. There is not a line in *Confessions* with the emotional power of the "through a glass darkly" passage in Paul's epistle to the Corinthians, nor could Augustine's obsession with original sin lure potential converts in the manner of Paul's promise that, although in our earthly lives we know only in part, in eternal life we will know fully, even as we are known. The author Christopher Hitchens, in a lagniappe to the King James translation written for *Vanity Fair* magazine several months before his death in 2011, felt the same way, in spite of his uncompromising atheism, about what has rightly been called the only great book ever written by a committee. For his father's funeral in 1987, Hitchens had chosen a Jesus-free reading (4:8) from Paul's Epistle to the Philippians: "Finally, brethren, whatsoever things are true, whatsoever things are honest, whatsoever things are just, whatsoever things are pure, whatsoever things are lovely, whatsoever things are of good report; if there be any virtue, and if there be any praise, think on these things." The "Contemporary English Version" published by the

American Bible Society translates the passage Hitchens quoted at his father's funeral as, "Finally, my friends, keep your minds on whatever is true, pure, right, holy, friendly, and proper. Don't ever stop thinking about what is truly worthwhile and worthy of praise." Hitchens correctly describes these verses as "pancake-flat," consistent with self-help psychobabble and lacking the power to penetrate "the torpid, resistant fog in the mind of a 16-year-old boy, as their original had done for me." He adds, "There's perhaps a slightly ingratiating obeisance to gender neutrality in the substitution of 'my friends' for 'brethren,' but to suggest that Saint Paul, of all people, was gender-neutral is to rewrite the history as well as to rinse out the prose."[4]

I read the "through a glass darkly" passage at my father's funeral for much the same reason as Hitchens selected his verses: as a daughter, I felt that the lines embodied the primary virtue—hope—that defined my dad's character. Paul's hold on Augustine can be attributed not only to theology but to the admiration of a very good writer for a great writer.

·

Confessions is a real autobiography as well as a real conversion story, and attempts to reduce it largely to a "prayer to God" minimize not only the degree of Augustine's emotional conflicts, egotism, and existential guilt but the importance of his having been raised in a family and spent his adult life in a society that provided fertile soil for every kind of doubt and belief—religious and nonreligious.

Periods of political change and uncertainty, such as the fourth and fifth centuries in the late Roman Empire, have nearly always been characterized by religious change. After the death of Constantine, the first Christian emperor (who was baptized not long before he died in 337), the empire was split into Eastern and Western sectors by his feuding sons—a division that would ultimately have a permanent impact on Christianity as well as politics. In the Western empire, the small Roman towns of North Africa, which had been prosperous from the first century B.C.E. until around the year 200, were literally crumbling. Public baths, aqueducts, and monuments—all of the material achievements of Roman civilization—would disintegrate steadily over the next millennium in the West—with the exception of the extraordinary feats of Moorish architecture and city planning at the height of the Convivencia (literally, the coexistence) of Muslims, Christians, and Jews in eighth-through-tenth-century Iberia. Repeated waves of attacks from the north stretched the material and military resources of the empire to the utmost. In 363, the last pagan emperor, Julian, was killed during an attempt to invade Persia, and in 376, Velens, emperor of the East, allowed Visigoths to settle within the borders of the empire. It took only another thirty-four years for Alaric and the Visigoths to invade and sack Rome—an event of incalculable economic and psychological importance that made the security of a church-state alliance even more appealing to those shaken by the once-invincible empire's fragility. But the union between Catholicism and what was left of imperial rule threatened the religious freedom of all who did not accept the teachings of the Roman church, including non-Christian Manicheans and Jews. In the theology that emerged from that union, especially with regard to Jews, Augustine was destined to play a fateful role.

The rise of a new, aggressive, proselytizing form of monotheism—and its attempts to form an alliance with imperial power—had even more negative consequences for Jews than for pagans, if only because most of the inhabitants of the empire were still pagans, and the Jewish minority had depended on a certain protected status to maintain its communal institutions within the imperium. A few historians, most notably Benzion Netanyahu (who died in 2012 and was the father of the current Israeli prime minister Benjamin Netanyahu), have argued that the Western persecution of Jews originated in the classical world's hatred of Jewish Scripture and culture and envy of the economic success attained by many Jews living outside Palestine (both before and after the destruction of the Second Temple in 70). Netanyahu argues that "the Jewish question in antiquity was produced by essentially the same factors that fashioned it in later times; that antisemitism in the Christian period was, fundamentally, a continuation of the anti-Jewishness that preceded it; and that the origins and manifestations of both phenomena were fundamentally the same."[5] But the Roman state, before the rise of Christianity, did not act to destroy Jewish institutions in the absence of open revolt, such as the uprising that led to the destruction of the Second Temple or the crushing, in 135, of the rebellion led by the "false Messiah" Simon bar Kochba. After the decisive battle in 70, it was said that Roman soldiers plowed the entire area around the temple under in an effort to destroy all of the original stones. According to the twelfth-century scholar Maimonides, what followed was the near-total destruction of the city of Jerusalem. Christians then used passages from the Gospels to praise the destruction of the temple and to argue that the catastrophe was foretold by Jesus. They were referring to a passage in the Gospel of Matthew (24:1–2), in which Jesus gathers his disciples in the temple in Jerusalem and says, "There shall not be left here one stone upon another, that shall not be thrown down." The same incident appears in Luke (21:5–8, 12):

> And as some spake of the temple, how it was adorned with goodly stones and gifts, he said, As for these things which ye behold, the days will come, in the which there shall not be left one stone upon another, that shall not be thrown down.
>
> And they asked him saying, Master, but when shall these things be? and what sign will there be when these things shall come to pass?
>
> And he said, Take heed that ye be not deceived: for many shall come in my name, saying, I am Christ; and the time draweth near: go ye not after them.
>
> . . . But before all these, they shall lay their hands on you, and persecute you, delivering you up to the synagogues, and into prisons, being brought before kings and rulers for my name's sake.

The final verse of this passage merits particular attention. Jesus the Jew would hardly have advanced the argument that delivering someone into prison was the same as delivering him to a synagogue. The verse is particularly significant because the author of the Gospel of Luke is also thought by most biblical scholars to be the author of the Acts of the Apostles, from which we derive so many of our impressions about the dawn of Christianity.

Even after Jerusalem was razed, however, Roman officials continued for another two centuries to protect Jewish communities dispersed throughout the Roman world. Netanyahu's analysis seems motivated more by the ideological position that Jew-hatred is endemic to all Western culture, or to all cultures with a history of extensive contact with Jews, than by a realistic assessment of the role of Jews in Greek and Roman culture (and vice versa). It is true that there were outbreaks of anti-Jewish violence in the classical world. Two of the most devastating, in Alexandria in 38 and 68, were described, respectively, by the historians Philo of Alexandria (a Hellenistic Jew) and Flavius Josephus (who had fought in the rebellion against Rome leading to the destruction of the Second Temple, was taken hostage—or, depending on one's point of view, defected to the Roman side—and eventually became a Roman citizen). Alexandria, however, was a special case, in that Roman authorities had encountered trouble for centuries when they tried to keep the lid on simmering tensions among Jews, Greeks, and Egyptians. The trouble only grew worse when Christianity was added to the mix, and Roman officials were no more successful in stopping later Christian violence against pagans than they had been in stopping earlier attacks focused on Jews.

Only when Christianity came into its own as a political force, and emperors as well as other Roman officials embraced the Christian faith and were subject to pressure from Christian leaders, did Jews every-where began to experience physical peril regardless of whether they had long maintained peaceful relations with governing authorities. The question of what to do about the Jews was far more pressing than what to do about pagans for the church fathers, given that Christian-ity developed out of Judaism and was seen as the fulfillment of Jewish prophecy. These prophecies eventually had to be twisted to fit the offi-cial events of the Christian story. The refusal of faithful Jews to accept that the story of *their* faith ended and was fulfilled by the arrival of Jesus was a constant challenge and reproach to Christianity in a way that the unrelated beliefs of pagans could never be.

Here Augustine enters the picture. *Confessions* says nothing what-ever about Jews. Augustine saved his ruminations about "the Jewish problem" for his massive theological work, *The City of God,* which he began writing at least fifteen years after *Confessions* appeared. The bishop of Hippo's unique and lasting contribution to the fate of Jews in Christendom rejected the exterminationist stance toward Judaism expounded in the writings of his contemporaries John Chrysostom of Antioch and Ambrose of Milan, the bishop and mentor who baptized him in 387. Augustine's particular contribution to the *Adversus Judaeos* genre of sermons, which permeates all of the patristic writings, was his admonition that Jews should be harassed, dispersed throughout the world at the pleasure of Christian rulers, treated as constant targets for conversion, but not, in the end, exterminated. To Augustine, the physical survival of some Jews—even though they were so wrongheaded and oblivious to God's grace as to reject Jesus as the Messiah—was necessary to attest to the truth of Christianity and its fulfillment of Hebrew prophecy. He writes:

> In fact, there is a prophecy given before this event on this very point in the book of Psalms. . . . It comes down in this passage, "As for my God, his mercy will go before me; my God has shown me this in the case of my enemies. Do not slay them, lest at some time they forget your Law," without adding, "Scatter them." For if they lived with that testimony and Scriptures only in their own land, and not everywhere, the obvious result would be that the Church, which is everywhere, would not have them available among all nations as witnesses to the prophecies which were given beforehand concerning Christ.[6]

In other words, if the Jews were not in every land to serve as a cautionary example and to be persecuted by Catholics, the universality of the church's truth would be harder to demonstrate. As James Carroll observes, Augustine's two-sided injunction—"preserve, but do not slay them"—resounds throughout Western history. "It was not only the Diaspora that provided Jewish witness to the truth of Christian claims," Carroll emphasizes, "but the negative condition of exile. Jews came to be seen as witnesses in the very desperation of their status. They must be allowed to survive, but never to thrive . . . Their homelessness and misery are the proper punishments for their refusal to recognize the truth of the Church's claims. And more—their misery is yet another proof of those claims."[7] Augustine's formula proved deadly for Jews over the long term because "the compulsively repeated pattern of that ambivalence would show in bishops and popes protecting Jews—but from expressly Christian mobs that wanted to kill Jews because of what bishops and popes had taught about Jews. A teaching that wanted it both ways was bound to fail, as would become evident at every point in history when Jews presumed, whether economically or culturally or both, to even think of thriving."[8]

I did not encounter *Confessions* as most readers, absent a special interest in theology, might encounter the book in a college course on the history of religion or (today) the oversubscribed category sometimes called history of memoir. I read *The City of God* first, when I was around sixteen—no doubt with glazed eyes and limited understanding—because my atheism had stimulated a strong interest in the history of religion and theology. One thing I did understand, though, was what Augustine wanted to do about Jews, and that certainly prejudiced me against him by the time I got around to reading *Confessions* some years later.

Though Augustine rejected extermination, he essentially believed that a people so foolish and evil as to refuse the truth claim of Christianity deserved almost every other form of abuse. Moses Mendelssohn, the eighteenth-century scholar and pre-eminent philosopher of the Jewish Enlightenment, once remarked that, had it not been for Augustine's "lovely brainwave, we would have been exterminated long ago."[9] Does a man deserve much credit, in any era, for being less brutal than his wholly brutal contemporaries? Human beings who are far in advance of their time—say, Spinoza on intellectual liberty and censorship—do deserve credit. But is there anything especially admirable about sanctioning every form of abuse short of murder to show people who disagree with you the error of their ways?

Augustine's prescription for the containment of Jewry within Christendom is directly related to his conviction that anyone who is exposed to the Gospels and refuses to accept them is committing the most grievous form of sin and perpetuating the evil error—not merely an intellectual but a moral error of the highest order—of choosing a life and philosophy without Jesus at its center. This conviction lies at the heart of the Christian conversion narrative—for most of European history, *the* conversion imperative—as a metaphorical and practical demonstration of the once-unbreakable connection between religious violence and belief in a religious truth so absolute that it is both the right and the duty of the state to enforce one faith. Augustine's conversion story—the first to explore the process in any detail—is no exception. *The City of God* meets *Confessions* in Augustine's denunciation of deliberate rejection of God's grace, by which he means grace and salvation through Jesus, as the ultimate sin. Paul's story does not really count in this regard, since Scripture has little to tell us about the psychological processes by which he was prepared, before his fall off the horse, for his transformation from an enemy of those who followed the prophet Yeshua into the indispensable publicist of the greatest story ever told. Paul's epistles tell us what he thought after being reborn in Christ after a bump on the head—not what he thought before.

Augustine's conversion was voluntary and heartfelt, but it holds out no help or hope for those—like believing Jews—who cannot and will not take the same spiritual path. In the Augustinian mind-set, there is only one right and happy ending to the quest for faith, and no alternative to Christianity qualifies. His unusual remedy for the offending Jewish presence in late antiquity, when the church was triumphing over other religions by using the state as an enforcer, affords powerful evidence of the closed nature of the Augustinian universe, whether cloaked in a Neoplatonic intellectual system or in Christian Scripture. In Catholic theology, there are two kinds of ignorance—vincible and invincible. Vincible ignorance is within an individual's power to overcome; a Jew or a pagan who had been presented with the arguments of Christianity but refused to accept them would normally be considered sinful, because he had been vouchsafed knowledge of the truth and deliberately turned away. Inhabitants of countries beyond the reach of the Christian message, by contrast, would not be deemed sinful for practicing other religions, because they were in a state of invincible ignorance that could not be remedied without help from an outside source.*

The enduring effects of Augustine's brainwave can be perceived in the assumption, made by many of my friends, that any history of conversion in the West must be concerned largely with conversions of Jews to Christianity. The interest in conversions, forced and unforced, of Jews has deepened since the Holocaust, as the relationship between Christian theology and modern anti-Semitism has been re-examined in many countries and in the Vatican itself. Were it not for Augustine's "harass, but do not destroy" formula, Christians and Jews would cer-

---

* The degree to which "vincible ignorance" can sometimes be a mitigating factor in sinfulness is a subject of some dispute among those who care about such distinctions. A child living in a community with strict penalties for desertion to another faith, for instance, might not be considered as guilty as an adult for failing to embrace the Christian message. Every adult Jew within reach of the Christian message in late antiquity— and that would have meant just about every Jew residing within the borders of the Roman Empire—would be in a state of vincible ignorance for which there could be no moral excuse.

tainly have had much less to do with each other throughout the many centuries before exterminationist anti-Semitism entered the West's historical consciousness and conscience. Moreover, many Westerners today see Christianity as the beginning of Western proselytizing and do not realize that Judaism itself, in its historical infancy, was a proselytizing religion using tactics, as recorded in the Hebrew Bible, that could sometimes be summed up as "harass and destroy."

One of the worst stories of forced conversion appears in Genesis, when Jacob and his family encounter a peaceful tribe in Canaan, and the son of the local ruler has sex with and proposes marriage to Dinah, the daughter of Jacob and Leah. (This bit of sex, which may well have been consensual, is treated by the Israelites as a rape, in much the same manner as the Taliban deals with consensual sex unauthorized by a girl's father or brothers.) In any case, the men of the tribe are told that Shechem, the son of the leader, may marry Dinah only if all of the tribesmen convert by undergoing the painful ritual of adult circumcision. Here is what happened to the new converts:

> And it came to pass on the third day, when they were sore, that two of the sons of Jacob, Simeon and Levi, Dinah's brethren, took each man his sword, and came upon the city boldly, and slew all the males. And they slew Hamor and Shechem his son with the edge of the sword, and took Dinah out of Shechem's house, and went out. The sons of Jacob came upon the slain, and spoiled the city, because they had defiled their sister. They took their sheep, and their oxen, and their asses, and that which was in the city, and that which was in the field, And all their wealth, and all their little ones, and their wives took they captive and spoiled even all that was in the house.
>
> —GENESIS 34:25–30

This account of forced conversion as atonement for rape (if it was rape) is surely a first in the history of religious conversion in the West; I could not say with certainty that it is a first in the annals of rape. In any event, the horrific story of Dinah surely demonstrates that Christians were not pioneers in the use of ethically indefensible conversion tactics. What Jacob's sons did would best be described as "bait and switch" conversion: tricking the men into undergoing the painful procedure of adult circumcision did not save their lives in the end. Jacob, it should be noted in fairness to the better angels of Jewish history, was said to have been angry at his sons for their deception. However, this chilling story illustrates and foreshadows a broader truth, ignored by Augustine, about group conversion from one religion to another. Whenever a significant number of people accept a new religious "truth" at the same time, some sort of force is apt to be involved. And there is a thin line between harassment and destruction when a politically ascendant religion is on the move in literal geographical as well as moral terms.

·

Even though I read *Confessions* long after I had read several of Augustine's other major works, I was aware of the book as a child because I attended Catholic elementary schools. Augustine himself was a saint not much talked about in catechism class, and the sexual parts of his autobiography would have been considered highly unsuitable for Catholic seventh- and eighth-graders, but one episode—the famous story of the pears—was recounted repeatedly as a moral lesson. Augustine's account of purloining pears that he could easily have obtained without stealing was a perfect object lesson for every teenage shoplifter.

> A pear tree there was near our vineyard, laden with fruit, tempting neither for colour nor taste. To shake and rob this, some lewd young fellows of us went, late one night (having according to our pestilent custom prolonged our sports in the streets till then), and took huge loads, not for our eating, but to fling to the very hogs, having only tasted them. And this, but to do what we liked only, because it was misliked. Behold my heart, O God, behold my heart, which Thou hadst pity upon in the bottom of the bottomless pit. Now, behold, let my heart tell Thee what it sought there, that I should be gratuitously evil, having no temptation to ill, but the ill itself. It was foul, and I loved it; . . . I loved mine own fault, not that for which I was faulty, but my fault itself.[10]

This sort of behavior is familiar to every teenager, not because of an innate propensity for evil, but because we all sense, from an early age, that in the presence of bad companions whom we wish to impress with our daring, most of us are willing to do things that we would never do on our own. We do such things not because we are stained with original sin—the point the nuns wished to impress on us by talking about Augustine's pears—but because we have failed to internalize standards of behavior independent of whatever punishment, human or divine, may ensue if we are caught. (Internet bullying is a classic modern example of the phenomenon, and one that does much more harm than stealing the pears of some burgher of late antiquity.) I always remembered the story of the pears, not because I considered it the epitome or even a particularly vicious example of the evil that dwells in the hearts of men, but because it was the embodiment of immature following-the-leader. The nuns' stories about stealing someone else's pears as an offense against a loving God had a good deal less impact on me than my mother's quotidian "If Rose Mary jumped off a bridge, would you jump off too?"

.

In addition to Augustine's complicated relationship with his mother, the girl of his dreams, the more prurient appeal of *Confessions* is inseparable from the author's obsession with chastity as the key to becoming a good Christian and from his fears about vulnerability to sexual desires that he could not control. The most important aspect of *Confessions,* however, is unquestionably Augustine's strong attraction to Manicheism, a major challenge to Christianity, as the answer to the theodicy question.

Why does evil exist if the world is governed by an all-powerful, all-good, all-seeing God? Pagans did not have to ask or answer that question, because their world was not governed by one perfect God. In the pagan supernatural realm, the gods themselves often behaved badly, in their relations with other divinities as well as with humans. Christians did have to ask and answer the theodicy question, because—this cannot be said often enough—their world was governed by one God who could do absolutely anything.

Manicheism, which viewed good and evil as independent forces, always in conflict, and saw the body as essentially corrupt, was one answer to the problem of evil in the dawn of the Christian era and the twilight of paganism. Augustine embraced this creed for nine years (though he was something of a follower, known as a "hearer," rather than an active believer and proselytizer). The sect's philosophy may be summarized in a Manichee verse: "I have known my soul and the body that lies upon it / That they have been enemies since the creation of the world."[11] R. S. Pine-Coffin, in his introduction to a 1961 translation of *Confessions,* considers it "incredible that a man of Saint Augustine's intellectual calibre could have been taken in by these fantastic theories, but the Manichees' plausible explanation of the problem of evil and his own inability to think of God except as a material being combined to win him over."[12] Why would this have been incredible to an intellectual of Augustine's era? Why, for that matter, should the notion of a dualistic universe seem any stranger to a twentieth-century intellectual than the idea of a magnificent being capable of preventing all the disasters that afflict his creatures but endowing them with the "free will" to doom themselves and others to endless suffering? The sect was founded in the third century by Mani, a charismatic Persian preacher considered a great prophet by his followers. The spread of Manicheism from Persia throughout the known world, from the Mediterranean portions of the Roman Empire in the West to Tibet in the East, reflects the rich interchange of religious ideas facilitated by trade routes extending from Asia to the heart of the Greco-Roman world. Rome was often at war with Persia, and Manichees were often persecuted because of the Persian origins of their faith. Nevertheless, Manicheism flourished, and its outsider status (much like Christianity itself) did nothing to diminish its appeal. The Manichees belong to the group of sects broadly classified as Gnostic—some of which were Christian, and others, such as Manicheism, non-Christian in their views on a wide variety of theological matters.

Like the Muslims whose faith would emerge several centuries later, the Manichees considered Jesus a great prophet and spiritual figure while viewing their own teachings as superior to Christianity. They were most closely connected to Christian teaching in their views on asceticism, although Manichees were more extreme in their ascetic leanings than Christian leaders in the fourth and fifth centuries—with the possible exception of the onetime hermit and church father Jerome. The chief importance of Manicheism was its relegation of good and evil to separate universes, literally consisting of the world of darkness and the world of light. Manicheans believed that particles of good were trapped in the evil matter that composed most of the human body. They believed not in original sin but in the possibility of human perfection, to be attained by rigorous self-discipline and eventual union with the pure, untainted light of goodness. Energy representing the light in man would rise toward perfection, in ways that contradicted contemporary observations of the movements of astral bodies. The phases of the moon, for example, were not seen by Manichees as objective phenomena, independent of man, but were thought to be caused by variations of pure light and impure darkness being released from earth as a result of human behavior. Even for that era, Manicheism was heavily dependent on pseudoscience; astrologers, building their business on the pseudoscientific premise that the stars affected the behavior of men, had nevertheless grasped the basic truth that the stars and planets were not controlled by human beings.

The pseudoscientific cast of Manichean dualism eventually drove Augustine away. Troubled by the contradictions between Manichean teaching and Greek scientific writings, Augustine turned to one Faustus, whom he tartly describes as a man with a reputation for learning "conveniently maintained by his frequent absences on missionary journeys."[13] When Faustus turned up in Carthage in 383, Augustine took his measure and was disappointed, discovering, to his disdain, that the Manichee's reputation for being "exquisitely skilled in the liberal sciences" proved unjustified for anyone who knew the Greek classics. "And since I had read and well remembered much of the [Greek] philosophers," Augustine recalled, "I compared some things of theirs with those long fables of the Manichees, and found the former more probable. . . ."[14] Ignorance of the classics would not do for Augustine as a pathway to religious faith. A year after meeting Faustus, Augustine was off to Rome and basically done with Manicheism.

Yet dualism, despite its weird cosmology, was certainly no more preposterous as an answer to the theodicy question than the "free will" used by the fathers of the church, including Augustine, to let God off the hook. No one describes the issue better than Augustine himself, in his musings in *Confessions* on the evil of babies:

> Who remindeth me of the sins of my infancy? . . . Who remindeth me? Doth not each little infant, in whom I see what of myself I remember not? What then was my sin? Was it that I hung upon the breast and cried? For should I now do so for food suitable to my

age, justly should I be laughed at and reproved. What I did then was worthy of reproof; but since I could not understand reproof, custom and reason forbade me to be reproved. For those habits, when grown, we root out and cast away. Now no man, though he prunes, wittingly casts away what is good. Or was it then good, even for a while, to cry for what, if given, would hurt? bitterly to resent, that persons free, and its own elders, yea, the very authors of its birth, served it not? that many besides, wiser than it, obeyed not the nod of its good pleasure? . . . *The weakness then of infant limbs, not its will, is its innocence.* Myself have seen and known even a baby envious; it could not speak, yet it turned pale and looked bitterly on its foster-brother. Who knows not this?[15] [Italics mine.]

A baby might look innocent to doting parents, but to Augustine, infants were only biding their time until they grew strong enough (thanks to all of those feedings on demand) to wreak real mayhem. There is certainly nothing incredible, by the standards of religious logic, about either Manicheism or free will as the answer for a man bound by faith to absolve God of being responsible for the evil committed by infants. One explanation is as plausible, or implausible, as the other—if, that is, you accept the premise that babies are born bad. Monica, characteristically, threw her son out of the house when he became a Manichee follower, although she never lost hope that he would return to the true path of Roman Catholic Christianity.

If *Confessions* is not a "tell-all" memoir in the modern sense (as ecclesiastical and scholarly commentators constantly remind Augustine's unwashed, prurient fans), it is a real autobiography, filled with stories about Augustine's earthly friends as well as his immortal Friend. It is no less a memoir or an autobiography because Augustine leaves out important episodes in his life (as all autobiographers do) or because twentieth-century scholars with a psychoanalytic bent have imposed historical anachronisms on certain episodes. Consider a famous passage in which Augustine expresses contempt for a father who was respected by the community because, in spite of sparse financial resources, he devoted what he had to financing his son's studies. "But yet this same father had no concern how I grew towards Thee, or how chaste I were; so that I were but copious in speech, however barren I were to Thy culture. . . ."[16]

Augustine then regrets that "the briers of unclean desires grew rank over my head, and there was no hand to root them out." When Augustine's father saw his nude son at the public baths, "now growing toward manhood, and endued with a restless youthfulness, he, as already hence anticipating his descendants, gladly told it to my mother; rejoicing in that tumult of the senses wherein the world forgetteth Thee its Creator, and becometh enamoured of Thy creature, instead of Thyself. . . ."[17] In other words (this translation was completed in 1838), Augustine's father saw his son's manly penis, probably in an erect state, and told Monica that they might anticipate becoming grandparents.

In his analysis of *Confessions,* Garry Wills takes two German psychiatrists to task for concluding that Augustine's father had seen him masturbating. It certainly does seem unlikely that public masturbation was a routine part of the experience of using Roman baths prized for their cleanliness.[18] Nudity, however, was a given. The point of the passage is not that the teenager was masturbating but that Augustine was repelled by his father's evident pleasure at the sight of his sixteen-year-old son's mature genitals. And the passage reveals a deeper truth about the young Augustine's formative emotional conflict, instilled by the contrast between his mother's devout Christian teachings and his father's paganism.

In spite of his father's vulgar earthly desires, Augustine continues, "In my mother's breast Thou hadst already begun Thy temple, and the foundation of Thy holy habitation, whereas my father was as yet but a catechumen, and that but recently. She then was startled with an holy fear and trembling; and though I was not as yet baptized, feared for me those crooked ways, in which they walk, who turn their back to Thee, and not their face."[19] As a Christian convert, Augustine would replay that conflict even after he became a bishop of the church. The role of mixed marriage is part of what makes *Confessions* seem modern and relevant in our society, which, like Augustine's own, is characterized by religious, racial, and ethnic intermarriage of many kinds. Augustine's harsh judgment of his father, and the clear line he draws between the moral values of his parents, is also entirely consistent with his attraction to Manicheism.

The book's best-known episode is its "conversion scene," when Augustine finally decides to be baptized. As Wills points out, the significance of this scene is not the conversion itself but Augustine's renunciation of sex. Chastity was not a condition for becoming a Christian; it was not even a condition for becoming a priest in the fourth century (although it was far from certain that Augustine—a respected teacher of rhetoric and the classics, thanks to his father's worldly ambitions and sacrifices—would become a priest). Exactly why Augustine was so focused on sexual sin, as opposed, say, to the sin of pride—which he demonstrated far more consistently and flagrantly throughout his life—is not entirely clear. In his *Soliloquies,* written shortly after his conversion, Augustine, who had already fathered his son, Adeodatus (c. 372–88), produces this charming description of woman:

> Portray woman as you will, endow her with every good thing, yet I have made up my mind that nothing is more to be shunned than union with woman. I know nothing that so topples a man from the defense of his own soul's battlements than female attractions and the carnal couplings that are the condition of having a wife. If a philosopher is allowed to beget children—a point I am not sure of—then he who has sex only for that purpose gets my admiration but not my imitation. . . . I have therefore laid this demand on myself (rightly and usefully, I believe)—to protect the freedom of my soul by giving up any concern or quest or contract with a wife.[20]

By this point, Augustine had already, at Monica's insistence, packed off his mistress and the mother of his son, but had also decided not to yield to Monica's wish that he take a wife of higher social status. For him, being a Christian and a philosopher had become antithetical to sex. In a long commentary, written in the mid-390s, on the Sermon on the Mount, Augustine added to the misogynist Christian template already provided by Paul. "Thus a good Christian [man] is found in one and the same woman to love the creature of God, whom he desires to be transformed and renewed; but to hate the corruptible and mortal conjugal connection and sexual intercourse; that is to love in her what is characteristic of a human being, to hate what belongs to her as a wife."[21] One can only imagine what a soul-nurturing experience it must have been to serve as Augustine's mistress and the mother of his son.

Suspicion of the body was a high-toned intellectual fashion not confined to Christians or Manicheans but also shared by pagans, and had a long tradition among ascetics in Roman civilization. The second-century emperor Marcus Aurelius, for example, is said to have given up the act of intercourse as soon as he had fulfilled his imperial duty of producing an heir. He memorably described the sex act between a man and woman in his *Meditations* as "the friction of an entrail and the expulsion of mucus accompanied by a kind of spasm."[22] Julian (332–63), the last pagan emperor of Rome and a convert from Christianity, held the same suspicious, disdainful view of the body and sexuality as Augustine. Religious conversion (to or from Christianity) required concentration and devotion to the gods or to God, but it did not require devotion to the natural expressions, such as sexual love, of divine creation.

In describing the moment of his conversion, Augustine quotes Paul's epistle to the Romans and says his eye was drawn to a passage advising the faithful to abjure any pleasure in "reveling and drunkenness . . . lust and wantonness . . . quarrels and rivalries. Rather, arm yourselves with the Lord Jesus Christ; spend no more on nature and nature's appetites" (13:13). Augustine declares that he has no desire and no need to read more of the passage in order to confirm his rejection of carnal pleasures and his embrace of faith. "For in an instant, as I came to the end of the sentence, it was as though the light of confidence flooded into my heart and all the darkness of doubt was dispelled." Augustine then told Monica that he "no longer desired a wife or placed any hope in this world but stood firmly on the rule of faith. . . ."[23] As a new Christian, Augustine rejected even those pleasures permitted to Christians. For him, it was better to burn than to marry.

•

This severe theology may explain the enduring fascination of *Confessions* for Christians, but it does nothing to illuminate the appeal of the book for some atheists, even though they regard the absolute truth cherished by Augustine as a fantasy and as the source of many of the world's ills. I certainly do not find Augustine a particularly appealing character. In his portrait of the church father as a young man, I see him as the sort of familiar male intellectual who spends most of his time in verbal joustings with male friends—especially the sort of acolyte friends who might consider him first among equals. And I despise

Augustine's views on Judaism, although it is possible that some of my ancestors—especially in regions that are now part of Germany and Poland—survived because of his formula for conversion and harassment that stopped short of extermination. I cannot, as a person shaped by Enlightenment thought and twentieth-century science, even begin to share Augustine's definitions of evil.

The real emotional power of *Confessions* lies in the spectacle of a man of high intellect struggling to reconcile his own reason with the acceptance of absolute truth required by his chosen faith. As he moves toward the conclusion of his personal story, Augustine presents a discussion of memory that belongs to the greatest Western literature of any era. These pages also demonstrate that Augustine was, for all the scientific ignorance of his time, an instinctive man of science: he was not the sort of person who trusted the evidence of his own eyes and ears as the measure of all things. And yet he was also a man who could call curiosity a disease, and the secrets of nature mysteries that should not be probed by human beings. It is not surprising that a man so deeply conflicted about the fundamental question of whether humans have the right to know and to understand nature—precisely because they are endowed with reason—should have taken many years to bow his head to a new faith and figure out a way to define it as reasonable. A world in which reason is seen as good and curiosity as evil cannot be a comfortable place for any thoughtful human being. The senses, Augustine points out in his discussion of memory, do not fully explain the storage of images in the mind. "All these things, each of which entered by its own avenue, are distinctly and under general heads there laid up: as, for example, light, and all colours and forms of bodies, by the eyes; sounds of all kinds by the ears; all smells by the passage of the nostrils; all flavours by that of the mouth; and by the sensation of the whole body is brought in what is hard or soft, hot or cold. . . . All these doth that great receptacle of memory, with its many and indescribable departments, receive, to be recalled and brought forth when required. . . . And yet the things themselves do not enter it, but only the images of the things perceived are there ready at hand for thought to recall. And who can tell how these images are formed, notwithstanding that it is evident by which of the senses each has been fetched in and treasured up?"[24]

Augustine did not, of course, understand either the sensory properties of memory or the ways in which the brain stores experience—in part because of the primitive state of medicine and biology, and in part because of the distinctions he made, as a Christian, between the physical and spiritual realms. But the question he asks—how does memory do what it does?—is the same question being posed in an age of biogenetic research. We know more, but by no means all, of the answers today—as evinced by the still-frustrating and frustrated search for any effective treatment for Alzheimer's disease, that fatal degeneration called "dying from the top" by Enlightenment thinkers, who were aware that men as brilliant as Isaac Newton had lost all memory before they died.

In one of the most beautiful, evocative passages about memory in the Western canon, Augustine observes:

> This same memory contains also the affections of my mind; not in the manner in which the mind itself contains them when it suffers them, but very differently according to a power peculiar to memory. For without being joyous, I remember myself to have had joy; and without being sad, I call to mind my past sadness; and that of which I was once afraid, I remember without fear; and without desire recall a former desire. Again, on the contrary, I at times remember when joyous my past sadness, and when sad my joy. Which is not to be wondered at as regards the body; for the mind is one thing, the body another. If I, therefore, when happy, recall some bodily pain, it is not so strange a thing. But now, as this very memory itself is mind (for when we give orders to have a thing kept in memory, we say, "See that you bear this in mind;" and when we forget a thing, we say, "It did not enter my mind," and, "It slipped from my mind," . . .)[25]

Augustine could not possibly have understood that the mind is inseparable from the body—nor would he believe that today if he held the same religious conviction, as many do, that man was created by God as an exception within nature. One need not be a religious believer to be disturbed by the fact that what we call the mind is entirely dependent on the proper operation of the physical human brain. There are even scientists who long for evidence that the human mind has a dimension independent of the body—a thoughtful, emotional, or spiritual dimension that cannot be quantified or measured in the laboratory. Such claims are necessary if one is to maintain that man is above the rest of the kingdom of nature—not only because of that undeniable fact, the superior human brain, but because of some other fundamental difference separating the human species from all other creatures. Augustine, though, was asking his questions about memory without being able to stand on the shoulders of giants. Both the limits of his scientific understanding and his conflicted sense that there might be more to understand are on display in the observation that the birds of the air and beasts of the field also possess memory—or they would not be able to return to their nests or earthly lairs.

Then, alas, Augustine the philosopher—curious in spite of his guilt about being curious—shifts from his general discussion of memory to what concerns him specifically as Augustine the Christian. How can it be that, before his conversion, he had no "memory" of God Himself? Again, he seeks to distinguish man from the birds and beasts. The knowledge of God, he argues, is nothing like either a bird's "memory" of its nest or a man's recollected emotion. "Where then did I find Thee, that I might learn Thee?" he asks. "For in my memory Thou wert not, before I learned Thee. . . . Place there is none; we go backward and forward, and there is no place."[26]

Augustine can come up with no answer other than the willful rejection of the presence of God by a man who has obscured any supreme being from memory—just as a baby commits sins without knowing what he is doing. "Too late loved I Thee, O Thou Beauty of ancient days, yet ever new! too late I loved Thee! And behold, Thou wert within, and I abroad, and there I searched for Thee; deformed I, plunging amid those fair forms which Thou hadst made. *Thou wert with me, but I was not with Thee.*"[27] (Italics mine.) Only when Augustine recognizes divine beauty through an act of free will—conversion—does God enter what would today be called his long-term memory. Thus, the gripping, extended passages on memory hold an atheist only until the appearance of the contrived (too contrived even for many devout religious believers) device portraying the entry of a supreme being— a real deus ex machina—into a previously empty storage unit. What follows, though—the conclusion of Augustine's personal story—is even stranger and more off-putting. Having renounced women and volitional, consensual sex, Augustine is still concerned about the sexual evil he may commit when his free will is weakened by sleep. He is concerned, to put it bluntly, about wet dreams. Despite his vow of continence, which he keeps by day, Augustine is unable to repress sexual images in his sleep. "But there yet live in my memory (whereof I have much spoken) the images of such things, as my ill custom there fixed . . . in sleep, not only so as to give pleasure, but even to obtain assent, and what is very like reality." He expresses the hope that God will increase his grace "to quench even the impure motions of my sleep!"[28]

Wet dreams do not fit the free-will paradigm explaining the existence of evil, but Augustine gets around this problem by reasoning, quite reasonably, that sleep is a state in which the will of human beings is considerably attenuated. Because we are stained by nature, there can be no complete and perfect union with God—no complete conversion, if you will—until the afterlife. There are limits, therefore, to "free will." Although Augustine explicitly denies this elsewhere in his memoir, he cannot ignore the evidence of his own experience.

The dispiriting conclusion of the long, initially splendid section on memory, which falls back on divine grace as the only possible antidote to the commission of unintended sin, explains (like his ruminations on infant sins) why Augustine's thought would one day become a pillar of Calvinist theology. It also explains why wet dreams figure less prominently than discourses about divine love in centuries of Christian commentary on *Confessions*. Nocturnal emissions strike a less-than-lofty note, although the note was supplied by the author himself, near the end of what is considered by many Christians to be the second-greatest conversion story ever told, outshone only by the rudely and divinely interrupted horseback ride on the road to Damascus.

2

THE WAY, THE TRUTH, THE LIFE,
THE EMPIRE

B Y 415, when Augustine was presiding as bishop of Hippo in North Africa and emerging as one of the church's most influential theologians for time and eternity, nearly 350 years had passed since stories began circulating around the Mediterranean world about the fateful fall off a horse by one Jew, Saul of Tarsus, on the road to Damascus. Improbably, Saul's embrace of another Jew, Jesus of Nazareth, as the Messiah foretold in ancient Hebrew prophecies had, by Augustine's time, begun to reshape the religious and political character of the Roman Empire in ways that would define and redefine Western history for the next fifteen hundred years.

The year 415 also marks the murder of Hypatia, a mathematician who has also been called the last pagan philosopher, by a Christian mob in Alexandria. Hypatia's birth date is uncertain; it may have been as early as 350 or as late as 360. We owe much, arguably all, of our modern knowledge about Hypatia's death to Edward Gibbon, who owed all of his knowledge to two Christian chroniclers—with very different views about the celebrated female scholar—who described the episode in the fifth and seventh centuries. Gibbon drew on the sources to provide a memorable description of the hacking to death of Hypatia. "On a fatal day, in the holy season of Lent," he recounts, "Hypatia was torn from her chariot, stripped naked, dragged to the church, and inhumanly butchered by the hands of Peter the reader and a troop of savage and merciless fanatics: her flesh was scraped from her bones with sharp oyster-shells, and her quivering limbs were delivered to the flames."[1] Peter was a minor cleric and rabble-rouser who, like many Christians, considered Hypatia's intellectual reputation especially scandalous because she was a woman.* A recent biographer describes her as a woman who stood for "intellectual values, rigorous mathematics, ascetic Neoplatonism, the crucial role of the mind, and the voice of temperance and moderation in civic life."[2] She probably received students at home, although legend says she also taught amid the ruins of the Library of Alexandria, which had been ravaged so many times in previous centuries (beginning in 48 B.C.E., when Julius Caesar set the Alexandrian fleet on fire in the harbor and the flames spread to the library). The remains of the building and its manuscripts were finally destroyed by Christians in the last decade of the fourth century, when Hypatia would have been in her thirties or forties. The fate of Hypatia, in what had long been one of the most cosmopolitan and cultivated cities of the ancient world, is in a sense a coda to a thirty-year period bracketing the turn of the century, during which the Catholic Church joined with Christian rulers to suppress paganism and other religions, most notably Judaism. These religions had been allowed to operate freely within the purview of Rome as long as they mounted no direct challenge to imperial rule. The church also enlisted the support of the state in fighting numerous heresies within its ranks; only the Roman church was recognized as the form of Christianity deserving of imperial privilege in the West.

The Christian narrative of this period is quite different. It skips over the decades when temples were razed, books of pagan philosophy burned, and pagan citizens threatened physically and financially if they refused to convert. Instead, the church's version of history jumps forward and emphasizes the role of Roman Catholicism in preserving the remains of classical culture during the medieval era, both in the Vatican and in monasteries throughout Europe. The church's own actions, in encouraging the devastation of repositories of Greco-Roman culture by fanatical Catholic mobs, are largely ignored. Where would the

---

* Peter is, however, described by John, the Coptic bishop of Nikiu—one of Gibbon's sources and hostile to Hypatia—as "a perfect believer in all respects in Jesus Christ."

written remnants of pagan culture be safer from barbarous Christians than in the fortresses of religion itself—in protected, elite ecclesiastical settings where Christianity's enemies would have no access to the classics? In its boastfulness about preserving pagan manuscripts, the church resembles the proverbial child who kills his parents and begs the court for mercy on grounds that he is an orphan. As Charles Freeman observes in *The Closing of the Western Mind,* "The historian is indeed deeply indebted to the monks, the Byzantine civil servants and the Arab philosophers who preserved ancient texts, but the recording of earlier authorities is not the same as maintaining a tradition of rational thought."[3]

By the opening decade of the fifth century, the once-invincible, increasingly shaky Roman Empire in the West had not yet become a monist Christian world. Not quite yet. The system by which historical events were assigned to the period B.C. or A.D., for example, as defined by the mythical date of the birth of Christ, was not even in use.* But as the chain of events in Alexandria demonstrates, the shift from paganism to Christendom was already well under way, as was the unholy or holy (depending on one's perspective) alliance between church and state. This was most evident in the urban centers of the empire, where Jews, Christians, and pagans, worshipping many deities, clashed as the ability of Roman civil authority to hold various religions in balance receded. Here the iconographic spiritual intellectuals like Augustine operated within a context of political power and turmoil that often applied strong economic pressure, with or without violence, to people who wanted to be on the right side of the new state religion.

The unpunished death of Hypatia occurred at a time when not only was it economically advantageous to be a Christian in urban areas

---

* Victor of Tennono, a seventh-century African chronicler, is believed to be the first historian who used the "A.D." dating system. The English monk Bede's *Ecclesiastical History of the English People,* completed in 731, is the first major, widely known historical work, beginning in the pre-Christian era with the Roman conquest of Britannia, to use the dating system based on the birth of Christ. This system was used in the West until the late twentieth century, when it was replaced, in many scholarly works, by the usage B.C.E. ("before the common era") and C.E. The locution "common era," of course, is a recognition that many peoples, including Jews, Muslims, and most Asians, do not consider the birth of Christ the most important event in history—if they consider it a historical event at all. Throughout this book, I have simply used the year for historical events after the beginning of the common era. Events before the common era are noted as B.C.E.

but when many wealthy Romans had embraced the faith and vastly enriched the church. One of Augustine's letters recounts the story of Pinianus and Melania the Younger, a wealthy Roman couple who fled the onetime capital of the empire after it was sacked by Alaric and the Visigoths in 410. The couple first stopped in Thagaste, Augustine's native city, where his friend Alypius (who is discussed extensively in *Confessions*) was bishop. After Pinianus and Melania gave generously to adorn what had once been a modest church in Thagaste, Alypius took them to visit his old friend Augustine in the larger city of Hippo. The laymen of Augustine's congregation crowded around the couple and demanded then and there that Pinianus be made a priest of the Hippo church. This conscription of laymen into the priesthood was increasingly common, especially if there was profit for the church in the clerical draft. (Marriage for priests was then a gray zone, but married men who entered the priesthood were almost always permitted to keep their wives.) Augustine said frankly that the purpose was "so as to retain among them a man of wealth who was known to despise money and give it away freely."[4] Such men and women gave most freely of all to the other Christians and Christian institutions, and the largesse from wealthy Christians strengthened the church in every city in its attempts to impose its religious agenda on once-secular Roman officials. The embrace of Jesus is viewed and portrayed by the church as an inevitable, supernaturally driven victory. And though there is no denying the spiritual power of the message proclaimed by the Jesus of the Gospels, there is also no denying that many Catholic authorities, especially as they gained political influence, used their new power to punish those who were not persuaded by the stories of the carpenter from Nazareth who rose from the dead. The shakiness of imperial authority provided opportunities for all proselytizers promoting different ways of life and faith, but only the Catholic Church, thanks to a unique confluence of its organizational strengths and the empire's weaknesses, managed to take full advantage of the anxieties of the era.

.

At the beginning of the transitional fourth century, almost no one would have predicted the triumph of Christianity in spite of the growing strength and visibility of Christians throughout the empire. The

Emperor Diocletian, who ruled from 284 to 305, inaugurated what would become the century of Christianity's ascendancy with a persecution of Christians that would come to occupy a mythological place in the history of the church. This era is worth revisiting, because Diocletian's moves against the church provided an organizing myth and memory that helped Christianity gain vast numbers of new converts later in the century. The emperor known today mainly for his hounding of Christians is recognized by most historians as the great administrative, economic, and military reformer of the late empire. By reorganizing the empire into a tetrarchy under four leaders (he was definitely first among nonequals), Diocletian was able to reinforce the borders so vulnerable to barbarian invasion, and to organize new systems of taxation. Historical apologists for Christianity, as distinct from historians of Christianity, are interested almost exclusively in Diocletian's antipathy to their faith.

A century earlier, all inhabitants of the empire (except slaves) had been made Roman citizens. Diocletian expanded the concept, "stressing that a common citizenship meant accepting common responsibility for the state, and so those whose allegiances were questionable suddenly found themselves more vulnerable."[5] Freeman observes that the Roman state had always regarded Christians with some degree of concern, even when they were not being persecuted, because they "posed the classic political dilemma: how far can one show tolerance to a group that itself condemns the tolerance of the state in allowing pagan worship to continue?"[6]

By the beginning of the fourth century, Diocletian was convinced that a large, well-organized community—and the church was already structured on a disciplined, hierarchical basis—did pose a threat to a centralized state that wished all citizens to accept equal responsibility for the common welfare (and pay equal taxes). The emperor's first action against the Christians focused on property, and the way his targeted enemies responded would lead to a permanent schism within Christianity. In 303, the emperor demanded that Christian congregations turn over their holdings—buildings, books and scriptures, valuable sacred vessels, and liturgical cloths—to the state. Some bishops told their communicants to give up their property; the Donatist clerics (especially in North Africa) not only refused to turn over the church holdings but condemned other congregations for doing so.

The Donatists' condemnation of other Christians—since the "others" ultimately won out—created the permanent schism that began in the fourth century. In Augustine's time, the Donatists considered themselves, not those affiliated with the Church of Rome, the "real" Christians—because no true Christian could have submitted to the state by giving up sacred writings and objects.

It is certainly true that resistance from some Christians had strengthened Diocletian's resolve to punish all Christians for their faith. Learning that some congregations had refused to give up their property, Diocletian issued a new decree that priests and bishops be imprisoned not only until they turned over the church's holdings but also until they made official sacrifice to pagan gods. In April 304, the death penalty was decreed for all Christians, clergy or lay, who refused to sacrifice. Ironically, the refusal of the Donatists to give up church property fueled the persecutions that would remain foundational to the Christian exegesis of history long after the Donatists had been rejected by Roman Catholicism and dismissed as schismatics.

Exactly how many Christians died in these persecutions is impossible to determine. Estimates based on the few contemporary sources range from a low of three thousand to a high of twenty thousand, and all depend on unverifiable statistics measuring the Christian population at the time. Historians agree that such estimates are inherently unreliable, if only because the religious landscape was shifting rapidly and Roman citizens in late antiquity had good reason, at various times, not to reveal their true beliefs. Also, Christians were more numerous in cities—and ancient census-takers (like modern demographers) could not keep up with immigration from the countryside into urban areas.

Even while Diocletian still ruled as emperor, the other members of the tetrarchy varied greatly in their interpretation of the edicts regarding religion. Galerius, appointed by Diocletian to govern the Danube regions, rounded up, tortured, and executed Christians en masse. Constantius, another member of the tetrarchy (and the father of Constantine the Great), is said to have avoided both torture and death sentences. Some local pagan governors permitted Christians to acknowledge only the existence of a supreme being, without specifying whether that being was Zeus, Jesus, or the Holy Trinity.* Diocle-

---

* Of the Trinity, I will only say here that the issue of whether Jesus was God—in substance, the equal of God the Father—was not settled theologically until 381, after a long evolution of the Nicene Creed of 325. By the end of the fourth century, Christians who

tian's persecution, and the more brutal follow-up by Galerius, was no exception to the rule that attacks on Christians were sporadic and did not outlast the ruler himself. When Galerius died in 311, the pressure on Christians eased almost immediately. Christians viewed Galerius's death as a demonstration of well-deserved divine vengeance. Lactantius, a Christian writer, exulted over the horrendous suffering of Galerius before his death, describing the illness in excruciating detail: "His bowels came out, his whole anus putrefied. . . . The stench filled not just the palace but the whole city. . . . His body, in intolerable tortures, dissolved into one mass of corruption."[7]

Because the roundups and executions that began under Diocletian came to such a swift end with Galerius's death, they strengthened Christianity in the short run as well as the long run by providing a powerful example of the faith for potential converts longing for a moral life that made more demands and provided more spiritual rewards than paganism.

The story of Diocletian's persecution has become a sustaining myth of official Catholicism in a fashion that resembles the place of American nineteenth-century persecution of Mormons in the official history of the Church of Jesus Christ of Latter-day Saints. Catholics educated in parochial schools in the twentieth century were immersed in the martyrology of the Diocletian era. (Apart from Augustus, whose census sent Mary and Joseph off to Bethlehem to be counted, and Nero, I believe that Diocletian was the only Roman emperor whose name I learned in Catholic school.) We schoolchildren, tainted as we were with original sin, took a ghoulish pleasure in the stories of exotic torture on behalf of the faith. After the apostle Peter (crucified upside down because he told his Roman tormentors that he was unworthy to die as his savior had), Paul (beheaded because, as a Roman citizen, he was entitled to a more dignified end than crucifixion), and Nero, who set Rome afire and blamed Christians, the nuns turned to the martyrs of Diocletian's era to praise and define the bravery of the early Christians.

One of my favorites was Saint Vitus (for whom the neurological

did not believe that Jesus was God were deemed heretics—a cause in which the church was able to enlist the aid of imperial authority. Of the Holy Ghost, whom most lay Catholics have always found incomprehensible, the less said the better. This spirit, however, is also an equal part of the Trinity in Catholic theology. For those who did not have a Catholic education, one of the more lucid explanations of the evolution of this theology in the morning of Christendom appears in James Carroll's *Constantine's Sword,* pp. 189–92.

disease Saint Vitus' dance is colloquially named), who supposedly died in 303. Vitus is also the patron saint of dogs, young people, actors, comedians, and mummers, and is asked to intercede in cases not only of Saint Vitus' dance (the correct scientific name is Sydenham's chorea, a neurological disorder) but also of epilepsy and insomnia. The details of his martyrdom, though, are obscure. Even the church classifies the Vitus stories as legend rather than fact, but of course I was not told that as a child. I was particularly enthralled by the tortures that Vitus was said to have survived through divine intervention before God finally let him be put to death. According to legend, he emerged intact from a cauldron of molten lead and then, when Vitus was thrown into a lion's den, the fearsome animal turned tame and cuddled against the future martyr. (The Vitus legends are yet another example of the appropriation of the Hebrew Bible by early Christianity. In the book of Daniel, the tyrant Nebuchadnezzar throws Daniel into the lion's den and his companions, Shadrach, Meshach, and Abednego, into a fiery furnace for refusing to bow down to idols. All emerge unscathed as testimony to the power of the God of Israel.)

Stories of Diocletian's martyrs provided perverse entertainment for Catholic schoolchildren in the twentieth century, but in the fourth century, they were the glue that helped bind together the Christians who were becoming a majority in the empire's cities. A pagan majority, pagan worship, and the shrines for pagan rituals persisted much longer—it is generally thought, for centuries—in the countryside.

The bravery of the Christians who went willingly to their deaths, especially when the persecutions were a relatively recent memory, was a powerful tool for attracting converts, in much the same fashion as secular martyrs serve to attract new adherents to political groups seen (rightly or wrongly) as a persecuted vanguard. Vitus was not just *my* favorite martyr; according to contemporary chroniclers, his devotional cult flourished in Central Europe and was responsible for many conversions in that part of the empire as the political tide was turning decisively against purely secular imperial authority.

·

Soon after the end of the persecutions, Constantine the Great, having succeeded his father, beheld his miraculous vision at the Milvian Bridge, and ushered in what was to be the first empowered Christian century of the decaying Roman Empire. Within the year, Constantine was sole emperor in the Western portion of the empire. The East was ruled by Licinius, who had succeeded to the throne after Galerius's little-mourned death. Despite Constantine's vision, after which he displayed the cross as a military standard in a manner that elevated Christianity in the imagination of his soldiers and his subjects, Constantine did not instantly impose Christianity; he began a long, slow, uneven process that would result in the victory of the faith by the end of the century. In 313, Constantine and Licinius jointly issued the Edict of Milan, a document that nullified all of the tetrarchy's edicts against Christians and stated that "freedom of worship ought not to be denied," and that decisions about faith, for Christians, pagans, and Jews, should be relegated to "each man's free choice."

It sounds good—almost like an Enlightenment document—if one ignores the fact that imperial edicts, unlike democratic constitutions, can be modified by the whim (or long-term plan) of a single ruler. Constantine soon began to renege on the promise of religious freedom as far as Jews were concerned. In 315, he issued a new edict, forbidding Jews—and only Jews—from proselytizing. Much later in the fourth century, however, Judaism demonstrated its continuing appeal for outsiders by attracting large numbers of Arabs, with whom the Jews had generally lived in amity throughout the early Diaspora, in Himyar (now Yemen). The Arab converts to Judaism proved just as intolerant of Christians as Christians were proving to be of Jews in late antiquity, and expended a fair amount of effort in the fifth century trying to wipe out the Christians among them. In the end, around 525, the Arab Jews of Himyar were vanquished when a much larger force of Ethiopian Christian troops crossed the Red Sea to attack them. (Today a tiny remnant of those Arab-descended Jews—no more than a few hundred—still live in a Yemen descending into chaos as militant Shia Houthi rebels—whose slogan is "Death to America, Death to Israel, Damnation to the Jews"—have seized power. The United States and Britain, which tried to get the remaining Jews out of Yemen, both closed their embassies as a result of escalating violence in 2015. Suleiman Jacob, the unofficial rabbi of a community of just fifty-five Jews in the capital of Raida, said in a poignant interview, "There isn't a single one of us here who doesn't want to leave. Soon there will be no Jews in Yemen, inshallah."[8])

•

Most conversions to Judaism in the late imperial period were undoubtedly the result of ordinary mixed marriages, demonstrating Jewish receptivity to outsiders rather than proselytizing in the active sense. Though not always an absolute requirement for a rabbi's approval of a mixed marriage, conversion was certainly a good idea for any pagan who wanted to get along with his or her (usually her) Jewish in-laws and the Jewish community. Mixed marriages, as demonstrated in the lives of both Constantine and Augustine, were also a factor in many conversions to Christianity. Unlike Jews, Christians were free to proselytize in any way they chose—in public and private, in churches as well as homes. During this period, there were also a good many conversions to paganism, especially Eastern cults, and Constantine made no move to prohibit pagan proselytizing. The most important reason for Constantine's hands-off policy regarding pagans was undoubtedly his awareness that most of his troops were pagan. They prayed to "God, the giver of victory and all good things," with no religious definition of the deity.[9]

Constantine's singular move against Jews was dictated by his understanding that the continuing existence of Judaism posed a unique challenge to Christianity's truth claim and was therefore of much greater concern than paganism to the church leaders whose loyalty the emperor wished to ensure. Although Constantine had not been baptized after his revelation at the Milvian Bridge—his formal christening would wait until he was much closer to death—the emperor soon began to give official preference to Christians, by filling the civil service from the ranks of the church. Delaying formal conversion until late in life, or even until death was imminent, was a common practice among Christian believers for the very reason Monica failed to baptize Augustine when he was sick as a child: the baptized Christian might go on to earn himself hell instead of being absolved at the last minute of sins committed before his formal admission to the church. The sacrament of Penance, also called the sacrament of Reconciliation, was not an individual confession to a priest in Augustine's time but a communal admission of wrong. The most serious sins—say, worshipping an idol or embracing a heresy—might eventually be wiped out after doing serious penances imposed by the bishop. The sacrament of Penance for healthy adults, by contrast, was more of a refillable get-out-of-jail-free card, in which the priest could absolve a penitent of the same repeated sin if he believed the sinner had sought forgiveness with a "firm purpose of amendment." This absolution had to be repeated if the sinner lapsed and repeated the same offense. Baptism, by contrast, wiped out all previous sins, so it made a certain amount of sense to delay being christened, as Constantine and Augustine's father, Patricius, did, until death seemed to be approaching and there was little time left to commit additional grave sins requiring penitential absolution. Of course, waiting too long, if the soul departed from the body before baptism, precluded the possibility of salvation. Timing was everything.

The delay in his baptism, however, did not prevent Constantine from becoming involved with church business in an unprecedented fashion. His real break with imperial tradition was not his favoritism toward Christians in office (what ruler does not make use of patronage to promote loyalty?) but his increasing tendency to involve himself, as ruler of Rome, in internal church quarrels. On theological matters, Constantine always sided with the Church of Rome. In 325, he did something no emperor had ever done before—or would even have thought of doing—by summoning all of the bishops of the church to a meeting in Nicaea, where the council gave birth to the Nicene Creed. The creed, which declared God the Father and God the Son to be one in substance, has probably been the cause of more controversy and bloodshed than any other doctrine in Christian history. It was as if the emperor had weighed in on the side of one rabbi over another in the interpretation of a crucial Jewish law, or chosen to displace Jupiter from pagan temples. The idea of the Trinity now had the imprimatur of not only the bishops but the head of state. Meanwhile, Constantine's mother, Helena, was traveling in Judaea in pursuit of the True Cross—a journey that, like the story of Vitus, is chronicled in unverifiable legend. What is verifiable is Constantine's aggressive program of using state money to build Christian churches. In 335, just two years before his death, Constantine presided over the dedication of the elaborate Basilica of the Holy Sepulcher in Jerusalem. After Constantine's death in 337, the status of both pagans and Christians fluctuated for the next half-century, depending on the religious convictions of the emperor. Christians continued to be subject to sporadic persecutions, but they never lost the economic and political foothold that Constantine had given them. Only Jews were on a clear, continuous downward track within the empire.

With a ruler who openly favored Christianity, the church began to attract more wealthy Romans. However, the interaction of wealth, Christianity, and the state was in its infancy during Constantine's reign. The process did not really accelerate and become a significant political force until mid-century, with the rise of a new middle and upper-middle class. The expansion in the number of newly prosperous and Roman citizens after 350 coincided with poverty and economic chaos for many in the lower classes, providing opportunities for religious appeals of every kind. In this competition, Christianity was better situated than any other faith, because it offered spiritual credit for charity in this life (a lure for the wealthy) and the promise of rewards in heaven for those who were poor enough to need charity. Paganism, by contrast, offered no coherent vision of an afterlife in which all of the sorrows of mortal existence would be wiped away.

The growing wealth of the Christian churches created a serious internal conflict within the Christian community, because there was an obvious contradiction between many of the anti-acquisitive themes of the scriptural Jesus and the church's approval and pursuit of riches and rich members. As Peter Brown notes, this dilemma was not easily solved, if it was solved at all, at either the communal or the individual level.

> The New Testament had passed on to the Christian communities of the later empire the challenge of Jesus to the Rich Young Man, along with his equally disturbing comment on the young man's failure to meet this challenge: that it was easier for a camel to go through the eye of a needle than for a rich man to enter the kingdom of God (Matt. 19:24). Once the truly rich had entered the churches, at the turn of the fourth and fifth centuries, these words took on a new immediacy. I am tempted to call this period the Age of the Camel. Christians of ascetic temperament watched expectantly to see which—if any—of the very large camels of their age were prepared to pass through the eye of the needle through renouncing their wealth. Those who did so received instant acclaim and have been studied with alacrity ever since. Compared with the heroes and heroines of renunciation, the silent majority of Chris-

tians who retained their wealth have been allowed to sink back into obscurity.[10]

The new wealth in the second half of the fourth century was not exclusively Christian, but neither Jewish wealth nor pagan wealth was under the control of a disciplined, centralized institution seeking converts in an organized way. The church was able to put its financial resources to use, in ways that less centralized faiths could not, in its effort to exercise more influence on the state. (One of the most unexpected developments in scholarship during the past two decades is the proliferation of new studies of the late Roman Empire emphasizing the role that economic factors played in the spread of Christianity. The indefatigable Brown—now professor emeritus of history at Princeton University—has examined the relationship in lively and illuminating detail. He observes that the new scholarship has opened "a vista of late Roman society from which many of the accustomed landmarks have vanished."[11] No one can read Brown's magisterial 2012 work, *Through the Eye of a Needle: Wealth, the Fall of Rome, and the Making of Christianity in the West, 350–550 AD,* without understanding that Christian money was essential to the proselytizing force of Christianity in the fourth and fifth centuries. Brown does not treat the subject as a heretofore unexplored scandal or as an argument against Christianity but as a complex historical association that has never received its due.)

·

Throughout the forty years after Constantine's death, most of the emperors, in both East and West, had Christian sympathies—though there were important exceptions. Licinius, who signed the Edict of Milan with Constantine, turned against Christians and purged them from the civil service even as Constantine was packing government offices with Christians in his portion of the empire. On the whole, though, Christianity made steady progress until Julian, a committed pagan who had been raised as a Christian, became emperor in 361. Known to Christian history as Julian the Apostate, he died in battle after a reign of just two years, in 363. Julian had attempted to undo Constantine's preferential treatment of Christianity and restore paganism as the state religion. He was brought up and educated as a Christian and only "came out" as a pagan after becoming emperor. It is probably inaccurate to describe Julian as a convert to paganism, since it seems likely that he had never accepted the Christian teachings of his childhood and waited prudently, until he gained imperial power, to declare his true religious allegiance.

A man with a clever and subtle mind, Julian took on the church at its two most vulnerable points. These were the proliferation of "heresies" within Christianity, and the continuing, maddening persistence of Jews, who rejected Jesus as the fulfillment of the Judaeo-Christian story. Like Constantine, Julian injected himself into the internal business of the church. Unlike Constantine, the last pagan emperor interfered to promote Christian diversity rather than uniformity—or, as the church fathers viewed it, to encourage heresies within their faith. Many bishops and priests of dissident Christian sects, like the Donatists, had been exiled by imperial officials who favored Catholicism. Julian ordered that all of the clergymen be allowed to return home and decreed that all forms of Christianity be tolerated within the empire. Nothing could have infuriated the church leaders more, since they considered freedom of religion a form of persecution, and freedom of conscience (if it conflicted with church doctrine) a sin against God.

The idea that the state would tolerate dissenting forms of Christianity—and call them Christian—was especially odious. Throughout most of Christian history, Roman Catholic and conservative Protestant leaders would take the same line. William Warburton, an eighteenth-century Anglican bishop and historian (who was as interested as Gibbon, from quite a different perspective, in the last pagan emperor and the role of Christianity in the decline of Rome as a secular power), described Julian's granting of full religious liberty not only to pagans but to all Christians as "this mask of moderation and equity for no other purpose than to inflame the dissensions of the Church."[12] (Warburton's analysis was untroubled by the fact that his own faith was, and had been since its inception under Henry VIII, deemed heretical by Rome.)

Aggravated as the Catholic hierarchy was by the emperor's extension of religious liberty to dissident Christians viewed as rebels and heretics, the church rulers were even more outraged by Julian's attempt to relegitimize Judaism as one of many religions sanctioned by imperial authority. One of the most provocative actions taken by Julian during his reign was his unsuccessful attempt to rebuild the temple that had been destroyed by the Romans. Julian saw Christians, not Jews, as a threat to imperial authority—and especially to the paganism he wished to restore as the empire's favored, albeit not exclusive, religion. He understood fully that the reason for the Catholic Church's *Adversus Judaeos* position was Catholicism's claim to have fulfilled and therefore superseded the predictions of the ancient Hebrew prophets. The destruction of the temple by the Romans, therefore, was seen as definitive proof of Jewry's defeat and of Christianity's claim to be the fulfillment of Jewish law and prophecy. What could deal the Christians a more decisive blow than the renascence of the site most sacred to Jews throughout the known world?

In 363, Julian issued an edict of toleration that allowed Jews to return to Jerusalem and provided for the rebuilding of the temple. He also wrote an extraordinary public letter, addressed to the Jewish community throughout the empire, in which he noted that the only difference (a rather big difference) between Jews and pagans was that Jews offered sacrifice to one god and pagans to many. Then Julian designated money from the imperial treasury for the specific purpose of rebuilding and restoring the temple to its former glory. After the edict was circulated, Jews converged on Jerusalem from distant corners of the empire to participate in the project so integral to their religion. Julian, with his Christian education, would have been familiar with passages in Matthew and Luke in which Jesus supposedly predicted the destruction of the temple. He understood that Christians would understand the literal rising of a new temple from the ashes and stones of the old site as a direct challenge to the words spoken by their god and savior.

Of course, the Third Temple was not to be. The Jews who had begun to gather stones were working on a site rich in natural gas deposits, and continual explosions gave Christians cause to rejoice. The explosions, probably caused by earthquakes, were naturally seen as the hand of God striking down Jewish efforts to rebuild their most sacred site. Still, this quixotic endeavor might conceivably have come to fruition had Julian lived and been able to pour the treasure of Rome into righting whatever went wrong with the project from geological causes or faulty engineering. But he was killed in battle in the same year that he had issued the orders to rebuild the temple. Christians naturally regarded his death as a miracle and as a demonstration of the victory of Christ. Legend has it that, at the moment of his death, Julian uttered the words "Thou has conquered, Galilean." Stories of deathbed recantations by "apostates" would surface repeatedly throughout Christian history, but they were of utmost importance when Christianity had not yet succeeded in conquering the Western world. Twenty-five years after Julian's death, as Jews were being systematically persecuted under the Christian emperor Theodosius I, John Chrysostom repeatedly referred to the debacle of Julian's attempt to rebuild the temple as an example of the divine wrath that had already been visited upon Jews for denying Jesus and that would be visited on anyone else who refused to accept the triune God.

Whether the Christian story would have unfolded differently, and less successfully, had Julian, like Constantine, exercised imperial power for a quarter-century is one of the unanswered and unanswerable questions of religious history. It seems unlikely that the Christianity would have died out, even if paganism had been restored as the official state religion. After all, Christianity and all of its "heretical" offshoots emerged when paganism was the official religion of the empire (however loosely interpreted). By the time of Julian's short rule, not only were there many more Christians throughout the empire—most of them converts from paganism, not Judaism—but the church possessed greater financial resources than it had just a half-century earlier. There is no reason to think that the faith would not have survived and constructed new martyrological myths if Julian had enjoyed a long reign, just as it had survived Diocletian's persecution. The only thing that can be said with some degree of certainty is that if Julian had been an effective ruler for decades, it would have taken much longer for Christianity to exert power over the state—and the nature of that power might have been more limited and therefore less devastating to those who did not share Christian beliefs.

·

The ascendancy of the church over secular authority accelerated in 379, when Theodosius I became emperor in the East. Theodosius ruled until 395, and the years of his tenure were characterized by even more serious economic troubles for the lower classes and even greater wealth for the upper-middle class. A number of important bishops, like Augustine, were themselves products of the new upper-middle class and depended on access to new money to finance their evangelical activities. More converts brought more money into the church coffers, and more money was required in order to reach out and attract more converts. The Catholic Church had much more appeal than ascetic sects (pagan or Christian) for the new bourgeoisie. If you were a wealthy exporter of, say, textiles in 390, would you join and give your money to a sect like the Manichees, who saw the flesh as evil (not a good marketing strategy for encouraging people to buy more cloth to drape around their bodies), or to an organized church that, even though it preached the gospel of eternal life, did not reject the comforts of this life? And if you were a displaced farmer who had not found a decent job in a city, would you seek solace from gods who promised nothing better in the future, or from a group that had the money to feed the poor even as it held out the promise of better things in the next world?

When Theodosius's rule began, the seat of empire was Milan, where Augustine's future mentor Ambrose presided as bishop (though years would elapse before the two future fathers of the church would meet). Meanwhile, Theodosius curried favor with church officials and well-off Christians and engaged in many conflicts with Ambrose over imperial versus church authority. In 388, Christians in Callinicus, a theretofore little-noticed town on the Euphrates River, destroyed a synagogue in what was to become a familiar theme. They were led by the bishop of the city—a once-unthinkable action that would soon become commonplace. They also torched a Gnostic house of worship, even though the Gnostics (who, like the Manichees, thought matter was generally evil) had just given in, under pressure from Theodosius, and pledged to practice the mainstream Christianity emanating from Italy. Theodosius, still under the illusion that his imperial authority trumped the church's power, ordered the offending Christians to rebuild both the synagogue and the Gnostic chapel—a common move by emperors when religious violence threatened civil order. Ambrose bluntly challenged Theodosius and declared any synagogue "a haunt of infidels, a home of the impious, a hiding place of madmen, under the damnation of God Himself."[13] Theodosius yielded, for what would not be the last time, to the implacable bishop.

In 390, another dispute between Theodosius and Ambrose had a similar outcome. In Thessalonika, a port on the Aegean in Greece and one of the earliest centers of the spread of Christianity, a civilian riot over taxes led to the death of a Roman garrison commander.* From Milan, Theodosius ordered military retaliation against the tax rebels, and thousands of civilians were said to have been killed. As news of the massacre filtered back to Milan, Ambrose threatened to refuse communion to Theodosius (many of the dead were Christians), and the Christian emperor was obliged to engage in damage control by humbling himself before the Christian community in Milan. Theodosius then took a step that would influence church-state relations for centuries: he volunteered to do penance publicly in Milan's Basilica Ambrosiana and seek absolution from Ambrose himself. As his surviving letters make clear, Ambrose viewed the penance as the emperor's acknowledgment of the church's authority over government. And the bishop was able to exact a significant price for having publicly rehabilitated Theodosius. Within weeks of the ceremony in the basilica, Theodosius gave his approval to laws banning, for the first time, all worship at pagan shrines. Throughout the empire, Christians soon began attacking and destroying shrines and cultural institutions with pagan associations.

The fallout from Thessalonika had a major impact in Alexandria, that longtime jewel of ancient culture. A mob destroyed the Serapeum, the city's oldest and most revered shrine. In 391, Jewish and pagan manuscripts were torched in what remained of the Great Library of Alexandria. After the destruction of the entire temple and its contents, it was said that the bishop of Alexandria had saved one image, "lest people should afterward deny that their forefathers had ever been so foolish as to worship such things. Some say that the image was a figure of Jupiter, the chief of the heathen gods; others say that it was the figure of a monkey, for even monkeys were worshipped by the Egyptians!" One of the greatest delights of the Christian attackers (second only to the destruction of ancient manuscripts) was identifying and breaking a wooden statue of the god Serapis and making the unsurprising discovery that the wood was infected with bugs and rodents. "The Egyptians' god had become an apartment block for mice," boasted the early Christian historian Theodoret (c. 393–c. 457), ". . . the head they

---

* Thessalonika is now the second-largest city in Greece, after Athens.

dragged through the whole city, so that his worshippers could see the impotence of the gods they had prayed to."[14]

From Milan, Theodosius issued formal congratulations to the Alexandrian Christians for their actions as defenders of their faith. Such kindhearted Christian efforts paved the way for the events of 415, which included the murder of Hypatia as well as the expulsion of unconverted Jews from Alexandria. This was not the first time the large and prosperous Jewish community of Alexandria had been attacked by the locals; it was the first time they had done it with a "bravo" from the emperor.

In the year 38, before Christianity existed as a religion, Alexandrian Jews, who had aided the Romans in their imperial administration of Egypt, were tortured and murdered in what has sometimes been termed the first real pogrom in Jewish history. Benzion Netanyahu cites this explosion in support of his rejection of Christianity as the main factor in Western anti-Semitism. He describes the violence in Alexandria as "the first manifestation of antisemitism in its fullest form. It originated in circumstances peculiar to Egypt in both the Greek and early Roman period. These were (a) the reliance of Jews for their protection and security on the country's rulers, who were mostly foreign; (b) the occasional assistance the Jews offered the rulers against the wishes of the non-Jewish population; (c) the stubborn insistence of the Jewish minority on equality of rights with the country's upper classes; (d) the rise of some Jews to high social levels; and (e) the projection by the Jews of a religious victory over the pagan cults and beliefs. These were the factors that set ablaze the Greek world with Jew hatred."[15] What Netanyahu ignores in his description of this pre-Christian pogrom was that the Roman authorities made a determined effort to bring the violence under control and eventually succeeded. Terrible as the assault had been, the Jews did not leave Alexandria, and their community grew larger and wealthier during the next century. There was no repetition of anti-Semitic atrocities on any large scale in the ancient city for several centuries—until the Christian Church and the state joined in their determination either to convert all Jews or to get rid of them by one means or another.

Theodosius was the key figure, even more significant than Constantine, in forging a working relationship between church and empire in opposition to all non-Catholic faiths. The sanitization—actually, a near canonization—of Theodosius, symbolizing that the church now possessed the right to legitimize the rulers of the state, was embodied in Ambrose's funeral oration for the emperor in 395:

> Relieved therefore of the doubt of conflicts, Theodosius of worshipful memory now enjoys everlasting light and eternal tranquility, and for the deeds which he performed in this body, he is recompensed with fruits of divine reward. And it is because Theodosius of worshipful memory loved the Lord his God, that he deserved the company of saints.[16]

The instigator of the massacre at Thessalonika was thus transformed into a meritorious resident of heaven. As for the once-secular authority of the empire, neither religious minorities nor the pagans who still constituted a majority could ever again count on imperial officials, as they had in the past, to crack down on those who used violence to stop others from practicing their religion.

.

When Christian mobs destroyed the Serapeum, Hypatia was a respected scholar and teacher. Theodosius's embrace of force to stamp out both non-Christian culture and non-Christian religion, including his official congratulations to the thugs who burned the non-Christian manuscripts, must have been a theretofore unimaginable blow to pagan intellectuals. Whatever her true age, Hypatia's life and fate must be viewed against the background of the growing imperial preference for Christianity and disdain for the classical pagan culture in which she was raised. Hypatia's father was the mathematician and astronomer Theon, best known for his surviving discourse on Euclid's *Elements*. A letter from one student, Synesius, indicated that Hypatia had taught him how to design and build an astrolabe, a portable astronomical calculator used into the nineteenth century. According to the historian of mathematics Morris Kline, the murder of Hypatia symbolized "the end of the era of Greek mathematics."[17]

Hypatia's death had nothing to do with heightened tensions between Christians and Jews, but it had everything to do with a political atmosphere in which the church was determined to attain a position as the only state-sanctioned religion. Brown writes that Egyptian Christian monks "shocked educated opinion by lynching a noble Alexandrian lady, Hypatia."[18] Hypatia's public slaughter, fueled by collective passions, did resemble a lynching, but she was much more than a "noble Alexandrian lady." Her death underscores the falsehood of the myth that Christianity won out solely by changing free hearts and minds and conveying a spiritual truth that the majority of the Roman Empire's subjects accepted naturally and voluntarily once they were exposed to the Gospels. Hypatia was not the victim of sudden mob passion; she was an exemplary victim of the hatred of non-Christians encouraged by the bishop of the city. Her brutal murder was an intellectual message delivered with the ultimate physicality.

There was no room for someone like Hypatia in a world where, only fifteen years earlier, an emperor had congratulated the Christian shock troops, known by the Greek word *parabolani,* for their destruction of early manuscripts. The *parabolani* did not arise as a spontaneous mob but were directly controlled by Bishop Cyril (that's Saint Cyril in Catholic history). Orestes, the prefect of Alexandria, who was a Christian but remained on good terms with both pagans and Jews, had asked Theodosius to limit the paramilitary force of Christian thugs to five hundred, but his request fell on deaf ears.

Orestes was also friendly with Hypatia, who corresponded extensively with both Christian and pagan intellectuals conversant with classical learning. Such relationships reflected the emergence of a new intellectual class dispersed in cities throughout the empire—the same group that would later provide an audience for Augustine's *Confessions.* Brown characterizes the era as one in which "able men, less burdened by the prejudices of an aristocracy and eager to learn, maintained a tone of vigor and disquietude that distinguishes the intellectual climate of Late Antiquity from any other period of ancient history."[19] In their energy and originality, these intellectuals resembled the thinkers of every era in which ancient certitudes give way to the doubts and enthusiasms of a new kind of society. That the men were willing to share ideas with an accomplished woman was one measure of their departure from classical tradition. Had Hypatia not engaged in a wide correspondence during her lifetime, the Christian sources upon which Gibbon based his account would not have known who she was or cared about her fate.

This intellectual flowering began when Christianity and paganism were still in rough equipoise under the weakening rule of Rome. The exchanges between Hypatia and male scholars represent yet another road not taken, a collaboration that might have been had Christianity not insisted on its absolute truth claim. For a continuing dialogue of enlightened intellectuals to have emerged from the cultural tumult of late antiquity, Christianity would have to have been, and subsequently developed into, a very different religion. There could be no better example of the stifling of the promising multireligious intellectual discourse than two commentaries by Christian scholars on the death of Hypatia—one written in the fifth century, the other near the end of the seventh century. The fifth-century Byzantine Christian historian Socrates Scholasticus provided an account of Hypatia's character and death that gave one of the last influential pagan intellectuals her due and deplored the manner of her death at the hands of Christians:

> There was a woman at Alexandria named Hypatia, daughter of the philosopher Theon, who made such attainments in literature and science, as to far surpass all the philosophers of her own time. Having succeeded to the school of Plato and Plotinus, she explained the principles of philosophy to her auditors, many of whom came from a distance to receive her instructions. On account of the self-possession and ease of manner, which she had acquired in consequence of the cultivation of her mind, she not infrequently appeared in public in presence of the magistrates. Neither did she feel abashed in going to an assembly of men. For all men on account of her extraordinary dignity and virtue admired her more.
>
> Yet even she fell victim to the political jealousy which at that time prevailed. For as she had frequent interviews with Orestes, it was calumniously reported among the Christian populace, that it was she who prevented Orestes from being reconciled to the bishop. Some of them, therefore, hurried away by a fierce and bigoted zeal, whose ringleader was a reader named Peter, waylaid her returning home, and dragging her from the carriage, they took her to the church called Caesareum, where they completely stripped her, and then murdered her with tiles. After tearing her body in pieces, they took her mangled limbs to a place called Cinaron, and burnt them. This affair brought not the least opprobrium, not only upon Cyril [the bishop] but also upon the whole Alexandrian church. And

surely nothing can be farther from the spirit of Christianity than the allowance of massacres, fights, and transactions of that sort.[20]

This denunciation of "fierce and bigoted zeal" was still possible among Christian intellectuals in the fifth century. But in a blink of historical time, fair-minded commentary about a pagan philosopher would be unthinkable for a Christian historian. In the seventh century, John, the Coptic bishop of Nikiu, told a completely different story about Hypatia. In John's view, Hypatia fully deserved what she got and had bewitched both the prefect Orestes and the Christian clerics with whom she corresponded about scientific matters. Of particular importance is the way in which John conflates Jews and pagans as enemies of the faith.*

And in those days there appeared in Alexandria a female philosopher, a pagan named Hypatia, and she was devoted at all times to magic, astrolabes and instruments of music, and she beguiled many people through Satanic wiles. And the governor of the city [Orestes] honored her exceedingly; for she had beguiled him through her magic. And he ceased attending church as had been his custom. And not only did he this, but he drew many believers to her, and he himself received the unbelievers at his house. And on a certain day when they were making merry over a theatrical exhibition connected with dancers, the governor of the city published an edict regarding the public exhibitions in the city of Alexandria. Now Cyril [the bishop] . . . was eager to gain exact intelligence regarding this edict. And there was a man named Hierax, a Christian possessing understanding and intelligence who used to mock the pagans and was a devoted adherent of the orthodox Father the

* The excerpts from Socrates Scholasticus and from the Chronicle of John, Coptic Bishop of Nikiu, were both originally written in Greek and have since been translated into English. Michael A. B. Deakin, an Australian historian of mathematics, provides a detailed history of these sources in a paper, "The Primary Sources for the Life and Work of Hypatia of Alexandria," dated August 1995. The document is available on the Web by entering the title in a search engine. (Since Web addresses of academic papers frequently change, I do not wish to frustrate readers by supplying one that may be out of date.) Deakin, author of *Hypatia of Alexandria: Mathematician and Martyr* (2007), points out that subsequent accounts of the death of Hypatia are all clearly derived from Socrates Scholasticus's account. They do not differ on the facts, as is clear from John's later hostile commentary, but on the meaning of Hypatia's death and its implications for Christianity.

patriarch and was obedient to his admonitions. . . . But when the Jews saw him in the theater they cried out and said: "This man has not come with any good purpose, but only to provoke an uproar." And Orestes the prefect was displeased with the children of the holy church, and Hierax was seized and subjected to punishment publicly in the theater. . . . And when [Cyril] heard this, he sent word to the Jews as follows: "Cease your hostilities against the Christians."

The chronicle goes on to talk about clashes between Jews and Christians, ending when "the Christians expelled Jews from the city, and pillaged all their possessions and drove them forth wholly despoiled, and Orestes the prefect was unable to render them any help." This attack on Jews was followed by the fatal attack on Hypatia. Bishop John exults in the fact that Hypatia was humiliated by being stripped and dragged through the streets of Alexandria before she died. The chronicle ends, "And all of the people surrounded the patriarch Cyril and named him 'the new Theophilus'; for he had destroyed the last remains of idolatry in the city."[21] And they lived happily ever after.

John's chronicle and its tone—including the use of the word "beguile"—remind us that Hypatia belongs as much to the history of feminism as to the history of the dominance sought by religions making absolute truth claims. Far from being a wily seductress, Hypatia did not marry and likely led a celibate life, in keeping with a variety of pagan and Christian sects and philosophies that embraced chastity at the time. What Christianity did not and could not embrace was chastity combined with a full intellectual life for a woman. Hypatia was a pagan ascetic to a fault, and she resembled the Emperor Julian in her contempt for the body—if even some of the legends handed down about her are to be believed. According to one story, she displayed a blood-soaked menstrual pad to discourage the attentions of one of her student-admirers. "That, young man, is what you have fallen in love with," she reportedly said, "and there is nothing beautiful about that."[22] The suspicion that Hypatia and Orestes were sexually involved fueled the rumors that she was responsible for preventing Orestes and the fanatical Cyril from compromising their differences over the relationship between church and state.

Respect for a female scholar was no higher among pagans and Jews than among Christians; the difference is that pagans and Jews did not take it upon themselves to kill Hypatia for being a woman who did not know her place. In 2009, the story of Hypatia was turned into a movie, *Agora,* examining Hypatia's history as a Neoplatonist philosopher and astronomer. The Chilean-Spanish director Alejandro Amenábar, amid the furor surrounding the release of the film in Europe (a controversy stoked largely by the Vatican), noted, "We are accustomed to seeing lions devouring Christians in films but not the transformation of Christians from a persecuted group to one that is powerful and armed."[23] In an effort to placate the Vatican, the film's Italian distributor invited high-level Catholic clergy charged with responsibility for religious orthodoxy to the premiere but described the reaction of those who did attend as "all on edge." Showings of *Agora* were canceled in Egypt, because the government feared attacks on its Coptic Christian minority, always a target for extreme Islamists in that country. (The fear that the film would instigate attacks is tragicomic, given that Islamic extremists today are every bit as opposed to science—and to learned women—as most fifth-century Christian theologians were to the influence of a female mathematician and philosopher.) However, the tense reaction of the Catholic Church to the movie offers a telling illustration of the investment that orthodox Catholicism still has in whitewashing its history regarding science and in presenting early Christians only as martyrs, not as persecutors who did everything possible to suppress learning that conflicted with church doctrine.

The Vatican's objections to a film depicting the ugly side of what Christians did to one female scholar more than seventeen hundred years ago is also motivated by the church's insistence that intimidation played no role in the growth of Christianity. The story of Hypatia challenges the myth that conversions came about only because of divine grace, reasoned persuasion, or both—and not because anyone was forced or intimidated into accepting the faith by seeing a pagan scholar murdered, a synagogue torched, or non-Christians losing jobs to those who had openly accepted Christ as their savior.

Not all of the church fathers initially agreed with tactics in which Christian violence against non-Christians was not only tolerated but, as in the case of Theodosius, supported by the state. Augustine had advised Christian government officials and church leaders to avoid combating heathenism by force. In a well-known sermon, Augustine preached, "We must first endeavour to break the idols in their hearts. When they themselves become Christians, they will either invite us to do the good work of destroying their idols, or they will be beforehand with us in doing so. And in the meanwhile, we must pray for them, not be angry with them."[24] This quote from Augustine appears today on a right-wing evangelical Christian Web site, accompanied by the assertion that "the wise teachers of the church knew that this would not be the right way of going to work, but that it would be more likely to make the heathens obstinate than to convert them."[25] The most conservative elements in both the Catholic and Protestant churches have adopted this line, because the idea of forced religious conversion is considered repellent today by most inhabitants of Western democracies.

It is hardly surprising that physical force remains a charged subject today for historical religions whose spread was facilitated by the unified power of church and state. But the concept and the practical reality of force should not be defined as purely physical, and should not be limited to exemplary cases like Hypatia's. Force is better defined as a state of mind, understandably shared by most people in societies where it is clear that official institutions, from the state to schools, allow no personal choice in matters of faith. It is entirely possible that many, perhaps the vast majority, of those living under this subtle yet all-powerful force sincerely adopt and adapt to the teachings of the approved religion and come to love them. We have no way of knowing, given that the only people who described their experience of conversion in the ancient world were the members of the rare minority of the literate. How did a pagan slave sold to a Christian master feel about the religious practices he would undoubtedly have to adopt? Slaves, before and after the spread of Christianity, were expected to follow the religion of their owners; this was a factor in early decrees preventing Jews from owning slaves. How did a pagan farmer feel when his region, and his tax obligations, came under the control of a Christian satrap? Perhaps, when a charismatic church leader like Augustine appeared on the scene in a city like Hippo, a religiously indifferent citizen was happy to join a new church that his neighbors had joined. We simply don't know. The only certainty is that, within a generation or two, the majority, in societies that predated the invention of the printing press, forgot that there ever had been a choice. At the beginning of the fifth century, in both the Western and Eastern sectors of the failing Roman Empire, just enough coercion was being applied to speed up and eventually ensure the triumph of forgetting.

3

COERCION, CONVERSION, AND HERESY

THE FOURTH-CENTURY rise of Catholicism, in a world of shifting imperial policy toward religion, was entwined with a variety of heresies (as defined by Rome) that have never disappeared from philosophical and religious discourse. In the modern world, yesterday's heretical cult often turns into today's respected religion, but in the fourth and fifth centuries, the reverse was true.

The average twenty-first-century American would laugh if the word "heresy" were used to describe the religious conversion of anyone close to her. If there are negative reactions, family heartburn is about as bad as it gets—although that can sometimes get pretty bad. Throughout most of history, however, social and family attitudes toward conversion depended mainly on whether the group in question was losing or gaining a believer. In the part of the world dominated by Christianity, intense feelings about religious conversion became integral to the bifurcated world of heresy and truth that emerged with the victory of Roman Catholicism, not only over paganism but over other forms of Christianity in the West. Only Judaism, because of its special historical and scriptural status as the predecessor of Christianity, stood outside the boundaries of this bifurcated theological universe.

The enduring power of the concept of true and false religions, even in an America where few citizens use the word "heresy" in public, can be seen in the appropriation of the word "Christian" by the religious right in the United States. When an American says, "I am a Christian," the declaration implies that those who disagree with the speaker's religious tenets, on either theological or philosophical grounds, cannot be "real" Christians. In the ancient world, the battle over heresies within and between various Christian groups always revolved around the questions of who the real Christians were; what sort of conversion and public testimony was required for "false" Christians to be reconciled with the "true" Christian community; and, eventually, whether the acceptance of a particular form of Christianity lined up with the prevailing political authority.

To muddy the religious landscape still further, heresies like Gnosticism included both Christian and non-Christian sects. It is often mistakenly thought that all Gnostics were Christians, largely because of the enormous attention paid in recent decades to the Gnostic gospels and their exclusion from the patristic canon. The only belief shared by all Gnostics was their vision of a world divided between spirit and matter. Manicheism, probably the largest of the Gnostic sects, drew heavily on Christian sources but was decidedly non-Christian. In retrospect, however, alternative versions of Christianity, professed by people who proudly proclaimed their reverence for Jesus, posed a more serious threat to the Roman church than any non-Christian heresy. Had the church not been able to suppress these dissenting Christian sects competing for and on the same turf, Catholicism would have looked more like Protestantism as it emerged from shards of the once-mighty empire.

Furthermore, the proliferation of heresies—not in small, isolated cults but in genuine movements that attracted converts—posed a special threat to the Roman church in regions like North Africa, where Catholics allied with Rome were a minority for many centuries among those calling themselves Christians. The Rome-based church's attempt, in concert with the state, to suppress dissenting Christians was accompanied by a change in attitudes on the part of many of Catholicism's founding fathers—Augustine among them—about the legitimacy of force to obtain converts and to prevent Catholics from converting to other branches of Christianity. The Augustine who had once said that Christians should not smash pagan idols but should persuade pagans to want to do the smashing themselves slowly changed his mind about coercion and about what ought to be done about all non-Christian religions, as well as heresies within the church.

Augustine initially thought that because Christianity represented a higher state of moral evolution than pre-Christian religions—including Judaism—there was no need for external pressure to spread the faith. Later in life, Augustine changed his mind and cited the punishments periodically visited upon the Israelites, God's chosen before the birth of the Messiah, as evidence that men undisciplined by superior external forces could not be expected to choose good or truth freely. Those Christians who gave in to the temptations of curiosity or carnality—and who did not, in Augustine's moral universe?—were no better than the ancient Israelites and must be made to obey God's laws through punishment administered by the church, the state, or both. Augustine took this attitude toward all of the heresies of his day, as well as toward pagans and Jews. He rejected the death penalty for Christian—and only Christian—heretics because it precluded any possibility of repentance. By the early 400s, Augustine had come to the conclusion that "rarely, no never, does it happen that someone comes to us with the wish to become a Christian who has not been struck by some fear of God."[1] He even noted that Paul's fall from the horse and his head injury were manifestations of divine force, without which Paul might never have embraced Christ. Augustine's adoption of the "a good knock on the head will set you straight" school of religious conversion is particularly remarkable in view of his own slow, unforced, and circuitous route to Christianity.

The words "heresy," "infidelity," and "apostasy" sound almost quaint today to liberal religious believers of many faiths as well as atheists—all of whom have been infected, according to the lights of traditional religion, by modernism. (In 1907, Pope Pius X declared in his encyclical *Pascendi Dominici Gregis*—"Feeding the Lord's Flock"—that "modernism embraces every heresy.") Conservative Islamists still use these words, especially "infidelity" and "infidel," but most Christian bishops do not—at least in public. What American Catholic bishop, exchanging quips with a Mormon and a nonsectarian Protestant running for the American presidency and eating a sumptuous dinner memorializing Al Smith, would wish to turn to his dinner companions on the dais and call them heretics or infidels?* In the fourth and early fifth

* The dinner in New York commemorating Al Smith, the first Catholic presidential candidate, is a quadrennial event before every presidential election. Smith's candidacy in

centuries, that is exactly what the fathers of the church did in public letters and sermons—and they were not obliged to have civic dinners with their religious enemies. But the church could never have waged such a vigorous fight against heresies, from without or within, had its leaders not benefited from the active help of the Roman state and its Christian emperors in the late fourth century.

In 382, Theodosius I became the first emperor to pronounce religious heresy a capital offense against the state. There is no evidence that the ultimate punishment prescribed by this law was enforced in any systematic way, given that groups like the Manicheans continued to flourish, but the edict's manifold provisions offered ample justification for a wide variety of lesser actions aimed at suppressing Christian, as well as non-Christian, sects abjured by the Roman church. "Heretical teachers were forbidden to propagate their doctrines publicly or privately," reports the Catholic Encyclopedia; "to hold public disputations; to ordain bishops, presbyters, or any other clergy; to hold religious meetings; to build conventicles or to avail themselves of money bequeathed to them for that purpose."* The law also permitted slaves who informed on heretical masters to buy their freedom by converting to Catholicism. The requirement of both conversion and money in exchange for freedom obviously calls the conventional spiritual narrative of conversion into question whenever and wherever slaves were concerned. We may not know how a pagan slave felt about having to follow his Christian owner's religion, but we know what he could do about it if he thought he could prove heresy on the part of the owner. (This interesting route to freedom would never be open to American slaves.)

·

It has been said by a number of scholars that Christianity introduced heresy into a pagan world that had never possessed such a concept. I would amend that generalization to emphasize a more important point

---

1928 was doomed from the start by anti-Catholic prejudice in an America that still looked askance at all non-Protestant religions.
* These prohibitions are cited in the *Codex Theodosianus*, under the heading "Regarding Heretics."

in the history of conversion: as Christianity consolidated its power, the church introduced the idea of individual religious heresy as a punishable offense and, on a collective scale, as a form of political treason. Absent punishment, heresy really has no meaning for heretics, apart from the knowledge that the majority religion rejects their ideas. Such knowledge—again, absent punishment—may be painful in some circumstances but a satisfying confirmation of superiority in others. Had Catholic bishops simply pointed fingers and yelled "heretic," without the support of the state to penalize those nonconformists, we might be reading books filled with pages about the Roman Catholic Heresy.

The Catholic definition of heresy was not limited to those who committed overt actions against Christians or Christian institutions; thinking differently, and refusing to accept the authority of the Roman church, was all it took to be stigmatized—first by the church, then by the state. The continued existence of a heretical group implied the legitimacy of a valid alternative within a given society, and that was as unacceptable to the Catholic Church as it had been to the ancient Israelites and would be in future Calvinist and Muslim theocracies.

The numerous religious movements considered heretical by the Church of Rome, even when confined to the first five centuries of Christianity, would provide (and have provided) material for a very large library. Dissident movements that flourished in the fourth and fifth centuries are of particular interest, because they were thriving, and attracting converts, at precisely the moment when the state weighed in on behalf of Catholicism. There would never be another time, until the post-Enlightenment world, when a new religion could be founded in the West without antagonizing an existing theocratic state. Even after the Enlightenment, new faiths often faced stringent social opposition. That people went right on founding new religions is a tribute to the irrepressibility of both heresy (let us call it "thinking differently") and the vainglorious prophetic impulse. Did Joseph Smith, when he walked into the woods in upstate New York in the 1820s and came back with wondrous tales of the golden tablets he had received from the Angel Moroni, differ in any fundamental way from the disciples who saw Jesus on the road to Emmaus after he had died on the cross and been buried? Was Smith's story any more or less plausible than the narrative of Manicheans who believed that the actions of men on earth poured light into the heavens?

•

Two of the most consequential Christian sects anathematized by the Roman church and state were Donatism and Pelagianism. These heresies are little-known today to anyone other than dedicated theological scholars, although the issues they raised (like those emphasized by the better-known Manicheans) continue to crop up in debate over religion. The Donatists, who outnumbered Catholics in North Africa until the religious balance of power was transformed by successive invasions and immigration of Muslims in the seventh, eighth, and ninth centuries, were obsessed with the high degree of purity and goodness that they considered essential to salvation. Pelagianism, even though its founder was a devout Christian from Britain, breathed religious air that contained a sulfurous whiff of what would be called secularism today, especially in its premise that humans alone are responsible for their moral decisions. In very different ways, both sects embodied many of the conflicts over conversion and religious liberty that would characterize Western culture for the next fifteen hundred years. The church rejected the right of such faiths to exist, or seek converts, whether the sects considered themselves Christian or not.

Some heretics who considered themselves "the true Christians" were just as adamant as Catholics about equating conversion to another sect with treason. Donatists required that any Roman Catholic who converted to their sect be rebaptized. They had no tolerance for any members—especially the clergy—who joined the Roman camp, whether the deserters had been convinced by the charismatic sermons of bishops like Augustine or because they saw the political handwriting on the wall in the pro-Catholic decrees of Christian emperors. In 404, the Donatist bishop of the city of Bagai in southern Numidia (today's Algeria) was attacked by members of his congregation and left for dead after he defected to the Roman Catholic camp. Unfortunately for his former congregants, the bishop survived and sought to punish them through an imperial court. It proved to be a case supporting the adage "Ask and ye shall receive." In 405, the Roman court classified the Donatists as heretics, making them subject to all of the provisions of the Theodosian code restricting the practice of non-Catholic religions. The Donatist church was officially outlawed, although Donatists were not—not exactly—forced to join the Catholic Church. Technically, their bishops were supposed to be removed and the Catholic Church was to take over their congregations. Imagine what a joyful task it must have been for a Catholic bishop to walk into a Donatist congregation in Carthage or Alexandria and tell people who considered themselves true Christians that their absent bishop was a heretic and they were, too, unless they immediately adopted an attitude of "out with the old, in with the new!"

The rupture between the Donatists and the Roman Catholics, which dated from the period when Donatist pastors and bishops had refused to surrender their sacred scriptures to Diocletian, was both bureaucratic and philosophical. In 311, just a year after the persecutions ended, the first dispute between the two groups came to a head. Caecilian, the bishop of Carthage, had been ordained by one of the bishops who had handed over his sacred books to be burned by Diocletian's minions. Because of his predecessor's sin, Caecilian's ordination was considered invalid by those who had taken a posture of absolute resistance to Diocletian. The Numidian bishops replaced him with another bishop, Donatus, after whom the sect would henceforth be called. Although this sounds like nothing more than a power grab, a deeper issue underlay the split. Donatists believed that the validity of the sacraments depended on the sanctity of those administering the sacred rites; hence, a man ordained by one who had committed treason against the faith by surrendering his books to the state had lost all claim to being a valid representative of Jesus, in a line of descent traced to the apostles. For Catholics, by contrast, the authority of the church and the validity of its sacraments did not depend on the sanctity of the priest, even though he was considered a mediator between God and man. The fundamental question was whether a sinner could transmit grace to other believers. Augustine was the most forceful exponent of the doctrine (as it was soon to be declared by Rome) that the validity of sacraments had nothing to do with the moral probity of priests. In *Confessions,* we also find an early hint of Augustine's eventual acceptance of the necessity of coercion—whether to reconcile a schismatic group like the Donatists to the true church or an individual to God. Referring to Manicheism, Augustine writes about having influenced a dear friend "to believe in the same superstitious, soul-destroying fallacies which brought my mother to tears over me." The friend, however, was pursued by a "god of vengeance" and fell ill from a fever. Expected to die, he was baptized (by whom, Augustine does not say) as he lay unconscious. At the time, Augustine assumed that this forced baptism, over which his friend had no control, would mean nothing if he recovered.

> . . . I chose to believe that his soul would retain what it had learnt from me, no matter what was done to his body when it was deprived of sense. But no such thing happened. New life came into him and he recovered. And as soon as I could talk to him—which was as soon as he could talk to me, for I never left his side since we were so dependent on each other—I tried to chaff him about his baptism, thinking that he too would make fun of it, since he had received it when he was quite incapable of thought or feeling. But by this time he had been told of it. He looked at me in horror as though I were an enemy, and in a strange, new-found attitude of self-reliance he warned me that if I wished to be his friend, I must never speak to him like that again.[2]

Augustine's friend then had a relapse and died. By the time he wrote *Confessions,* Augustine found the forced baptism a source of deep spiritual consolation. Since the friend had died in a state of grace—even though, had he been in his right mind, he would have not consented to baptism in the first place—Augustine might meet him again in the next world.* And if the validity of a sacrament does not depend on the conscious, active consent of the recipient, how much less could it depend on the moral perfection of the priest administering the rites of the church? Sanctity and authority rest in the church itself, not in its fallible administrators and messengers. (I suspect that I would have been on Augustine's side on the latter point had I been alive and Christian in the fifth century. The human fallibility of priests and bishops, whether considered apostolic successors or not, must have been as obvious to Christians then as it is to Christians today. I have not

---

* Passages like these have, of course, led to speculation that Augustine might have been gay. This strikes me as equivalent to the claims that Abraham Lincoln was gay because, on the frontier, he slept in the same bed with male friends in whose homes he had found lodging. For all I know, both Augustine and Lincoln were gay, if gayness is assessed by the intensity of male friendships in the ancient world or the shortage of beds in houses on the nineteenth-century American frontier.

heard of any mass movement demanding rebaptism for Catholics who discover that they may have been christened by a pedophile priest.)

The other issue between Donatist Christians and Catholics was the proper relationship to the larger society and the state, and this offers a perfect example of the relevance of early heresies to modern disputes over the same subject. The Donatists saw themselves as a saving remnant, a pure (or purer) group that could only be corrupted by association with the state. The Catholic Church saw itself as a part of society and as a transformative force; thus, its leaders were not only able but eager to form alliances with the state and its rulers. In this context, it is easy to understand why the Catholics won out. Nondemocratic states and rulers favor religions and religious leaders who want to cooperate with the governing authorities in return for the secular government's enforcement of their religious beliefs. The Donatists, like dissenting Quakers, Baptists, and Anabaptists in the seventeenth and eighteenth centuries, wanted nothing from the government except to be let alone. Roman emperors were always coming to the rescue of Roman Catholicism when it could not win over "heretics" by persuasion. With regard to religious conflict, the rulers of a declining empire played the role of a judge ordering an unhappy wife who has left her husband to return or face being flogged and stripped of her possessions and means of support.

•

Pelagianism, also a genuinely significant movement representing a breach within Christianity in Augustine's time, takes its name from Pelagius, the teacher from Britannia who had the temerity to reject the doctrine of original sin. Although Pelagius is often called a monk by scholars (including Augustine), he never calls himself a monk in his writings, which stress the role of the Christian layman as teacher. He repeatedly cites Paul's allusions to the duty of all Christians to instruct one another and rejects the church's emphasis on the exclusive teaching authority of the clergy.* (This could be the reason Augustine calls Pelagius a monk while disputing his ideas. Pelagius was definitely not

---

* Many of Paul's epistles contain passages specifically emphasizing the responsibility of the laity to "edify one another."

a priest, but the idea that a mere layman's ideas could be worthy of refutation may have been distasteful to Augustine.)

We know little about Pelagius's life before he turned up in Rome, around 400. When he did look into the heart of the empire and the aspiring heart of the church, his reaction seems to have resembled that of Jimmy Stewart's character in the movie *Mr. Smith Goes to Washington*. Here were men claiming to be the direct successors of the apostles while living sumptuously and co-opting imperial officials (and, in many instances, being co-opted by them) for financial and political gains that had little to do with faith and goodness. Yet Pelagius also moved in highly educated circles, including laymen and scholarly monks who debated and wrote about theological issues (such as original sin) that were already resolved as far as many clerics, intellectual or not, were concerned. Pelagius believed in the Christian God as devoutly as Augustine, but he did not believe that God's grace or withholding of grace determined the actions of men.

Adam's fall was not the cause of man's sinfulness, Pelagius asserted: each human being is solely responsible for his virtues and vices. Nor is death the penalty for original sin, as traditional Christian theology maintains. Adam was nothing more or less than a man, and he would have died whether he sank his teeth into the fruit of the tree of knowledge or not. Poor Pelagius! Small wonder that he was condemned by more church councils than any other heretic of the pre-medieval Christian era. His analysis belongs much more to the history of skepticism and humanism than to the history of faith, although he certainly—like the Donatists—considered himself a "true Christian." However, Pelagianism proved far more important than Donatism in the intellectual long term—notwithstanding the larger number of Donatists in late antiquity. Pelagius was concerned with what it means to be human and how much God has or does not have to do with the choices humans make, for good or for evil.

Pelagius's assertion that human choices are determined not by original sin or by divine grace but by each human being might well be described as the ultimate heresy—hence, the condemnation by so many Vatican councils and by theologians ranging from Augustine to far-right evangelical Protestants today. As one conservative evangelical scholar puts it, "It is this heresy that lies at the bottom of much of popular psychology (human nature, basically good, is warped by its environment), political crusades (we are going to bring about salvation and revival through this campaign), and evangelism and church growth (seeing conversion as a natural process, just like changing from one brand of soap to another)."[3] This commentator makes Pelagius sound like a fifth-century Rousseau, and nothing could have been further from the truth. Pelagius's concern about the impact of the physical environment on humanity's moral choices has led some commentators on the religious left to see him as a prototype of nineteenth-century Christian Socialists—in its own way, as ludicrously anachronistic a conclusion as the idea that he believed in man as a noble savage. Pelagius was influenced by the many ascetic movements of his time, but he advocated a more moderate form of asceticism than either the Manichees or, to cite a Christian example, Jerome. Pelagius's view of wealth and poverty might be summed up with one word—enough. He believed neither in the exaltation of riches nor in the passive notion that "the poor ye shall always have with you." Although Pelagius did believe that a corrupt environment corrupted its inhabitants, he held humans solely responsible for the quality of the environment they established—a view that, it must be emphasized, does no better than original sin in attempting to lay the theodicy problem to rest. Pelagius's most consistent position was his belief in the capabilities of man and woman—he clearly took women's intellectual and spiritual faculties seriously—and his refusal to assign blame or credit to the supernatural.

"Whenever I have to speak of laying down rules for behavior and the conduct of a holy life," he wrote Demetrias, a young woman from an old and noble Roman family who had decided to become a nun, "I always point out, first of all, the power and functioning of human nature, and show what it is capable of doing . . . lest I should seem to be wasting my time, by calling on people to embark on a course which they consider impossible to achieve."[4] In the same letter, Pelagius elaborated on his belief that, although God had endowed humans with the intelligence and understanding to choose between good and evil, He wants our choices to be the product of our own reason rather than fear of his punishments—"*volutarium, non coactum.*" God wants the fulfillment of His plans to come from our own willing collaboration, not the divine will. God wants a lot: in the Pelagian philosophy, He wants to have it both ways. It is obvious that Pelagius was no more successful than Augustine and his orthodox contemporaries in his effort to reconcile free will with divine power. What separates him from the rest is a much higher opinion of human capacities; the balance in Pelagian thought is tilted in favor of human reason rather than divine intervention through grace. A man or woman might seek divine grace but cannot rely on it to ensure a sound moral life. Nor, in the Pelagian scheme of things, may human beings blame the evil they do on the Divinity's withholding of grace.

Pelagius's rejection of original sin also calls into question the doctrine of Christ's death on the cross as a onetime atonement for the curse inflicted on all men by Adam. "If mankind's sin is, so to speak, not solid but atomic," he argues, "there can be no single and solid act of redemption for mankind en bloc."[5] For Pelagius, it is the earthly example of Jesus—not his death—that makes the Christian religion worthwhile. This emphasis on Jesus's earthly good works rather than his death points in the opposite direction from the Nicene Creed and every doctrine that revolves around Christ's death on the cross and resurrection.

Augustine, who also knew the aristocratic family of the nun Demetrias, recognized the Pelagian threat immediately when he learned of Pelagius's letter to Demetrias. Augustine wrote to Demetrias's mother, Juliana, to assert "that the virtues of Demetrias, great and outstanding as they were, did not come from her own strength, but were the gift of God: she must be humble and honour the Savior to whom she alone owed her high merits."[6] He also warned Juliana that an inflated opinion of human reason and capacity for good could lead men and women to deny the need for prayer and divine guidance. Why ask God for anything if you have the power to choose good on your own? Augustine must have been on close terms with Juliana to send her such a letter, but scholars report that she cooled considerably toward the bishop of Hippo after receiving this unsought advice. It is a rare mother who wants to hear that her daughter's excellence comes not from her own independent mind and spirit, not from her upbringing in a learned and devout family, but from an outsider—even if the outsider is, as in this case, God Himself.

There is another element distinguishing Pelagius from the orthodox fathers of the church: a sense of humor. Regarding original sin, the bête noire that led to his condemnation at so many church councils, he remarked, "There are enough things for which we are morally accountable, without blaming us for the things for which we are not."[7]

There is a tendency on the part of all who have a passion for the past to cherry-pick aspects of biography that mesh with the authors' views. This human shortcoming of historians, which only divine grace might be capable of eliminating, can lead to awful anachronisms of the sort that would turn Augustine into a repressed homosexual and Pelagius into an Enlightenment philosopher or a Marxist. Of the two, Augustine is the religious rock star, because Catholicism won out. Pelagius was nothing more or less than a brilliant philosopher speaking for a part of Christianity that was suppressed for a millennium. If he is a precursor of anyone or anything, it is of Erasmus and Christian humanism. The probative evidence of Pelagius's humanism, and a reason for profound regret that he was on the heretical losing side, is that the possibility of moral justification for forced conversions never seems to have occurred to him. He is another figure thrown by the wayside in the Christian narrative, for his brand of early humanism could never have led to a union of government force and religious faith. If the writings of Pelagius had been handed down through generations of Christians, as Augustine's were, the road of Christianity might have taken a detour around both the Spanish Inquisition and Calvin's Geneva. Wouldn't it be pretty to think so?

· **PART II** ·

FROM CONVIVENCIA TO THE STAKE

4

BISHOP PAUL OF BURGOS (c. 1352–1435)

Formerly Known as Solomon ha-Levi, Rabbi of Burgos

> *Midway in our life's journey, I went astray*
> *From the straight road and awoke to find myself*
> *Alone in a dark forest. How shall I say*
> *what a forest that was! I never saw so dreary,*
> *so savage, so stern a wilderness!*
> *Its very memory imparts form to fear.*
>
> —CANTO I, DANTE'S *Inferno*

WHAT A DIFFERENCE a year can make in the interpretation of an iconic conversion story! Solomon ha-Levi, a Talmudic scholar who converted to Christianity approximately midway in his life's journey, was one of the most famous converts from Judaism of his time and place—an exemplary catch for Christians who ardently desired the conversion of all Jews. So it is not particularly surprising that some fourteenth- and fifteenth-century Christian sources would date his conversion from 1390 rather than 1391.[1] In 1391, a wave of savage attacks against long-established Iberian Jewish communities—some with origins in Roman times—was carried out by Christian mobs throughout the peninsula. Had Solomon ha-Levi, born into one of the most eminent Jewish families in the kingdom of Castile, embraced Catholicism a year earlier, his decision could be more easily seen by Christians as a purely spiritual choice, uninfluenced by Christian persecutions of Jews. For Jewish life throughout Iberia, the assaults that began in 1391—which resulted in the deaths, departures, or forced conversions of tens, perhaps hundreds of thousands of Jews—signaled the beginning of an end that would come just a century later, when all Jews who refused to convert were expelled in 1492 by order of King Ferdinand and Queen Isabella. The first wave of conversions lasted about twenty-five years, and, although exact numbers are a matter of considerable dispute, the most conservative estimates suggest that half of the Jews in Iberia submitted to baptism.[2] Conversions by eminent Jews like ha-Levi could not have failed to provide a powerful example for less educated, less prosperous members of the Jewish community. He would eventually become a bishop and counselor to kings, cardinals, and a pope (actually, an antipope in Catholic history).

But there could be no more appropriate epigraph than the famous opening lines of Dante's *Inferno* for the conversion to Catholicism, as he was nearing age forty, of a man steeped in Jewish learning.* For the threatened Jews of his community, the world in which Solomon became Paul embodied fear in its most concrete forms. The rejection of Judaism by a scholar as eminent as ha-Levi (known both as "Pablo" and as "Pablo de Santa Maria" in his new incarnation), had it occurred before the 1391 attacks, could be seen and exalted by Christians as a straightforward recognition on the part of a once-devout rabbi that Christianity was the completion of Jewish prophecy.† That is how Paul himself, in his subsequent Christian theological writings, presented his conversion. The same conversion could be and was seen by some Jews (then and now) as loathsome, pure, unforced apostasy—a voluntary act of treachery against the Jewish people.

Most twentieth-century scholars, however, concluded that ha-Levi converted not in 1390 but in 1391, at the height of violence that had already ravaged the Jewish quarters of Seville, Toledo, and Córdoba and would soon spread to Barcelona, Valencia, and Majorca. The later date makes much more sense in view of ha-Levi's status as a Jew who was influential among both Jews and Christians and enjoyed the protection of the Christian rulers of Castile for his services to the monarchy. Why would a respected Talmudic scholar—moreover, one with powerful connections at the Christian court—suddenly decide to have himself and his family baptized for purely religious reasons?

---

* Since Dante wrote in the Tuscan vernacular, which Solomon ha-Levi certainly did not know, he would not have read *The Divine Comedy* before his conversion.

† In the United States today, proselytizing right-wing Christian groups frequently refer to Jewish converts as "completed Jews."

He was an ambitious man, versed not only in the Torah and Talmud but in Christian theological argument, classical philosophy, and, as a product of the Convivencia, most likely in Islamic writings. He read Hebrew, Arabic (the language in which Maimonides usually wrote), and Latin, a language whose mastery was unusual among his Jewish contemporaries.

Since the first Muslim invasion of Iberia, Muslims, Christians, and Jews had accommodated one another with varying degrees of tolerance and suspicion, and occasional violence—the latter usually, but not always, committed by Christians against Jews. For the most part, though, Muslim rulers had not only allowed but encouraged a cross-fertilization of cultures that did not exist anywhere else in Europe during the Middle Ages. The cultural flowering of the Convivencia had included everything from plumbing unknown since Roman times to translations of the vast body of classical Greek literature into Arabic—awaiting the time when it would be retranslated from the Arabic into Latin and the emerging vernacular languages of Europe. This renascence lasted well into Paul's time, even though the long Christian Reconquista—its irreversible victories beginning with the recapture of Toledo in 1085 and ending with Ferdinand and Isabella's triumphal entry into Granada in 1492—created unpredictable combinations of latitudinarianism and persecution for both Jews and Muslims.

The conversion of a Jew like Paul of Burgos, however, attested to the weight of one military victory after another by the Christians over the Moorish rulers. The fabled city of Córdoba fell in 1236; Valencia, in 1238; and Seville, in 1248. At the time of Paul's conversion, only Granada survived as the last outpost of what a learned tenth-century Saxon nun, Hroswitha of Gandersheim, had described as the "ornament of the world." Another century would pass before Ferdinand and Isabella—having conquered the last Moorish city and its monarch, Boabdil—would expel all Jews from Spain unless they agreed to convert to Christianity. But the handwriting was already on the wall in the 1390s for ancient Jewish communities throughout the peninsula. The Conversos of Paul's generation were known as New Christians, to distinguish them from Old Christians, who presumably had no Jewish ancestors—or none who could be identified.

The ha-Levi family, including Solomon, was among the most influential clans within the Jewish community of Burgos—one of the three largest, richest, and most politically influential Jewish population centers in Castile. It makes little sense that Solomon, having assumed his role as the community's leading rabbi, would suddenly have seen the light of Christ unless he had been given a push by outside events leading to the inescapable conclusion that there was no future in Spain for Jews who remained Jews. Many scholars mention the oft-told tale that ha-Levi was convinced of the truth of Christianity by the writings of Thomas Aquinas. "There is no need to doubt this tradition," asserts Benzion Netanyahu, who considers the influence of Muslim, Christian, and classical pagan thought on the Jews of Spain a historical tragedy.[3]

There is every need and reason to doubt such a tradition (though it is certainly likely that a scholar like ha-Levi, who was literate in Latin, would have read Aquinas). I daresay that more Jews have converted to Christianity because they saw other Jews being murdered, deprived of their property, and stripped of royal protection than because they had encountered Aquinas's use of logic and reason in the service of Christian religious beliefs (just as Maimonides had used classical logic in the service of Judaic beliefs). Attributing ha-Levi's conversion to his reading of Aquinas is just another way of saying that no Jew in the Diaspora can be a real Jew. That is a political and moral position, but it is hardly a historical fact.

This is not to say that Jewish, Christian, and Muslim intellectuals in Iberia were not unusually well acquainted with one another's beliefs throughout what were still the Dark Ages in much of Northern Europe. The Jews, obviously, were in a very different position from both Muslims and Christians, in that their fate depended on the religious liberality or repressiveness of particular Muslim and Christian rulers. Both Muslim rulers before the Reconquista and Christian rulers afterward made use of Jews as high-level political advisers as well as ordinary tax collectors. But the events of 1391, which demonstrated the combined inability and unwillingness of Christian authorities at that time to protect even their favorite Jews from mobs, made it clear that even court Jews at the highest level of the realm would have to convert in order to retain their former occupations and privileges. The collection of taxes in Castile, for instance, was carried out by the office of the chief treasurer, who was a Jew. By the end of the fourteenth century, the treasurer's office was staffed by Conversos. Whether taxes were collected by religious Jews or Conversos made little difference to the rulers, who in either case were able to insulate themselves to some degree from the ordinary populace's natural hatred of tax levies. And it seems unlikely, given the profound suspicion of the sincerity of Conversos that led to the establishment of the Spanish Inquisition by the Vatican in 1478 (at the request of Ferdinand and Isabella), that ordinary people made any distinction between tax collectors who remained faithful to Judaism and those who converted to Christianity.

It should be superfluous to state that the vast majority of Jews in Spain were neither moneylenders nor tax collectors; what is true is that nearly all lenders and tax collectors, before the wave of persecutions began in 1391, were Jews. Representing the royal treasury was one way in which elite men of the Jewish community made a living and exercised political influence. After 1391, that influence would become increasingly constricted for ambitious Jews. Converting to Christianity was the smart thing to do, if your interest lay in kingdoms belonging to this world.

•

Ha-Levi's conversion was no more "ordinary" than Augustine's, because ha-Levi, like Augustine, was a man of extraordinary intelligence and learning. Given his subsequent career in the church and his defenses of Christian theology, it is impossible to regard him as a member of the *anousim,* the Hebrew term for Iberian Jews who were forced to convert to Christianity but nevertheless continued to practice certain Jewish traditions in secret in order to preserve their identity. Historically, such people were more commonly called Marranos (a pejorative probably derived from the Spanish word for "swine"); or Conversos (literally, the converted).* The dilemma posed by the transformation of Solomon ha-Levi into Bishop Paul of Burgos is that, although his subsequent opportunistic church career can hardly

---

* I will generally use the term "Conversos" in this book, because it is more neutral than either of the other words for Jews who converted under duress as well as their descendants. *Anousim* is a term used mainly by observant Jews and rabbinical authorities and has often been used historically by rabbis to determine what degree of force can remove the moral opprobrium attached to conversion in the observant Jewish community. "Marranos," although it has long been a term used by many Jews, has derogatory origins.

be regarded as anything but treason by devoutly observant Jews, his original change of faith cannot be viewed outside the context of the death and destruction then being wreaked upon Jewish communities. It is natural that, over generations, many Conversos would sincerely embrace Christianity and lose touch with their origins (insofar as the Inquisition would let them). Solomon ha-Levi's instant makeover, though, has nothing to do with the attenuation of old religious loyal- ties may occur over many generations. It is certainly within the realm of psychological possibility that a man might rationalize a forced con- version in spiritual terms rather than acknowledge his own legitimate fear as well as vaulting ambition.

•

Before his conversion, ha-Levi was already a promising diplomat. In 1389, he was chosen by King Juan I of Castile to serve, along with other diplomats and nobles, on a diplomatic mission to Aquitaine in France (then under English rule). In a sense, ha-Levi and the other nobles were hostages to guarantee the payment of a dowry promised by Juan to the duke of Lancaster, in return for the marriage of the duke's daughter Catalina (Catherine) to Juan's son Enrique. Unlike tax collection, diplomacy at such a level was not ordinarily engaged in by Jews, and most monarchs in Christendom would never have countenanced such participation. During this period, negotiations for an armistice between England and France (the latter an ally of Cas- tile) were also under way. As a representative of Castile, ha-Levi would surely have met many important European diplomats, including rep- resentatives of both church and state. They would become valuable contacts throughout his post-conversion career.

There is ample evidence, however, that at the time Solomon ha-Levi was a believing Jew, albeit one with doubts. In a letter written on Purim—apparently, the first such holiday he had ever spent among Gentiles—he wrote to a friend, Rab Don Meir Alguadex, of his loneli- ness in Aquitaine.

When the Lord cast me out from my father's house, and my sins drove me out from abiding in the inheritance of my forefathers . . . I was thrust into the pit [i.e., the service of the Castilian king], then did I see many terrible happenings . . . but all this means nothing to me when I reflect upon that which my tender soul hath suffered because of the inadequate observance of the commandments required of it. . . . Here I sit, apart from the camp of the *Shekhinah*, Levites and Israel, and even those commandments which can be performed in private and of which one makes little, such as *kiddush* and *havdalah*, I have not had the benefit of these many days.[4]

In the letter, ha-Levi regrets that he has no wine and cannot participate in the inebriation that has always been a part of the Purim celebration for many observant Jews. He declares that he must reach into his own soul for intoxication and that he will celebrate the holiday with his own songs and verses.[5] As the historian Yitzhak Baer notes, this letter was written with a combination of humor and melancholy and "should not be studied for auguries of the writer's eventual conversion and tragic political fate."[6]

And yet these sentiments were expressed only two years before the pogroms and ha-Levi's conversion (if one accepts, as I do, that the conversion took place during the savagery of 1391 and not before). It certainly displays the state of mind of a man who was aware of the conflicts between his worldly ambitions and the faith of his fathers. The letter is of particular interest because it is the only Hebrew text that remains from his pre-conversion life.*

What the letter does not explain is why, after his conversion, ha-Levi went on not only to pursue his ambitions at the highest level of the Catholic hierarchy (as opposed to simply serving as an adviser to the monarchs of Castile) but also to support a wide variety of restrictive laws against Jews. If Solomon ha-Levi felt compelled to become Paul of Burgos in 1391, as so many Iberian Jews did feel compelled to convert, something happened to make him pursue his new faith with an ardor, and a callousness toward his people, unshared by most other Conversos. One need not believe that Jews are obliged to become martyrs to view Paul of Burgos as a turncoat.

---

* This may not be surprising, given that, by the time Paul died in 1435, suspicion of the sincerity of all Conversos was on the rise. Even a bishop might not have thought it advisable to keep examples of his old Talmudic scholarship lying around, and many of Paul's friends had also converted, in the first decade of the fifteenth century.

Before his conversion, Paul had been known to both Christians
and Jews as a powerful spokesman for Judaism in the theological disputations with Catholics that were a recurrent feature of cultural life
throughout Iberia in the late fourteenth century. There are essentially
two ways of reconstructing Paul's conversion, and they reflect differing, though occasionally intersecting, historical views about how Jews
are to be judged for abandoning Judaism and what justifies such abandonment in a moral sense. The first judgment, articulated forcefully
by Netanyahu, is that Paul was already corrupted by his contact with
and knowledge of Christian and Muslim teachings, as well as the free-
thinking philosophy of the Muslim scholar Averroës, who in many
respects anticipated some of the key tenets of Enlightenment deism.
In Netanyahu's portrait, Paul was undone as much by his attraction
to non-Jewish cultural and religious thinking as by his own worldly
ambitions. The persecutions of 1391 were an added inducement that
did not, however, rise to the level of irresistible "force." Netanyahu
does not pretend to have documentation for his imaginative reconstruction of what Paul did, and why he did it, but that does not stop
him from offering a fairly detailed scenario, which goes something
like this:

By the time the pogroms neared Burgos, the Jewish communities
of Seville, Córdoba, and Toledo had already been devastated. Paul
(still Solomon) tells his people that it would be pointless for the Jewish
community of Burgos to suffer the same assaults when, by converting
right now, they can save themselves, their homes, and their businesses
from destruction. The rabbi convenes a general meeting and presents
a hopeless portrait of the condition of Jews throughout Iberia. He may
even talk about the conditions of Jews in other countries of the West,
mentioning past and contemporary persecutions in England, France,
and Germany (including the devastation of Jewish communities in the
Rhineland by the warriors of the First Crusade in 1096) and conclude
that the end is coming for Jewish life in the Iberian Peninsula as well.
The Catholic Church is on the rise everywhere west of the Bosporus.
Solomon does not try to convince those in his audience that Christianity is superior to Judaism as a religion (that would be a bit much, in
that he has been their chief rabbi). He does remind the Jews, though,
that even the Muslim rulers of Andalusia have had to retreat, one by
one, before the power of Christian soldiers. Netanyahu continues:

Whatever arguments Paul used in that address, which, as we conjecture, he most probably delivered, it was not received with general acclaim . . . and the grave insults hurled at him on that occasion may have been so offensive and so hard to take that he could never forget or forgive them. Perhaps the seed of his future hatred of the Jews—that is, of the Jews who had stuck to their religion—that hatred which seethed in his later writings, had its origin in that bitter experience and his subsequent encounters with the faithful Jews of Burgos in those crucial days.[7]

Yes, *perhaps. Probably,* as one may *conjecture.* What is known to have happened is that many members of the Jewish community of Burgos, like Jews in other cities, converted—and many did not. Some wealthy Jews found a haven during the attacks in the homes of wealthy Christians, whom they paid for offering them shelter. "Thus," Netanyahu argues, "Paul's presumed prognostication did not prove entirely true. Rich Jews *could* have saved themselves without being converted."[8] Well, that settles it. Jews with enough money to save themselves by paying off the goyim are morally superior to those who converted to save their lives and possessions. Although Paul of Burgos is far from an inspiring figure in Jewish history, there is something arrogant and anachronistic about the passage of judgment from late-twentieth-century Israel (or, for that matter, America) on Diaspora Jews of a distant era who could, possibly, have saved themselves from both death and apostasy by paying off Gentiles. However, the same judgment was also passed by a number of fourteenth- and fifteenth-century rabbis in North Africa and the Middle East; though few of them had lived in Iberia themselves, they parsed the conditions for distinguishing between a Marrano and a member of the *anousim.* With friends like this, what Jew seeing his world collapse around him needs enemies? (These assessments seem particularly harsh in view of our knowledge about what money could—and could not—buy from Gentiles when twentieth-century European Jews attempted to escape the Nazis.)

The second reconstruction of Paul's conversion, offered by Baer and many other mainstream Jewish historians, is no more flattering about Paul's career as a Christian prelate and diplomat but is uncontaminated by an ideology maintaining that it is possible to speak with certainty of "voluntary" conversions in circumstances like those prevailing in

Spain in the 1390s. Though also using the blunt word "apostasy" to describe Paul's conversion, Baer emphasizes that this famous change of faith and communal loyalty was inextricably "connected with and symptomatic of the general destruction."[9] Although Baer agrees with Netanyahu that Paul soon turned into an outright enemy of Jews who refused to convert, the former never suggests that freedom of religious choice could truly exist in an environment where Jews were threatened with the loss of both their lives and their property. Baer is also somewhat less convinced than Netanyahu that forced converts were seduced by the theological appeal of Christianity as a result of the rich (and, no doubt, doubt-provoking) contacts among religious scholars in Andalusia during the most tolerant period of the Convivencia. If familiarity with the religious thinking of others had been sufficient to seduce Jews and Muslims away from their faiths, there would never have been any reason for Christian persecutions designed to force conversions. In any era, familiarity with other faiths, or at least *one* other faith, is necessary but not sufficient for religious conversion.

Whatever the original combination of motives for Solomon ha-Levi, he began propagandizing for Christianity among his Jewish acquaintances soon after his official change of faith. In a letter to his friend Joseph Orabuena, he asserted, as any convert from Judaism to Christianity must, that the Old Testament prophecies of the coming of the Messiah had been fulfilled by the coming of Jesus. The letter was widely circulated among Jewish intellectuals. One of Paul's old friends, Joshua ha-Lorki, a physician and Talmudic scholar who later converted to Christianity himself, asked, "Did you perchance lust after riches and honors? . . . Or did the study of philosophy cause you . . . to regard the proofs of faith as vanity and delusion? Or, when you beheld the doom of our homeland, the multitude of the afflictions that have recently befallen us, did it then seem to you that the name of Israel would be remembered no more? Or perhaps . . . you saw that our fathers had inherited falsehood . . . ?"[10] Ha-Lorki, who eventually became the antipope Benedict's personal physician while he was still a Jew, converted to Christianity in 1412 and took the name Hieronymus de Santa Fide.

Ha-Lorki's side of the correspondence—much more extensively preserved than Paul's—does reflect the doubts and questioning that attested to the influence of Averroism on Iberian intellectuals of all faiths. Ha-Lorki asks whether it is the duty of a religious believer to investigate his faith and determine whether it is true. The conundrum ha-Lorki cites is that, if investigation of religious truth is a moral duty, "then no religious man anywhere in the world would be faithful to his religion, but would be constantly doubting and questioning." Yet, if it is forbidden to inquire, "it follows that any believer can be saved by his own religion, and that one religion is not superior to another."[11] That is precisely what the thinkers of the Enlightenment *would* say in another three hundred years.*

It certainly does not follow that Averroism would have led Jewish intellectuals in Spain to turn to the Catholic Church. The dogmas of Catholicism were, after all, even more antithetical to Averroës's early form of freethought than Talmudic inquiry was. Baer, though acknowledging that Catholic dogma was irreconcilable with the Averroist "religion of the intellect," argues that the church offered men like ha-Lorki and Paul of Burgos "a rich tradition of humanism and secular culture."[12] This seems to me yet another example of the tendency of religious believers of every era to "spiritualize" conversions for which there are overweening secular reasons, ranging from economic self-interest to fear of extermination. No institution detested Averroism more than the Catholic Church, and the "rich tradition of humanism and secular culture" associated with Catholicism was, for the average Christian believer, a cloud no bigger than an artist's hand or a writer's pen at the end of the fourteenth century. The rediscovery of vital Greek texts ranging from treatises on engineering and mathematics to lost plays of Aeschylus and Sophocles did not really begin until the third decade of the fifteenth century in Italy.† At the time when the Jews of Iberia began their mass conversion in the 1390s, the full emergence of Christian humanism—in art, science, and critical thinking—lay roughly a century in the future. What Christianity had to offer Jews was power and protection, not humanism.

The language of educated discourse among intellectuals of differ-

---

* The answer Thomas Paine would have given ha-Lorki appears in the author's profession of his personal faith in Part I of *The Age of Reason*: "Infidelity does not consist in believing, or in disbelieving; it consists in professing to believe what he does not believe." This, of course, was not an acceptable conclusion for anyone of any faith in fifteenth-century Spain.

† See Ross King, *Brunelleschi's Dome* (New York: Penguin, 2001), p. 63.

ent faiths in Iberia was Arabic, not Latin. Both the towering twelfth-century Jewish scholar Maimonides, writing in Arabic, and the thirteenth-century Christian Aquinas, who of course wrote in Latin, were intent on reconciling classical Greek philosophy, specifically Aristotle, with their respective religious traditions. Maimonides attempted this task first, and he was certainly no Averroist. Aquinas's conclusions were far more hostile to Averroism, particularly in his rejection of Averroës's belief that at a fundamental level—regardless of religion—all humans share the same intellect that makes them part of something greater. Nothing could be further removed from the reasoning of Aquinas, who, though he was certainly a part of secular culture (to the extent that it existed in medieval Christendom), was definitely not a humanist or a precursor of secular humanism in the modernist sense.* It is utterly anachronistic to believe that a fourteenth-century Jewish convert in Spain (even if that convert was an admirer of Averroës) would have considered Catholicism more hospitable than Judaism to Averroist humanism.

Paul's reply to ha-Lorki, of which only a small segment has been preserved, is, in its own way, a classic of the hairsplitting that characterizes so many converts who have exchanged one absolute truth for another, or a lesser truth for what they consider a higher truth. It was, in Paul's view, the duty of Jews to question the truth of their religion, and consider the possibility that Christianity was superior, precisely because Messianic prophecy was a fundamental principle of Judaism. Paul reasons that "scrutiny is the door of hope through which I entered the New Covenant—I and my friends—and this is the gate of the Lord through which the righteous enter."[13] In a triumph of circular reasoning, however, Paul absolves Jews of any responsibility to investigate the claims of Islam, because Islam is demonstrably a false religion—since no one but Jesus of Nazareth could possibly be the fulfillment of Hebrew prophecy. In spite of his tortuous analyses of who is, and is not, bound to question his faith and examine the claims of other faiths, Paul—like Augustine—concludes that faith itself is not

---

* Nor can Aquinas be considered, as Averroës is, a precursor of secular humanist or Enlightenment thought. When the Texas Board of Education decided to replace Thomas Jefferson with Aquinas in textbook discussions of thinkers who influenced revolutionary movements, it failed to take into account what Aquinas would have thought of a Declaration of Independence that rejected the divine right of kings.

the product of human reason but is granted only by the grace of God. Christian faith demands that humans use their reason—but only insofar as reason, augmented and guided by divine grace, leads them to a deeper belief in the truth of Christianity.

In Paul's theological scheme, Christians, like Jews—if they are living in a place like Spain, where they have contact with other religions—are bound to question the truth of their own faith. But if a Christian is living on an island and never meets people of any other faith, he is not required to ask such questions. Perhaps what was lost in the incomplete record of Paul's reply to ha-Lorki was his explanation of exactly how one formulates questions in the absence of any challenges. This type of convoluted rationalization is inevitable for intellectual converts to religions with absolute truth claims; the need for justification is evident in converts not only to monotheistic religions but to rigid, politically driven secular ideologies. Censorship—whether exercised by religious institutions or totalitarian governments—is simply an attempt to suppress the questions that Paul considered a moral duty even for medieval Christians.

·

The state of Paul's ambition as well as his theology may be inferred from the fact that he left Burgos within the year after his conversion, to study Catholic theology in Paris. There he met Cardinal Pedro de Luna of Aragon, who was Pope Clement VII's representative to France, England, Scotland, and what are now the Benelux countries. In 1394, Cardinal de Luna, who is considered an antipope by the Roman Catholic Church today, was elected pontiff by his supporters; took the name of Benedict XIII; and played an important role in perpetuating a papal schism that eventually saw three different men, in several different places, from Avignon to Rome, lay claim to the office of head of the Holy Roman Catholic Church between 1378 and 1417.

Exactly when Paul was ordained a priest is uncertain, but his rise in the church hierarchy began after his alliance with Benedict. In 1398, Benedict appointed Paul archdeacon of Treviño and made him the official papal representative to Castile. During this period, Paul also became an adviser to King Enrique III. Paul's close association with Enrique was a key factor in the Castilian king's agreement to side with

Benedict in the continuing papal schism. Paul was so close to Enrique that he was made one of the three executors of his will in 1406. It was during the period of Paul's close friendship with the king that new anti-Jewish legislation was enacted. Enrique ordered bishops in Castile to excommunicate any Catholic judge or official who honored and enforced contracts obliging Christians to pay interest to Jewish money-lenders. In one particularly interesting twist, Enrique also decreed civil penalties for Christians who confessed, before a lay or an ecclesiastical court, to having borrowed money from Jews. Any Jew who demanded such an admission would be penalized the same amount. Don't ask, don't tell.

After Enrique's death in 1406, Paul remained close to the two regents, the king's widow, Catalina (the same Catalina who had been the prospective bride when Paul, then Solomon, was a diplomatic hostage in Aquitaine), and his brother, the Infante Fernando. Many scholars blame Paul's influence for a major piece of anti-Jewish economic legislation prohibiting Jews from engaging in their previous role of collecting taxes for the monarchy. Even though the evidence of Paul's involvement is probative rather than definitive, there is one certainty: Paul never made any attempt to help unconverted Jews (unless pressuring them to convert is considered "help"). Paul's silence, given his influence with monarchs since the 1380s, would have provided support for anti-Jewish economic laws even if he himself did not propose them.

Nor did Paul ever speak out against the much harsher laws issued by the Castilian government in 1412 in the city of Valladolid. The Valladolid Laws, also known as Laws of Catalina, affected both Jews and Muslims (although the economic impact on the former was much greater). For the first time, Jews were to be confined to their own quarters in cities. In a wide variety of businesses and professions—from medicine to shoemaking—Jews were forbidden to deal with Christian customers (although this law was not always enforced). Jewish men, in another spottily enforced edict, were ordered to let their hair and beards grow in order to distinguish them visibly from their Christian neighbors. They were no longer entitled to the honorific "Don." Whatever the levels of enforcement in different cities, the Laws of Catalina added social humiliation to the economic strictures of earlier statutes restricting Jewish moneylending and tax farming. It could not have been clearer that the remnants of the golden age (arguably always closer to bronze than gold) of the Convivencia in Spain were losing their luster for both Jews and Muslims.

Paul remained at the Castilian court until 1416, dividing his time between his duties as tutor to the future King Juan II (fulfilling a wish expressed by Juan's father, Enrique) and his functions as a bishop. When he retired from court, he devoted more of his attention to ecclesiastical than royal politics (although the two were always intertwined). Paul's departure from court took place as the fortunes of the antipope Benedict, the former Cardinal de Luna, waned. He would be deposed as pope at the Council of Constance in 1417, which officially ended the papal schism. But Paul remained in the church's good graces, as demonstrated by his elevation to archbishop of Philippi in Macedonia shortly before his death in 1435.

After leaving court, Paul wrote two Spanish-language works of Christian apologetics and history. The best known is *Siete edades del mundo* (*The Seven Ages of the World*), dedicated to his former pupil King Juan II. The work was probably completed at some point in the 1420s. *Seven Ages* is a deeply boring, conventional work based on the mistaken classical and medieval concept that the stages of man's development are analogous to the universe's stages of development. One of the few "original" aspects of this work is that it divides the history of the world into seven stages, instead of the six stages used by Augustine in *The City of God*—a convention normally followed in the Middle Ages. The first stage deals with biblical history (treated as if it is literally true) from the Creation until the birth of Noah, and the book proceeds until the final age, which ends with a summary of Castilian history from Noah through the reign of Juan II. No doubt the biblical-era inhabitants of modern Castile had heard all about the Ark! Juan is presented as the redeemer of Castile, in a fashion not at all dissimilar to the presentation of Jesus as the Messiah. Judith Gale Krieger, in an essay comparing *Seven Ages* with the Purim letter, contrasts the "energy and exuberance" of ha-Levi's Purim observations from Aquitaine with the "perfunctory and unaesthetic style" of Paul's post-Christian writing. For Krieger, *Seven Ages*—which makes no reference either to Paul's Jewish background or to what was happening to Jews in Castile—"attests to the tragic historical circumstances which pressured him and thousands of others into conversion and the suppression of their ethnic identity." She asserts that the Purim poem and

Seven Ages speak "not only of medieval Jewish life and the history of the world and Spain respectively. They tell also of Solomon Halevi [*sic*] and Pablo de Santa Maria and of the artistic sterility born of the usurpation of man's freedom."[14] She sees the obliteration of Solomon ha-Levi in the writings of Paul, whereas Netanyahu sees religious and ethnic treason. The interpretations are not mutually exclusive.

We cannot know exactly what proportion of Jewish conversions to Christianity were undertaken for entirely pragmatic rather than spiritual reasons during this period, but it defies reason to attribute more than a small number of such conversions to a genuine change of faith. Paul of Burgos may have been one of the few, but I doubt it. If his was a true change of faith, it was conveniently timed. Paul likely convinced himself, as the years passed, that his opportunistic behavior truly was motivated by a deep recognition that Jesus, and the Catholic Church, were the fulfillment of Jewish prophecy. I see him as the kind of chameleon who appears in every culture and every era of human history—the pagan merchant in the late Roman Empire who becomes a Christian after Constantine; the English Catholic landowner who sides with Henry VIII when he breaks with Rome in the sixteenth century; the revolutionary idealist who becomes a brutal apparatchik under Stalin; the mainstream American Protestant who, contemplating a political career in heavily Mormon Utah or Nevada, converts to Mormonism. To rationalize their behavior, such converts frequently transform opportunism into righteousness in their own minds. They are living a lie, but they may not be lying consciously.

5

IMPUREZA DE SANGRE: THE CRUMBLING
OF THE CONVIVENCIA

I N 1997, I VISITED BARCELONA and met a Catalan bookseller who traces his lineage, on at least one side of his family, to Conversos who submitted to baptism in the early fifteenth century. There is also a family legend, he told me, that a more distant Jewish ancestor had married a Morisco (a Christian convert from Islam) who translated Greek classics into Arabic. "Of course," he said, "it's quite fashionable now to brag about having an ancestry that recalls the glories of al-Andalus— the gardens of Córdoba, the libraries when Northern Europe was going through the Dark Ages, the courts of the caliphs, the brilliant Jewish and Arab scholars. No one will ever tell you that he's descended from a Jewish or a Muslim janitor. The one thing we do know is that the whole idea of 'purity of blood' in Spain was a terrible, lethal joke. You only invent the idea of blood purity if you know that the blood of your people is impure—or, rather, mixed together. No one will ever know what really happened, because people were forced to lie and lie for generations about their religious origins, until it all dissolved into what you call 'tall tales' in English."

For most modern Spaniards with a Muslim or a Jew in their distant family trees, the precise nature of their ancestors' occupations will certainly remain a tall tale or a mystery. But the widespread influence of intermarriage and religious conversion, whether voluntary or forced, since the first Muslim Arabs and Berbers crossed the Strait of Gibraltar into Iberia in 711, is no longer in doubt. In 2008, a study published in *The American Journal of Human Genetics* found a mean incidence of 10.6 percent North African Muslim patrilineal genetic markers in a sample from the current population of Spain and Portugal, and a 19.8 percent incidence of Sephardic Jewish markers.[1] In practical terms, the figures mean that roughly one in ten Spaniards possesses genes, on the father's side, originating in those distant centuries of emigration from Muslim North Africa, and one out of five has Sephardic Jewish genes. Some surely possess both sets of markers, although the study does not address that question. The higher incidence of Sephardic Jewish than of North African genetic indicators reflects, among other possible influences, the continuous presence of Jews in Sepharad (the Hebrew word for "Spain") in Iberia since the early Christian era, while no Muslims arrived until the eighth century. There may also, in later centuries, have been a higher rate of intermarriage between Conversos and "Old Christians" than between Moriscos and Old Christians. The possible explanations are numerous and speculative, given the unreliability of demographic data from the medieval era and the tremendous impetus to lie about one's religious lineage in a country where non-Christians could never feel safe from persecution after the Reconquista.

The cult of *limpieza de sangre,* which began to develop about fifty years after the conversion of Paul of Burgos, eventually became a Spanish obsession, even though it was never codified in a national set of laws. At first the concept of a "purity of blood," independent of one's professed religion, was intended to limit the influence of Conversos within Christian society. Soon enough, it would also be applied to Moriscos. The first local law based on blood lineage rather than religion was passed by Toledo's city council in 1449. Known as the Judgment Statute, the legislation prohibited Conversos from holding local public office. At the time, prominent Spanish clerics condemned the statute and excommunicated the legislators who had framed it, basing their rationale on the church's position that acceptance of the faith, not ethnicity or previous beliefs, defined a Catholic. (During the Nazi era, this position would lead the church to protest persecution of Jewish converts to Catholicism but not of unconverted Jews.) Despite the initial response of church leaders, the Toledo legislators were eventually forgiven and restored to the church. More important, the original Toledo law became the template for new restrictions on Conversos in other cities, universities, and even religious orders. As my Catalan friend rightly observed, there is no reason for a society to become obsessed with purity of blood unless its people know, deep down, that they have already mingled their flesh and blood. And Spanish society would remain obsessed with bloodlines for centuries after the expulsion of the unconverted Jews in 1492 and the Moriscos in 1609. Byron captures this nicely in his 1819 satiric poem *Don Juan,* in a description of Don Juan's father:

> *The father's name was Jose—Don, of course,—*
> *A true Hidalgo, free from every stain*
> *Of Moor or Hebrew blood, he traced his source*
> *Through the most Gothic gentlemen of Spain. . . .*

The mocking tone perfectly fits the larger satiric theme of the poem, which portrays Don Juan not as an expert seducer of women but as easy prey for any clever, attractive lady. A father who is proud to be descended not from Jews or Muslims but from the Visigoths fits the family story.

The genetic study of modern Iberia's population is valuable precisely because the genes tell a story that adds some flesh to the maddening, intractably invisible religious conversions of the pre-modern era. We need not speculate here about the inner spiritual lives of religious converts: the diversity of such a large gene pool, after so many centuries of religious persecution and repression (in the Freudian as well as the literal sense), demonstrates the inevitability of conversion on a large scale when people from different religious and ethnic groups mingle closely. Ordinary people may have changed their religion in large numbers, for a variety of reasons, but only the most extraordinary converts told or were able to tell their stories for posterity.

We may make reasonable inferences (as distinct from ideologically driven generalizations) about Paul of Burgos, because he rose to an eminent position in the church and was both a chronicler of his own life and an object of commentary by others. But who knows what it felt like, when the first invading Muslim forces from North Africa crossed into Iberia, to be a Christian Visigoth woman swept off her feet (through either rape or mutual desire) and married to a Muslim? She would, certainly, have converted to Islam, but did that feel strange? Or was conversion to the religion of the new masters as natural as the conversion of many Roman pagans to Christianity had been in the fourth and fifth centuries, as one secular imperial ruler after another embraced the new religion of Jesus and brought along his subjects? If you were a Jewish man who had suffered persecution, and the threat of forced conversion, under the late rule of the Christian Visigoths, were you simply relieved to be able to practice your religion under the more tolerationist outlook of the Muslims who replaced them as rulers in the eighth century? Or did you look one day with desire at a seductive stranger—one who honored your Holy Book but regarded Muhammad, not Moses, as the most important prophet in history? If you married that stranger, did she convert to Judaism? Was she then dead to her Muslim family? Or, when your first baby was born, did your families get together for a pork-free meal? Did the Convivencia—and the mixing of genes evident in modern Spain—begin then and there for some of the inhabitants of Iberia? We can never know the answers to these questions, and all of the subjunctives used by scholars with ideological axes to grind cannot produce a convincing story—although they can produce a persuasive story for those already of a mind to be persuaded.

Whatever the proportions of religious toleration and religious persecution at any point in history, it is never possible to eradicate the evidence that people of very different beliefs, given sufficient propinquity and proximity, often engage in sexual relations and adopt different religious loyalties as a result of those unions. "Ethnic cleansing" can never fully succeed, because it is impossible to kill or exile everyone before men and women leave their unique genetic mark on the future. Absent force and violence, intermarriage has always been one of the most important secular causes of religious conversion. I say "one of" only because mixed marriages have also been entangled, in proportions that vary greatly according to the level of tolerance within a society, with purposeful social climbing that leads to better financial and educational opportunities. Intermarriage really is a threat to purity of faith as well as purity of blood, if one cares about either.

·

Although many of the highest cultural achievements of the Convivencia—from excellence in translation to the splendors of Moorish architecture—were still very much in evidence at the end of the fourteenth century, the cultural cross-pollination that produced these achievements had slowed at least two centuries earlier. The "ornament of the world" had always been an anomaly, and with the onset of severe anti-Jewish violence in 1391, it became a shattered anomaly that would never quite be eradicated from history but would linger as a religiously and politically contested memory and, one day, as a contributor to Iberian DNA.

•

The contested history of the Convivencia begins with the first documented arrival of Muslims in the Iberian Peninsula in 711, when the Berbers led an army of some ten to fifteen thousand men. The estimated population of Iberia at the time was seven to eight million, ruled by a Christian Visigoth minority of around two hundred thousand.* A Jewish minority—there are no reliable estimates of its size—had definitely existed since the destruction of the Second Temple in 70 and may have been present before the Christian era. Nevertheless, it took the Muslim invaders just four years to conquer most of the peninsula, with the exception of the Basque country, Cantabria, Galicia, Asturias, and the northern Pyrenees.[2] How did such a relatively small army manage to conquer such a large population?

First, the Muslims really were an army (although there was already a considerable tension between the Berbers and their Arab leaders, who looked down on the tribesmen they had conquered and claimed for Islam). It should be recalled that Muhammad died in 632, so the conquest of the Middle and Near East and much of Iberia was completed in less than a century by the warriors of the new religion.† Second, the Visigoths were not exactly popular with the much larger indigenous population of the old Roman province of Hispania. After sacking Rome under Alaric in 410, the Goths moved westward and wound up as the rulers of the peninsula, although not, as one historian notes,

---

* These population estimates vary enormously among scholars, and the precise numbers are highly questionable. The proportions of different ethnic groups, however, are considered accurate by most experts.
† The Arab-Berber invaders were stopped in their northward advance by the Frankish king, Charles Martel, in a number of battles in the vicinity of Poitiers in 732.

without centuries of "destructive battling over the territory with the Vandals and then among themselves."[3] The invaders named their new territory "al-Andalus," which literally means "land of the Vandals" in Arabic. The Roman refugees who had fled to the west after the sacking by the Goths made a bad choice by comparison with those who went to North Africa (and who eventually helped solidify the alliance between North African bishops like Augustine and the Roman Catholic Church). The Visigoth rulers in Hispania did not formally renounce their half-pagan brand of Christianity until 589, when they formally accepted the authority of Rome. The time line is important: less than 125 years separate the acceptance of Roman Catholic authority in Hispania from the Muslim occupation of most of the peninsula. But the Muslims, especially the Arabs who would lay the foundations for the splendors of Córdoba in the mid-750s, represented a vastly more sophisticated culture. And that is the most important reason why territory occupied by millions was conquered by a relatively small force representing a new religion.

The invaders arrived to find the ruins of Roman civilization, left to rot after centuries of misrule by the Vandals and Visigoths. About the only action the Visigoth rulers found the energy to take during the closing decades of their control was the persecution of Jews. That changed when the Muslims—especially those of the Umayyad tradition—crossed the thirteen-mile Strait of Gibraltar. Persecutions and forced conversions of Jews ceased, and Christians (once they stopped fighting the invaders) were also allowed to practice their religion freely. Both Christians and Jews were regarded by Muslims, especially the Umayyads, as *dhimmi,* the Arabic term for "Peoples of the Book," who shared monotheism and a common descent from Abraham. However, both religions, though regarded as "protected," were legally subordinate to Islam—a fact glossed over in many perorations about the glories of coexistence in al-Andalus. The protected minorities were allowed to administer their own religious affairs but were forbidden to proselytize and were subject to a special poll tax.[4] Moreover, this protection did not extend to pagans, who had survived not only in Visigoth-ruled Hispania but in rural areas throughout Europe. Under Muslim rule during this period, Christians were considered neither better nor worse than Jews—a theologically based Muslim attitude that permitted and encouraged a new efflorescence of Jewish learning and commerce.

That learning was soon to be expressed in Arabic, the language of scholarship throughout most of the region.

As the Cuban-born historian María Rosa Menocal notes, many of the early Muslim immigrants to Andalusia were an ethnic mix of Arab and Berber (another example of intermarriage despite cultural tensions). Abd al-Rahman, the first Muslim ruler of Córdoba, had an Arab Umayyad father and a Berber mother. "As with the Christians before them," Menocal argues, "the Muslims' distinctive power and authority resided in a faith to which conversion was not only possible but desirable and encouraged, pragmatically coerced by the range of civil advantages to any Muslim, whether he had converted the day before or descended from the most prestigious Bedouin tribe, the Quraysh of the Prophet himself. And convert the population did, in droves."[5] (Menocal deserves a gold star for that felicitous phrase, "pragmatically coerced," which describes so many religious conversions from minority to majority religions.) Naturally, it became prestigious, within a century or two, for Muslims to claim that they were descended from the first Arabs who had led the expeditions westward from Syria and then across the Strait of Gibraltar. No one wanted to claim descent from a Muslim slave, any more than today's Spaniards want to claim descent from a Muslim or Jewish janitor. But even the emirs and caliphs were nearly all children of mixed marriages between Arabs and mothers from the North who had once been Christians. The light skin and blue eyes of Umayyad-descended Muslims were noted by contemporary Eastern travelers during the Middle Ages, and this heritage is evident in southern Spain today. The story written on the faces of so many residents of Andalusia is the same story told by the DNA study. In the eighth and ninth centuries, another attractive feature of Islam for the indigenous population was that even a recent conversion provided opportunities for immediate social advancements. Unlike the later Christian cult of *limpieza,* the Muslim incorporation of converts in eighth- and ninth-century al-Andalus did not take into account how far back the faith went in the family tree.

•

We know how the story ends—with the relentless Christian Reconquista; the expulsion of countless Jews and Moors; the official denial

of centuries of "impure" non-Christian cultural influences; the burning of Arabic books and the prohibition of spoken Arabic; and the
Spanish Inquisition. But let us linger, for a moment, in the brightest
period of the Convivencia, which began when Abd al-Rahman arrived
in Córdoba, having fled Baghdad after the rest of his family was murdered by a rival dynasty. Al-Rahman founded an Iberian caliphate—a
term that should not be confused with its use either by modern terrorist groups or by conservative scholars who insist that everywhere,
in every period of history, there was always a "clash of civilizations"
between Islam and "Judaeo-Christianity," and that things could never
have turned out any other way.*

Even before the establishment of a caliphate with Córdoba as its
capital, the Moorish presence rejuvenated Iberian agriculture, which
had stagnated during the long rule of the Vandals and Goths. Building on and reconstructing old Roman aqueducts and roads, Muslims
re-established effective irrigation and introduced crops already familiar in the Arab world—including citrus fruits, sugar, rice, and coffee.
Amenities such as public bathhouses, unknown since Roman times,
were rebuilt. "At its peak in the tenth century," writes the British journalist Matthew Carr, "Córdoba was a metropolis without parallel in
the Christian world, boasting paved roads and streetlights, hospitals,
schools, public baths, and libraries. At a time when the largest library
in Christian Europe had no more than six hundred volumes, a cottage
industry of Arabic calligraphers in Córdoba was churning out some
sixty thousand handwritten books every year."[6]

In recent years, depictions of the culturally fruitful encounter among
Muslims, Jews, and Christians during the Convivencia have provided
a much-needed corrective to right-wing stereotyping of all Muslims,
throughout history, as barbarians and terrorists. But some of these
scholarly accounts, animated by an understandable but not necessarily fact-based nostalgia, tend to minimize the tensions that always lay
beneath the surface, and sometimes boiled over violently. Menocal's
Ornament of the World (2002), an evocative and justly praised history focusing on the literary and artistic achievements of that unique

---

* *The Clash of Civilizations and the Remaking of World Order* was the title of a 1996 book
by Samuel P. Huntington, a conservative scholar associated with the American Enterprise
Institute. "Judaeo-Christianity" is, of course, a modern term and, in my view, belongs in
quotation marks when applied to much of Western history.

culture, nevertheless downplays both the long-term refusal of Spanish Christians to accept the cultural intermingling in al-Andalus, and the outbursts of Muslim as well as Christian violence against Jews, as tolerationism began to recede in the waning decades of the eleventh century. In her lengthy book, for example, she sums up the 1066 massacre of some four thousand Jews with one sentence, noting that "ferocious anti-Jewish riots broke out in Granada."[7] This was one of the more grisly pogroms in Jewish history, following as it did the murder of Joseph Ibn Naghrela, the Jewish vizier to the Berber king of Andalusia. Naghrela was apparently accused by political rivals of plotting against the king (an accusation the monarch did not believe, because he gave Joseph asylum in his own palace). But on December 30, 1066, Joseph was seized by a Muslim mob and crucified. It seems likely, according to most scholars, that the Jews were caught between battling Muslim factions—invading fundamentalists from North Africa versus the more tolerant Andalusians, who created the marvels of a sophisticated civilization. The Muslims in Granada at the end of the eleventh century could hardly have been unaware of the symbolic importance of crucifixion as a way of murdering a Jewish official, and the butchering of thousands of other Jews afterward followed a familiar pattern of punishing an entire community for what was originally portrayed and seen by the mob as the crime of one Jew. Minimizing the cracks that always existed in the "ornament of the world" actually diminishes the magnitude of the cultural achievement: we are not surprised when people who love one another collaborate in great endeavors, but it is remarkable when people who sometimes find it difficult merely to tolerate one another produce a high civilization. The historian Joseph Pérez aptly describes the relations between the three monotheistic religions during the Convivencia as "a *de facto* tolerance, suffered rather than desired."[8] Pérez's analysis of the Realpolitik that characterized the Convivencia is more plausible than idealization based on the desire to emphasize the better angels of the Islamic past for today's political purposes.

.

Two of the most brilliant tolerationists of the era, the near contemporaries Maimonides (c. 1135–1204) and Averroës (1126–98) were both natives of Córdoba. Yet it was their fate to come along at just the point when things were going wrong, and there is no better indicator of what was happening than the fact that neither man could live out his life in the civilization into which he was born. Averroës, the rationalist Muslim philosopher who can, in many respects, be viewed as a precursor of Spinoza, was detested not only by Catholics but by the more militant fundamentalist Muslims, the Almohads, who, in the 1150s, replaced more tolerant Muslim rulers. Like Maimonides, Averroës was both a physician and a sophisticated scholar. He was a religious judge in Córdoba and Seville and a personal physician to the caliph in Marrakech. But the caliph, under pressure from Almohad religious authorities, banished Averroës in 1195 and ordered that his philosophical writings be burned. (He was apparently permitted to return to the court in Marrakech, on the other side of the Strait of Gibraltar, shortly before his death.) Because Averroës was such a controversial figure in his own lifetime, many of his works survive only in Hebrew and Latin translation, not in the classical Arabic that was the glory and lingua franca of his culture. Two of Averroës's core beliefs provided ample reason for the loathing he incited in conservative Muslim and Christian authorities. First, he argued that the physical world has always existed, just as God has—that God and nature are, in effect, one. Second, in contrast to Aquinas, he believed that all humans share a common higher intellect—a position leading him to conclude that only the soul, not the body, is eternal. Thus, Averroist philosophy denies the core tenet of both Islam and Christianity. There are no virgins awaiting martyred jihadists in paradise, no risen Jesus and saints sitting at the right hand of God the Father in heaven. One scholar cites an Arab proverb, relying on a homonym meaning both "logic" and "speech," to explain the hostility incited by Averroës in his Muslim contemporaries: "Their fate has struck all the falsifiers who mix philosophy with religion and promote heresies. They have studied logic (*mantiq*), but it is said with reason that misfortune is passed through speech (*mantiq*.)"[9]

Maimonides, unlike Averroës, is revered (indeed, no Jewish scholar is more revered) as a teacher and philosopher in his own religious tradition as well as within many other cultures. He entered manhood at a time when persecution of the long-established Jewish community of Córdoba was beginning under the city's first Almohad ruler. Jews were pressured to convert, or to put on the appearance of converting, by reciting the basic Muslim creed: "There is no God but God, and Muhammad is His prophet." The young Maimonides wrote a famous response to a Moroccan rabbi who insisted that all Jews were required to die rather than feign conversion and practice their religion secretly. (By the early twelfth century, the view that Andalusian Jews were bad Jews in any case because of their close association with Arabs was widespread in Jewish communities outside Iberia, and a similar view of Andalusian Muslims was held by many non-Iberian Arabs.) In his lengthy reply, written in Arabic, Maimonides noted that some Jewish sages had feigned apostasy in order to save their lives and that the obligation to preserve life was primary in Jewish law. "Even heretics," he argued, "were worthy of reward for a *single* act of piety. Those who practice the *mizvot* secretly are even more worthy of reward despite the circumstances of their forced conversion."[10] Nevertheless, Maimonides and his family (his father, Maimon, was a religious judge) decided in 1160 to leave Córdoba for Morocco, which was also under Almohad rule but where the persecutions were, at the time, less severe. Eventually, the family moved on to Palestine and then to Egypt, where Maimonides died. Although Maimonides' attitude toward forced converts was one imbued with charity and fellow feeling, his own desire to avoid forced conversion drove his actions as a young man. The persistent rumors that Maimonides once lived as a Muslim, or that he actually went through a conversion ceremony himself, have been largely rejected by mainstream Jewish and non-Jewish scholars. Shaul Magid, professor of Jewish studies at Indiana University Bloomington, says flatly that there is "no credible evidence" in Jewish sources that Maimonides or his family ever converted to Islam.[11] Norman Roth, author of *Jews, Visigoths and Muslims in Medieval Spain* (1994), points out that the rumors about Maimonides, though dismissed by most scholars, have been accompanied in recent years by equally unsubstantiated theories that Jewish soldiers actually fought against Almohad troops and that the Almohads deliberately entered certain Andalusian cities on Saturdays because Jews would not fight on the Sabbath. Had Jews fought at all, their behavior would have broken with a history of adaptive behavior toward previous waves of invaders in al-Andalus. Moreover, the real hatred was between the Almohad invaders and the Muslim Almoravids who had controlled al-Andalus for several hundred years.) The intense strife between competing Muslim sects aided the Christian Reconquista, which gained momentum in 1236 with the fall of Córdoba to the Christian King Ferdinand III (who was later canonized).

Maimonides and Averroës were the brilliant heirs and late creators of a vibrant but doomed culture. Maimonides, like Averroës (and Aquinas after them), was determined to reconcile his religion with classical Greek culture. And his incalculable contributions to the body of Jewish law were also shaped by his encounters with and deep knowledge of Muslim law in the society in which he was raised. "It has been said without exaggeration that to know Maimonides is to know Judaism," writes David Shasha, director of the Center for Sephardic Heritage. Maimonides' genius lay in his adoption of "the parochial traditions of Judaism, its laws, its rituals, and its particular understanding of God and the Covenant, and merging them with philosophy, science and history."[12] Despite their different traditions, both Maimonides and Averroës can be described as religious humanists—a movement that did not gain strength within Christianity until the late fifteenth century.

Nothing could be more central to the achievements of a Maimonides and an Averroës than the right to practice one's religion unmolested. That ended with the onset among Muslims in twelfth-century al-Andalus of what would today be called "sectarian violence"—the stupid, religiously correct euphemism beloved by those who refuse to admit that faith can do any wrong. Soon the Reconquista—and the advance of Christian absolutism—would become irreversible. Freedom of conscience in Spain and Portugal could never again be taken for granted by Jews, Muslims, or, eventually, by practicing Christians with a Jew or a Muslim in their backgrounds. Conversion as a weapon would replace conversion by choice.

6

THE INQUISITION AND THE END

THE FATEFUL YEAR 1492 began in Spain with the fall of the peninsula's final piece of Muslim-held territory, Granada, to the Christian monarchs Ferdinand and Isabella. Boabdil, the last Muslim ruler in Iberia, had no choice but surrender if he wished to avoid the destruction of his own people. As legend has it, Boabdil's Mommie Dearest responded to her son's tears upon leaving the city with the reproach, "You weep like a woman for what you could not defend like a man." Acting like a man would, presumably, have meant fighting a hopeless battle against the combined forces of the kingdoms of Aragon and Castile. Boabdil's beloved Alhambra palace and the lush gardens of the Generalife, which survive today as a testament to the grace and splendor of Spain's Moorish past, would have overlooked the bodies of Granada's slain Muslims. By signing the articles of capitulation to Ferdinand and Isabella, Boabdil thought he was assuring the city's Muslims of the right to practice their religion—although the monarchs' promise would, in a relatively short time, turn out not to be worth the parchment on which it was written. For the moment, though, Ferdinand and Isabella left Muslims alone and focused their attention on Jews.

In the second historic turning point of 1492, the monarchs expelled all Jews from Spain unless they agreed to convert to Christianity. The expulsion edict, dated March 31, 1492, is a document—like a fair number of notorious historical pronouncements—that elicits strong opinions from nearly everyone but that few people have actually read. It is understandable but unfortunate that the media do not reprint odious public declarations as regularly as, say, *The New York Times* reprints the Declaration of Independence every Fourth of July. Understandable, because there isn't much of an audience, in modern Spain or anywhere else, for a screed inveighing against "wicked Christians who Judaized and apostasized from our holy Catholic faith." Unfortunate, because considerable benefit can be derived from the realization that powerful leaders and would-be leaders sometimes spell out their bad intentions in words that say exactly what they mean. Ferdinand and Isabella's expulsion edict, like *Mein Kampf,* is one of those instances.

Today, many who know or care about the expulsion of the Jews from Spain tend to assume that it was all about anti-Semitism, or Jew-hatred, in the modern sense. It was not. It was about the centrality of valid conversion to the Catholic faith in general, and the specific fears of two Catholic rulers who themselves had many advisers, born into Jewish families, who had converted. The monarchs feared that the very presence of recalcitrant religious Jews in Christian Spain might induce Conversos to revert to the faith of their forefathers. In the view of the king, the queen, and church authorities, Conversos could not be counted on to embrace Catholicism fully as long as faithful Jews were around—Jews who might be relatives or friends—to remind them of the old ways and seduce them from the True Faith. The edict says so explicitly. As long as unconverted Jews "continue to engage in social interaction and communication" with New Christians, they find "means and ways they can to subvert and to steal faithful Christians from our holy Catholic faith . . . instructing them in the ceremonies and observances of their law . . . achieving that the Christians and their children be circumcised, and giving them books from which they may read their prayers and declaring to them the fasts that they must keep, and joining with them to read and teach them the history of their law . . . carrying to them and giving to them from their houses unleavened bread and meats ritually slaughtered . . . and persuading them as much as they can to hold and observe the law of Moses, convincing them that there is no other truth except for that one."

The pernicious influence of unconverted Jews on New Christians, the edict asserts, had been "proved by many statements and confessions, both from these same Jews and from those who have been perverted and enticed by them." Since the Spanish Inquisition had been given the go-ahead by the Vatican at Ferdinand and Isabella's request, there certainly were a good many "statements and confessions" that "proved" the truth of the danger to the faith posed by the very presence of observant Jews. Autos-da-fé do have that effect, and the first was held in Seville on February 6, 1481—less than five months after the appointment of two inquisitors, both Dominicans, for the diocese. Between 1481 and 1488, more than seven hundred were executed in Seville alone, and thousands of others received life imprisonment for "Judaizing" or encouraging others to Judaize.[1]

The 1492 edict, before spelling out the specific conditions of the expulsion, actually explains—with a combination of regret, petulance, and outright indignation—that the monarchs themselves had preferred less draconian measures to expulsion. These milder measures had included targeted arrests, torture, imprisonment, executions, and expulsions from areas that were supposedly hotbeds of Judaizing. Ferdinand and Isabella had, to their regret, been too softhearted.

> Notwithstanding that we were informed of the great part of this before now and we knew that the true remedy for all these injuries and inconveniences was to prohibit all interaction between the said Jews and Christians [Conversos] and banish them from all our kingdoms, we desire to content ourselves by commanding them to leave all cities, towns, and villages of Andalusia where it appears that they have done the greatest injury, believing that that would be sufficient so that those of other cities, towns, and villages of our kingdoms and lordships would cease to do and commit the aforesaid acts. And since we are informed that neither that step nor the passing of sentence against the said Jews who have been most guilty of the said crimes and delicts against our holy Catholic faith have been sufficient as a complete remedy . . . because every day it is found and appears that the said Jews increase in continuing their evil and wicked purpose wherever they live and congregate, and so that there will not be any place where they further offend our holy faith, and corrupt those whom God has until now most desired to preserve, as well as those who had fallen but amended and returned

to Holy Mother Church, the which according to the weakness of our humanity and by diabolical astuteness and suggestion that continually wages war against us may easily occur unless the principal cause of it be removed, which is to banish the said Jews from our kingdom . . .*

Here is the straightforward rationale for expulsion, and I see no reason to doubt it. As Joseph Pérez puts it, "The intention was to create an irreversible situation. By eliminating Judaism, it was hoped to discourage reversion to it."[2] But the expulsion of unconverted Jews did not stop suspicion of Conversos (including some who remained in the service of the monarchy).

Even as the king and queen prepared to expel unconverted Jews from their kingdom, they paid for the voyage of Christopher Columbus with loans from the Converso financiers Luis de Santangel and Gabriel Sanchez. Columbus's journey—he set sail on August 3—would have been the third front-page story of 1492, had there been newspapers at that time. As he prepared his ships to set out from the port of Palos de la Frontera, Columbus actually watched the stubbornly unconverted Jewish exiles leaving on other ships and described the scene in his ship's log as a "fleet of misery and woe."[3] Columbus himself had five Conversos as members of his crew, including a physician and an interpreter who spoke Arabic. (It is not clear why Columbus thought an Arabic-speaking interpreter would be useful wherever he landed; the inclusion may simply attest to the history—soon to be brought to a close—of Arabic as the language of the educated in Spain.)

In any event, the involvement of Conversos at so many levels of Castilian and Aragonese society and government does not lend support to the idea that pursuit of blood purity was the chief motivation for the expulsion of unconverted Jews. Even Tomás de Torquemada (1420–98), the first Grand Inquisitor, had familial Converso connections. He was the nephew of Cardinal Juan de Torquemada (1388–1468), an important theologian who had a Converso grandmother and

---

* All quotations from the edict are contained in an excellent translation from the Castilian, by Edward Peters, provided online by the Foundation for the Advancement of Sephardic Studies and Culture, http://www.sephardicstudies.org/decree.html. The translation is based on the fullest version of the original text, *Documentos acerca de la expulsión de los Judios,* edited by Louis Suárez-Fernández.

wrote a defense of the Converso community of Toledo, in which he criticized the idea that New Christians should be treated differently from Old Christians. Even if the number of secretly observant Jews among the Conversos amounted to an insignificant handful, it does not follow that Ferdinand and Isabella believed this to be so and were therefore motivated by something akin to modern anti-Semitism. A Christian ruler did not have to be an anti-Semite as the term has been understood since the nineteenth century (and especially since the Holocaust) to hate and fear Judaism as a religion and to translate that hate into suspicion of individual Jews' loyalties.

Furthermore, people who play an active role in forcing others to convert, as both the monarchy and the Spanish ecclesiastical hierarchy did, are almost certain to be suspicious of all converts on some level. Those who compel people to give up one religion for another, whether through the pragmatic coercion described by María Rosa Menocal or through direct threats to their lives, have good reason to be suspicious of the resulting conversions. Surprisingly, few historians have emphasized the obvious psychological truth that inquisitors and absolute monarchs are in an excellent position to know exactly how much deception people will employ to keep what they have when their only alternative is being crushed by a superior power. Jews and Muslims who were forced to convert may not have remained good Jews and Muslims, but many of them must not have been very good Christians, either. That was the suspicion, but it was also, in unknown numbers of instances, the truth.

Perhaps the most difficult aspect of the old Roman Catholic inquisitorial mentality for the modern mind to grasp was its absolute conviction that anyone who had been baptized, regardless of the circumstances, was to be considered an apostate if found by the Inquisition to be practicing any other religion, or even cherishing remnants of another tradition. This would remain a crucial point not only throughout the Spanish Inquisition but well into the nineteenth century for the Roman Inquisition operating in the Papal States of Italy. Forced baptisms of all kinds—whether they were performed by a priest in a mass sacrament administered at the point of a gun (or within sight of a pyre for an auto-da-fé) or by a Christian servant splashing holy water on the head of a Jewish infant—were considered valid forever. (Too bad for you if you were a circumcised Jewish baby sleeping in your crib and a Christian servant girl came along and sprinkled water on your head, baptizing you in the name of the Father, the Son, and the Holy Ghost. In this scenario, which occurred more than once in the history of forced conversion, baptism became the spiritual equivalent of the involuntary transformation portrayed in the movie *Invasion of the Body Snatchers*.)

Suspicion of sacramental betrayal, justified or unjustified, would eventually lend support to anti-Jewish actions based on impurity of blood—a concept originally decried by influential Spanish church officials when it first emerged, in the 1450s in Toledo. As Pérez notes, the demand for blood purity rather than only for religious purity "was a prejudice that eventually poisoned the very spirit of the Spanish public."[4] But the centrality of the concept of "true" conversion to Catholicism came first, *limpieza de sangre* second.

The real fusion of *limpieza de la fe* with *limpieza de sangre* would not take firm hold until the sixteenth century, with intensifying suspicion of all Conversos, the extension of the Inquisition from Jews to Muslims, and the forced baptisms of Muslims throughout Iberia. In 1609, King Philip III ordered the expulsion of all Muslims, including the converts to Christianity known as Moriscos. During the same period—although there were almost no Protestants in Spain—fear of the Reformation in the North added a new urgency to religious oppression in a land where there had once been coexistence among the three monotheistic faiths.

•

The term "Spanish Inquisition" is used so commonly (and has appeared in so many satirical guises) that a fair number of people are under the impression that it was a purely Spanish phenomenon. There were several inquisitions, with distinct local as well as general religious characteristics involving the defense of Catholic orthodoxy. The initial phase, which began in the early thirteenth century, was aimed at Catharism, a sect that emerged in Europe in the eleventh century and whose adherents were concentrated in the Languedoc region of southern France. The Cathars were dualists, and their beliefs were a revival of the oldest split within Christendom. Catharism (called the "Albigensian Heresy" by the Vatican) was based on a philosophy in which an all-good creator vied with an independent evil power for supremacy. Medieval Cathars also embraced elements of the asceticism that had characterized Manicheans in the early Christian era. The Roman Catholic Church, with its immense secular as well as religious power in the medieval world, was not about to overlook the same type of heresy it had refused to tolerate in the fifth century, when its secular power was not yet fully established. Beginning in 1208, Pope Innocent III decreed a formal Crusade against the Cathars. His first appointee as a leader of God's army was a Cistercian abbot, Arnaud Amaury (also known as Arnaud Amalric), whose battle cry, "Kill them all, God will know his own," was the very model for a Christian soldier in that era. That was his reply when the wholesale slaughter was questioned by a knight who had qualms about the possibility that some Catholics would be massacred along with the Cathars in the city of Béziers, a Cathar stronghold. According to the abbot himself, in a letter to Pope Innocent, twenty thousand people were slaughtered on July 22, 1209—a death toll far exceeding that on any of the worst days (or years) of the Spanish Inquisition.[5] Eventually, what was truly a war of extermination was taken over by French Catholic rulers. Then, in 1231, Pope Gregory IX installed "inquisitors of heretical depravity," directed by the Vatican—an action that marked the true beginning of the Catholic crusades against heresy and heretics lumped together today as "the Inquisition."

The investigation of the Cathars was conducted under the supervision of the recently founded Dominican Order, and its explicit purpose was to wipe out Cathars who had survived the military actions initiated by Pope Innocent. (The Spanish founder of the order, Dominic Guzmán, was lauded in the saccharine Number One hit song of 1963, "Dominique," by a performer known as the Singing Nun—also a Dominican.* Needless to say, none of the song's lyrics—which featured an unforgettable, mind-numbing refrain that still pounds in my cortex as "Dominiqua-niqua-niqua"—mentioned the role of the sainted Padre Dominic's order in finishing off the Cathars. Dominic

---

* The Singing Nun is not to be confused with the sixties' American television series titled *The Flying Nun,* starring the young Sally Field. The nun who recorded "Dominique" was a Belgian, Soeur Sourire, who sang in French. Field did not sing (at least not well), but she did fly with the aid of television's then primitive special effects.

died in 1221 and was canonized by his friend Pope Gregory in 1234.)
The physical destruction of the Cathars was completed by the end
of the thirteenth century, although many Cathar ideas would resur-
face during the Reformation—particularly with the emergence of
Protestant denominations dissenting from mainstream Calvinism and
Lutheranism. The campaign against the Cathars, unlike later inquisitions, did not have to contend with that most formidable of enemies,
the printing press.

The Spanish Inquisition, which, as already noted, was approved
by the Vatican only after Ferdinand and Isabella requested the pope's
assent, was quite different in its aims and more sophisticated in its
methods than the medieval inquisition of the Cathars. The specific
character of the Spanish Inquisition was determined by the history
of the Iberian Peninsula as a place where two large groups, Jews and
Muslims, had generally been left alone to practice their non-Christian
faiths. It was therefore of ultimate importance to the inquisitors to
establish the spiritual authenticity of conversions, as demonstrated not
only by the original convert but by his or her descendants. From the
Vatican authorization of the Inquisition in 1478, through the widen-
ing investigations of Conversos and Moriscos in the sixteenth century,
and ending in the expulsion of Moriscos at the beginning of the seventeenth century, the religious preoccupations of Spanish monarchs
formed a mirror image of the preoccupations of monarchs in parts of
Europe being divided by the Reformation. As Christendom in Northern Europe was splitting into different sects, and rulers were forced,
albeit not without endless wars, to make political accommodations to
encompass large numbers of people with different religious beliefs, the
rulers of Christendom in Spain were attempting to ensure uniformity
of belief in a land that, in the medieval era before the Reconquista, had
made such accommodations.

It is fair to state that most Western historians have paid much more
attention to the 1492 expulsion of Spanish Jews, and to the Inquisition's subsequent treatment of Conversos, than to the Inquisition's
treatment of Muslims and their expulsion of Moriscos. Most scholars
agree that fewer Moriscos were placed on trial for heresy, and many
fewer received the death sentence, than Conversos. Nevertheless, the
destruction of the crucial Muslim element in the culture was progressive and relentless under a succession of monarchs. It took Ferdinand

and Isabella only a few years to renege on the pledge of religious freedom that they made in their agreement with Boabdil. By 1500, the
rulers decided that all Muslims in Castile must submit to baptism
(although, for reasons that are obscure, the same policy was not instituted in Aragon for another twenty-five years). The edict ordering
Muslims to convert or leave Castile was followed by bans on the use
of the Arabic language and the wearing of traditional dress. But, as
one historian notes, the baptized Muslims in the first two decades of
the sixteenth century "were left mostly to their own devices . . . when
the Inquisition was busy directing its attention towards the Converso
community."[6] In other words, a Morisco in 1510 did not have to worry
that informers listening at the window might report a spoken word of
Arabic to the Inquisition, but Conversos during the same period did
have to worry that a neighborly informer might report suspicions that
the family was observing the Jewish Sabbath.

By the last quarter of the sixteenth century, though, with Spain
engaged in military conflict with Turkey and various Protestant states,
both the monarchy and the church had come "to regard the Moriscos
as a kind of fifth column, enemies within, ready to ally themselves with
the Turks or the Protestants of Béarn."[7] (Béarn, an independent state
since the mid-1400s and eventually a Huguenot Protestant stronghold, was annexed to France in 1620. The area was a center of conflict
between Catholics and Protestants throughout the Reformation.) Even
within the Spanish church, there was disagreement about how to solve
the Morisco "problem." The Grand Inquisitor was opposed to expel-
ling the Moriscos in 1609 precisely because they had been baptized,
whatever the circumstances, and were therefore considered Christians.
But the archbishop of Valencia, which had a large Morisco population, disagreed and insisted that the Moriscos had all secretly remained
Muslims. He carried the day, and Philip III signed the expulsion order
on April 9, 1609. It is estimated that some three hundred thousand
Moriscos—about 5 percent of the total population of Spain—were
expelled. Some forty thousand went to Morocco, where, as Pérez dryly
observes, they were greeted with contempt "on the grounds that they
were Christians!"[8] Exiled Jews and Muslims who had refused to convert were affected by this irony in the history of forced religious conversion and persecution. Spanish Jews were regarded with contempt by
many Jewish communities in other parts of Europe and North Africa

because of their long, close association with both Muslim and Christian rulers. They were considered bad Jews by many rabbis, just as the Moriscos—expelled for their Muslim lineage—would be considered bad Muslims.

Suppression of books in both Hebrew and Arabic was a preoccupation of the Spanish Inquisitors almost from the start. In 1497, the *Suprema* (Supreme Council of the Inquisition) ordered the civil courts of Valencia and Barcelona to burn books in Hebrew concerning surgery and medicine as well as Judaism. A year later, Catholic theologians were tasked with examining Qurans and other religious texts before burning them. The preface to the 1583 Spanish Index of forbidden reading materials (not to be confused with the Vatican's Index, compiled in Rome) provides the best insight into the motivation of the censors. All records of famous disputations between rabbis and priests were to be banned. So, too, would any Christian writings *refuting* the Quran. The reason explicitly cited was that "such polemics enabled people to form some idea of what infidels believed."[9]

In Rome, where the third phase of the Inquisition began in the sixteenth century in response to the Reformation, what was called the Sacred Congregation of the Universal Inquisition worked closely with the Congregation of the Index. The campaign against intellectual and religious heresy—it was the Roman Inquisition that put Galileo on trial in 1633—was never divorced from the absolute power the church believed it had the right to wield over baptized Catholics. Even in the nineteenth century, as one European country after another limited the power of the church over both non-Catholics and civil government, the threat of being placed on the Index could still be used by the church against Catholic writers. (Non-Catholics generally regarded being placed on the Index as a compliment.)

The compilers of the Index in Rome, like the Spanish inquisitors, were worried about any book—even one antagonistic to non-Catholic faiths—that provided information about other people's beliefs. As the cardinal and inquisitor Robert Bellarmine wrote to a Jesuit friend on July 13, 1598, "I myself hardly ever read a book without feeling in the mood to give it a good censoring."[10] (Bellarmine was canonized by Pope Pius XI in 1930 and declared a Doctor of the Church in 1931, and the timing certainly suited what proved to be the best decade since the Inquisition for ideological censors, as demonstrated in Hitler's Germany, Stalin's Soviet Union, Franco's Spain, and Mussolini's Italy.)

One specific reason for the occasionally disproportionate focus on the Spanish Inquisition in the United States was its influence during the colonial period in the Western Hemisphere. Along with the Portuguese Inquisition, which did not begin until 1536, the Spanish Inquisition was close enough geographically, through its New World colonies, to remind the English settlers in New England of how much they hated Catholicism. In 1492, many expelled Spanish Jews had originally fled to Portugal, which had a policy of greater toleration than Ferdinand and Isabella did at the time. When the Portuguese launched their own inquisition, a fair number of these Jews eventually wound up in Amsterdam—then the most religiously tolerant city in Europe—the Portuguese colony of Brazil, or Spain's colony of Mexico. Many immigrated to the colonies, in the misguided hope that an ocean would place them beyond the reach of the Inquisition. Fat chance: the shepherd was not about to let his sheep escape on ships.

A full-scale Inquisition tribunal was established in Mexico City in 1569, and some Conversos fled north to what is now Santa Fe, New Mexico, in the persistent hope of finding a place far enough away from civilization to escape religious barbarity. We will never know how many Jews settled in the Santa Fe area, but we do know that there were prosecutions of both Jews for Judaizing and converted Indians for having reverted to their pagan ways. With the Indians, as with Conversos, the issue was their status as Christians after baptism: only Indians who had been foolish or unlucky enough to be converted through baptism were subject to the New World Inquisition. Executions were conducted in Santa Fe's main plaza, now an upscale tourist destination. The story is not over yet, because a number of residents of New Mexico have discovered through recent DNA testing that they, like much of the population of Spain, have Sephardic Jewish ancestry. Both Portugal and Spain have offered citizenship to the descendants of Jews who were expelled or forcibly converted. However, the procedures for obtaining citizenship are in limbo in Spain, because descendants of Moriscos have asserted that they should receive the same apology and offer of citizenship. (The strains between Spaniards and new Muslim immigrants—legal and illegal—are beyond the scope of this book. The assimilation of Muslim immigrants is a major issue in much of Europe, but the tension has an added dimension in Spain because of Iberia's Muslim past. Since the 2004 terrorist train bombings near Madrid, in which at least 181 were killed and thousands injured, there has been considerable Spanish sentiment against Muslim immigration—and the granting of citizenship to everyone of Morisco descent seems unlikely. The terrorists who bombed the trains had the chutzpah to cite the Reconquista as one of their justifications.)

In general, families of Sephardic Jews who originally came from Portugal have better documentation of their long connection to Judaism than those who came from Spain. The first Jews to arrive in the Dutch colony of New Amsterdam had left Portugal for old Amsterdam and immigrated to northern Brazil when it was a Dutch colony, in the first half of the seventeenth century. After the Portuguese regained full control of Brazil by taking Recife in a war with the Dutch that ended in 1650, the Jews who had settled in that city left for both Holland and New Amsterdam.

In the Old World, the activities of the Inquisition continued in late-sixteenth- and early-seventeenth-century Spain even as Christendom continued to splinter throughout Northern Europe. The battle for uniformity of religious belief—with one faith, one monarch, and one law for all—was already lost to the continuing Reformation. That Protestant reformers, such as John Calvin in Geneva, could be just as brutal and repressive as Torquemada when they attained political power only underlined the depth of religious division throughout Christendom, from England to the borders of the tsarist empire.

•

In 1826, in a kind of coda to religious conformity that could no longer be enforced in most of Western Europe, the last execution conducted by the Spanish Inquisition took place, in Valencia. The victim, Cayetano Ripoll, was a deist and schoolteacher accused of spreading free-thinking ideas (such as freedom of speech and religion) to his students. A soldier in the Spanish Army during the Peninsular War (1807–14) between Spain and France, Ripoll was captured by Napoleon's forces. While a prisoner of war, he was exposed to deist writings, which circulated freely in the territories controlled by Napoleon's army, and became deeply influenced by writings that certainly included Voltaire and possibly even Thomas Paine (whose works were more highly regarded in Napoleonic France than in either England or the United States). Soon after he returned home from the war, he was arrested by the Inquisition for his classroom forays into deism. Ripoll was held prisoner for two years, then sentenced to death, not by burning but by the more merciful method of hanging. The rope, however, was not quite enough to satisfy the blood lust of the inquisitors; when Ripoll was pronounced dead, his body was stuffed into a barrel decorated with flames. Both barrel and body were burned in unconsecrated ground. It is said that Ripoll's last words were "I die reconciled to God and man."

Ripoll was executed on June 26, just over a week before the fiftieth anniversary of the signing of the Declaration of Independence—written by the deist Thomas Jefferson. The new American government, unlike European societies that still thought it was possible to stamp out heresy, was able not only to accommodate but to welcome (some of the time) a diversity of religious belief that emerged from the bottom up. From the beginning of the Inquisition, the Spaniards had been trying to put Humpty Dumpty back together again, even though printing presses could now spread dissident religious ideas to anyone who could read. But the proliferation of Protestant denominations in Northern Europe would leave no doubt—despite the best efforts of Protestant as well as Catholic inquisitors—that the emergence of new religions attracting millions of new converts was an unstoppable and irreversible process.

· **PART III** ·

REFORMATIONS

7

JOHN DONNE (1572–1631)

To our bodies turn we then, that so
Weak men on love revealed may look;
Love's mysteries in souls do grow,
But yet the body is his book.

—"THE ECSTASY"

Batter my heart, three-person'd God; for, you
As yet but knock, breathe, shine, and seek to mend;
That I may rise, and stand, o'erthrow me, and bend
Your force, to break, blow, burn and make me new . . .
Divorce me, untie, or break that knot again,
Take me to you, imprison me, for I
Except you enthral me, never shall be free,
Nor ever chaste, except you ravish me.

—"DIVINE MEDITATIONS," 14

JOHN DONNE was the first great English-language writer to ally him-self openly and unequivocally with Protestantism. His choice of the Protestant Church of England over the Roman Catholic faith in which he was raised was one of the two most significant decisions of his life—the other being what was considered a socially unsuitable marriage for love. Absent conversion to Protestantism, the poet would never have become the dean of Saint Paul's in London and one of the most influ-ential preachers of his era. He would doubtless have been a great poet regardless of his religion, although he might not have lived as long had he chosen Catholicism at a dangerous time in England for those who adhered to the old faith.*

Donne was born in 1572, fourteen years after the Protestant Queen Elizabeth I ascended the throne and sixteen years before the defeat of the Spanish Armada. The Donnes were a family of Roman Catholics known as recusants—those who considered the pope in Rome, not the English monarch, the head of the only true church. Donne's childhood and adolescence took place during a period of intense religious controversy and suspicion, as Elizabeth struggled to consolidate the gains of the Protestant reformed church while many who remained loyal to the old faith still longed for a reconciliation with Rome that would replace Elizabeth (presumably by killing her) with her Catholic cousin, Mary, Queen of Scots. Elizabeth herself was a Protestant moderate, more interested that her subjects behave in a fashion loyal to the Crown (and not openly contemptuous of the English church) than she was in the fine points of doctrine. She once described the dispute of theologians, over which so much blood had already been shed, as "ropes of sand or sea-slime leading to the moon."[1] As one scholar sums up the situation, "From Donne's earliest childhood, the fight over God was everywhere."[2] It was everywhere within England, everywhere in Europe, and everywhere between the Protestant and Catholic European powers. Donne himself would play a bit part in the military struggle over religion, when he joined an English expedition in 1596 to capture the Spanish Catholic city of Cádiz.

Today, lovers of Donne's poetry are unlikely to give much thought to him as a religious convert or warrior (albeit a halfhearted one), mainly because the secular love poems of the wild, seductive young

---

* The question of whether Shakespeare was a Protestant or a Catholic—or any sort of conventional religious believer—like so much of Shakespeare's sparsely documented personal history, has never been settled definitively, nor should it be. Shakespeare's writings do not, of course, provide the undeniable evidence of Protestant convictions that Donne's status as an ordained priest of the Church of England, as well as his polemics against Roman Catholicism, did. However, the idea that Shakespeare was some sort of "secret Catholic" in Elizabethan England is considered unlikely or downright preposterous by most historians and literary scholars. The claim that Shakespeare was a Catholic—or, for that matter, an ardent nationalistic supporter of the Church of England—may originate in the same wishful thinking that has made some American Christians claim Abraham Lincoln as a devout believer in Jesus. In fact, Lincoln never joined a church, never mentioned Jesus in his public speeches, and wrote in private correspondence that he did not believe Jesus was divine. When you are as great as Lincoln and Shakespeare, everyone wants to own a piece of your soul.

Jack Donne are much better known—and much more suited to modern sensibilities—than the religious explorations of his later poems. However, all of Donne's most famous sensual poems deal, on some level, with the relationship between body and soul. "The Ecstasy," which Donne probably wrote for his wife, Anne, whom he married secretly in 1601 against her father's wishes, is a passionate man's poem of both spiritual love and carnality.* It is also a statement of the mind-body problem that has more in common with Spinoza, whose *Ethics* lay three-quarters of a century in the future, than with Augustine, to whom Donne has often been compared. "Divine Meditations," by contrast, was written by an older, more intensely and overtly religious man, who, after converting to the Protestant, state-established Church of England, became a priest and one of the most admired clerical orators of his time.† Here he does sound like Augustine, who was certain that only divine grace could suppress shameful bodily urges. The body is no longer the book upon which the soul's love is written, but an object that can be purified only through the overwhelming force of God—"except you ravish me." Or, as Augustine put it, "Our hearts are restless till they rest in Thee." The contrast, and conflict, between Donne the poetic student of the body and the priestly Donne lasted a lifetime, because the older poet-priest wrote as precise an anatomy of the sick and dying corpus as the young man had of the sensual body at the height of health and desire.

•

Donne's father was a successful, rich ironmonger who, although he died when John was only four years old, left enough money to provide the best possible education for his children (at least, for his two boys).

---

* See John Stubbs, *John Donne, The Reformed Soul,* p. xxi. The date of this poem, like many of Donne's verses, cannot be established with certainty. Few of his poems were published in his lifetime. "The Ecstasy" may well have been written for Donne's wife, but many of his sentiments in the poem are not far removed from earlier verse associated with the rake and seducer Donne was said to have been before his marriage at age twenty-nine. The reader should also bear in mind the cautionary preface to John Donne's complete poems by its editor, A. J. Smith, who observes, "We rarely know when he wrote this poem or that." This was true even in 1635, when the first collection of Donne's poetry was published four years after his death.

† Then as now, one important difference between the Anglican and the Roman Catholic churches—at least for clerics—is that Anglican priests may marry.

In an England ruled by a queen who had declared that she had no desire to "make windows into men's souls," an English family could remain true to its Catholic roots—although its male members could not aspire to any significant state office—as long as its religious practices were private and did not involve an attempt to convert others or plot against the monarch. Donne's father seems to have been that sort of circumspect Catholic.

The maternal side of Donne's family, however, belonged to the unreconciled branch of Roman Catholicism. Elizabeth Heywood Donne, John's mother, was a great-niece of Thomas More, the Catholic chancellor of England executed by Henry VIII in 1535 for refusing to recognize the king as head of the church. More, canonized in 1935, was already considered a martyr by English Catholics at the time of Donne's birth. Donne's maternal grandfather, John Heywood, a singer and comedian at Henry's court, was actually convicted of treason and condemned to die in 1542 after becoming involved in a plot against the powerful archbishop of Canterbury, Thomas Cranmer (who had first obliged his king by declaring his marriage to Anne Boleyn ecclesiastically valid and then, three years later, by declaring it invalid so that Anne could be executed and Henry could marry his new favorite, Jane Seymour). Heywood, whose performances had apparently pleased Henry in happier days, was pardoned by the king at the last minute, after he had already been brought from the Tower of London to the execution ground at Tyburn.

Nor had the Heywood family's involvement in what was defined as treason come to an end by the time of Donne's birth. Donne's uncle Jasper Heywood had fled the country and become a Jesuit in Rome. In 1581, when his nephew was nine, Jasper returned to England after meeting Father Edmund Campion, who had already secretly entered the country in order to encourage the recusants. By then, Jesuits were banned from England altogether. Jasper was arrested in 1583, along with five other priests, and, like his father, convicted of treason and sentenced to death. But—again like his father—he was allowed to live, and his sentence was commuted, certainly by order of the queen herself, to exile. He died in Naples—not a terrible fate for one who might have perished as his friend Campion did in 1581, by being drawn, quartered, and having his sexual organs cut off at Tyburn. Campion was arrested, tried, and convicted of treason after several hundred copies of his pamphlet, *Ten Reasons* (against the Church of England), were found on benches at the 1581 commencement ceremony of Saint Mary's College, Oxford. These were the years when Elizabeth was receiving many reports (some true) of plots against her life, with the ultimate aim of placing Mary on the throne. The issue was not settled definitively until an indecisive Elizabeth finally signed the order for Mary's execution in 1587, just a year before the Spanish Armada sailed against England and united most of its citizens behind their Protestant queen. The wreck of the Armada, greatly aided by a fierce storm at sea, was regarded by the English as a sign of God's providence and approval, not only of their nation but of their reformed religion. This defining event in the history of England would surely have made a powerful impression on the sixteen-year-old Donne.

Given the religious affiliations of Donne's mother, it is all but certain that he was privately baptized and instructed in the teachings of the old faith. Many of those basic doctrines did not differ greatly from the theology of the Church of England, which—like Roman Catholicism—accepted the stain of original sin and that perennial religious conversation stopper the Holy Trinity. What the Church of England did not recognize was the supremacy, religious or secular, of the pope in Rome. There were other differences as well—the ascendancy of the vernacular over Latin in English church rituals; a lessened emphasis on saints and the role of the Virgin Mary; and, most of all, an affinity for, if not total agreement with, Calvin's acceptance of the Augustinian view of divine grace, not free will to do good works, as the key element in salvation. Article 9 of the Church of England's Thirty-nine Articles of Religion, ratified at a convocation in 1564, even takes a swipe at the forgotten Pelagius (whose works were as unknown to the average sixteenth-century Englishman as they are to the average churchgoer in the United States and Europe today). "Original Sin standeth not in the following of Adam, (as the Pelagians do vainly talk), but it is the fault and corruption of the Nature of every man, that naturally is ingendered in the offspring of Adam; whereby man is very far gone from original righteousness, and is of his own nature inclined to evil, so that the flesh lusteth always contrary to the spirit. . . ."[3]

However, the Church of England was always a halfway house between Roman Catholicism and Puritanism and would remain closer, in many respects, to both of those branches of Christianity than to the more liberal, individualistic Protestant sects, such as the Quakers, that began to proliferate in the seventeenth century. The views on predestination laid out in the crucial Article 17 of the Articles of Religion never approached the absolute belief in divinely determined damnation or salvation from birth that led to (or at least provided one doctrinal rather than political excuse for) the religious wars between Puritans and the adherents to the established English church in the seventeenth century. The article declares that "godly consideration of Predestination, and our Election in Christ, is full of sweet, pleasant, and unspeakable comfort to godly persons, and such as feel in themselves the working of the Spirit of Christ, mortifying the works of the flesh, . . . and drawing up their mind to high and heavenly things . . . because it doth fervently kindle their love towards God." Yet it would be wrong, according to the article, for "curious and carnal persons" to behave in an ungodly fashion because they "have continually before their eyes the sentence of God's Predestination." In other words, faithful communicants of the English church are bound, exactly as a Roman Catholic is, to act as if good works matter and to behave well in this life if they desire eternal life. There is not a word in this compromise theology, despite the church's affirmation of the doctrine of original sin, to make any Protestant English parent worry that his or her baby, sleeping peacefully in the crib, might already be damned for all eternity. Many of the articles, based on earlier drafts by Cranmer and approved by the Queen, were deliberately designed to provide a middle path for those within the realm who held differing interpretations of church doctrine. But even as new Protestant sects emerged and diverged widely on doctrinal matters, "batter my heart, three-personed God" would remain a sentiment that the Church of England and the Church of Rome could share, whether one emphasized "batter" or "three-personed."

•

The date of Donne's conversion is unknown, since it was certainly a process rather than a Pauline bolt from the sky or the sort of specific occasion described by Augustine in *Confessions*. In any case, there would have been no special ceremony. Conversion from Roman Catholicism to the Church of England (the Anglican Communion today)—or vice versa—does not require "rebaptism."* There are good biographical reasons to conclude that Donne, in spite of his Catholic background, was more inclined toward Protestantism as a young man than the rest of his family. In 1593, Donne's brother, Henry, with whom he had studied at Cambridge, died in Newgate Prison, where he was being held on charges of harboring a Jesuit. The following year, Donne accepted his share of Henry's inheritance.

In 1596, Donne signed on for the English expedition to Cádiz under the command of Sir Walter Raleigh and Robert Devereux, the Earl of Essex and a favorite of Queen Elizabeth (though he would eventually lose his head). It should be noted that Donne paid his own way as a sort of gentleman adventurer—not quite a professional soldier—attached to an enterprise that would, if successful, reward him with stories to tell his children and connections with the right people. Many such expeditions failed (as one of Donne's later ventures would), but the attack on Cádiz did not. The Catholic city was captured and looted by the English in late June, and the expedition returned home in August. It is highly unlikely that a young man with strong Catholic sympathies, in spite of old family ties and friendships, would have joined this expedition to sack a city in a Catholic nation that, only eight years earlier, had launched a major attack on England. In 1597, his bellicose seafaring adventures concluded, Donne became secretary to Thomas Egerton, the Lord Keeper of England.† This position, though advancing his connections, did not provide him with the financial means to launch an adult life of substance. As the poet and lover approached age thirty, he needed an income sufficient to fund a marriage.

In 1601, Donne secretly married sixteen-year-old Anne More, the daughter of a well-off Protestant landowner whose economic and social standing was higher than that of the Donnes. The ceremony was performed, with only a few close friends in attendance, by a priest of the Church of England, because Anne's father, Sir George More,

* Anglican converts to Roman Catholicism must, however, be reconfirmed, and if priests, they must be reordained. But former Anglican priests who convert to Roman Catholicism are allowed to remain married if they already have a wife. Marriage is, of course, forbidden to priests originally ordained in the Roman Catholic Church.
† The Lord Keeper had physical custody of the Great Seal of England. The actual importance of the office varied greatly, depending on the relationship between the particular monarch and the particular Lord Keeper.

strongly opposed the match. For decades—even after Anne had died in 1617 after giving birth to a stillborn baby (she was pregnant at least twelve times in sixteen years of wedlock), their marriage was summed up by the pun, "John Donne, Anne Donne, Undone."*

What was so terrible about this marriage that Sir George (who later was appointed lord lieutenant of the Tower of London) refused to recognize the union, arranged to have Donne fired from his job as secretary to the Lord Keeper, and even helped engineer the brief arrest of his son-in-law? Money. Or, rather, Donne's lack of a reliable income. Moreover, Sir George had lost a marital pawn—which all daughters were at the time—who might have increased his own influence and fortune. Then, too, John and Anne had violated church law. Marriages were supposed to take place only after publication of banns in church—and there were no banns, because Anne's father would never have allowed the wedding to take place. Also, marriages were not supposed to be solemnized during Lent and Advent, and the couple was married in December—which always falls within Advent, because Christmas, unlike Easter, is not a movable feast. Needless to say, these church rules were far from inflexible in view of the undeniable fact that many couples committed the sin of having sex before marriage, and it was better to have a wedding in Advent or Lent than to have a visibly pregnant bride or a baby born too soon to stop tongues from wagging. But Anne More either was not pregnant at the time of her marriage or suffered a miscarriage soon afterward; the couple's first child was born in 1603. Had she turned up visibly pregnant within a few months of the marriage, her father might have been forced to take a less harsh line toward his son-in-law.

There has always been controversy, among Donne's contemporaries as well as scholars for the past four hundred years, about whether the poet married Anne for love or for the status and money he could hope to obtain through an alliance with the More family. The flowering of enduring love poems like "The Ecstasy," generally dated from the beginning of John's relationship with Anne, would argue for love. The clandestine nature of the wedding also provides strong evidence that John knew exactly how angry his new father-in-law would be when

* One tale was that Donne himself had scribbled the line on the door of his lodgings on their wedding day.

he learned about the marriage. He may have hoped that Sir George's attitude would soften sooner than it did; five years would pass before Anne's father granted her a marriage settlement of eighty pounds a year—only a portion of what would have been her dowry had she married a man considered suitable by her family. The money enabled the couple to establish a home of their own for the first time; until then, they had moved from place to place, depending on the kindness of friends for shelter.

Another piece of evidence supporting the case that Donne's was a love match was his failure to marry again after Anne's death. He was only forty-five: most men whose wives died in childbirth did remarry, if only to provide a mother for the young children left behind. By then, however, Donne did not have to find a new wife, as most widowers (nobles and commoners alike) did to manage their domestic affairs. In 1615, he had been ordained as a priest and deacon at Saint Paul's and appointed a royal chaplain. By the command of King James I, he received an honorary doctor of divinity degree from Cambridge. At the time of Anne's death, the family was living in a well-appointed rectory supplied by the church; a prominent preacher who was a royal favorite did not have to worry about who would take care of his children if he chose not to marry again. It is certainly possible that, even if Donne was still deeply in love with his wife at the time of her death, he decided that he would be able to pursue his own endeavors, both as a writer and an increasingly prominent preacher, without the distraction and demands of a wife (not to mention the possibility that the birth of more children in a new union would inevitably increase those demands).

Anne Donne, dead at age thirty-two and undoubtedly exhausted by repeated childbearing, is simply one of many—most—women tragically lost to history. But she must have been a woman of great spirit and courage to marry a man whose inappropriateness, in the eyes of her father, was certain to deprive her of the social standing and financial comfort to which her family background would ordinarily have entitled her. John Donne wrote no elegy for his wife, and none of her letters to him survive. We may infer, from Donne's poems to her, that she was unusually educated for a woman of her time, perhaps by sharing in the knowledge that would have been extended to her brothers through private tutors. There is no question that John and

Anne's relationship was intellectual as well as sexual, and that she was acquainted with the scholarship and philosophy of her time in ways that few women were. Donne's poem "A Valediction: of the Book" clearly conveys his regard for Anne's learning and intellect.

> *Study our manuscripts, those myriads*
> *Of letters, which have past 'twixt thee and me,*
> *Thence write our annals, and in them will be*
> *To all whom love's subliming fire invades,*
> *Rule and example found;*
> *There, the faith of any ground*
>
> *No schismatic will dare to wound,*
> *That sees, how Love this grace to us affords,*
> *To make, to keep, to use, to be these his records.*
>
> *This book, as long lived as the elements,*
> *Or as the world's form, this all-graved tome*
> *In cypher write, or new made idiom;*
> *We for Love's clergy only are instruments,*
> *When this book is made thus,*
> *Should again the ravenous*
> *Vandals and Goths inundate us,*
> *Learning were safe; in this our universe*
> *Schools might learn sciences, spheres music, angels verse.*

•

Although we do not know the timing of Donne's spiritual conversion to the Church of England, his Protestant loyalties had been publicly displayed long before his ordination to the priesthood. In the first decade of the seventeenth century, he became a protégé of Sir Thomas Morton, chaplain to the earl of Rutland and a favorite of James I, who had succeeded to the throne of both England and Scotland (the latter as James VI) after Queen Elizabeth's death in 1603. (The son of the executed Mary, Queen of Scots, James had been raised a Protestant. His rule was characterized by consistent support for the more moderate doctrines of the Church of England over the more radical Puritanism spearheaded by the dour John Knox in his native Scotland.)

Morton was a leading anti–Roman Catholic polemicist, and he frequently consulted Donne while drafting his manuscripts. Although James was a "moderate" in theological terms, the political split between the Church of England and the "papist" recusants had grown deeper and more bitter since Elizabeth's death. Shortly after he ascended the throne, James had made an overture to the Vatican that seemed to offer the possibility of liberalization regarding Catholics. Fidelity to Protestantism, James wrote, should "beget no such severity toward those who are otherwise persuaded, but that they may enjoy under us the same fruits of justice, comfort, and safety, which others of our people do, till we shall find that disloyalty is covered with the mask of conscience."[4] The key phrase in this sentence, however, turned out to be "till we shall find that disloyalty is covered with the mask of conscience." James's attitudes would harden in 1605 as a result of the infamous Gunpowder Plot, which would have blown up Parliament and killed the king, his sons, and many nobles. The conspirators included Guy Fawkes, a Protestant convert to Roman Catholicism, who, along with other conspirators, rented a cellar underneath the Parliament building and stowed away at least twenty barrels of gunpowder—more than enough to blow up the entire establishment, had the plot not been discovered.* Fawkes was convicted of treason and hanged, drawn, and quartered, according to the traditional Christian concept—adhered to by both the Vatican and the Church of England—of the mercy deserved by traitors. After the Gunpowder Plot, King James adopted harsher policies toward recusants than Elizabeth had; pardoning convicted traitors on their way to Tyburn was not his style. Parliament passed a new Oath of Allegiance requiring Catholics to acknowledge

* The anniversary of the Gunpowder Plot, November 5, is still celebrated as Guy Fawkes Day or Bonfire Night throughout the United Kingdom. The celebrations include bonfires and fireworks, and no one seems to care about the irony of commemorating with incendiary displays a plot to blow up Parliament. Guards, however, still perform a ritual search of the Houses of Parliament to make sure that no twenty-first-century arsonist is lurking—just another English tradition in the spirit of having a town crier, in the digital age, announce the birth of an heir to the throne. In 2007, the libertarian conservative Representative Ron Paul, who was then running for the presidency, set up a Web site honoring Guy Fawkes and raised more than four million dollars for his campaign on the anniversary day alone. Why Paul would consider Fawkes a hero is something of a mystery, since Catholics of that era wished only to substitute one theocratic state for another—a goal inconsistent with Paul's professed libertarianism. Perhaps Paul's attraction to Fawkes has something to do with the American right-wing libertarian position that everyone should have access to guns and ammunition without government regulation.

that the monarch could not be removed by any papal decree and to "abhor, detest, abjure, as impious and heretical, this damnable doctrine and position, that princes which be excommunicated or deprived by the Pope, may be deposed or murdered by their subjects." The heart of the matter was that Catholics had to swear not to try to assassinate the English monarch. In the bitter controversy that ensued in the years after the oath became law, Donne sided publicly with the Crown and the English church.

The affair led, in 1610, to the publication of his first book, *Pseudo-Martyr*, dedicated to King James. Donne made it clear that, in spite of, or perhaps because of, a family history that included recusants convicted of treason, he held radical Catholics—not the English monarchs or English church—responsible for the misguided choices of his relatives.

The title itself reflected the bitter contemporary dispute between English Catholics and Protestants over whose martyrs were the real martyrs. Executed Jesuits like Father Campion, the friend of Donne's uncle Jasper Heywood, and political figures like Thomas More were traitors—pseudo-martyrs—to English Protestants, and saintly heroes to Catholics. Archbishop Cranmer, executed by Mary Tudor, was a martyr to Protestants. To the modern reader, *Pseudo-Martyr* is a tedious, politically tendentious work; it might be used to make a case that Donne the convert has deservedly been forgotten. The tract should be read not as a spiritual meditation but as the statement of an ambitious man coming out, irreversibly and unmistakably, on the winning side of an ongoing religious and political war. This means not that Donne's religious convictions were insincere but that they were certainly expedient in that they fell on the side of the victors—the *English* side. "The king therefore defends the liberties of the Church," he wrote, "as the nature of his office, which he has acknowledged, and declared, and sealed to his subjects by an Oath, binds him to do, if he defend the Church of England from foreign usurpation."* It could not have been more evident that Donne's religious and secular allegiances were fused. He noted that "the title by which the Prince has to us by

---

* I have taken the liberty of altering seventeenth-century spelling and punctuation in some quotations from *Pseudo-Martyr*, which, unlike most of Donne's essays, sermons, and poetry, is extraordinarily difficult for a general reader to follow today.

Generation, and which the Church has by *Regeneration,* is all but one now. For we are not only subjects to a Prince, but Christian subjects to a Christian Prince, and members as well of the Church as of the Commonwealth in which the Church is."[5]

In a preface pointedly addressed to "the Priests, and Jesuits, and to their Disciples in this Kingdom," Donne speaks candidly about the time and personal sorrow it has taken for him to overcome the loyalties instilled by his Catholic upbringing.

> They who have descended so low, as to take knowledge of me, and to admit me into their consideration, know well that I used no inordinate haste, nor precipitation in binding my conscience to any local religion. I had a longer work to do than many other men; for I was first to blot out, certain impressions of the Roman religion, and to wrestle both against the examples and against the reasons, by which some hold was taken; and some anticipations early laid upon my conscience, both by persons who by nature had a power and superiority over my will, and others who by their learning and good life, seemed to me justly to claim an interest for the guiding and rectifying of my understanding in these matters. And although I apprehended well enough, that this irresolution not only retarded my fortune, but also bred some scandal, and endangered my spiritual reputation, by laying me open to many misinterpretations; yet all these respects did not transport me to any violent and sudden determination, till I had, to the measure of my poor wit and judgement, surveyed and digested the whole body of Divinity, controverted between ours and the Roman church. In which search and disquisition, that God, which awakened me then, and has never forsaken me in that industry, as he is the Author of that purpose, so is he a witness of this protestation; that I behave myself, and proceeded therein with humility, and diffidence in myself; and by that, which by his grace, I took to be ordinary means, which is frequent prayer, and equal and indifferent affections.[6]

Nearly every reference to theology in *Pseudo-Martyr* is related, in some way, to the conflict between the secular authority of the English Crown and the claim of a foreign pope to authority not only in matters of faith and morals but over the ways in which monarchs might interpret and choose to resolve secular controversies in their own lands. The Roman Catholic religion, Donne concluded, had undermined secular laws and lawmakers—first, by giving priority to ecclesiastical privilege; second, by teaching that martyrdom was the way to expand the influence of the church ("that the treasure of the Church, is by this expense of our blood increased"); and, third, by the doctrine of purgatory, which supposedly allows people to escape just punishment for their actions on earth.[7] The English church's article of religion on purgatory, unlike many other articles of faith, could not have been more straightforward: "The Romish Doctrine concerning Purgatory, Pardons, Worshipping, and Adoration as well of images as of Reliques, and also invocation of Saints, is a fond thing vainly invented, and grounded upon no warranty of Scripture, but rather repugnant to the Word of God." Without purgatory, there could be no reason for the buying and selling of indulgences that played such a critical role in Luther's rebellion: once you were in hell, no prayers offered up for you on earth, whatever their price, could help you.

It is somewhat paradoxical that Donne mentions his reluctance to bind himself to a "local religion" in *Pseudo-Martyr,* because his later writings are filled with a love of England—a sense of "chosenness" that resembles the writings of the Puritans who founded the Massachusetts Bay Colony. Although Donne was well aware of the many manifestations of the Reformation in continental Europe, and shared many of the views of German and French Protestants, it is likely that the particular, more moderate national character of the English Reformation decided him, once and for all, against Rome. "God shin'd upon this Island early," he observed in a sermon delivered in 1622, "early in the plantation of the Gospel, (for we had not our seed-Corn from Rome, howsoever we may have had some waterings from thence) and early in the Reformation of the Church: for we had not the model of any other Forreign Church for our pattern; we stript not the Church into a nakedness, nor into rags; we divested her not of her possessions, nor of her Ceremonies, but received such a Reformation at home, by their hands whom God enlightened, as left her neither in a Dropsie nor in Consumption. . . . Early in the Plantation, early in the Reformation, *Illuxit Nobis,* and we have light enough, without either seeing other light from *Rome, or more of this light from other places.* . . . We shall not need any such re-Reformation, or super-Reformation, as swirling brains will need cross the Seas for. *The Word of God is not above thee, says Moses, nor beyond the Sea.*"[8]

For Donne, England is what the Massachusetts Bay Colony, "a city on a hill," would be for John Winthrop. The Church of England, not the Church of Rome—and not, for all Donne's affinities with other forms of Protestantism, the churches of Calvin or Luther—is its moral center. It is worth noting that Winthrop was only fifteen years younger than Donne and that their views about history and theology, although they reached different conclusions, were shaped by many of the same events. Donne's thinking about matters of religious doctrine, apart from the elephant of papal authority, did not differ radically from that of moderate Roman Catholics in England. Yet the Augustinian importance he assigned to the role of divine grace in individual human destiny did have much in common with the Puritans who, feeling stifled by the political demands of the Church of England and displeased by a theology that seemed too "Romish," set out for the New World. "O, my America, my Newfoundland." Some recent revisionist scholarship has attempted to turn Donne into a believer in predestination akin to Augustine (the elderly Augustine, that is) and contemporary Puritans. But Donne's later "Holy Sonnets," as well as the sermons he delivered from the pulpit of Saint Paul's, indicated that he could never resolve the issue of predestination to his own satisfaction as a theologian or as a human being. Even as a committed Protestant priest, he could not bring himself to conclude that there was no salvation for those outside his church. In one sonnet, he expresses the conviction that his father, whom he barely remembers and who died a Catholic, must, or at least might, be in paradise: "If faithful souls be alike glorified / As angels, then my father's soul doth see. . . ."[9] The Articles of Religion provided plenty of wiggle room for those similarly reluctant to consign recalcitrant or religiously suspect relatives and friends to the fires of hell. That cruel brand of predestination was left for those who, in Donne's words, sought light from other places.

Would Donne ever have become a Protestant had the Reformation not unfolded as it did in his native land, any more than Paul of Burgos would have become a Catholic had the persecution of Jews not intensified in Spain at the end of the fourteenth century? I will go out on a strong limb and say no and no. Although Paul of Burgos was not, as far as we know, a great writer in any language, he and Donne had one important characteristic in common—ambition. Donne wanted to be not only a man of letters but a man of influence, and he tried unsuccessfully to obtain positions at court during the many years when he resisted his patron Morton's urging that he take Holy Orders and enter the service of the church. Only in his early forties, with no other sure route to a secure financial future and public position, did Donne finally accept ordination.

And yet, when one reflects on Donne's lifelong preoccupation with the relationship between the flesh and the spirit, even when he is at his most carnal in his youthful poems, it is apparent that the Protestantism of the established English church offered a broader template for his philosophy than Roman Catholicism did. Throughout his life, Donne referred to his own faith as "Catholic"—meaning universal, in the sense that would now be spelled with a small "c." As an adult, he came to regard the *Roman* Catholic Church as exclusionary, attempting to circumscribe and control not only the actions but the thoughts of men, and the English church as the more expansive, inclusionary faith. The greatest of Donne's small-"c" catholic writings are the meditations he produced when, in November 1623, he was stricken and nearly died in an epidemic of what was called "spotted," or relapsing, fever—probably typhus. No one survived this fever unless he or she broke out into a rash, which doctors attempted to induce by, among other brilliant methods, the application of dead pigeons to the patient's feet to draw the "evil humours" of the fever away from the head. In Donne's case, the rash did appear, but it was known that the fever might return and that patients who succumbed to a second bout nearly always died. The only remedy, it was thought, was to administer laxatives and induce a long cycle of vomiting and diarrhea. Patients who survived the "purge" generally did live—undoubtedly because their ability to endure this treatment indicated that they had been unusually hardy physical specimens when they caught the fever in the first place. Between November, when he was first diagnosed, and January, by which time it seemed likely that he would remain among the living, Donne had written his *Devotions upon Emergent Occasions,* a great humanistic work that extends—in spite of itself—beyond the boundaries of purely Christian humanism.

In Meditation IV, wryly titled "The physician is sent for," Donne combines philosophy with sharp, direct observation of the limits of whatever "treatment" he is receiving.

Man consists of more pieces, more parts, than the world; than the world doth, nay, than the world is. And if those pieces were extended, and stretched out in man as they are in the world, man would be the giant, and the world the dwarf, the world but the map, and the man the world. If all the veins in our bodies were extended to rivers, and all the sinews to veins of mines, and all the muscles that lie upon one another, to hills, and all the bones to quarries of stones, and all the other pieces to the proportion of those which correspond to them in the world, the air would be too little for this orb of man to move in, the firmament would be but enough for this star; for, as the whole world hath nothing, to which something in man doth not answer, so hath man many pieces of which the whole world hath no representation. Enlarge this meditation upon this great world, man, so far as to consider the immensity of the creatures this world produces; our creatures are our thoughts. . . . Inexplicable mystery; I their creator am in a close prison, in a sick bed, any where, and any one of my creatures, my thoughts, is with the sun, and overgoes the sun in one pace, one step, everywhere.

As the larger physical world produces vipers and other dangerous beings, Donne observes, so does the singular world of the human body produce "venomous and infectious diseases" for which "as yet we have not names." In falling victim to diseases that cannot be named, much less cured, Donne observes, "we shrink in our proportion, sink in our dignity, in respect of very mean creatures, who are physicians to themselves." Dogs know enough to eat grass to induce vomiting, he notes, but "man hath not that innate instinct, to apply those natural medicines to his present danger, as those inferior creatures have; he is not his own apothecary, his own physician, as they are." Therefore, a sick man must send for the physician, but the physician is himself no more than a man.[10]

These meditations were written even though fever patients were supposed to be forbidden to read, much less write, as part of their treatment. The dean of Saint Paul's had enough power to get reading and writing materials past the proscriptions of the doctors, who included the king's personal physician.

The devotions also include what is surely Donne's best-known prose work, the meditation, mistakenly thought by many to be only metaphoric, that asks for whom the bell tolls. Donne was listening to real bells. In the depths of his fever, he paid close attention to London church bells to keep himself informed about weddings, funerals, and other events signaled by the chimes. The title of the meditation could hardly be more specific: "Now, this bell tolling softly for another, says to me: Thou must die." In opening, Donne clarifies what "Catholic" meant to him.

Perchance he for whom this bell tolls may be so ill, as that he knows not it tolls for him; and perchance I may think myself so much better than I am, as that they who are about me, and see my state, may have caused it to toll for me, and I know not that. The church is Catholic, universal, so are all her actions; all that she does belongs to all. When she baptizes a child, that action concerns me; for that child is thereby connected to that body which is my head too, and ingrafted into that body whereof I am a member. And when she buries a man, that action concerns me: all mankind is of one author, and is one volume; when one man dies, one chapter is not torn out of the book, but translated into a better language. . . . God's hand is in every translation, and his hand shall bind up all our scatterd leaves again for that library where every book shall lie open to one another.

Later in that meditation come the famous lines: "No man is an island, entire of itself; every man is a piece of the continent, a part of the main. If a clod be washed away by the sea, Europe is the less, as well as if a promontory were, as well as if a manor of thy friend's or of thine own were: any man's death diminishes me, because I am involved in mankind, and therefore never send to know for whom the bell tolls: it tolls for thee."[11]

Donne delivered his final sermon, "Death's Duel," from the pulpit of Saint Paul's on February 25, 1631, less than a month before his own death. Izaak Walton, Donne's friend and first biographer, recalled that the congregants were terrified by Donne's skeletal appearance. Walton wrote, in 1840, "When to the amazement of some beholders he appeared in the pulpit, many of them thought he presented himself not to preach mortification by a living voice: but, mortality by a decayed body and dying face." For the congregation of Saint Paul's it was as if "Dr Donne had *preached his own Funeral Sermon.*"[12]

Donne's final sermon is a grim treatise, primarily focused, as befitted the Lenten season, on the meaning of Christ's voluntary death to redeem man from sin. There is little of the optimism that portrayed the afterlife as a great library in which "every book shall lie open to one another." And Donne reflects on life from the perspective of a dying man who seems capable of remembering the pleasures of his youth only as sins. "Our youth is hungry and thirsty after those sins which our infancy knew not," he told the congregation, "and our age is sorry and angry, that it cannot pursue those sins which our youth did. . . ."[13]

In spite of its bleakness, there is a raw honesty in this image of old age; the thought is no less unsettling if one substitutes the word "pleasures" for "sins." Donne, after all, was equally insistent on the intermingling of body and soul when pleasure, not sin, dominated his writing. We remember "License my roving hands, and let them go / Before, behind, between, above, below," but often forget the lines that follow in short order in the elegy "To His Mistress Going to Bed."

> Then where my hand is set, my seal shall be.
> Full nakedness! All joys are due to thee;
> As souls unbodied, bodies unclothed must be
> To taste whole joys.

Would Donne have viewed the stages of life—his own or anyone else's—in a significantly different way had the Reformation and his ambitions not pulled him away from the faith of his fathers? Did conversion, in his case with a whiff of Calvinist damnation of the sensual, cast Donne's earlier joyful analogies between body and soul into darkness, or was his last sermon simply a product of his last illness? These are unanswerable questions about a convert for whom the secular and spiritual dimensions of his changing faith were inseparable.

8

"NOT WITH SWORD . . .
BUT WITH PRINTING"

J OHN FOXE, in his popular sixteenth-century English *Book of Martyrs,*
summarized his support for Protestantism by calling the printing
press an instrument of divine providence. "God works for his church,"
he wrote, "not with sword and target . . . but with printing, writing,
and reading. . . . Hereby tongues be known, knowledge groweth, judgment increaseth, books are dispersed, the Scriptures are seen . . . stories
be opened, times compared, truth discerned, falsehood detected. . . ."*
Either the pope must abolish knowledge and printing, Foxe asserted,
or "printing must at length root him out."[1]

Twenty-first-century Americans have repeatedly expressed astonishment at the rapid change in public attitudes toward gays and same-sex
marriage during the past two decades. We know that twenty years,
even in an era of instantaneous communication, remains an extraordinarily short period for large numbers of people to change their minds
about any sensitive, fundamental social value. And yet that is exactly
what happened in roughly three decades on the continent of Europe
five hundred years ago, on a subject far more basic than any single

* The formal title of this book, first published in English in 1563, is *Acts and Monuments,*
which emphasizes sixteenth-century Protestant martyrs. Even then, however, the work
was popularly referred to as the *Book of Martyrs.*

social issue such as modern gay rights. Between, roughly, 1517 and 1550, huge numbers of Europeans changed their minds about what constituted the foundation of their lives—encompassing their view of the universe, of relations between God and man, and of the proper way for individual human beings to seek truth.

For a millennium, the Roman Catholic Church had been the lodestar, the sole route to salvation for Western Christians—even though the relationship between religious and secular authority varied from country to country and region to region. That the majority of illiterate Europeans—95 percent of the population, by most estimates, at the beginning of the sixteenth century—did not concern themselves with abstract theological matters such as the Trinity or transubstantiation made the church more, not less, powerful in its role as keeper of the gate to the afterlife. Dissident movements, like the Cathars in the early thirteenth century, were ruthlessly extirpated by the combined power of Christian soldiers and the newly established Inquisition. Three hundred years later, the printing press made it impossible for the church to do the same thing to a new generation of dissidents and reformers.

In any analysis of the secular factors affecting religious conversions on a large scale, it is always tempting, and often correct, to place primary emphasis on shifts in political power, the acts of churches themselves, and the relationship between the two. In the early Christian era, the triumph of the Gospel of Jesus cannot be seen apart from the decay of the Roman Empire and the pro–Roman Catholic position taken by certain politically effective (notwithstanding the continuing deterioration of the empire itself when viewed in retrospect) emperors in the West. The conversions of vast numbers of Jews and Muslims in Iberia would not have happened had they not been forced by cycles of violence during the Reconquista, the stark choice of conversion or expulsion later presented to the Jews by Ferdinand and Isabella, and the support of the church throughout the Inquisition. The Protestant Reformation—if one views it in a broad sense as the emergence of multiple forms of Christianity, each with its own political turf—could not have been accomplished without bloodshed and outright civil war in much of Northern Europe and England. Yet there can be no doubt that the printing press was the single most important secular factor in the development of the Reformation in Europe and in the eventual arrival of Protestantism on the shores of North America. In each country, the Reformation had a distinct national character, depending in significant measure on the religious sentiments and political power of secular rulers. The one common factor was movable type and its power to spread religious dissent as well as new ideas of all kinds. It is hardly a coincidence that there was never anything resembling a large-scale religious reformation in tsarist Russia, and that the only printing press in Russia from 1565 until the last quarter of the seventeenth century was owned and operated by the Russian Orthodox Church. Ivan the Terrible (Elizabeth I's contemporary, let us not forget) had permitted foreigners to bring one printing press to Moscow, and the first book published in Russia, *The Acts of the Apostles,* appeared in 1564. Only a year later, though, Ivan pacified Slavophiles who hated all foreign inventions by allowing them to burn the press. After that, until the reign of the westernizing Peter the Great began in 1682, the church controlled the only press. In the spread of the printed word beyond an elite, Russia was two full centuries behind Western Europe.

"We must root out printing, or printing will root us out," the Vicar of Croydon supposedly said in a sermon preached at Saint Paul's Cross during the reign of Henry VIII—presumably before Henry broke with Rome in order to marry Anne Boleyn. The vicar was right, but by the time he voiced these sentiments, it was already too late to stop the revolution initiated by the publication in 1455 of the first vernacular Bible produced by Johannes Gutenberg's printing press. Ironically, at a time in the 1520s when Martin Luther's first German translations of the New Testament were being widely read in his homeland, the English scholar William Tyndale (c. 1494–1536) had to flee to Germany and to Luther's town of Wittenberg to finish his English translation of the Bible—copies of which were then smuggled back into Henry's realm. When a priest attacked Tyndale for his desire to make the Scriptures available to ordinary, ill-educated people without the approval of the church, the translator replied, "If God spare my life, ere many years, I will cause a boy that driveth the plow in England to know more about the Scriptures than thou dost."* This quotation echoes Tyndale's onetime teacher, the Catholic humanist Erasmus, who wrote in the preface to his 1516 Greek-Latin New Testament, "I would to God, the

---

* Accounts of the details of this incident vary, but the quotation was widely circulated in sixteenth-century England and appears in John Foxe's *Book of Martyrs* (1563).

plowman would sing a text of the scripture at his plowbeam, and that the weaver at his loom, with this would drive away the tediousness of time. I would the wayfaring man with this pastime, would express the weariness of his journey." Erasmus's works were all placed on the Index of Forbidden Books, an arm of the Inquisition in Rome, by Pope Paul IV in 1559. Unlike Tyndale, who was pursued by agents of Henry VIII and tried, convicted of heresy, strangled, and burned to death in 1536 in Belgium by a special commission of the Holy Roman Empire, Erasmus died a natural death in that same year.

The spread of vernacular Bibles, which took place much earlier on the continent than in England, did allow every literate person direct access to the Scriptures without the mediation of priests—the result long feared by Catholic satraps as well as the pope. Luther's first translation of the New Testament was published in 1522, and though he was not the first to translate the Bible into German since the invention of the printing press, his was the best and most influential version. His sermons, as well as his Bible translation, were published and made him a best-selling author in the 1520s and the most widely read writer in Germany throughout the early Reformation.[2]

The King James Bible, which adopted much of Tyndale's once-forbidden language, was not published until 1611, and the English-speaking world finally had a Protestant vernacular Bible that not only was a glory to the language but, unlike Tyndale's Bible, was approved by both church and state. Puritans did not use the King James Version but the English translation of Calvin's Geneva Bible, published in English in 1560. The Pilgrims brought the Geneva Bible along on the *Mayflower*. The language of the King James translation, however, ultimately won out in America. Whether one is listening to Lincoln's Second Inaugural Address, Martin Luther King's 1963 "I Have a Dream" speech, or the tribute paid to that speech fifty years later by President Barack Obama, the Bible being quoted is the King James Version, not Calvin's. (Even though the King James Version has been replaced in many churches by pedestrian translations designed to eliminate all of the supposedly archaic, beautiful, lyrical phrases presumed to be too challenging for the readers reared on text messages, the King James text has a way of creeping into important public speeches and occasions that seem to call for more elevated language. Somehow, the New Living Translation version of Psalm 23—"Even when I walk through

the darkest valley / I will not be afraid, for you are close beside me"—
doesn't quite measure up to the King James's "Yea, though I walk
through the valley of the shadow of death, I will fear no evil: for thou
art with me.")

In the sixteenth century, there proved to be no way, despite the
ardent efforts of ecclesiastical censors, to suppress the widespread questioning of dogmas and practices promulgated by the church but never
mentioned in the Bible. Purgatory—the church teaching that led to
the sale of indulgences—was only one of the concepts that readers
of the Bible in their native languages could see was never mentioned by
the authors of the New Testament. Those who could read—many of
them monks and priests—spread doubts and questions to the illiterate
in sermons preached from the pulpits of German and Swiss churches
once loyal to Rome. Moreover, there is no question that literacy itself
was encouraged by the new possibility of access to the Gospels in a language that people already spoke; many who would never have learned
to read Latin did learn to read German, English, French, or Italian—
thereby spreading heresy even in the Papal States, under the direct
political authority of the Vatican. When Luther supposedly nailed
his theses against indulgences to the door of the Chapel Church of
the University of Wittenberg on October 31, 1517, he touched a chord
in huge numbers of people—educated and uneducated, literate and
illiterate—who were ready to think for themselves about religion and
to say no to the inquisitors.* But the printing press not only made
it possible to publish Bibles; it also encouraged the dissemination of
discussions about theology by both laymen and clerics. The swift
appearance of pamphlets written by educated laymen (and even a
few women) was one of the true marvels of the Reformation, because
the Catholic Church had long permitted only clerics to write about
what were considered theological matters—and only in Latin. The
motto of Christian humanists of the Renaissance was *ad fontes* (back
to the sources)—meaning sources of classical learning from Greece
and Rome, as well as manuscripts of the Bible in Greek and Hebrew,
and not only in Latin translations approved by the church. This was,

---

* Although the story of Luther nailing the theses to the door of the university chapel in
Wittenberg, where he taught theology, may be apocryphal, it is certain that on October 31 he sent a copy of the theses to the archbishop of Mainz.

of course, an elite movement, but with the invention of the printing press, it began to have an impact, as one historian of religion puts it, that "outpaced the increase in actual literacy rates" and rendered books—and the ideas they contained—important even to people who could not themselves read or write.[3]

Miriam Usher Chrisman, in her pioneering studies of early Reformation-era pamphlets published in Germany and Switzerland, observes that as early as 1522 there were already numerous printed lay responses to the doctrinal questions raised by Luther.[4] (It is impossible to exaggerate the value of Chrisman's work, and the studies of microhistorians in many countries, in illuminating and elucidating the diverse grass-roots effects of a movement that is often portrayed only through the actions of its most famous leaders.) Many pamphlets dealt directly with the issue of conversion and with the strain created by religious dissension within families that had members in both camps. Some were actually composed in the form of a dialogue between relatives.

One pamphlet is addressed by a married woman to her sister, a cloistered nun who had been deeply disturbed to hear (family gossip apparently penetrated the convent walls) that her sister and brother-in-law had become Protestants.* The wife tells her sister that Christ taught, "I am the door through which you must go to the father." Religious orders, however, had established all sorts of other requirements— setting themselves apart from and above fellow Christians trying to please God simply by following Gospel teachings. "One [order] wears black, another grey," the married sister writes. "One does not handle money, another does not touch the plough in the field. The conventuals had set up their own rules, forgetting the unity of the spirit, the bond of peace which Christ had preached." The married woman then implores her sister to read the Bible herself, in her own language. "How

---

* Chrisman believes the internal evidence provided by the style and subject matter of the pamphlet indicates that the author was indeed a woman. The writer, as Chrisman notes, talks about her recently born baby and expresses sorrow that the nun will not use the baby's name (possibly because a Catholic nun would not consider any Protestant baptism valid and would see the infant as unentitled to a "Christian name"). Although women were much less likely to be literate than men at a time when the vast majority of the population could not read, many women from well-off, educated families—among the mercantile class as well as the aristocracy—did partake of the tutoring accorded their brothers.

much," she asks, "do you and your cloistered sisters understand of your Latin songs and chants? Probably not much more than the miller's donkey."[5] If this pamphlet originated as a real letter from one sister to another, it can hardly have been comforting to the nun! Its tart rather than conciliatory tone offers real insight into the less-than-equable effect of conversions on relations between family members on opposite sides of the growing religious divide.

Another pamphlet, also revealing the process of proselytizing within a family, takes the form of a dialogue between a Protestant son and a Catholic father. Published in 1523 under the signature of Steffan von Büllheym, the pamphlet deals with the dismissal of a number of priests by the Catholic bishop of Strasbourg for expressing what were considered Lutheran views from their pulpits. The son tells the father that he should not place any faith in the Catholic authorities, because they have shown themselves to be corrupt by selling indulgences and peddling phony relics—such as a stone said to have been thrown at Stephen, the first martyr, and a saint's bone that was really a sheep's bone. The father initially replies that he sees nothing wrong with many such time-honored religious practices, like his own habit of placing a penny on the altar every morning to save a soul from hell. The son laughs and observes that he never knew such power could be found in a mere penny. The argument focuses on the possible arrest of another priest, one Matthias Zell, who had begun to preach directly from the Gospels instead of relying on church doctrine. Here the father, who has heard Master Matthias preach and likes what was said, begins to change his mind and agrees with his son that there is no justice to be expected from clerical judicial authorities. The father's change of heart is hastened by the son's references to the church's corrupt practice of providing priests with concubines instead of allowing them to marry the women who, in many cases, had shared their lives for years. The author's tone is somewhat unusual, in that it expresses sympathy rather than contempt for the female concubines, who "willingly submitted to hatred and abuse because they loved their consorts." The fault is attributed not to the priests and not to their women but to the church itself. The father, convinced by these arguments, finally agrees with his son that he can no longer believe the Catholic clergy but will henceforth live by "the Evangelical teaching and the truth of God's word."[6] The pamphlet wraps up the father's conversion neatly and swiftly, rather in the manner of a police procedural that must solve a crime and restore justice within one television hour. It is reasonable to assume that most family battles over religion went on for years and were resolved—if they were resolved—in messier and slower fashion, with hurt feelings all around. A Protestant's making fun of her Catholic sister's knowledge of Latin, and the sister's refusing to recognize the baptism of a Protestant baby, sounds like the behavior of real families when their members rebel against a fundamental "family value."

Yet, as Chrisman observes, both of these pamphlets "show that lay men and women did not simply repeat, parrot fashion, the arguments of the theologians." Although statements about such issues as priestly celibacy, indulgences, and the direct relationship between Scripture and individual conscience had already been made by Luther, Huldrych Zwingli in Switzerland, and other, less known Protestant reformers, "in each case the lay person constructed his own argument, reflecting his particular view of the problem."[7] The pamphlets were strongly anticlerical, but it was an anticlericalism directed more at what the authors considered false doctrines than, as in the pre-Reformation era, at individual instances of corruption or lavish living by church officials. The shift from individual to institutional anticlericalism was the intellectual turning point of the Reformation; dissatisfied Catholics struggling to remain loyal to Rome could no longer say that, if only the pope knew what was going on, he would rectify the injustices perpetrated by his priest and bishops. Corrupt and oppressive systems dependent on centralized power can only exist as long as subjects do not challenge the ultimate goodness of the ruler. This was as true in pre printing press Europe as it would be half a millennium later in Joseph Stalin's Soviet Union; many memoirs by camp survivors talk about prisoners who were convinced that Stalin had been betrayed by his subordinates and that, if only the Leader knew about the injustices, their sentences would be reversed.

Some of the most extraordinary sixteenth-century pamphlets were written by literate laymen who, lacking any formal education, demonstrated how the reading of the Bible in the vernacular had led them to tackle theological questions that, since the earliest patristic writings, had been reserved for highly educated church (and church-approved) scholars. Clement Ziegler, a Strasbourg gardener, took it upon himself to preach to his fellow gardeners after he experienced a vision of Christ in a 1524 flood. Ziegler's preaching, it should be noted, angered Protestant as well as Catholic authorities, since he was an uneducated man by the standards of both. He needed no articles of faith promulgated by any church, Catholic or Protestant, to develop his own rationale for rejecting, say, the doctrine of the transubstantiation. For Ziegler, the Last Supper and Jesus's breaking of bread were brilliant symbols, not a sacrament, and the belief that bread and wine were actually the body and blood of Christ amounted to idol worship. It was ridiculous, he wrote, to conclude that even when the Communion wafer "is broken into a hundred pieces, still the body of Christ remains in every piece, just as though it still hung on the cross. . . ."[8]

Ziegler cannot have been an "ordinary" gardener, because ordinary gardeners, even those who were already extraordinary by virtue of being literate in the early sixteenth century, do not read the Bible and then begin to develop and publicize their own theories about transubstantiation. But he and his fellow pamphleteers provided irrefutable evidence that the genie could never be returned to the bottle. Once people had claimed the right to read words long forbidden unless filtered through ecclesiastical mediators who understood ancient languages, there was no stopping the proliferation of religious ideas. Soldiers of the Inquisition might smash printing presses, but the knowledge of how to construct another one remained. Calvin might rejoice (to the extent that his dour philosophy allowed him to rejoice about anything) at the burning of Michael Servetus's book on the errors of the Trinity along with the man, but somewhere, in the era of printing, another copy would—and did—survive. (In fact, three copies survived.) And even at a time when paper was much more expensive than it is today, it was relatively cheap to print pamphlets by all of those irrepressible lay theologians. The small pamphlets were not glorious art objects like illuminated manuscripts, but those older, beautiful one-of-a-kind manuscripts never reached the sort of people who could easily grasp the assertion that most Catholics understood no more Latin than "a miller's donkey."

The printing press turns up everywhere, regardless of what particular national form the Reformation took, in accounts of major shifts in public opinion that led to conversions from Catholicism to Protestantism. One comical (today) incident that speeded the Reformation in Zürich in the early 1520s involved the forbidden consumption of ordinary *Wurst,* German sausage, during Lent. (History does not record whether the sausage was bratwurst, knockwurst, or some other variety.) As Kenneth G. Appold, professor of Reformation history at Princeton Theological Seminary, tells the story in a lively short history of the Reformation on the continent, the sausage controversy began on March 9, 1522, when the printer (print, again) Christoph Froschauer offered a plate of the forbidden *Fleisch* to a group of friends gathered in his shop. "Church law prohibited eating meat during Lent," Appold reminds us. "Froschauer knew this, as did those who partook of the unholy communion."[9] Zwingli, already a well-known preacher, who held the post of "people's priest" at the city's Grossmünster Church, remained at the forbidden feast but did not actually eat the sausage—his own abstinence enabling him to declare his approval of breaking Lenten custom without having to defend himself personally against charges of having sinned. Zwingli soon delivered a sermon supporting the breaking of Lenten rules, noting that fasting was a purely human, ecclesiastically invented and prescribed custom, not mentioned in the Bible. His sermon, titled *Von Erkiesen und Freiheit der Speisen* (*On Choice and the Liberty of Foods*), was then published on April 16.

Publication of the sermon set off a citywide debate, which, in less than six months, resulted in the Zürich city council's siding with Zwingli against the Catholic bishop and establishing a new post of "city preacher" for him. Of primary importance was the fact that this new post removed Zwingli from ecclesiastical jurisdiction and made him responsible only to the city's secular magistrates. These actions—beginning with the consumption of a humble sausage and the publication of a sermon—led to the Zürich Disputation of January 1523, between Zwingli and Catholic authorities. The disputation, a key event in the Reformation in Switzerland, resulted in Zwingli's being acquitted of heresy by secular magistrates. The debate drew an audience of more than six hundred, and many of the speeches were republished in pamphlet form. Absent the printing press, there is simply no way to imagine that events would have moved so swiftly, or moved at all, after one man broke Lenten fasting rules in the presence of a few friends.

The new force of the printed, infinitely reproducible word added both a public and a private dimension to the worldly calculus involved in previous eras of large-scale religious conversion. The public dimension, perfectly embodied by the Lenten *Wurst* rebellion in Zürich, involved the ability of publications to multiply the effect of word of mouth.

The private dimension enabled the individual to engage directly with sacred writings and encouraged the idea that the capacity to seek and grasp religious truth extended not only beyond ecclesiastical bureaucrats but also beyond visionaries like Luther. Conversions to Protestantism—like conversions to Christianity in the late Roman Empire—could certainly be opportunistic. This was true whenever and wherever secular rulers took sides against Catholicism, whether in various cities and regions on the continent or in England, as the half-century reign of the powerful, popular, and politically astute Elizabeth I provided time for the reformed faith to take root as the norm rather than as a dissident creed. But most of these conversions in Northern Europe and England, whatever worldly advantage may have accrued to the convert (as in the case of John Donne), were not forced in the sense that nearly all conversions to Christianity from Judaism and Islam after 1391 in Spain must be suspected, if not presumed, to have been forced. When the blood of a people is running in the streets, its communities being destroyed, and its possessions confiscated, how is it possible to speak of truly "voluntary" conversion? By contrast, the rise of Protestantism in its many forms was a widespread shift of ideas, spread by a medium with greater power to disseminate information and change cultures than the world had ever seen.

Yet the printing press had another effect: it was also a more efficient medium for spreading hatred. The idea of the Reformation as a movement for "religious tolerance" in the modern sense, with the big, bad Catholic Church as the sole villain, is both an erroneous and an anachronistic concept. Nowhere is this misguided notion more prevalent than in the United States, where we love to tell ourselves that, from the very beginning, we were a people who upheld religious tolerance. It does not fit our national religious myth to acknowledge that the Puritans who established the Massachusetts Bay Colony lost no time in exiling religious dissidents. It took 150 years, the Enlightenment, and more instruction in the horror of theocracies in the Old World before the United States of America became the first nation on the planet to uphold the legal separation of church and state. The early Puritan immigrants had learned their lessons from Old World forebears who were fanatics as well as visionaries. Zwingli, Calvin, and Luther were all great figures in religious history, but they were as hostile to freedom of conscience for those who disagreed with them as the leaders of the Catholic Church were to all Protestants. The printing press spread not only Luther's and Calvin's vernacular translations of the Bible but the former's scurrilous polemics against Jews and the latter's prescriptions for informing on any fellow citizen suspected of religious unorthodoxy. The early Reformation, precisely because its voluntary conversions were rooted in the idea that individuals could approach God and the truth for themselves, contained the seeds of more conversions and different faiths. But the Protestant churches that had already achieved majority status and political power were not ready or willing to tolerate those faiths on their own turf. Not then. Not there. Not yet.

9

PERSECUTION IN AN AGE OF
RELIGIOUS CONVERSION

O N JULY 22, 2010, the Council of the Lutheran World Federation held
a formal service of repentance in Stuttgart, Germany, expressing
"deep regret and sorrow" for the sixteenth-century Lutheran persecution of Anabaptists in Europe. The Lutheran council requested forgiveness from God and from many religious denominations descended
from the Anabaptists, whose name literally means "baptized again."
American denominations whose origins can be traced to the Anabaptists include Seventh-Day Adventists, Amish, Mennonites, and Hut-
terites. (The Catholic Church, busily fighting against all of the new
forms of Christian faith, did not single out the Anabaptists for special
censure.) Anabaptists fled many parts of Europe as a result of persecution by Lutherans and later by Calvinists, and they brought ideas
to the New World—specifically, the concept of being "born again"
through adult baptism—that have influenced many evangelical faiths
since the First and Second Great Awakenings.* Zwingli and his followers in Zürich, who had been in real danger of being killed for their
Lutheran-influenced beliefs in the early 1520s, needed only a few years

---

* The First Great Awakening in the United States is generally dated from the 1730s to the
1760s; the Second Great Awakening began after the Revolution and lasted until, roughly,
the early 1840s.

to begin killing believers in a new Protestant faith that practiced adult baptism. The Anabaptists rejected infant baptism because it is not mentioned in the Bible, and because (just imagine!) they were perceptive enough to understand that an infant could hardly be expected to make an informed decision embracing a particular religious faith.

It all began—like Luther's rebellion over indulgences—with a dispute over money. This time, the issue was tithing; to be more precise, the issue was tithing that did not concede the right of a church community to select its own minister. A small village near Zürich had the temerity to elect its own pastor, one Wilhelm Reublin, without applying for approval from the Zürich Grossmünster chapter headed by Zwingli. This straightforward worldly conflict was also developing in Germany, where Luther had taken the side of wealthy central communities against peasant villages, and the Zürich city council did the same. The issue was clearly one of taxation without representation, and it set some of Zwingli's inner circle, including an influential preacher named Konrad Grebel, against their leader. To make a long story short, the initial dispute over tithing (again, like the battle over selling indulgences) soon escalated into a larger conflict over the authority of individuals, and individual congregations, to interpret the Scriptures according to their own consciences. Baptism, at that point, became the critical issue, and after a 1525 disputation, the busybody Zürich city council issued a decree that all babies be baptized within eight days of birth; parents who refused to comply would be banished from the community.

Further discussion of the infant baptism issue was forbidden to biblical study groups in Zürich. Whereupon Grebel, Reublin, and others promptly began baptizing one another and people who agreed with them in nearby communities. In one of the more comical (had it not led to executions) turns in the argument, Zwingli, while acknowledging that infant baptism was not mentioned in the Scriptures, compared the christening of babies to the rite of circumcision, the foundational biblical covenant of Abraham with God that established the Jews as his chosen people (before Jesus appeared as the Messiah). The irony of using this analogy to argue for infant baptism should have been evident even in the sixteenth century. Simply being circumcised was not the death sentence at the time of the Inquisition that it was to become for Jewish males in the Nazi era, but the circumcision of any boy born into a family of what were supposed to be New Christians would certainly, if discovered, have meant a death sentence for the parents, if not for the baby himself. Such a circumcision would have been incontrovertible proof that the New Christian family was really a nest of "Judaizers." Also, it is entirely possible that there was a comical and confused equation between the Hebrew Bible's precise requirement, mentioned in both Genesis and Leviticus, that a Jewish baby boy be circumcised on the eighth day after birth and the eight-day window of opportunity for infant baptism prescribed by the Zürich city council.

In any event, the Zürich magistrates, with Zwingli's strong backing, cited a provision of Roman law from the Theodosian Code of 412 that prohibited rebaptizing and had been used against the Donatists in North Africa. (The Inquisition had also employed this ancient provision against the Cathars.) In 1526, rebaptism became a capital offense in Zürich. The form of capital punishment for heretical rebaptizers was drowning, considered a particularly appropriate penalty for those who used the water of baptism to declare their independence from the (barely) established Lutheran churches. Moreover, immersion in water, as practiced by John the Baptist in the Gospels, was beginning to take hold as the standard procedure for adult baptism, and remains popular to this day in many evangelical faith communities in the United States. But in sixteenth-century Lutheran-dominated regions, it was a decidedly bad idea to gather at the river if you wanted to stay alive. The first recorded Anabaptist martyr, Felix Manz (who had been a friend of Zwingli's), was captured, dragged to a fishing hut on a local river, and drowned. Anabaptist communities also emerged in areas that are now part of Germany, Austria, Hungary, and western Russia—and they were persecuted everywhere. Balthasar Hubmaier, who led Anabaptist movements in the Black Forest and Moravia, was captured and burned at the stake in Vienna in 1528. His wife Elisabeth was executed by being thrown off a bridge into the Danube River with stones tied around her neck.

In the midst of this targeted carnage, the Anabaptists nevertheless managed to get together in the Swiss town of Schleitheim in early 1527 and agree on seven articles of faith, which included adult baptism as a form of recommitment to a new life in Christ—the experience of being "born again." The second article of faith—one practiced within communities like the Amish today—rejects physical violence and prescribes "shunning" if a member, after being counseled privately within the group, refuses to abandon what is considered a sin. Shunning can hardly be considered a benign practice, in that it substitutes what might be considered emotional abuse for physical violence. An Amish parent who secretly remains in contact with a child who has been shunned, for instance, may be shunned herself and driven out of the only community she has ever known. Though shunning seems both severe and cruel by modern secular (and many religious) standards, it was less cruel than being killed for dissenting religious beliefs, as the Anabaptists were at the time the Schleitheim articles were drafted. (The present Amish custom of Rumspringa—derived from a Dutch word that means "running around"—embodies the seriousness with which the descendants of Anabaptists regard adult religious vows. When Amish children turn sixteen, they are allowed a period in which they may sample all the wares of what is called the "English" world, including alcohol, mass media and entertainment, and unsupervised contact with the opposite sex. After the Rumspringa interlude, they must decide whether to join the Amish church as full adult members or to remain in the outside world. Should they choose the latter, they will be shunned by their families.) The Anabaptist tradition certainly did involve proselytizing in its early European incarnation, in that it reached out to orthodox Protestants and actively encouraged a form of baptism that bound adherents to a new church in defiance of state-favored religions. However, Anabaptists never tried to induce conversions by force. In the New World, descendants of the Anabaptists basically wanted only to be let alone by government—a position that was not confined to small denominations like the Amish or Adventists but also influenced mainstream Baptists in the eighteenth century and led to cooperation between Baptists and freethinkers in framing the Establishment Clause of the First Amendment.

•

In Western Europe, the Reformation meant that one state-approved religion, Roman Catholicism, was replaced by a multiplicity of establishments, which encouraged religious conversions and produced new political majorities supported by different monarchies in different regions. To say that conversions to Protestantism were voluntary is not, as would eventually become evident in England as well as on the continent, to imply that Protestants were more "tolerant" than their Catholic brethren in Christendom. Protestantism is short-hand for what, in the interest of historical truth, ought to be called protestantisms—though some protestantisms were certainly more tolerant than others. And it cannot be emphasized enough that conversions from majority to minority religions were never secure or easy until the onetime minority became a majority or acquired solid secular political protection—usually around the same time. The paradox of protestantisms, beginning with Luther himself, lies in the incompatibility of a core belief in the right of individuals to engage directly with God's truth through reading the Bible, and a quickly emerging intolerance of divergent conclusions about that truth.

·

The most intolerant of the major founders of the Reformation was, without question, John Calvin (1509–64). Born Jean Cauvin in France, he would eventually flee the Catholic monarchy. After many false starts and twists and turns of political as well as religious fortune, Calvin was able to create a repressive religious polity in Geneva that the Catholic Church, for all the historical intransigence of its absolute truth claims, had never quite been able to manage, even in the territory of the Papal States. Calvin cared not only about doctrine—especially predestination—but about strict social discipline, maintained not only by civil magistrates and ecclesiastical pooh-bahs but by a network of neighborhood informers united in their determination to ferret out anyone who did not subscribe to strict Calvinist practices and beliefs about everything from the basic sinfulness of humanity to any pleasure that might be derived from such inventions of the devil as colorful clothes, music, sweet foods—in short, anything that might please any of the human senses. Having been kicked out of Geneva by city fathers who considered his ideas of discipline too strict (and too threatening to secular power), Calvin returned for good in 1541 as the political and ecclesiastical winds shifted. Pastors of individual churches were approved both by the city council and the Calvinist clergy (there would be no such rebels as emerged from the Grossmünster Church in Zürich). Excommunication from the church was to be enforced

The fifth-century terracotta statue is believed to represent the Alexandrian philosopher and mathematician Hypatia (c. 350–415), who was literally torn to pieces by a Christian mob for the dual offense of being a female intellectual and expounding classical pagan philosophy as Christianity triumphed throughout the Roman Empire. *(Ancient Art and Architecture Collection Ltd./Bridgeman Images)*

The future church father Augustine of Hippo (354–430) was encouraged to convert to Christianity from paganism by his mother, Monica. This 1855 painting by the Dutch-born Romantic artist Ary Scheffer presents an idealized, somewhat saccharine image of their devotion to each other. *(Louvre, Paris, France, Peter Willi/Bridgeman Images)*

MICHAEL SERVETVS HISPANUS DE ARAGONIA.

Born in Spain in 1511, Michael Servetus was a physician and Renaissance humanist whose challenges to orthodox doctrine, especially the Holy Trinity, were equally offensive to Catholics and Protestants. He was burned to death at the stake in Geneva, with the complicity of John Calvin, on October 27, 1553.

John Donne (1572–1631) is portrayed here by an anonymous artist, c. 1595, as the romantic, rakish young poet he was. Raised in a Roman Catholic family, Donne converted to the Church of England and eventually became one of the most prominent preachers of his day. *(National Portrait Gallery, London, U.K./Bridgeman Images)*

Anne Marbury Hutchinson (1591–1643) ran afoul of the male theocrats in charge of the Massachusetts Bay Colony when she led prayer meetings and preached in her own home. She was convicted of heresy and expelled from the colony in 1638 for her views on salvation by grace alone and for being a woman who dared to lead biblical discussions. This 1901 illustration originally appeared in an article in *Harper's Monthly*. *(Library of Congress, Prints & Photographs Division)*

Womens Speaking

Justified, Proved and Allowed of by the SCRIPTURES,

All such as speak by the Spirit and Power of the Lord JESUS.

And how WOMEN were the first that preached the Tidings of the Resurrection of JESUS, and were sent by CHRIST's Own Command, before He ascended to the Father, John 20.17.

And it shall come to pass, in the last dayes, saith the Lord, I will pour out of my Spirit upon all Flesh; your Sons and Daughters shall Prophesie. Acts 2.27. Joel 2.28.

It is written in the Prophets, They shall be all taught of God, saith Christ, John 6.45.

And all thy Children shall be taught of the Lord, and great shall be the Peace of thy Children. Isa. 54.13.

And they shall teach no more every man his Neighbour, and every man his Brother, saying, Know the Lord; for they shall all know me, from the least to the greatest of them, saith the Lord. Jer. 31.34.

London, Printed in the Year, 1666.

Margaret Fell (1614–1702), an outspoken English Quaker advocate for female intellectuality and equality with men in religious affairs, wrote one of the earliest defenses of women's speaking in public, nearly three decades after Hutchinson's conviction in Massachusetts. The first edition of Fell's then controversial pamphlet was published in London in 1666. *(Copyright © Religious Society of Friends [Quakers] in Britain)*

Fell converted from Puritanism to the new Quaker religion and is often called the "mother of Quakerism." She never had her portrait painted during her lifetime, in keeping with Quaker ideas about personal humility. In this nineteenth-century engraving, Robert Spence envisions Fell as a young girl (third from left, standing), surrounded by the Lancashire family into which she was born. *(Copyright © Religious Society of Friends [Quakers] in Britain)*

The great German lyric poet Heinrich Heine (1797–1856) was born a Jew and later regretted his conversion to Lutheranism. This 1831 portrait by Moritz Oppenheim captures the romantic appeal that led some to call Heine a "German Apollo." *(Hamburger Kunsthalle, Hamburg, Germany/Bridgeman Images)*

Elizabeth Ann Seton (1774–1821), pictured here as a young married woman, came from a prominent New York Episcopal family but converted to Roman Catholicism—scandalizing her relatives—after the death of her husband. She later founded the Sisters of Charity in the United States and became the first American-born saint canonized by the church. *(Library of Congress, Prints & Photographs Division)*

Raised in an observant German Jewish family, Edith Stein (1891–1942) converted to Catholicism and became a Carmelite nun. But she was murdered at Auschwitz because she had been born a Jew. This stamp was issued by the German postal service in 1983 to honor Stein, who would later be canonized by the church in a move that offended many Jews.

Whittaker Chambers (1901–61), pictured here at the trial of Alger Hiss in 1949, wrote about his embrace of Communism in the 1920s as a form of conversion and emphasized his return to belief in God after he left the Party. He is best known as Hiss's chief accuser and wrote about all of his conversions in his best-selling autobiography, *Witness*. *(Photo by Ed Jackson/New York* Daily News *Archive via Getty Images)*

G. K. Chesterton (1874–1936), a prominent English journalist, literary critic, Christian apologist, and author of the Father Brown mystery series, was raised in a Unitarian family and moved steadily in the direction of ultra-orthodox Christianity. In the 1920s—the same decade in which left-wing intellectuals like Chambers were converting to Stalinist Communism—Chesterton chose the most conservative brand of Roman Catholicism over the Church of England. *(Library of Congress, Prints & Photographs Division)*

An English convert from atheism to the Church of England, C. S. Lewis (1898–1963), pictured here at Oxford University, was one of the most eloquent literary defenders of Christianity in the twentieth century. A Renaissance scholar as well as a theologian, he is best known in the United States as the author of the children's fantasy series *The Chronicles of Narnia*. *(Photo by Hans Wild/ The* Life *Picture Collection/Getty Images)*

The future world heavyweight champion Muhammad Ali (second from right), then named Cassius Clay, represented the United States at the 1960 Olympics in Rome when he was eighteen and won the light-heavyweight Olympic gold medal. Raised a Baptist, Ali would become the most famous American convert to Islam in the mid-1960s. *(Photo by Central Press/ Getty Images)*

Though he had been reviled in the 1960s for his conversion to Islam and opposition to the Vietnam War, Muhammad Ali was awarded the Presidential Medal of Freedom, the nation's highest civilian honor, by President George W. Bush in 2005. *(Photo by Mandel Ngan/AFP/ Getty Images)*

by a combination of civil and ecclesiastical authority. All gambling, card playing, and dancing were banned; fornication was added to the usual crimes of murder, assault, and theft as grounds for civil penalties and excommunication. Witchcraft and sorcery, as might have been expected, were capital offenses. Homes of loyal Calvinists were searched once a year, just in case they possessed books or any signs (such as a pack of playing cards) of dissent from the moral and civil order. A legal enforcement agency called the Consistory, including representatives of both the Geneva city council and the church, was established, and the city's residents (Geneva then had a population of about fifteen thousand) were to report violations ranging from fornication to the skipping of sermons, as well as to practices, such as naming children after saints, that might indicate some atavistic attachment to Catholicism. Like the Spanish inquisitors, authorities in Geneva kept meticulous records of denunciations. We know, for instance, that in 1550 exactly 160 cases of sexual immorality were reported.[1] Since this meant that a report was filed by someone at least every other day, it certainly betokens a high level of Christian neighborly surveillance. The array of prohibitions covering the most minute aspects of daily life was seemingly endless. Women's dresses were checked to make sure the skirts were neither too long nor too short. There were limits to the number of rings a woman (or a man) could wear on his or her fingers, and a prescribed number of shoes allowed each citizen. Even the amount of meat that could be eaten at any specific meal was regulated by law. Almost anything with the taint of pleasure was forbidden, including family dinners to which more than twenty people were invited. (Perhaps the authorities felt that twenty was the magic number for producing too much sinful laughter. How could so many people get together in one room without telling jokes?) Pastries and candied fruits were specifically prohibited. The Genevan Consistory, like the office of the Holy Inquisition in Rome, gave an imprimatur to books; woe unto the household where books without the imprimatur were found. During the first five years after Calvin's triumphalist return to Geneva, ten people were beheaded, thirty-five burned at the stake, and seventy-six driven from their houses after their property had been seized. Prisons were so crowded with citizens being prosecuted for heresy that the wardens had to tell city officials that there was no more room.

No one has described Calvin's regimen with a more scathing accuracy than Stefan Zweig, who wrote in 1936 that, after Calvin returned to Geneva to stay, "it is as if the doors of the houses had suddenly been thrown open and if the walls had been transformed into glass. From moment to moment, by day and by night, there might come a knocking at the entry and a number of 'spiritual police' announce a 'visitation' without the concerned citizen's being able to offer resistance." Calvin had inaugurated "a Protestant orthodoxy in place of a papistical one; and with perfect justice this new form of dogmatic dictatorship has been stigmatized as bibliocracy." Zweig also argues that any "reign of force which originates out of a movement towards liberty is always more strenuously opposed to the idea of liberty than is a hereditary power. Those who owe their position as governors to a successful revolution become the most obscurantist and intolerant opponents of further innovation."[2] Zweig, an Austrian Jew who left his country in 1934 and committed suicide in Petrópolis, Brazil, in 1942, offered his opinion of Calvin in a world living between the two poles of revolutionary repression represented by Nazism and Stalinism. He knew all about living in a house suddenly turned to glass.

•

Unlike Queen Elizabeth, Calvin intended to peer into men's souls and to punish them for thoughts as well as deeds. The well-known severity of the Calvinist regime in Geneva makes it difficult to understand why the Aragonese-born Michael Servetus, who was both an iconoclastic theologian and a medical thinker, made the mistake of thinking that he would find refuge from Catholic persecution in what had become, by the 1550s, a near-totalitarian Calvinist domain. Born into a Catholic family in 1511 in the village of Villanueva de Sigena, young Miguel was originally educated by his father, a low-ranking noble, scholar, and notary to the nuns in the local convent. Miguel was a linguistic prodigy; it was said that he could read French, Greek, Latin, and Hebrew—in addition to his native Spanish—by age thirteen. The study of Hebrew was a sensitive subject, and Miguel would likely have been taught by a "secret" Jew. The young scholar's facility with Hebrew would lead to rumors that he was himself from a Converso family. Most scholars dismiss this possibility, but I am not at all sure that they are right. Lawrence and Nancy Goldstone, in *Out of the Flames* (2002), argue that it is "more likely that Miguel, growing up in a time of political and religious upheaval, was bombarded by heterodoxy on all sides. He watched the Jews and Muslims resist Catholicism and the Navarrese resist Spain, both powerless minorities fighting a desperate battle for freedom. He learned to identify with the outcast long before he was to discover that he would be one himself."[3] What the Goldstones ignore in this scenario is that it was dangerous to study or know Hebrew in Spain in the early sixteenth century. Why would Christian parents take such a risk with their brilliant child in the absence of a connection to Judaism? It is a biographical question—like many of the gaps in Shakespeare's life—that will probably never be answered.

At age sixteen, Miguel was sent by his father to study at the University of Toulouse, located in Catholic France but then a hotbed of religious disputes generated by the Reformation. In 1531, Servetus published his first book on what he considered the senseless concept of the Trinity (appropriately titled *De Trinitatis Erroribus* in Latin). For Servetus, Jesus was an intermediary between God and man and could not have been eternal because he was the son of God—not God Himself. Servetus also rejected infant baptism because he, in contrast to Augustine, did not believe that infants had the mental capacity to sin. Although Servetus considered himself a Christian, both Catholics and Calvinists deemed him a heretic. Where, after all, would both Augustine and Calvin be without original sin and the Trinity? Servetus was not a convert to anything; he might well be considered the exemplary anti-convert. That is why he has been revered by generations of humanists and freethinkers, beginning in the seventeenth century. In 1890, the American freethinker Robert Ingersoll, in a statement opposing vivisection, would use Calvinism as a metaphor for sadism. "We can excuse, in part, the crimes of passion," Ingersoll wrote. ". . . But what excuse can ingenuity form for a man who deliberately—with an unaccelerated pulse—with the calmness of John Calvin at the murder of Servetus—seeks, with curious and cunning knives, in the living, quivering flesh of a dog, for all the throbbing nerves of pain?"[4] The eminent physician and medical educator William Osler observed in 1910, in an article in the *Johns Hopkins Hospital Bulletin,* that Servetus could have saved himself from the stake even at the last minute by modifying his public views about the Trinity. In extremis, Servetus was said to have cried out, "Jesu, thou Son of the eternal God, have mercy upon me." Osler notes that the chains would have been removed and the fire doused had Servetus instead cried out, "Jesu, thou Eternal Son of God." The latter would presumably have upheld orthodox Calvinist (and Catholic) doctrine that Jesus was a co-equal of the three persons in God and was not inferior to or created by God the Father.[5] Servetus was executed and burned with a copy of his most recent work, *Christianismi Restitutio* (*The Restoration of Christianity*). One unusual aspect of this book—and the reason a prominent doctor was writing about Servetus in the twentieth century—is that it contains the first written description in Western history of the minor circulation of the blood (the circulation and oxygenation of blood through the heart and lungs). Servetus argued against Galen's incorrect belief that blood was created in the liver from ingested food and flows from there to the right side of the heart. Servetus's comments on blood circulation were ignored at the time, since they constituted a small portion of a controversial theological treatise. Nevertheless, he was at least on his way to a correct theory of blood circulation seventy-five years before the English physician William Harvey (1578–1657), who published his findings in 1628 and is generally given full credit for the correct explanation of blood circulation in standard medical histories.*

The earliest and—because he was the earliest—the greatest defender of Servetus was a man whose name has largely been lost to history: Sebastian Castellio (1515–63), a professor of Greek literature, originally attracted by Calvinism, who did not have the luxury of commenting on the execution from the safe distance of centuries. After the execution of Servetus (whom Castellio did not know personally), the professor at the University of Basel took on Calvin directly. In a manifesto on behalf of religious toleration, *Concerning Heretics and Whether They Should Be Punished by the Sword of the Magistrate,* Castellio outlined one of the first arguments against civil punishment for religious offenses to circulate in the Western world. (The work was

---

* The Arab physician Ibn al-Nafis (c. 1213–88), born in Damascus, also wrote a treatise questioning Galen's theory. His theories—which, like those of Servetus, were not complete but were a major step toward the truth about blood circulation—were largely ignored by his Arab contemporaries, as well as by later Europeans.

published under the pseudonym Martinus Bellius, but, as would be the case more than four centuries later with many Russian samizdat works, the real identity of the author did not long remain a secret in a police state.) Castellio wrote that men "are so strongly convinced of the soundness of their opinions that they despise the opinions of others. Cruelties and persecutions are the outcome of arrogance, so that a man will not tolerate others' differing in any way from his own views, although there are today almost as many views as there are persons. Yet there is not one sect which does not condemn all the others and wish to remain supreme. That accounts for banishments, exiles, incarcerations, burnings, hangings, and the blind fury of the tormenters who are continually at work, in the endeavor to suppress certain outlooks which displease our lords and masters."[6] In denouncing the execution of Servetus, Castellio also uttered the unforgettable sentence "Who burns a man does not defend a doctrine, but only burns a man." (The statement is often mistakenly attributed to Servetus himself.) Finally, Castellio declared with immense courage, given Servetus's recent execution for heresy, "When I reflect on what a heretic really is, I can find no other criterion than that we are all heretics in the eyes of those who do not share our views."[7] Soon, as a result of Calvin's personal intervention, Castellio was dismissed from his post at the university. He had no means of support, and was about to be brought to trial (thanks to Calvin's behind-the-scenes machinations) for stealing firewood when he died, supposedly of natural causes, at the age of forty-eight. After Castellio's death, his friends—finding that nearly all of his possessions had been sold to provide food for his family—paid for his funeral. Almost every member of the university faculty marched to Basel's main church for the funeral, and students carried the coffin on their shoulders. They also paid for a tombstone with the inscription "To our renowned teacher, in gratitude for his extensive knowledge and in commemoration of the purity of his life." (One wonders where all these academic supporters were while Castellio was still alive.) Castellio's ideas on religious toleration, originally circulated in pamphlets, were not published until the seventeenth century, after Locke and Spinoza had written similar treatises on the folly of forced conversion and religious persecution. As one Unitarian minister notes (the Unitarian Universalist Church is one of the few religious institutions in which the names of Servetus and Castellio are mentioned), Castellio "is honored by no memorials. No churches are named after him, not even rooms in churches. . . . There remains only that tomb in Basel, overgrown with weeds and neglected by a perfidious people." This minister reported that, on the four hundredth anniversary of Castellio's death, he had asked a meeting of the Unitarian Universalist General Assembly to take up a collection to restore Castellio's grave, "but the motion was ruled out of order."[8]

Unlike the Lutherans, who have apologized for past persecutions, the small numbers of unreconstructed Calvinists remaining in the twenty-first century are still trying to defend their founder's role in the murder of Servetus. "It is true that Calvin and his fellow pastors in Geneva were involved in the death of Servetus," acknowledges a historical Web site maintained by Calvin College in Grand Rapids, Michigan.* "However, it would be difficult to find any church leader in the sixteenth century who advocated a more gentle approach. . . . Toleration and acceptance of doctrinal differences were simply not sixteenth-century concepts."[9] That is exactly the point. Of course it would have been difficult to find any church leader in the sixteenth century who advocated a "gentler" approach. But there were dissidents and humanists of Calvin's generation who saw him for exactly what he was. To think about the religious conversions that took place throughout the Reformation as a great step forward for freedom of conscience is to look back, in anachronistic fashion, from a world of religious pluralism to a world in which reformation usually meant the substitution of one absolute truth for another.

•

Throughout the sixteenth and seventeenth centuries, strife between Protestant sects was accompanied and often overshadowed by the continuing battle of the Catholic Church to regain the hegemony it had enjoyed before the Reformation. The Saint Bartholomew's Day Massacre of August 24, 1572, in which thousands of prominent Huguenots were slaughtered by Catholics in Paris, was the era's most notorious and inflammatory event, with far-reaching consequences that influ-

* Many of the early settlers of Grand Rapids were Calvinists who emigrated from the Netherlands in the 1820s and 1830s. The area was long known as one of the most religiously conservative in the state of Michigan and the Midwest.

enced later Enlightenment thinkers as well as contemporary attitudes. The initial massacre took place on a day when thousands of the most prominent Huguenots in France had traveled to Paris for the wedding of Henry of Navarre, who later succeeded to the French throne as King Henry IV, to Marguerite of Valois, a daughter of Catherine de' Medici. Henry was raised as a Protestant, and his marriage to the Catholic Marguerite was supposed to promote harmony between the Protestant minority and the Catholic (90 percent) majority. Instead, soldiers (in a plot possibly organized by Catherine as well as French Catholic nobles) took advantage of the celebration to surprise the Huguenots. The first to die was Admiral Gaspard de Coligny, whose body was chopped to pieces by a soldier in the service of the Catholic duke of Guise. But the massacre did not stop there; for at least two months, Huguenots were hunted down in provincial cities, and contemporary reports describe rivers running red with Protestant blood. These gory accounts soon reached England and resulted in new repressive measures against English Catholics. Mary, Queen of Scots, was a member of the Guise family, and her cousin Elizabeth could hardly have failed to draw a cautionary lesson about the threat to her monarchy posed by wealthy Catholics with strong connections to the Vatican. Even today, many official Catholic publications deny that the Vatican had any role in instigating the Saint Bartholomew's Day Massacre, but there is no question that the church was pleased by the slaughter. Pope Gregory XIII commissioned a special medal in honor of the event and sent the memento to Catherine de' Medici and to every Catholic bishop in France. The massacre set off decades of religious wars in France, where members of the Huguenot minority were mainly followers of Calvin. Henry of Navarre would lead Protestant forces against Catholics in the decades after his wedding had been spoiled—to understate the case—by blood in the streets. In 1598, as King Henry IV, he issued the Edict of Nantes, which permitted, with strict limitations, the practice of the Protestant religion. The king's caution about offending Catholics was exemplified by a provision for the feast of Corpus Christi, in which houses along the route of elaborate Catholic processions were supposed to be decorated with banners to honor the day. Huguenots were not required to do the decorating themselves, but the edict allowed Catholics, at their own expense, to hang decorations on Huguenot houses. Given the religious invasion of citizens' homes, it is easy to understand why Corpus Christi became an occasion for violent clashes between Catholics and Huguenots. "The matter occasioned dozens, perhaps hundreds, of confrontations in France," notes one religious historian. "Houses that were not properly decorated were attacked and looted. Even after the revocation of the edict [of Nantes], Huguenots would sometimes 'forget' to decorate their homes, risking draconian punishment."[10]

No religious settlements in Europe really involved tolerance in the modern sense; at best, they allowed toleration—a recognition that someone's disagreement with the majority about, for instance, the Holy Trinity, was not grounds for chopping him to pieces. Nevertheless, the limited Edict of Nantes was revoked in 1685 by that great progressive King Louis XIV. Louis' retrograde legislation not only prohibited the practice of Protestantism in France but also ordered Huguenots to renounce formally their allegiance to their faith. The death penalty was established for Huguenots caught attempting to flee France. Louis commissioned three hundred thousand special troops specifically to hunt Huguenots and confiscate their property for the throne. Nevertheless, it is believed that at least a quarter-million Huguenots did succeed in leaving France, mainly for the Netherlands, England, Protestant regions of Germany, and the dour Geneva created by Calvin (which many of the French Huguenots did not find agreeable, since their version of Calvinism did not always extend to the renunciation of wine, fine clothes, and other worldly pleasures). One of the unintended consequences of the persecution of French Huguenots was the immigration of many of their ancestors to the American colonies. Paul Revere's father was Apollo Rivoire, a goldsmith. George Washington was the grandson of a Huguenot on the maternal side of his family.

Another seven hundred thousand Huguenots were legally prevented from emigrating and forced to attend Catholic services.* The forced conversion and/or exile of the Huguenots is comparable in pre-modern European history only to the forced conversions and expulsions of Jews and Muslims from the Iberian Peninsula. Huguenots themselves frequently made the comparison between their fate and that of the

---

* These figures represent the lower end of standard scholarly estimates. Huguenots who refused to attend Catholic ceremonies were frequently imprisoned, tortured, killed, or sentenced to become galley slaves (the equivalent of execution, given that the life span of a galley slave was no longer in seventeenth-century Europe than it had been in Roman times).

Jews in fifteenth- and sixteenth-century Spain. In 1682, the French Huguenot minister Pierre Jurieu explicitly compared the forced baptisms of Jewish children by King Manuel I in Portugal in 1497 to the removal of many children from their French Huguenot homes in order that they might be "adopted" by Catholic families and raised as Christians.[11] (The identification of French Huguenots with persecuted Jews was to last for centuries. During the Second World War, a number of Huguenot pastors and parishioners in Vichy France would play a major role, rooted in religious principles, in hiding and rescuing Jews attempting to escape both the Nazis and the French collaborators.*)

The Saint Bartholomew's Day Massacre was still celebrated by French Catholics in the eighteenth century, even as it was decried by Enlightenment freethinkers as a symbol of everything wrong with an autocracy and absolutism that united church and state. French supporters of the American Revolution were deeply impressed by the flourishing of a multiplicity of faiths in the colonies even before independence. The Marquis de Lafayette, the greatest French friend of the American founders, was well aware of the Huguenot descent of many prominent members of the American revolutionary generation. In 1787, Lafayette cited the loss of Huguenots to the New World as an argument in favor of a law guaranteeing religious toleration for Protestants remaining in France. King Louis XVI was persuaded to agree, but that decision did nothing to help him keep his head in the bloody Jacobin phase of the French Revolution.

The European religious wars of the sixteenth and seventeenth centuries were critical factors in the thinking of the authors of the U.S. Constitution. One of the great ironies of life in seventeenth-century England and continental Europe was the juxtaposition of bitter religion-driven political conflict with the dawn of an Enlightenment that gave primacy to liberty of individual conscience. The same century saw the birth of the first modern faiths, most notably Quakerism, that truly viewed religious belief, in practice as well as theory, as an individual choice rather than a social imperative to be imposed by force.

---

* For an account of what happened in one Huguenot village, Le Chambon-sur-Lignon, see Phillip P. Hallie, *Lest Innocent Blood Be Shed* (New York: HarperCollins, 1994).

· PART IV ·

CONVERSIONS IN THE DAWN
OF THE ENLIGHTENMENT

10

MARGARET FELL (1614–1702):
WOMAN'S MIND, WOMAN'S VOICE

> You that deny Women's Speaking, answer: Doth it not consist of
> Women, as well as Men? Is not the Bride compared to the whole
> Church? And doth not the Bride say, *Come*? Doth not the Woman
> speak then, the Husband, Christ Jesus, the Amen? And doth not the
> false Church go about to stop the Bride's Mouth?
>
> —MARGARET FELL, *Women's Speaking Justified,* 1666

FOR THE OBVIOUS REASON that a literate woman was an even rarer
creature than a literate man throughout most of recorded history,
we know relatively little about the women whose religious conversions
played a critical role in transmitting new faiths to future generations.
The stories of iconographic female converts in early Christian history,
such as Augustine's mother, Monica, and Constantine's mother, Helena, were told by men.

Margaret Fell, one of the founders of the Society of Friends in
England, told her own story.* This remained exceptional in the seventeenth century, even though more women, at least among the gentry,
were learning to read and write than in previous centuries. Known
to her co-religionists as the "mother of Quakerism," Fell became a
prolific correspondent and activist in the only contemporary faith that
encouraged women to take an influential role in spiritual matters. In a

---

* Eleven years after the death of her first husband, Thomas Fell, Margaret married
George Fox, whose preaching had originally impelled her to embrace the new Quaker
faith. I refer to her as Margaret Fell rather than Margaret Fox not only because it would
be confusing to call her by different surnames but because Fell was, in the modern sense,
the equivalent of her professional or public name.

long life—spanning wars between anti-monarchist Puritans and supporters of the Church of England (and the Crown), the Puritan dictatorship of Oliver Cromwell, the Restoration, and the dawn of the Enlightenment—Fell spoke out against war, religious persecution, and the treatment of women as inferior moral beings. She spoke in a voice of early Enlightenment religious liberalism that preceded, but is linked to, the more secular "High Enlightenment" voices of the eighteenth century. *Women's Speaking Justified* was written from prison, where Fell spent nearly four years, from 1664 to 1668, for holding Quaker meetings in her home and failing to take an oath of loyalty to the government. Quakers refused to take all oaths, on the grounds that Jesus himself denounced the practice.* Fell made countless personal appeals for the release of persecuted religious dissidents, to rulers of different faiths (including Cromwell, and King Charles II after the Restoration). A voluminous correspondent with Quakers at home and abroad, and a ceaseless proselytizer for a faith that operated with little ritual and regard for traditional ecclesiastical hierarchies, Fell left a legacy that was not fully realized until religious feminists in the last quarter of the twentieth century began to battle for an equality that had been pioneered (although in decidedly uneven fashion) by Quakers.†

The wife of an influential judge, Thomas Fell, and the mother of eight children, Margaret Askew Fell originally belonged to an ordinary parish and practiced a Calvinist-influenced brand of Puritanism. In 1652, while Margaret's husband was away carrying out his duties on the judicial circuit, the charismatic, self-educated preacher George Fox visited the Fell home, Swarthmoor Hall, in Lancashire. Fox's teachings, during a period of intense religious strife, differed radically from all of the other contending faiths. The basis of Quakerism was its

* In the Gospel of Matthew (5:33–36), Jesus tells his followers, "Again, ye have heard that it hath been said by them of old time, Thou shalt not forswear thyself, but shalt perform unto the Lord thine oaths. But I say unto you, Swear not at all; neither by heaven, for it is God's throne: Nor by the earth, for it is his footstool: neither by Jerusalem, for it is the city of the great King. Neither shalt thou swear by thy head, because thou canst not make one hair white or black."

† Although women were encouraged to speak at Quaker meetings, mainstream Quakers—especially in America during the battle over slavery in the early nineteenth century—were often opposed to women's speaking in public, on public issues, in non-Quaker venues. See my discussion of Sarah and Angelina Grimké in *Freethinkers: A History of American Secularism* (New York: Metropolitan, 2004), pp. 74–77.

reliance on an "Inner Light" that lived in each man and woman and required the intervention of neither a church hierarchy nor the state. Even Baptists, who also adhered to a much more individualistic brand of faith than establishment Protestants and opposed state involvement with religion, did not approach the Quakers in their disdain for state-established churches. The Quakers' distaste for authority imposed from above, whether ecclesiastical or political, was later demonstrated not only by their abjuring of oaths but by the refusal of their men to tip hats, or their women to curtsy to their putative superiors.

Another important difference between Quakers and other Protestant denominations, whether mainstream or nonconformist, was their rejection of a literal interpretation of the Bible. Although Quaker leaders, including Fox and Fell, knew their Bible from Genesis to Revelation and quoted extensively from both testaments in theological argument, they believed that God resided within each man and woman, and it must therefore follow that the individual's Inner Light was the final authority. The nature of the Trinity and distinctions among the Father, Son, and Holy Spirit—a subject over which other Christians were still killing one another—never became an absolutist loyalty test for Quakers.

When Fell first heard Fox speak, she said he had "opened us a book that we had never read in, nor indeed never heard that it was our duty to read in it (to wit) the Light of Christ in our consciences. . . ."[1] That Margaret made her own religious choices in her husband's absence is itself a demonstration of her extraordinary independence of mind. Conversion to a dissident Protestant faith in the sixteenth and seventeenth centuries was a decision that could result in loss of property, torture, imprisonment, and death—sometimes all of the above. In England, varying degrees of religious persecution—its targets depending on the sympathies of the head of government—were the rule rather than the exception. The Glorious Revolution of 1688, which brought the Dutch William of Orange to the throne (he ruled England jointly with Queen Mary II), brought an end to religious violence in England, established Anglicanism as the state religion, provided limited toleration for nonconformist Protestants, and imposed stronger civil penalties on Catholics. (Even today, bishops of the Church of England are formally appointed by the monarch from a list supplied by Anglican officials, and any non-Anglican prime minister is explicitly forbidden, under a law passed in 1829, to advise the sovereign on ecclesiastical affairs. Although the Crown's role in ecclesiastical appointments is only a formality under today's constitutional monarchy, Tony Blair waited until he left the prime minister's office in 2007 before converting from the Church of England to Roman Catholicism. Benjamin Disraeli, born a Jew, would have been legally barred from becoming prime minister in the nineteenth century had his father, Isaac, not had him baptized in the Church of England at age thirteen. Isaac, a man of letters who spelled his name D'Israeli and did not convert to Christianity himself—though he broke formal ties with his Reform synagogue after his father died—knew that an unconverted Jew's professional and social opportunities would be severely limited.)

Fell was aware of the personal as well as the political implications of her embrace of Quakerism. "I was struck into such a sadness," she wrote years after Fox's death. "I knew not what to do, my husband being from home. I saw it was the truth, and I could not deny it; and I did as the Apostle saith, 'I received the truth in the love of it'; and it was opened to me so clear, that I never had a tittle in my heart against it; but I desired the Lord that I might be kept in it; and then I desired no greater portion."[2]

During Fox's first visit to Swarthmoor, Margaret took him along to "lecture day" at her church—much to the dismay of her own minister, William Lampitt. When the singing ended, Fox stood up in his pew and asked for permission to speak about the Inner Light and the irrelevance of outward symbols and rituals (many of which he had just witnessed). Fox used a peculiar reference to Jews to underline his point, observing that a man "is not a Jew that is one outward: neither is that circumcision which is outward: but he is a Jew that is one inward; and that is circumcision which is of the heart." He then spoke out strongly against pedantic, literal interpretations of the Bible that lacked "the illumination of the spirit of Christ."[3] Margaret, whose later writings showed her complete familiarity with both the Old and New Testaments, wept when she heard Fox's excoriation of those who treated every word of the Bible as literally true. She wrote that Fox's remarks "opened me so, that it cut me to the heart; and then I saw clearly that we were all wrong . . . and I cried in my spirit to the Lord, 'We are all thieves; we are all thieves; we have taken the Scriptures in words, and know nothing of them in ourselves.'"[4]

Margaret's minister was so incensed by Fox's statements that he directed the church wardens to throw the itinerant preacher out of the chapel. Fox, undeterred by his expulsion from the consecrated precincts, continued his talk in the churchyard and on the walk back to Swarthmoor Hall.

This first meeting and its aftermath are envisioned in *The Peaceable Kingdom* (1971), a popular novel by the Dutch writer Jan de Hartog.* A key issue in the novel's depiction of Fell and Fox's first meeting is the Quaker mandate that all believers be addressed as equals with the familiar "thou." Margaret tells Fox (their real names are used in the novel) that her entire household requires more instruction in understanding the new equality of which he has spoken. "As I told thee," says the fictional Fox, "it is not I but God. . . ." "God, fiddlesticks!" Margaret cries, realizing too late that this was hardly the language of a meek, unquestioning convert.[5]

•

When Judge Thomas Fell returned home about three weeks later, he was greeted on the riverbank near his house by an angry group of local burghers, including the vicar. They told the judge that a spiritual catastrophe had taken place in his own family while he was away, that his wife and entire household had been bewitched by Fox, and that he must send the Quaker preachers away to avoid the further catastrophe of the spread of a false faith throughout the area. Poor Judge Fell! After a long business trip, he must have been looking forward to a joint of roast lamb or beef, perhaps accompanied by a tankard of ale, in the bosom of his family. Instead, he was greeted by an outraged parish priest, who suggested that his wife had fallen under the spell of a wizard—an accusation that was anything but harmless in an era when most Christians believed in witches, and death was the penalty for sorcery. At home, Judge Fell was met by a wife who, as she later wrote, was torn by the realization that "either I must displease my husband, or offend God."[6]

---

* The Dutch-born novelist moved to the United States in the early 1960s and became a Quaker. De Hartog became interested in the role of women in Quakerism after he and his wife became involved in Quaker activities protesting the Vietnam War.

This recollection suggests that the Fells enjoyed a close relationship even though the judge was more conservative than his wife in matters of religion. Fox's friend was waiting to talk to Thomas Fell about the spiritual equality of believers, and Margaret noted that her husband became noticeably calmer and quieter when he saw that his dinner was ready. There is no record of whether the repast included a roast and ale, but Judge Fell was content enough to tell Margaret that he was willing to hear, upon her recommendation, what Fox had to say. After Fox had spoken to the judge, Margaret reports, her husband "came to see clearly the truth, of what he [Fox] spoke, and said no more, and went to bed."[7] We do not know whether Thomas Fell was more impressed by Fox's arguments or by the prospect of peace in the home, but, the very next day, he offered the use of the great hall of Swarthmoor for the area's first Meeting of Friends. He also continued to attend services at the Puritan parish church, displaying an uncommon flexibility at a time when choosing one church over another was generally considered mandatory and often a matter of life and death. The judge died in 1658, but he and Margaret had had another child in 1653. Remarkably for that era, all eight children survived to adulthood. It was said that, sometime before his death, Judge Fell stopped going to the parish church and left a door open between his study and the large hall where the Quaker meeting was held each week—a solution reflecting a preference for compromise that was rarely a feature of religious life anywhere in the seventeenth century. Judge Fell was clearly not as convinced of the truth of all Quaker beliefs as his wife, but he was a highly unusual man to have created no obstacles to Margaret's intense involvement in the birth and dissemination of a religion that he did not fully share.

Possibly because she was one of the few founding Quakers who were members of the landed gentry, Margaret was often asked—when she was not in prison herself, for holding Quaker meetings in her home or refusing to take oaths—to intercede with the authorities on behalf of her imprisoned co-religionists. She met with King Charles in London on June 22, 1660, only a month after his restoration to the throne. Shortly afterward, she issued a long statement, addressed to the king and Parliament, that is credited today with being the first comprehensive declaration of Quaker opposition to all war and violence. Despite her importance in her own time, attested to repeatedly in correspondence from men whose names we know well—such as William Penn, who founded the colony of Pennsylvania—Fell's contributions were largely overlooked and "seriously underestimated" before twentieth-century feminist scholarship cast a new light on the role of women in religion.[8]

In her declaration, Fell pointed out that Quakers had been persecuted under each new regime at times of political change because they refused to take oaths or doff their hats to superiors. "We who are the people of God called Quakers, who are despised and everywhere spoken against, as People not fit to live . . . we have been a Suffering People under every Power and Change, and under every Profession of Religion, that hath been, and born the outward Power in the Nation these Twelve Years. . . . Even some [have been] persecuted and prisoned till Death . . . and this done, not for the wronging of any Man, nor the breach of any just Law of the Nation, nor for Evil-doing, nor desiring any Evil, or wishing hurt to any Man, but for Conscience sake towards God, because we could not bow to their Worship."

Fell's statement emphasized that their religious resistance to practices such as taking oaths in no way implied any rejection of lawful governing authorities. "Our Intentions and Endeavours are and shall be Good, True, Honest, and Peacable towards them," she declared, "and that we do Love, Own, and Honour the King, and these present Governors, so far as they do Rule for God, and his Truth, and do not impose anything upon peoples Consciences. . . . We do not desire any Liberty that may justly offend anyone's Conscience; the Liberty we do desire is, that we may keep our consciences clear and void of Offence towards God and toward Men, and that we may enjoy our civil Rights and Liberties of Subjects as Freeborn Englishmen."[9] (That little caveat, "so far as they do Rule for God," would not have escaped the scrutiny of any perceptive monarch and goes a long way toward explaining why a religious movement committed to nonviolence was nevertheless viewed as threatening to the established order.)

•

Margaret married George Fox in 1669, eleven years after her first husband's death. While Thomas Fell was alive, and during her long period as a widow, Margaret worked closely with Fox as one of the main founders of Quakerism. It is somewhat surprising, although Quakers were regarded—even by their religious enemies—as people of unusual rectitude, that there were so few rumors of any improper sexual relations between Margaret and Fox. Their marriage was solemnized and witnessed at a large Quaker meeting (attended by many non-Quakers as well) on October 27, 1669. The form of Quaker marriage was and is simple: the bride and groom stand before the congregation, with no clerical officiant, and declare their love for and intention to be faithful to each other. After Fell's wedding to Fox, the marriage certificate was signed by ninety-four witnesses, including Margaret's children by her first marriage. The certificate of marriage was legal (and remains in a county record office in England today), but the religious form of the ceremony was not. Although there were few accusations of sexual impropriety before their wedding, the nature of the Quaker ceremony would be used to insult Margaret when she was imprisoned during the winter of 1683. Her indictment for holding Quaker meetings in her home and refusing to attend an officially approved church was addressed to "Margaret Fell, widow," with the clear intention to declare her second marriage illegal and sinful in the eyes of church and state. After she was released from jail, Margaret protested the use of her first husband's name in the indictment and reminded the judges, the king, and the public that she had been married to George Fox for fourteen years.

It is unlikely that Margaret's pleas on behalf of religious dissenters would have been respectfully received, or that she would have been seen personally by Cromwell or King Charles, had these men considered her anything but a morally unimpeachable representative of her faith. Fox's intellectual appeal to women is certainly easy to understand; a frequent cause of his falling out with clerics of other Christian faiths was his insistence not only that women had souls but that their souls, spiritual faculties, and intellectual abilities were as capable of full development as those of men. Even the most misogynistic of the church fathers in the early Christian era did believe that women possessed souls, but not that women's intellectual (not to mention theological) faculties were equal to those of men.

Most scholars agree that Fox and Fell considered their marriage a primarily, even exclusively, spiritual union in which they joined forces as advocates of Quakerism. They were separated for much of their marriage, by imprisonment (his and hers), Fox's frequent travels abroad to spread the faith, Margaret's religious activism throughout England, and her heavy family responsibilities to children and grandchildren. However, the sexlessness of the marriage is certainly debatable, and the scholars' views may well have been influenced by the ages of the bride and bridegroom at the time of their marriage. Fox was in his mid-forties and Margaret in her mid-fifties in 1669. Many people (yes, even respected historians) still have trouble imagining that a man in his forties might desire a woman in her fifties—even if the most powerful component of their relationship was a spiritual affinity. Fox also took care to renounce, in writing, any claim to the estate bequeathed by Margaret's first husband. Under English law at the time, he could have assumed total control of her fortune and spent it as he wished. This renunciation of male financial privilege was as much a statement of Quaker religious principles of equality as of Fox's feelings for his bride.

.

The birth of Protestantism—whether Anglicanism in England, Calvinism in Switzerland and France, or Lutheranism in Germany—took place in a pre-Enlightenment world. It should not therefore be surprising that many of these denominations were as insistent on their absolute rightness and righteousness as the Catholic Church had been (and remained). Seventeenth-century Quakerism, however, belongs to the early Age of Enlightenment, to an era when religious toleration was beginning to be seen by pioneering Enlightenment thinkers like John Locke not only as politically desirable but as morally virtuous. In a paradox that makes perfect sense, the same period was one of fierce religious intolerance in England and on the continent, with the Catholic Church making a violent and repressive effort to return to the pre-Reformation status quo in France, and conservative Protestants attempting to stamp out nonconformist Protestantism, which included Quakerism and all of the Anabaptist sects, in England and Europe. In the 1680s, when Margaret Fell was working ceaselessly for the release of Quaker prisoners in England, Locke was writing some of his most important works promoting religious toleration. Fell, then nearly seventy, was imprisoned in the fall of 1683—heading into the coldest winter ever recorded in England. She was released after six weeks, but more than a hundred religious dissenters died in prison, mainly of starvation and hypothermia, during that winter. By 1685, some fifteen hundred Quakers were imprisoned. Many Quaker meeting houses were either reduced to rubble or nailed shut, and the Friends were forced to meet outdoors through the "great, severe, and long frost and snow . . . when the river Thames was so frozen up that horses, coaches, and cars could pass to and fro on it." When children tried to keep the Quaker meetings going in the absence of their imprisoned parents, some were put in the stocks or imprisoned themselves.[10] (Quakers, unlike other religious denominations, considered children equals in the spiritual sphere and allowed them to speak at meetings. They also opposed corporal punishment—a natural outgrowth of their belief in nonviolence.) In no other religion of her time and no earlier era could a fully articulate female convert like Margaret Fell have functioned as she did—as an advocate for her specific beliefs and for freedom of conscience in general, in both the public and private spheres. The very word used by the Quakers for conversion—"convincement"—implies a voluntary, individual process and rules out the forced conversions long practiced by the Catholic Church, and more recently adopted by both Calvinists and Lutherans when Anabaptists appeared on their turf. Like other Christian denominations, Quakerism was a proselytizing religion, but argument—not violence—was its only method of obtaining convincements.

Quakers were certainly as interested in converting Jews, for instance, as every other Christian sect was at the time. In 1651, the famous rabbi Menasseh ben Israel, a leader of the Amsterdam Jewish community originally formed by refugees from persecution in Spain and Portugal, wrote to Cromwell to request the admission of Jews to England. (King Edward I had expelled all Jews from England in 1290, and Cromwell did permit them to return—in exchange for considerable contributions to the treasury—in 1657.) Throughout the 1650s and early 1660s, both Jewish and Christian messianists believed that the coming of the Messiah was imminent and would take place in the year 1666. Faithful Jews were waiting for the first Messiah, and Christians, including Quakers, for the second coming of their Messiah, who had already walked the earth. Ben Israel alluded to this common belief in his plea to Cromwell, which observed that the "opinion of many Christians and mine concurre herein; that we both believe that the restoring time of our Nation into their Native County, is very near at hand . . . and therefore this remains only in my judgment, before the Messia come and restore our Nation, that first we must have our seat here [in England] likewise."[11] (Exactly why the appearance of the Messiah should have anything to do with the admission of Jews to England is unclear. In any case, Cromwell did wait to readmit the Jews until the fateful year 1666 had passed, as all such deadlines for Judgment Day have passed since then.)

Before and after the re-entry of Jews into England, there were numerous connections between English Quakers and Dutch Jews. Between 1656 and 1658, Fell wrote four tracts specifically appealing to the Jews to convert; she was the first Quaker writer whose works were translated into Hebrew and Dutch, and her books were imported into Holland. Her initial appeal to the Jews was titled *For Manasseth-ben-Israel: The Call of the Jews Out of Babylon*. Although as convinced as other Christians that those who rejected Christ would be judged harshly at the Second Coming, Fell in *For Manasseth* does not actually mention Jesus but says, "This is the Way, walk in it." She does not cite the New Testament but tactfully confines herself to Old Testament imagery. Above all, Fell emphasizes what she sees as the connection between her particular branch of Christianity and Judaism. Among the words substituted for Christ in her early tracts, she uses "Light," "Living Water," "Spirit," "Tree of Righteousness," and "Ancient of Days."[12] Nowhere in Fell's writings is there any mention of the cornerstone of Christian persecution of Jews—the notion that the Jewish "race" was tainted by hereditary guilt for the crucifixion of Jesus. Hers was a forward-looking appeal based on the joy that would come to anyone who saw the light of God, rather than a backward-looking condemnation of Jews for deicide. This is not to say that believing Jews would have been any more responsive to Fell's appeals (or those of any other Quaker) than to harsher Christian appeals charging them with deicide. The important point is that Jews who were unpersuaded and unconvinced by Quaker proselytizing had nothing to fear from missionaries dedicated to nonviolence.

One of the more intriguing connections between Quakers in England and Jews in Amsterdam—accepted by many but no means all scholars—involves the philosopher Baruch Spinoza, who was excommunicated by the Amsterdam synagogue in 1656, when he was just

twenty-three. William Ames, another member of the founding generation of English Quakers, led what proved to be a fruitless effort to
convert Amsterdam Jews at roughly the same time. While in Holland,
he wrote a letter to Fell describing a meeting with an apostate Jew who
may well have been Spinoza. "There is a Jew at Amsterdam," Ames
wrote, "that by the Jews is Cast out (as he himself and others sayeth)
because he owneth no other teacher but the light and he sent for me
and I spoke to him and he was pretty tender . . . and he said to read
of Moses and the prophets without which was nothing to him except
he came to know it within. . . . I gave order that one of the Dutch
copies of thy book should be given to him and he sent me word he
would Come to our meeting but in the meantime I was imprisoned."[13]
Since Ames's letter to Fell was written in 1657, both the timing and the
description do fit Spinoza. Ames himself, despite the greater tolerance
extended to Quakers in the Netherlands than in his native England,
wound up at one point in the city insane asylum in Rotterdam, where
he was visited by Job's comforters in the person of Dutch Reformed
ministers attempting to show him the error of his missionary ways.

•

No account of Margaret Fell's life as a Quaker would be complete
without acknowledging that her conversion—or convincement—
provided her with worldly opportunities inaccessible at that time to
most women, regardless of their social station and religion. They also
gave her a way to combine her work in the public sphere with her
role as the mother of a large family. Proselytizing on behalf of a new
religion—unless a woman happened to have inherited a throne—may
have been the only semi-respectable way for a wife and mother to
step onto the public stage. It may sound strange to apply the adjective
"worldly" to activities promoting a faith that rejected the rituals and
riches of established churches. But how else can one describe the life
of a woman who used not only her Inner Light but her valuable estate
and web of family and social connections to speak her truth to the
highest powers in the land and, ultimately, to help transform a new
religion from the ridiculed creed of a persecuted, oddball fringe to a
respectable and respected minority? Furthermore, Fell also stood up
for her own sex by organizing women's meetings as a regular feature

of life in the Society of Friends. These meetings were based on considerable female autonomy and had nothing to do with the women's subservience preached by Paul, or with the segregation of men and women in Orthodox Jewish rituals. The Quaker groups did, however, honor conventional expectations about female virtues by emphasizing what were considered the special gifts of women with regard to providing relief for the poor, aiding prisoners and the homeless, and, above all, educating children. It would certainly be a grievous anachronism to describe Fell as a feminist in the modern sense, or the women's meetings as seventeenth-century consciousness-raising groups. Fox was a strong supporter, but many other Quaker men initially opposed Fell's activities for reasons ranging from antagonism toward all formal organization to resentment at having to provide financial support for "women's work." There may even have been suspicion of meetings that brought together women of varying social positions and levels of education. Who knew what they might be talking about without any men listening? Perhaps the men did fear that a certain amount of seditious talk against patriarchy might be heard at gatherings that were for women only.

One major impact of the women's meetings, in both England and later in America, was the establishment of Friends' schools and an emphasis on education for all. Because Quaker boys and girls were educated together, in the New World as well as the Old, the literacy rate among Quaker women was unusually high. In 1692, the women's meeting in Fell's home county of Lancashire pushed hard for the appointment of teachers in every Quaker community. This recommendation was initially resisted (again, mainly by men) but eventually became the norm in every sizable Quaker congregation on both sides of the Atlantic. The nineteenth-century woman suffrage movement in America owed much to the emphasis placed on education by Fell and her contemporaries in England. (Lucretia Mott, the famous American abolitionist and suffragist, played the pivotal role in organizing the 1848 Seneca Falls convention, which marks the beginning of the nineteenth-century women's rights movement in the United States. As a devout Quaker, she denounced the discrimination against women that remained within her own religion as well as others.)

Although Fell was not a crusader for women's rights in either the nineteenth- or twentieth-century sense, she spoke in an authoritative,

often aggressive manner that had nothing to do with traditional images
of desirable womanhood in England or anywhere else. It is in her proselytizing for Quakerism that Fell's sometimes downright contemptuous voice comes through. As the historian Bonnelyn Kunze notes, Fell
often wrote to her theological opponents in a "polemical style . . . not
unusual for religious discourse in her era."[14] It was unusual, though,
for a woman to employ the sort of invective Fell displayed in a letter
to Allen Smallwood, the Anglican priest of Carlisle. "Thou has manifested thy ignorance and unskillfulness in the things of God," Fell
declared, "though thou art called a Doctor and art got up in as high
as thou could. . . . Thou never had the true knowledge of the Father
nor of the Son . . . whereby the simple and innocent might be deceived
and beguiled . . . [by] thee who art outwardly appearing to be great
and in esteem, but it is in that which will vanish as the dust before
the wind."[15] These are not the words of a deferential gentlewoman, or,
for that matter, of a Quaker who found it easy to practice the humility exalted by her faith. One can only wonder if Fell, in the silence of
a Quaker meeting where Friends meditate and consider their lives,
reflected upon the sin of pride.

This arrogant strain is seldom evident, however, in Fell's rich trove
of correspondence with her children and grandchildren. Her mission to promote her faith began with her family: All of her daughters
and many of her grandchildren married Quakers. The Fell daughters became leaders in the Quaker movement themselves, and many
of their signatures can be found on petitions protesting government
persecution. In her large family, only her son, George, opposed his
mother's religious activities.

After Fox died in 1691, Margaret spent nearly all of her second
widowhood at Swarthmoor—the estate to which her second husband
had renounced any claim. But she remained actively involved, through
her extensive correspondence, with a Quaker movement that, as it
became more respectable and established, was developing more ritual-
istic practices and rules than Margaret deemed appropriate for those
who sought to live by their Inner Light rather than social conformity.
One of her best-known letters to the Quaker community, written in
1700, when she was eighty-six, sharply criticized the relatively recent
custom—it would become a requirement—of wearing drab gray
clothes. Fell regarded outward conformity of dress as a haughty prac-

tice intended to designate Quakers as a special, identifiable, and better group than others. "Let us beware of this," she wrote, "of separating or looking upon ourselves to be more holy, than in deed and in truth we are. Away with these whimsical, narrow imaginations, and let the spirit of God which he hath given us, lead us and guide us. . . .

> But Christ Jesus saith, that we must take not thought what we shall eat, or what we shall drink or what we shall put on; but bids us consider the lilies how they grow in more royalty than Solomon. But contrary to this, they say we must look at no colours, nor make anything that is changeable colours as the hills are, nor sell them nor wear them. But we must be all in one dress, and one colour. This is a silly poor gospel. It is more fit for us to be covered with God's eternal Spirit, and clothed with his eternal Light, which leads us and guides us into righteousness and to live righteously and justly and holily in this present evil world.[16]

It is impossible not to like a woman who, having devoted her life after conversion to spreading her new religion, warns against confusing inner faith with dreary outer garb and signifying a conformity as rigid as the latest worldly fashion. Goodness, for Fell, could be clad in red silk just as easily as in gray homespun. Not only her words but her household account books, which record many purchases of attractive and costly cloth, say so.

Her mind intact, Fell died at Swarthmoor on April 23, 1702, at age eighty-seven. Following an early Quaker custom, she was buried with no stone marking her grave.

11

RELIGIOUS CHOICE AND
EARLY ENLIGHTENMENT THOUGHT

No man's mind can possibly lie wholly at the disposition of another,
for no one can willingly transfer his natural right of free reason
and judgment, or be compelled to do so.

—BENEDICTUS (BARUCH) SPINOZA,
Tractatcus Theologico-Politicus, 1670

That any man should think fit to cause another man—whose
salvation he heartily desires—to expire in torments, and that even
in an unconverted state, would, I confess, seem very strange to me,
and I think, to any other also. But nobody, surely, will ever believe
that such a carriage can proceed from charity, love, or goodwill.

—JOHN LOCKE, "A LETTER CONCERNING TOLERATION," 1689

Toleration is not the opposite of Intolerance, but is the counterfeit
of it. Both are despotisms. The one assumes to itself the right of
withholding Liberty of Conscience, and the other of granting it.

—THOMAS PAINE, *The Rights of Man,* 1791

FROM THE FIRST STIRRINGS of the Enlightenment in the mid-
seventeenth century through the High Enlightenment of the late
eighteenth century, both the morality and the social utility of forced
conversions were challenged by philosophers, and eventually by states-
men of the age of reason. Margaret Fell's embrace of Quakerism represents only one familiar type of seventeenth-century conversion—a
"conversion of conscience," often involving a transition from one of the
mainstream Protestant denominations to nonconformist Protestantism. Another kind of conversion—what my grade-school nuns used

to call a "conversion of convenience"—was encouraged by religious intermarriage, as it has been throughout history. The few religious paintings among Johannes Vermeer's surviving works, for example, are dated within two years after his conversion to Catholicism, when he married a Catholic, Catharina Bolnes, in 1653.* Then there were forced conversions under the least tolerant governments, most notably in France under Louis XIV, who, during his fifty-four-year reign, offered Huguenots the same choice that Spanish and Portuguese monarchs had offered Jews and Muslims two centuries earlier: convert or be prepared to lose everything, including your life.†

The religious turmoil and violence accompanying the Reformation, the Counter-Reformation, and the proliferation of Protestant sects varied greatly according to the national character and traditions of each people and state, the degree of political power wielded by the majority religion, and the disposition (in a temperamental as well as a political sense) of various monarchs. By the middle of the seventeenth century, however, it was clear in England and every country on the continent that the existence of so many religious denominations challenged the fundamental rationale for the legitimacy of forced conversion. That rationale, played out in states where the divine right of kings was coupled with the divine authority of the church, took for granted the willful sinfulness of the religious dissenter as a threat to public order. The obvious relativity of divine truth in societies where the voice of God said different things to different people only encouraged absolute monarchs like Louis, supported by religious authorities, in their effort to deny the obvious by forcing their subjects to recant "heretical" beliefs.

The Enlightenment was a process, not an event. Nothing demon-

---

* Religious intermarriage in the seventeenth century, even in the Netherlands, the most tolerant country in Europe, was a serious matter that nearly always involved the conversion of one spouse to the other's faith. Little is known about Vermeer's life, and the extent of his devotion to his adopted faith remains a matter of dispute among scholars, but he lived in the house of his mother-in-law, Maria Thins, in an area of Delft known as Papists' Corner. The Vermeers, who had fifteen children (eleven of whom survived infancy), named one of their sons Ignatius, after the founder of the Jesuit order, Ignatius of Loyola. Maria Thins had many connections among Jesuits in Holland—some of them wealthy enough to be art patrons.

† The boy who would one day be known as the "Sun King" was crowned at age fifteen, in 1654, but his rule as an absolute adult monarch, unanswerable to a chief minister, began in 1661 and continued until his death in 1715.

strates that more clearly with regard to religion than the philosophical gap between John Locke's use of the word "toleration" in his famous essays on religion, at the end of the seventeenth century, and Thomas Paine's dismissal, only a century later, of the idea that any rulers should feel entitled to congratulate themselves for allowing wide latitude in religious practices and beliefs. George Washington, in his second year as president of the fledgling United States, would underline the distance between the limited toleration expounded by Locke and other early Enlightenment thinkers and the liberty guaranteed by the First Amendment to the new U.S. Constitution—itself a product of the High Enlightenment. In an extraordinary letter to the Jewish community of Newport, Rhode Island, Washington would declare in 1790, "It is now no more that toleration is spoken of, as if it was by the indulgence of one class of people, that another enjoyed the exercise of their inherent natural rights. For happily the Government of the United States, which gives to bigotry no sanction, to persecution no assistance requires only that they who live under its protection should demean themselves as good citizens."[1]

It is remarkable, given the long history of violent religious oppression and repression in Europe, that it took only one century for the most advanced forms of Enlightenment thought to progress from a limited toleration of religious pluralism to the assumption of freedom of conscience as a natural human right. It cannot be emphasized enough that seventeenth-century toleration was not tolerance in the modern sense, which implies, at least in the West, that one religion is as good as another. Tolerationism, at the dawn of the Enlightenment, meant not that you approved of your neighbor's differing religious beliefs or thought that he might be as right in his own way as you were in yours, but that you would refrain from inflicting violence on him in this world for not sharing your view of how to achieve salvation in the next. You would suffer the heretic or the infidel to live—a not-inconsiderable accomplishment by the standard of recent as well as ancient history. This limited tolerance, which Washington rightly dismissed as insufficient to fulfill the young American republic's constitutional guarantee of complete liberty of conscience, was still a revolutionary idea everywhere in Europe in the second half of the seventeenth century. The voices of religious tolerationists—whether they took a moderate, limited stance like Locke or the rarer absolutist freethought position of Baruch a.k.a. Benedictus Spinoza—were greatly outnumbered by the voices of those who defended and encouraged religious intolerance.

The historically intolerant Catholic Church was joined, as we have seen, by so-called magisterial Protestants in their attacks on heretics. The term "magisterial," in this context, refers to mainstream Reformation figures such as Luther, Calvin, and Zwingli, who (like Catholics) supported the right of civil magistrates to enforce uniform religious belief. Nonmagisterial or, as they are more commonly called, nonconformist Protestants, including Quakers and Anabaptists, opposed any association between religion and government and were therefore considered heretics by both Catholics and mainstream Protestants. The last two decades of the seventeenth century, in which both Spinoza's and Locke's writings were circulated among the small but influential educated classes of all European countries, were also characterized by a level of religious repression and forced conversion that many today (especially in the United States, which escaped this history) associate with the Dark Ages rather than with the dawn of the Enlightenment.

This was true throughout most of Europe with the exception of the Netherlands, a de facto haven of tolerance. Toleration of religious pluralism prevailed even though the Dutch Reformed Church—one of the most dour offshoots of Calvinism—was the only religion receiving public funds. Things were so much worse for minority religions nearly everywhere else on the continent. Louis XIV's repeal of the Edict of Nantes meant that, even as Locke was writing his essays on religious toleration, Huguenot children in France were being taken from their parents' homes at age seven—the "age of reason," according to the church—to be educated as Catholics.* Before 1680, there were roughly nine hundred thousand Huguenots in France, making up about 5 percent of the population. By the end of the 1680s, it is estimated that seven hundred thousand French Huguenots had converted to Catholicism. (If anyone believes those were voluntary conversions

---

* Seven is the age at which the church historically deemed children to be morally responsible for their actions. Catholic children made their First Communion, and were also obligated to take part regularly in the sacrament of Penance, when they reached that age. To the modern mind, it may be somewhat unclear why this was used as a rationale for wrenching children from their parents, but the general idea was that at seven a child would be capable of "freely" choosing Catholicism if exposed to Catholic teachings— which, of course, would be impossible in a Huguenot family.

of conscience, she might also want to place a bid at auction for a bridge between Manhattan and Brooklyn. Many of the Huguenot converts to Catholicism undoubtedly continued to profess their original faith in secret, or Protestants would not exist—which they do—in today's France.) Another two hundred thousand Huguenots left France, although it was a crime to do so, for the Netherlands and England. As John Marshall notes in his magisterial (in the nonreligious sense) work *John Locke, Toleration, and Early Enlightenment Culture* (2006), the exile of the Huguenots in the 1680s gave rise to the widespread use of the term "refugee" in the modern sense as a definition of those fleeing religious or political persecution.[2]

Moreover, England itself—despite the horror of English Protestants at the persecution of the Huguenots across the channel—was hardly a tolerant society. Seven years after Locke's first letter on religious toleration was circulated in 1689, Thomas Aikenhead, a twenty-year-old Edinburgh medical student, became the last person to be executed in England or Scotland for blasphemy. He was said to have mocked the Trinity, characterized the dual nature of Jesus as God and man as a logical impossibility, and, worst of all, expressed the wish on a cold Scottish day to find warmth in hell. He was convicted on the testimony of five terrified fellow students who had been his friends and confidants. It was said that Aikenhead, as he mounted the scaffold, carried a Bible to attest to his contrition. It seems unlikely, if he did carry a Bible, that the action represented his true beliefs, since, on the morning of his execution, he wrote a letter to his friends stating, "It is a principle innate and co-natural to every man to have an insatiable inclination to the truth, and to seek for it as for hid treasure."[3] Aikenhead must have considered himself fortunate to face the hangman's noose instead of the more painful death by burning at the stake that had awaited most heretics at the beginning of the seventeenth century.

The distinction of having been the last person in the British Isles to be executed for heresy by burning belonged to one Edward Wightman, a cloth trader. Wightman, who was drawn to a particularly strict form of Puritanism that rejected the Book of Common Prayer (as heretical a position as rejecting the King James Bible during the reign of James I), eventually wound up quarreling with church authorities about everything from demonic possession to—what else?—the Trinity. On his execution day, Wightman screamed and recanted his views when he felt the first heat of the flames. As a local history of the town of Burton-on-Trent recounts, "A written retraction was prepared and Edward, in pain and weakness, orally agreed as it was read to him. Later, however, no longer fearing the flames, he refused to sign the retraction and blasphemed louder than before."[4] After the Wightman case, King James decided that burning heretics had no exemplary value and that religious dissenters would be imprisoned in solitary confinement rather than burned publicly (though, as can be seen from Aikenhead's hanging in 1697, that mercy was not extended to bar other forms of capital punishment for religious dissent).

The penalty of burning occupies a special place in the history of the criminalization of both religious and political dissent. Throughout Europe, burning at the stake was originally a punishment reserved for women convicted of treason; this was considered more merciful than the punishment inflicted on treasonous men—being hanged, cut down alive, and drawn and quartered. From the late Middle Ages through the seventeenth century, however, burning was imposed on both sexes for heresy, blasphemy, and, above all, witchcraft. In many instances, the charge of witchcraft involved not only the alleged conjuring of demonic forces but the seduction of others from whatever the "true faith" was considered to be by the governing authorities. The right of the English king to sentence heretics to death by burning, instituted in 1401 in the reign of Henry IV, was only removed by Parliament in 1677, although courts still had the power to impose such sentences.* Another 114 years would pass before the idea that there ought to be some limits on penalties imposed by all government institutions would find full expression in the Eighth Amendment to the U.S. Constitution, which prohibits "cruel and unusual punishment." (The definition of "cruel and unusual" naturally remains the core issue in the continuing procession of American court cases about everything from mandatory sentences to capital punishment.)

---

* The law, *De Heretico Comburendo,* was aimed at the Lollards, followers of John Wycliffe. Wycliffe translated the Bible into Middle English, and his was the first vernacular translation to be widely used by those who could read. The literate population at the time consisted almost entirely of priests, monks, and some members of the nobility. Nevertheless, making the Bible available to even the small numbers of the literate, about forty years before the invention of the printing press, was considered a serious threat to religious orthodoxy.

One of the most striking example of the degree of religious intolerance in Restoration England was the 1670 trial of William Penn, the future founder of the commonwealth of Pennsylvania. Penn was charged with rioting for holding a Quaker meeting outdoors. The al fresco services were necessary because Charles II had ordered the destruction of all meeting places for dissident Protestants. In what would become an ironic historical footnote, the task of reducing nonconformist Protestant churches to rubble was supervised by Christopher Wren, the architect of Saint Paul's Cathedral, in his capacity as surveyor general of England. There are no records of Wren's personal feelings about building one of the most glorious examples of Restoration church architecture while presiding over the destruction of other, more modest places of worship.

Throughout Penn's trial, he foreshadowed Locke and Adam Smith by linking the right to liberty of conscience and worship with the right to property. Penn argued before the jury in the Old Bailey that unless the "ancient fundamental laws which relate to liberty and property" also apply to people regardless of their religion, no one "can say that he hath the right to the coat upon his back."[5] Penn's ability to speak eloquently and wittily in his own defense had been demonstrated at the opening of the trial in an exchange with the presiding officer:

PENN: I desire you would let me know by what law it is you prosecute me, and upon what law you ground my indictment.
JUDGE: Upon the common-law.
PENN: Where is that common-law?
JUDGE: You must not think that I am able to run up so many years and over so many adjudged cases, which we call common-law, to satisfy your curiosity.
PENN: This answer I am sure is very short for my question, for if it be common, it should not be so hard to produce.[6]

The jury was persuaded by Penn's argument and refused to convict him, and the Recorder of the Court responded by announcing that he at last understood "the reason of the policy and prudence of the Spaniards, in suffering the Inquisition among them." He added, in a statement that would have been considered treasonous at the time of the Spanish Armada, that "certainly it will never be well with us, till something like the Spanish Inquisition be in England."[7] The Recorder, Sir John Howell, then jailed the jury members when they refused to change their verdict. Penn was kept in prison for failing to pay a fine, imposed because he refused to take off his hat in court. A year later, a higher court reversed the decision that had imprisoned the jury (though not the incarceration of Penn). But the very fact that a judge had cited the Inquisition as a desirable example for England—and had directly sabotaged the cherished institution of trial by jury—demonstrated the degree of intolerance in a country that prided itself (sometimes justifiably, sometimes not) on being more tolerant and observant of individual rights than the Catholic nations of Europe.

•

In France, there were no juries to stand up to the Crown when it came to religious dissent. Forced conversion—by any means necessary—was the aim and core of the religious violence against Huguenots both before and after the revocation of the Edict of Nantes. One matter-of-fact document, dated 1680, in the town of Alençon, listed all of the local Huguenot children scheduled to be taken forcibly from their parents. In the margins, the man in charge had written, "Take Jean and Anne Marie," "Take Louise and Marie," and "Take Anne if she is in [good enough] condition." Anne, if she was too sick to be safely moved, would presumably be taken later, when she was well enough to begin her new life in a new Catholic home.[8] One is reminded by this cool bureaucratic memo, resembling earlier accounts kept by the Spanish Inquisition, that the Nazis were not the first to keep unashamed, meticulous records of the most repulsive and revealing details of their crimes.

It is against this background—in which all societies upheld, to a greater or lesser degree, the right of the community and the state to control the consciences of their citizens—that the importance of the early Enlightenment must be assessed. This was a world where nearly everyone believed in witchcraft and in subjecting witches to the death penalty, and where governments decided which worship services could be conducted in public, which could be conducted only in private, and which could not be held at all. It was a world that had, in some ways, changed immensely since the heyday of the Spanish Inquisition in the late fifteenth and sixteenth centuries, but in other ways had changed very little. One thing that had changed was the insistence of large numbers of people in the realm of Christendom on the right to choose new, different forms of Jesus-centered faith. What had not changed was the determination of the leaders of dominant religions, backed by the power of government, to force people to convert to their own faiths or to keep them from converting to another.

.

In this environment, it is not surprising that thinkers advocating religious toleration were greatly outnumbered by philosophers and theologians, Catholic and Protestant, advocating stringent religious intolerance as a moral and political necessity. Only the toleration-ist writers are widely read today (insofar as any seventeenth-century thinkers can be said to be read "widely"), because religious toleration proved to be a necessary, though far from sufficient, condition for the establishment of modern political democracies.

Of the then outnumbered tolerationists, the two whose works are especially important in terms of the future Enlightenment argument against forced conversion are Locke and Spinoza.* Spinoza, the outcast Jew whose ancestors had fled the Inquisition in Portugal, was called an atheist because he was far ahead of his time in upholding absolute liberty of thought rather than mere toleration. Locke, by contrast, was a man only somewhat ahead of his time. Contemporary (and, later, Enlightenment) opinion was always split between critics who consid-ered Locke too orthodox a Christian and those who considered his form of Christianity a mask for "infidelity." Both views have some validity: in retrospect, Locke's essays may be seen as a bridge between the religious and political culture of the early Enlightenment (and late

---

* There are many, especially in the Anglo-American world, who would include Thomas Hobbes (1588–1679). Hobbes's writings in old age—he went on publishing prolifically until his death at age ninety-one—did show certain affinities with Spinoza. However, the views presented in *Leviathan* (1651), which endorses many kinds of censorship by the sovereign and provides wide latitude for deeming ideas subversive, could not be further from either Spinoza or Locke.

Reformation) and the more radical Enlightenment that influenced many American as well as French revolutionaries. Spinoza's philosophy, by contrast, was a beacon from a far-off lighthouse, a message from a world that did not even begin to take shape until the late eighteenth century. One may read Spinoza's exegesis of divine action, for example, without finding any contradiction between his philosophy and Darwin's theory of evolution by means of natural selection. "By the help of God," Spinoza wrote in the 1660s, "I mean the fixed and unchangeable order of nature or the chain of natural events: for I have said before and shown elsewhere that the universal laws of nature, according to which all things exist and are determined, are only another name for the eternal decrees of God, which always involve truth and necessity."[9]

.

Spinoza and Locke were exact contemporaries, born in 1632 in Amsterdam and Wrington (a parish in Somerset), respectively. Unfortunately, the two men never met: Spinoza had been dead for six years by the time Locke arrived in the Netherlands as a political refugee in 1683. Locke left England because he feared that he might be persecuted on account of the political problems of his friend and patron, the Earl of Shaftesbury, and he did not return to his native land until after the Glorious Revolution of 1688. (After that revolution, the Dutch William of Orange and his Protestant English wife, Mary, succeeded the Catholic James II on the throne of England. The settlement surrounding these events confirmed the Church of England, once and for all, as the state-established religion.)

It is impossible to overstate the importance of the Netherlands as a shelter, providing a protective cultural space for the refugee writers and thinkers who helped give birth to the Enlightenment. Despite the status of the Dutch Reformed Church as the state-financed religion, there was no legal compulsion (as there was in Calvinist Geneva and sometimes in England) for people to attend services. There were certainly advantages in belonging to the "public" church for those who wished to hold public office, but there was no punishment for those who kept their distance from the Dutch Calvinists, or even for those, like Vermeer, who apparently converted to another faith. The power and severity of the Dutch Reformed Church administration varied from city to city, and the conservatism of Dutch Calvinists was, ironically, reinforced by the arrival of even more conservative Calvinist Huguenot refugees from France in the 1680s. There was a double irony attached to the large-scale arrival of French Calvinist refugees, in that Holland also provided a haven for the few tolerationist French Protestant philosophers, most notably Pierre Bayle. The lack of national uniformity in enforcement of anti-heresy policies produced an everyday society of religious pluralism that simply did not exist elsewhere on the continent. (The relative liberty of conscience exercised by residents of the Netherlands is best described by the difficult-to-translate Dutch term *gedogen,* which means, roughly, "technically illegal but tolerated and not punished." Today, the term is used to describe Dutch legal practices regarding prostitution and the sale of marijuana.)

Gedogen was far from a perfect solution for seventeenth-century religious conflicts. Religious pluralism (especially with regard to Catholics and anti-Trinitarian Protestants) could never be taken for granted, since it was never guaranteed and was actually opposed by many laws. In Rotterdam, for example, where the English Quaker missionary William Ames had been thrown into the city insane asylum in 1657, disruptions of Quaker meetings and violence against Quaker meeting places remained a regular feature of life into the 1690s. When Quakers protested, the response of the civil authorities was to blame the victim by banning Quaker gatherings, thereby ensuring that there would be no further violence directed against them.

And yet the Netherlands continued to provide an environment in which dissenting intellectuals of every variety, from every country, could work out their ideas in relative peace and security. In no area of culture was this more apparent than in the Dutch publishing business, one of the marvels of the seventeenth-century Western world. The main reason we know so much about religious dissent in Holland is that the dissidents were constantly publishing first-person accounts of their travails—something impossible in England and France. Ames, for example, wrote an entertaining personal history, in Dutch, of the many visits made to him in prison by Dutch Reformed ministers. In *An Account of the Persecution and Imprisonment of William Ames and Maerten Maertensz,* Ames noted that the preachers disagreed on whether the Quakers should be banished from Holland, burned at the stake, or burned with their books. The story of his incarceration appeared in 1659, not long after his release.

By the 1680s, the Netherlands had five cities with concentrations of important publishers—Amsterdam, Rotterdam, Leiden, The Hague, and Utrecht. There were more urban publishing centers in Holland than in France, England, and Germany combined. Because of its large Jewish refugee community, the Netherlands also replaced Venice as the center of European Jewish book publishing. In addition to printing classic Judaic texts for export to Jewish communities throughout Europe, some Jewish publishers even produced non-Jewish books—including, in at least one case, the New Testament. The Jewish printer Joseph Athias was granted the exclusive right to print English Bibles for export by the States of Holland in 1670 and even claimed to have produced a million Bibles for the reading of every "plow boy or servant girl" in the British Isles.[10] (The numbers in this claim were surely exaggerated. Athias had undoubtedly heard about the doomed William Tyndale's promise that if God spared his life, Tyndale's vernacular translation would "cause a boy that driveth the plow in England to know more about the Scriptures" than theologians.)

The economic dependence of the Netherlands on trade, and the importance of the Jews in every aspect of international trade and finance conducted within the Dutch states, was the critical factor creating a sense of safety for the Jewish community that did not exist elsewhere in Europe. In what was meant as a compliment to, not a criticism of, the Dutch, Spinoza remarked, "All they bother to find out, before trusting goods to anyone, is whether he is rich or poor and whether he is honest or a fraud."[11] In a society that placed a high value on honest dealing and sound financing, a Jew might feel secure—certainly more secure than Spinoza's ancestors had felt in Catholic Portugal and France. That the importance of Jews in trade and finance would not protect them from "racial" and ultimately exterminationist anti-Semitism in nineteenth- and twentieth-century Europe has little bearing on the situation of Sephardic Jews in seventeenth-century Holland. Trade was lifeblood, not a sideline, in a small country (actually, a collection of states) whose low-lying agricultural land was perilously exposed to the sea. Jewish businessmen were not merely tolerated but welcomed—a phenomenon that surprised even Quaker missionaries from England. William Caton, who, along with Ames, was among the first Quaker missionaries to Holland, wrote Margaret Fell that he had discussed religion many times with Jews, but "they could scarce endure to hear Christ mentioned." He added that although the Jews were a "high, lofty, proud and conceited people, far from the Truth . . . there is a seed among them, which God in the fulness of Time will gather into his garner."[12]

Spinoza's ancestors had fled Spain for Portugal in 1492—a move that did not prevent the family from being forcibly converted in 1498. When the Inquisition cracked down on all Portuguese Conversos in 1536, the Spinozas left the Iberian Peninsula and settled in France. Spinoza's father, Miguel, moved to Amsterdam in 1627, renounced Catholicism, and returned to the Judaism of his ancestors. It might be seen as one of the great ironies in the history of conversion that Miguel's son, Baruch, would one day be excommunicated by the Amsterdam synagogue for claiming his own right to freedom of conscience and thought.

As Rebecca Newberger Goldstein notes in her provocative study *Betraying Spinoza* (2006), Spinoza's circle included freethinking* Christians as well as longtime Jewish friends not scared off by the order of excommunication. In Amsterdam's Jewish community, excommunication was not the absolute penalty implied by its usage in Christian terminology. "Whereas others among the chastised had obediently—and sometimes desperately—sought reconciliation," Goldstein writes, "Spinoza calmly removed himself from any further form of Jewish life. Nor did Spinoza seek out another religion. In particular, he did not convert to Christianity, although it would have been convenient for him to do so. Spinoza opted for secularism at a time when the concept had not yet been formulated."[13] Like the unclassifiable Christian Servetus, Spinoza was an anti-convert. It is known that the philosopher, both before and after his excommunication by the synagogue, met with dissenting Amsterdam Protestants, including Quakers and Mennonites, who called themselves Collegiants. The term was derived from bimonthly meetings, or "colleges," in which the dissenters studied the Bible, argued with one another, and took for granted that each had the right to interpret the Scriptures for himself.

Some would contend that Spinoza opted not for secularism but simply for an individual's right to formulate his or her religious beliefs, but

* The word "freethinker" in English dates from the seventeenth century and was often used to describe not only the antireligious but denominations, such as Quakerism and, later, Unitarianism, whose members were committed to freedom of conscience for all.

this is a distinction without a difference. The right to believe or not believe as one wishes is a secular idea that vitiates every form of religion based on absolute truth claims.

It is certainly understandable that Spinoza's ideas were as repellent to rabbis as they would be, once they began circulating in print, to orthodox Christians. One can only imagine the reactions of both a rabbi and a minister of the Dutch Reformed Church if either happened to read, in 1670, this "anonymous" author's analysis of the so-called chosenness of the Jews.* When the biblical God spoke to the Hebrews, according to Spinoza, the Lord's law revealed itself "only according to the understanding of its hearers." The Jews "would have been no less blessed if God had called all men equally to salvation, nor would God have been less present to them for being equally present to others; their laws would have been no less just if they had been ordained for all, and they themselves would have been no less wise."[14] Oh my. The chosenness of a covenanted people is the foundation of historical Judaism, and insistence on the Gospel of Christ as the fulfillment of Hebrew prophecy is the foundation of Christianity. Spinoza was the philosopher who offered something to offend everyone. The inscription on the frontispiece of the *Tractatus* says it all:

> *A Theologico-Political Treatise*
> *Containing certain discussions*
> *Wherein is set forth that freedom of thought*
> *And speech not only may, without prejudice*
> *To piety and the public peace, be granted;*
> *But also may not, without danger to piety and the public*
> *peace, be withheld.*[15]

Spinoza consistently rejected the claim that only supernatural punishments and rewards could induce humans to behave virtuously, and this struck at the heart of all Christian belief. Replying to one of many who criticized him for his nonbelief in heaven and hell, Spinoza wrote, "I see in what mud this man sticks. He is one of those who would follow after his own lusts, if he were not restrained by the fear of hell.

* The *Tractatus* was first published anonymously, but the real identity of the author was known to many intellectuals in Amsterdam.

He abstains from evil actions and fulfills God's commands like a slave against his will, and for his bondage he expects to be rewarded by God with gifts far more to his taste than Divine love, and great in proportion to his original dislike of virtue."[16]

Spinoza also rejected the doctrine that the desire to sin is as evil as the actual commission of a sin, and this rejection had obvious political as well as religious implications. If looking on a woman with lust is essentially the same as actually committing adultery, then it follows that religious authorities have every right to inquire into and judge a man's beliefs—to, in Elizabeth I's words, "make windows into men's souls." And if thinking about the deficiencies of one's civil rulers is equivalent to chopping off their heads, then it follows that a government has both a right and a duty to gain access to the thoughts of its citizens. Religious and governmental authorities have that right because their power is derived not from the consent of the governed but from a divinity. Yet Spinoza insists that men be judged, whether by church or state, according to their actions alone and not their thoughts—whether suspected or publicly expressed. "If we hold to the principle that a man's loyalty to the state should be judged, like his loyalty to God, from his actions only—namely, from his charity towards his neighbours; we cannot doubt that the best government will allow freedom of philosophical speculation no less than of religious belief."[17] But the religious loyalties of men were not judged only by their charitable or uncharitable actions but by their beliefs, or in many instances suspected beliefs, about supernatural matters having nothing whatever to do with natural charity. From this passage alone, it is easy to understand why Spinoza was considered an atheist and a dangerous political as well as antireligious radical.

Spinoza would not have become the philosopher he became in a less liberal atmosphere. He might conceivably have been the same man, with the same beliefs (although that too seems doubtful), but his thoughts would certainly not have been published, circulated, and debated in the same way had they only been written "for the drawer."* The same might be said of Locke. When he arrived in Amsterdam at

---

* This expression was used by Russian writers during the Soviet period to describe writing that could never be officially published in their own country. Eventually, frustration with writing "for the drawer" gave rise to the samizdat phenomenon of the 1960s and 1970s.

age fifty-one, Locke had published nothing. During what was clearly a transformational period, he used his time in Holland to talk with other independent thinkers who had been hounded into exile by the governments and churches of their own countries. Although Spinoza was dead, Locke certainly met many of the philosopher's admirers and enemies. He was well acquainted with nonconformist Protestant Collegiants, and his later writings would advocate complete toleration for all forms of Protestantism.

At the time of Locke's death, his library contained all of Spinoza's published works as well as many political and religious disputations, in many languages, in which Spinoza's ideas were vigorously debated. Locke, like Hobbes, Adam Smith, and David Hume, is much more widely recognized than Spinoza in the United States as an influence upon the Enlightenment views of the American founders, but the more radical Spinoza's voice can be heard in both the Declaration of Independence and the Bill of Rights. It is not surprising that Thomas Jefferson's library contained Spinoza's collected works, which were more readily available at the end of the eighteenth century than in Locke's time. Goldstein observes: "We can hear Locke's influence in the phrase 'life, liberty and the pursuit of happiness' (a variation on Adam Smith's Locke-inspired 'life, liberty and the pursuit of property'), we can also catch the sound of Spinoza addressing us in Jefferson's appeal to the 'laws of nature and of nature's God.' This is the language of Spinoza's universalist religion, which makes no reference to revelation, but rather to ethical truths that can be discovered through human reason."[18]

It is generally agreed that Locke's first two complete works—his *Essay Concerning Human Understanding* and *A Letter on Religious Toleration*—were published and widely circulated in England in 1689. The date—so soon after his period of exile in Holland—leaves little doubt that they were the product of his contacts with tolerationist thinkers in Amsterdam and that his studies abroad had not been disturbed (or unduly disturbed) by English politics. But Locke had already expressed his unequivocal opposition to forced conversion in a 1667 *Essay Concerning Toleration* that was not as widely circulated as his later works.

> ... the forcible introducing of opinions keeps people off from closing with them by giving men unavoidable jealousies, that it is not truth that is thus carried on, but interest and dominion that

is sought in making proselytes by compulsion. For who takes this course to convince anyone of the certain truths of mathematics? 'Tis likely 'twill be said that those are truths on which depends not my happiness. I grant it, and am much indebted to the man that takes care I should be happy, but 'tis hard to think that that [which] comes from charity to my soul should bring such ill usage to my body, or that he is much concerned I should be happy in another world who is pleased to see me miserable in this. . . .

But, after all this, could persecution not only now and then conquer a tender faint-hearted fanatic, which yet it rarely does and that usually by the loss of two or three orthodox, could it I say at once drive in all dissenters within the pale of the church, it would not thereby secure but much more threaten the government and make the danger as much greater as it is to have a false, secret but exasperated enemy rather than a fair open adversary. . . . At least this is certain that compelling men to your opinion any other way than by convincing them of the truth of it, makes them no more your friends, than forcing the poor Indians by droves into the rivers to be baptised made them Christians.[19]

Despite Locke's opposition to all forced conversion, his overall appeal for toleration had definite limits. The first cautionary boundary was drawn around Catholics, because the Catholic Church did not recognize the religious rights of non-Catholics. "Papists are not to enjoy the benefits of toleration because where they have power they think themselves bound to deny it to others," he wrote. "For it is unreasonable that any should have a free liberty of their religion, who do not acknowledge it as a principle of theirs that nobody ought to persecute or molest another because he dissents from him in religion."[20] Unlike the judge at Penn's trial, Locke was not calling for a counter-Inquisition as a way of limiting the rights of Catholics. But he certainly was implying that the state has the right to regulate, if not the private worship, the public proselytizing of a religion that would, if it ever regained power, persecute non-Catholics.

Then there is the famous "atheist exception" to Locke's general argument for toleration. This passage is of particular importance in the United States, because it is the main argument used to this day (albeit by many who have doubtless never read Locke himself) to but-

tress the political position that the American government was founded
on religion rather than on the separation of church and state. Locke
could not have been more explicit about the atheist exception in his
writings on toleration, and he never recanted this position (although
there is some evidence in his later works that he accepted the possibility
that atheists might be good citizens even if their ideas about morality
were not based on religion). But he clearly laid out his basic objection to tolerance for atheists in his 1689 letter. *"Lastly,"* he emphasized,
"those are not to be tolerated who *deny the being of a God.* Promises,
covenants, and oaths, which are the bonds of human society, can have
no hold upon an atheist. The taking away of God, though but even in
thought, dissolves all; besides also, those that by atheism undermine
and destroy all religion, can have no pretence of religion whereupon to
challenge the privilege of a toleration."[21] Again, this passage does not
suggest that Locke wanted to burn atheists, any more than Catholics,
at the stake. Opposition to forced conversion, from the standpoint of
both civil peace and religious freedom, was an enormous step forward,
coming as it did from advocates of tolerance who were not atheists but
religious believers themselves. Locke would doubtless be described as
a "moderate" in today's political parlance (although that wishy-washy
term, generally used by members of the mainstream media who believe
devoutly that truth is always equidistant from two points, does not do
justice to him). Spinoza would probably be considered a radical or an
"extremist" by today's pundits—as he was in his own time.

The ground on which Locke and Spinoza undeniably do converge
places them both on the right side of a history that was just beginning
to assimilate the foundational principle of the age of reason—the right
of people to think for themselves. In this new world, human beings
might change their religious or political opinions, but they could
not and might not be forced to do so. The philosophers of the early
Enlightenment recognized that anyone who converts to a new ideology because his or her property or person has been threatened is most
assuredly lying, and that any religious or civil government presiding
over such forced conversions can only fear the communion of liars it
has created.

12

MIRACLES VERSUS EVIDENCE:
CONVERSION AND SCIENCE

I N AUGUST 1663, Baruch Spinoza received a letter from Henry Oldenburg, secretary of the recently founded Royal Society in London.
The Society, established in 1660, was England's first organization
dedicated to the advancement of scientific knowledge.* Oldenburg
expressed the hope that Spinoza might join intellectual forces with
Robert Boyle (1627–91), the chemist and physicist who was then the
most prominent English scientist, and "unite your abilities in striving
to advance a genuine and firmly based philosophy." He urged Spinoza "especially, by the acuteness of your mathematical mind, to continue to establish basic principles, just as I ceaselessly try to coax my
noble friend Boyle to confirm and illustrate them by experiments and
observations. . . ."[1]

Boyle, born in Ireland, was the youngest son of the first earl of Cork,
who was also the lord high treasurer of the English-ruled island (and,
as such, the epitome of the class of overlords most hated by the Irish).
He became a prolific experimental scientist, interested in everything
from the improvement of agricultural methods to the possibility of

* A group of twelve men, including Robert Boyle and Christopher Wren, met and
resolved to form an organization "for the Promoting of Physico-Mathematical Experimental Learning." In the Royal Charter granted by King Charles II in 1663, the group is
called "The Royal Society of London for Improving Natural Knowledge."

preserving foods through vacuum packing, and is best known in the history of science for his experiments on the nature of air and the relationship among gases.* Along with Robert Hooke, another member of the Royal Society, Boyle invented a vacuum pump to carry out his experiments.†

Boyle was also a devout Christian, whose theological writings were as prolific as his scientific work. The relationship among Boyle, Oldenburg, and Spinoza is one of the more revealing episodes of the rapidly changing and increasing international body of religious and scientific interchanges throughout the seventeenth century. Boyle and Spinoza indirectly conveyed their irreconcilable views about the relationship between faith and science, as well as about the limits of individual experiments in explaining the natural world, to one another via their mutual friend Oldenburg. The correspondence sheds light on the challenge posed both by experimental science and by reason-based philosophy to religious orthodoxy, and on the many contortions used by men of reason to accommodate faith (and vice versa).

The Royal Society's motto, *Nullius in verba*, which may be translated as "take no one's word for it," was unintentionally ironic in that it was a true emblem of the challenge that real science—including both experiments and naturalistic philosophy—posed to orthodox religion. Many members of the Society (including Boyle and Oldenburg) held theological beliefs incompatible with the motto, because their faith depended entirely on the sacred, unchallengeable, unverifiable accounts in the Bible.

The German-born Oldenburg (1619–77) was not himself a scientist

---

* His most famous equation, Boyle's Law, states that for a given mass of gas, at a constant temperature, the pressure exerted on the gas times the volume is a constant ($pV = C$).

† It is understandable that Boyle's research on gases would have led him to envisage the possibility of vacuum-packed foods, which depend on removing oxygen before packaging to impede the growth of bacteria. In Boyle's time, the industrial tools and procedures needed to actually produce vacuum-packed products did not exist. The history of vacuum packaging is tangled, with inventors of various generations on at least two continents claiming to have invented the machines and processes enabling extended, sanitary food preservation. The nineteenth-century American inventor Amanda Jones, who was awarded two patents for canning procedures, is often credited with founding the vacuum-canning industry in the United States—though her own all-female company, established in the early 1890s, was a commercial failure. Jones attributed the failure of the venture to her unwillingness to give up ownership and executive authority to men, which meant that men were unwilling to invest in the company.

but had studied theology. As a tutor (mainly for English boys), he traveled widely throughout Europe and became a master of networking for scientists and philosophers who wished to communicate their findings and opinions to one another. That is how he knew Spinoza, and it explains why Spinoza and Boyle used him as an intermediary.

These informal networks connecting scientists of different countries, and enabling them to share findings through unofficial channels, posed a formidable challenge to the attempt of churches to control knowledge. A Galileo might be forced by the Inquisition to recant his views on the heliocentric solar system officially, but scientists throughout Europe knew about and discussed those views. Oldenburg was one of many who facilitated such communication.

In his role as head of the Royal Society's network, Oldenburg was frequently the recipient of communications from scholars who disagreed about science as well as philosophy and theology, and, as so often occurs with go-betweens, he was frequently blamed for the conflicts and misunderstandings of others. (He was long held accountable for the hostility between Isaac Newton, who developed the theory of gravity, and his competitor Hooke, who formulated the theory of planetary motion. Oldenburg was largely absolved by late-twentieth-century scholars, who not only noted the gigantic egos of Newton and Hooke but blamed the conflict on the seventeenth-century procedure of "knocking men's heads together to make the intellectual sparks fly . . . that the truth might emerge from the conflict of rival views."[2])

Yet it is difficult to imagine that Boyle and Spinoza could ever have agreed on what constituted truth—or even the proper method of searching for truth. Boyle was more than devout; his was not the pro forma behavior of a man who could publicly accept the practices of an established church while carrying on, in untroubled fashion, with scientific experiments that might call into question the very existence of a purposeful Creator. Boyle had undergone what he described as a conversion at age thirteen, during a terrifying, unseasonal December thunderstorm in Switzerland. This was not a conversion from one faith to another but from the reflexive, tepid observances of the Church of England, in which he, as the son of a Protestant noble appointed by the monarch, had naturally been baptized, to an ardent form of faith— what would be seen by later standards as a "born-again" awakening. (Boyle's experience certainly qualifies as a conversion by my standard of a shift in faith that radically changes one's way of life. Most born-again Christians today do not call themselves converts unless they were not Christians at all before they developed a personal relationship with Jesus as their savior. Yet the difference between a born-again Christian whose faith requires him to take every word of the Bible literally, and one who simply regards the Bible as a human document depicting beliefs of a particular period in time, could certainly be deemed greater than, say, the difference between many Unitarians and Reform Jews.)

As Boyle himself described his conversion, he woke up in a storm with claps of thunder and flashes of lightning so numerous and dazzling that he feared the imminence (and probably the immanence) of Judgment Day. The frightened boy vowed then and there that "all further additions to his life should be more Religiously & carefully employ'd." Feeling guilty about having found faith only because of fear, he repeated his pledge in tranquil weather "so solemnly that from that Day he dated his Conversion; renewing now he was past Danger, the vow he had made whilst he fancy'd himselfe to be in it . . . yet at least he might now owe his more deliberate consecration . . . of himselfe to Piety, to any less noble Motive than that of it's owne Excellence."[3]

Boyle's overnight adolescent conversion differs markedly from the long, thoroughly considered movement toward Christianity by the young Augustine, but it cannot be dismissed as the overwrought self-dramatization of an impressionable teenager; the scientist's intense devotion to religion and theological writing throughout his life rules out such an interpretation. If his had been a spur-of-the-moment teenage conversion, he probably would have gone through numerous subsequent conversions—as so many of his contemporaries did. Precisely because Boyle was a scientist, his awakening to a more orthodox form of faith remains important to educated evangelical Christians today. An entry in the archives of *Christianity Today,* the evangelical magazine founded by the Reverend Billy Graham, misleadingly asserts that Boyle's scientific inquiries can be dated from the time of his conversion. "The 'science' of the day disagreed with the Bible," the article states. "Was the Bible true, or the science? Robert would have committed suicide over this troubling issue if he had not believed that God forbade it. Instead, he determined to press hard after truth. He had become one of the Protestant thinkers who exposed the nonsensical and inaccurate ideas of the time and replaced them with ideas based on experiments."[4] The quotation marks around the word "science" in this passage imply that Boyle's religious conversion was somehow intended to help him distinguish between so-called false science, which disagreed with the Bible, and true science, which could be reconciled with biblical super-naturalism. However, nearly all of the insights of the dawning age of science—whether they turned out to be scientifically true or false in light of later knowledge and discoveries—contradicted the Bible. This was as true of Leonardo da Vinci's fifteenth-century observations of marine fossils, which could not be reconciled with the biblical story of Noah's flood because the fossils had been deposited in different strata of rock at different periods of time, as it was of the many anatomical and astronomical insights of Boyle's century.* The out-of-season thunderstorm that triggered Boyle's religious awakening would have been seen as a purely natural phenomenon by a great many contemporary scientists and philosophers. We can be as certain as it is possible to be of anything that Spinoza, Leibniz, Galileo, William Harvey, or, for that matter, seventeenth-century popes were no more disposed to believe that thunderstorms predicted Armageddon than that lightning was instigated by Thor's hammer.

What seems more likely than *Christianity Today*'s tortuous attempt to attribute Boyle's conversion to his worries about false "science" is that the young Robert, educated at Eton and traveling through Europe in order to broaden his cultural and linguistic background, was already quite aware that it would take stronger religious convictions than those inspired by a reflexive adherence to an established church to deal with the philosophical implications of science *without* quota-tion marks. Throughout his life, Boyle would be subject to doubts about his faith—some evoked by ancient philosophers, and some by contemporaries, who included Spinoza. Boyle viewed these doubts as bearing the same relation to the spirit as a toothache to the body—"for tho it be not mortal, 'tis very troublesome."[5] He even acknowledged

---

* This was so even though Leonardo's observations were intended to prove the truth of a complete misconception—that the human organism is a microcosm of the macrocosm of earth. For a full and lively account of this episode in scientific history, see Stephen Jay Gould's essay, "The Upwardly Mobile Fossils," in *Leonardo's Mountain of Clams and the Diet of Worms* (New York: Harmony Books, 1998).

that "the greatest number of those that pass for Christians, profess themselves such only because Christianity is the religion of their Parents, or their Country, or their Prince, or those that have been, or may be, their Benefactors; which is in effect to say, that they are Christians, but upon the same grounds that would have made them Mahometans, if they had been born and bred in Turkey."[6] Even today, this insight remains uncommon among people convinced (as Boyle was) that their own religion embodies absolute truth. Boyle's disdain for reflexive, unexamined, "inherited" faith was responsible for his determination to contribute as much as possible toward the conversion of "heathen" peoples under the control of the expanding British Empire. Born to wealth and privilege, Boyle became even richer as a director of the East India Company and personally financed translations of the (Protestant) Bible into Malay, Turkish, Lithuanian, and Gaelic. The Catholic Irish did not appreciate having greater access to the King James Bible, which was used by the hated English Protestants. Turks of Muslim persuasion may not have been excited, either. But no matter: attracting potential converts was the whole point of Boyle's underwriting of foreign-language translations of his Bible. He believed not in conversion by the sword but only in conversion by proselytizing. In his will, Boyle set up a fund for lectures on the relationship between religion and new discoveries in science, but these lectures were aimed at atheists, Muslims, Jews, and other non-Christian "infidels." They were not supposed to deal with differences among Christian sects (which Boyle considered deeply regrettable), although many of the early lectures did take up the issues raised by Christian deism.

Boyle became one of the chief authors of what is today called the intelligent design argument for the existence of a divine creator— a being who set the universe in motion and allows most corporal affairs to be governed by mechanistic natural laws but is also capable, for reasons beyond human understanding, of suspending those laws to perform miracles. The inadequacy of human understanding in the face of mystery and miracle is the a priori assumption underlying the impossible attempt to truly reconcile empirical science with the miraculous. In his 1675 essay *Some Physico-Theological Considerations about the Possibility of the Resurrection,* Boyle clearly sets forth the crucial, not-to-be-questioned assumptions supporting the existence of miracles. "For supposing the truth of the history of the scriptures," he writes, "we may observe that the power of God has already extended itself to the performance of such things as import as much as we need infer, sometimes by suspending the natural actings of bodies upon one another, and sometimes by endowing human and other bodies with preternatural qualities."[7] More than three centuries later, the current director of the U.S. National Institutes of Health, Dr. Francis Collins, would say essentially the same thing in an interview about his conversion, at age twenty-seven, from atheism to evangelical Protestantism. "If God is who God claims to be, and who I believe he is, then he is not explainable in natural terms," Collins told the Public Broadcasting Service. "He is outside the natural world; outside of space and time. So if God chose to intervene from time to time in the natural world by allowing the occurrence of miraculous events, I don't see why that is an illogical possibility. Once one accepts that idea that there could be something outside the natural, then miracles become possible."[8] The seventeenth-century chemist and the twenty-first-century head of all federally financed American scientific research say essentially the same thing: it's a mystery. (Unlike Boyle, Collins was not converted suddenly in a thunderstorm, but struggled with doubts for many years. His decision to embrace religion was made, however, at a particular time during a hike in the mountains, when he felt, "I cannot resist this another moment.")

For Spinoza, the reconciliation of science with belief in miracles was impossible. To him, what people called a miracle was simply a phenomenon insufficiently exposed to the light of reason and insufficiently examined (and examinable) by contemporary science. The absence of a reasonable and natural explanation for what is generally considered a miracle in no way precluded the discovery of such an explanation in the future. Eclipses of the sun, violent earthquakes, great floods, Boyle's conversion-inducing thunderstorms, long considered supernatural manifestations of the Creator's power (or the power of the Creator's nemesis), were already known to have natural causes, and there was no reason why the natural causes of other mysterious (to the contemporary mind) phenomena should not be unraveled in the future. Spinoza's scathing assessment of miracles was one element of the *Tractatus* that would eventually place him beyond the pale for Boyle, Oldenburg, and any number of liberal religious believers. (I found it easy, while reading the famous opening paragraphs of Spinoza's chapter "Of Miracles," to understand why a devout student at a religious college once told me that he was "shocked" and unable to sleep for several nights after reading the passages. If it is strong stuff for a believer today, one can only imagine how Spinoza's rejection of miracles must have affected religious thinkers 350 years ago.)

> As men are accustomed to call Divine the knowledge which tran-scends human understanding, so also do they stile Divine, or the work of God, anything of which the cause is not generally known: for the masses think that the power and providence of God are most clearly displayed by events that are extraordinary and contrary to the conception they have formed of nature, especially if such events bring them any profit or convenience: they think that the clear-est possible proof of God's existence is afforded when nature, as they suppose, breaks her accustomed order, and consequently they believe that those who explain or endeavour to understand phenom-ena or miracles through their natural causes are doing away with God and his providence. . . .
>
> The masses then style unusual phenomena "miracles," and partly from piety, partly for the sake of opposing the students of science, prefer to remain in ignorance of natural causes, and only to hear of those things in which they know least, and consequently admire most. In fact, the common people can only adore God, and refer all things to His power by removing natural causes, and conceiv-ing things happening out of their due course, and only admire the power of God when the power of nature is conceled as in subjection to it.[9]

As Boyle made clear in his rationalization for that most miraculous of all miracles, the resurrection of the dead, his views on the subject could not have been more alien to Spinoza's philosophy. Boyle also objected strongly to the use of the term "nature" as identical to, or even as a substitute for, God. In his 1686 essay, "A Free Enquiry Into the Vulgarly Received Notion of Nature," Boyle argued that the word "nature" should never be used when what is really meant is the Divin-ity and Creator. To write of nature instead of God "seems not to me very suitable to the profound reverence we owe the divine majesty, since it seems to make the *creator* differ too little by far from a *created* (not to say *imaginary*) being. . . ."[10] The use of nature was "harsh and needless" and "in use only among the schoolmen."*

Boyle also objected—and here is the heart of his disagreement with Spinoza and with the later philosophers of the High Enlightenment—to references to the "laws of nature" (while admitting that even he was wont to lapse and use the vulgar phrase when referring to well-established facts such as the movements of heavenly bodies). But Boyle emphasized that philosophers should never use language so loosely on matters of ultimate importance—such as nature itself. It is impossible to overstate the degree of danger, from the perspective of orthodox religious thinkers, inherent in the Spinozan idea that God and nature were one and indistinguishable. The 1697 indictment of Thomas Aikenhead, which served as the rationale for his execution for blasphemy, excoriated the young student for claiming "that God, the world, and nature, are but one thing, and that the world was from eternity."[11] Boyle also considered such views blasphemous. A law, according to Boyle, could only be "a *notional role of acting according to the declared will of a superior.*" He further argued that "nothing but an intellectual being can be properly capable of receiving and acting by a *law*. For if it does not understand, it cannot know what the will of the *legislator* is; nor can it have any intention to accomplish it, nor can it act with regard to it, or know what it does, in acting, either conform to it or deviate from it. And *it is intelligible to me* that God should at the beginning impress determinate notions upon the parts of matter, and guide them as he thought requisite for the primordial constitution of things, and that, ever since, he should by his ordinary and general concourse maintain those powers which he gave the parts of matter to transmit their motion thus and thus to one another."[12]

The intelligent designer, then, accounts for miracles and the ordinary workings of nature, for the demonstrable and the undemonstrable. Boyle's work laid the foundation for the most famous argument for intelligent design, articulated in the late eighteenth century by the English philosopher William Paley, whose "watchmaker God" served

---

* The strange use (to modern readers) of "schoolmen" in this context referred to both medieval and contemporary Aristotelians, who believed the universe had always existed—a position that Boyle, who believed there was no universe before God created it, could never accept. That the divine Creator had always existed was (and is), of course, a tenet of orthodox Christianity, Judaism, and Islam.

as the foundation for Christian deism during the High Enlightenment and frequently appears on anti-evolution Web sites today.* Boyle, too, had used images of clocks in his seventeenth-century arguments for intelligent design. Neither Boyle nor Paley came to grips with the fact that all of the marvelous inner workings of a clock or watch are useless if they lack an outside source of energy—in their day provided by human hands winding a mechanism, in ours mainly by batteries or digital chips. This does not pose a logical (or theological) difficulty if man himself is the product of intelligent design (apart from the question of why an intelligent designer would not make a man who could invent an everlasting battery).

·

It is difficult to evaluate the influence of seventeenth-century science on the prevalence of religious conversion in an era characterized by large new religious movements, notable individual conversions, and religious violence connected with widespread political instability. Knowledge of science, like philosophy, was available primarily to a literate elite. And yet, as was already evident from the early decades of the Reformation, the printing press fostered more general discussion of all ideas that would once have been solely the province of a literate few. If one literate man in a seventeenth-century household read a pamphlet about contemporary science's conclusions concerning the solar system, it is unlikely that he would fail to share the information that the earth moved around the sun with other members of his family.

Certainly, many conversions—Margaret Fell's, for example— would seem, on the surface, to have little or nothing to do with the new science. Yet the Quaker ideal of the primacy of individual conscience over hierarchical thinking and authority fitted well with the

---

* The orator Robert Green Ingersoll (1833–99), known as the Great Agnostic, summarized Paley's argument in this fashion: "A man finds a watch and it is so wonderful that he concludes that it must have had a maker. He finds the maker and he is so much more wonderful than the watch that he says he must have had a maker. Then he finds God, the maker of the man, and he is so much more wonderful than the man that he could not have had a maker. . . . According to Paley, there can be no design without a designer— but there can be a designer without design. The wonder of the watch suggested that the watchmaker suggested the creator, and the wonder of the creator demonstrated that he was not created—was uncaused and eternal."

hierarchy-shattering implications of experimental research that was overturning mistaken concepts, held since antiquity, about everything from the motion of planets to the circulation of blood. As Boyle's case demonstrates—and he was far from alone—even leading figures in the new science might convert to a more personally demanding form of faith and insist that there was no conflict between their religion and their experimental work as researchers. There is not the slightest indication that medical luminaries such as William Harvey (1578–1657) were even slightly worried about the implications of new medical discoveries for religion. Yet the new science and its inventions did frighten many dissident Protestants. The large Anabaptist movements, whose traces remain today in relatively small Amish, Mennonite, and Hutterite communities in North America, turned into faiths noted for their rejection of changing science and technology.

The inarguable and most important impact of early Enlightenment science on religion was its inevitable challenge to the notion of unchanging, accepted truth. The most earnest, if literally fantastic, attempts by religious scientists like Boyle and Newton to reconcile the validity of experimental science with belief in the supernatural could not halt the process by which the questioning of one long-established truth often, and inevitably, leads to the questioning of another. The unstoppable expansion of doubt, once loosed upon the world, also had a personal dimension: scientists of different religions (whether they were considered heretical or devout by the guardians of their own faiths) often knew one another personally and corresponded directly instead of through intermediaries. Spinoza exchanged letters, displaying a mixture of respect and rivalry, with Christiaan Huygens, the preeminent Dutch scientist of the 1660s and 1670s. Born into a wealthy Dutch Calvinist family, Huygens respected Spinoza as a naturalistic philosopher but also looked down on him as a Jew, referring to him in letters as "*nostre Juif*," "*le Juif de Voorburg*," or, plainly, as "*l'Israelite*."[13] This prejudice was no less strong for being rooted more in social class than in religion, but the fact is that, a century earlier, it would have been unlikely for Huygens and Spinoza to know each other at all. Moreover, Huygens's affinity (to the degree that he possessed it) for Spinoza's mathematically grounded, mechanistic philosophy was made possible by the former's brand of deism. Like Spinoza, Huygens rejected miracles. Huygens refused to see a Dutch Reformed minister when he was thought to be on the brink of death, and his brother remonstrated with him after his recovery for showing "insufficient concern for the salvation of his soul."[14] (Huygens seems to have been an unusually prickly character even when measured against the other vainglorious geniuses of his era; he broke off correspondence with Newton in 1673 over a dispute probably rooted in the entirely correct perception of Western Europeans that Newton was the greater scientist of the two.)

Another setting for once-unthinkable personal relations between scientists, and scholars in general, of different religions was the Renaissance and post-Renaissance university. In Italy, so many Protestants and Jews studied at the University of Padua that Pope Pius IV, who occupied the papal throne from 1559 to 1565, had issued a papal bull forbidding non-Catholics from receiving college degrees. La Serenissima, the Republic of Venice, which controlled Padua, foiled the pope by giving degree-granting power to an official appointed by the Venetian Senate. Harvey, after receiving his bachelor of arts degree from Caius College of Cambridge in 1597, became another in the distinguished group of European scholars who went to Padua to study medicine, philosophy, and even theology in the atmosphere of cosmopolitan freedom that had so offended several popes.* Harvey's most notable predecessor at Padua in the history of medicine is the Belgian Andreas Vesalius, who in 1543 published his *De Humani Corporis Fabrica* (*On the Fabric of the Human Body*), the first accurate portrait of human anatomy. Galileo was also a member of the faculty, as professor of mathematics, during Harvey's time at the university. But the major attraction for Harvey, it seems, was Girolamo Fabrizio, also known as Hieronymus Fabricius (1537–1619), an anatomist in the tradition of Vesalius.† Harvey would later tell Boyle that Fabricius's research on chick embryos was a key factor influencing the British scientist's historic discoveries about the true function of the heart, lungs, veins, and

---

* At the Council of Basel in 1434, the church had attempted to impose an absolute ban on granting degrees to Jews at any university, in what was still a monist Catholic Christendom. Not every church official considered this a wise decision. In 1555, Pope Julius III— just a few years before Pius IV's unsuccessful bull—had actually ordered the University of Padua to allow a Jewish student to take an examination for his doctorate. Julius believed that allowing Jews access to Christian universities would foster religious conversions.

† The adviser for Fabricius's doctoral thesis was Gabriele Falloppio, for whom the Fallopian tubes, where fertilization takes place before the egg is transported to the uterus for implantation, are named.

arteries in the circulation of blood. (Harvey had certainly never read Servetus's passages about blood circulation in the suppressed book that was incorrectly thought to have perished in the flames that consumed its author.) Most of the Catholic, Protestant, and Jewish scientists who had direct contact with one another during the seventeenth century neither converted to another religion nor went through a profound "born-again" conversion like Boyle. They were compartmentalizers—able to erect barriers between what they learned from their experiments and what their sacred scriptures preached. It is also reasonable to suspect that lapses into secularism—as exemplified by Huygens's refusal, while he thought he was in extremis, to see a clergyman—were common not only among scientists but among the small but significant scientifically educated elite.

Most pioneering researchers of the early Enlightenment would never have accepted the proposition that science and religion were inevitable enemies. But neither was it possible for a scientifically educated religious believer to adopt a seventeenth-century version of Stephen Jay Gould's twentieth-century argument for science and religion as separate magisteria. For minds rooted in the age of faith, too many intellectual and emotional contortions were required to envision science and faith as polite but distant friends, careful not to step on each other's toes by inquiring too closely into beliefs that could never be reconciled. In the early years of the Enlightenment, conversion and belief were becoming matters of choice rather than grace, as Boyle himself recognized when he wrote of the religious doubts that continued to plague him throughout his life. The doubts were not mortal—yet—but they were potent disturbers of the peace.

13

PRELUDE: O MY AMERICA!

EVEN AS THE OLD WORLD struggled toward a form of religious tolleration that would take shape only after the deaths of hundreds of thousands of Europeans in religious wars, a new kind of society was emerging in the English and Dutch colonies of North America. In most American public schools and textbooks, students have always been taught that the United States was founded upon religion, because its first settlers were seeking freedom from religious persecution. This is an incomplete story, well suited to the purposes of those who wish to dismiss the importance of the separation of church and state in American history by writing secularism out of the first narratives told to children about their country. The desire for religious freedom was indeed the chief factor in immigration to the New World for some settlers, but it played little role for others.

The Puritans and Pilgrims who settled the Massachusetts Bay Colony in the 1620s were fleeing religious persecution in England, but their credo might well have been "freedom of conscience for me but not for thee." Their hostility to any form of theological opposition led, only fifteen years after the first settlers landed at Plymouth Rock, to Roger Williams's exile and the founding of the new colony of Rhode Island. It was Williams who later offered the Puritan dissident Anne Hutchinson her first shelter after she was tried and convicted of, among other offenses, encouraging women to preach and teach. If the first Puritans had prevailed, the absolutist religious prejudices of the Old World could have become so firmly established here that the Christian-government fantasy of today's religious right might have become a reality. But they did not have their way—even in areas of the new land where it looked, for a time, as if they might.

Religious persecution had nothing at all to do with the establishment of the first permanent English colonial settlement, in 1607, at Jamestown in Virginia. The earliest settlers were profit-seeking adventurers who adhered to the reformed Church of England, under both Queen Elizabeth I and King James I, and were in search of New World resources (eventually settling on tobacco after a rough start) upon which they might build their own fortunes and the fortunes of the Crown. Most did not have the slightest quarrel with the established church across the sea.

Later in the century—between the Virginia profit-seekers and the Massachusetts Puritans—a third religious way emerged with the establishment of the colony of Pennsylvania. In 1681, William Penn—convinced that the Quaker ideal of religious toleration could never be achieved in England—founded the colony with a charter from Charles II. After the public debacle of Penn's trial in London for holding a Quaker meeting outdoors, the king was only too happy to get rid of this persistent religious pest. Penn's First Frame of Government for Pennsylvania, adopted in April 1682, specified toleration for all religions, established freedom of the press, and prohibited military conscription. In the late seventeenth century, Pennsylvania's combination of religious toleration with anti-militarism attracted European as well as English Protestants, Catholics, and Jews, all of whom had personally suffered religious persecution or lived with a constant, tension-producing awareness that religious violence might erupt again even if peace prevailed at the moment. The prohibition of military conscription was equally important. Nonconformist Protestant denominations, like the Quakers, Mennonites, and Amish, proclaimed pacifism as a tenet of their religion, but the absence of conscription also appealed to nonpacifist Lutherans and Catholics who, in Europe, had feared being drafted and having to fight wars that might bring them into conflict with their co-religionists. Penn's haven of toleration, which provided not only de facto religious freedom (as in Amsterdam) but de jure recognition of all religions, was established during the period of the seventeenth century when Huguenot children were being torn from their homes by the soldiers of Louis XIV in France, when the Inquisition still functioned as vigorously as it could in Spain and Portugal (and in their New World colonies), when Anabaptists were being persecuted throughout Europe by Calvinists and Lutherans, and when nearly everyone on the continent had reason to fear if he found himself in the wrong place at the wrong time when a new monarch of a different religion assumed power.

The major factor in the hospitality of the English colonies to numerous religions was the abundance of unsettled land. Even if an official church like the one in Massachusetts was as quick to cry "heresy" as it would have been in Europe, the consequences were not nearly as dire, because there was ample room for convicted heretics to move on and practice their religion in a more hospitable space. The Massachusetts Puritan John Cotton dismissed concern about the banishment of Williams from the Bay Colony on the ground that exile, in America, simply meant moving on to what might be a more agreeable place. "The Jurisdiction (whence a man is banished) is but small," he said, "and the Countrey round about it, large and fruitful: where a man may make his choice of variety of more pleasant, and profitable seats, then [*sic*] he leaveth behinde him. In which respect, Banishment in this countrey, is not counted so much a confinement, as an enlargement."[1] One colony's heresy was another's dissent, and in some of the colonies, dissent itself was simply another form of religion.

The first century of colonization on the East Coast was characterized by constant pressure for religious freedom from a variety of immigrants, and conflicts were resolved or avoided—with some notable exceptions, like the Salem witch trials—through political negotiation and machinations rather than bloodshed. The story of Hutchinson's theological rebellion, trial, and expulsion from Massachusetts is a singular case in point.

Anne Marbury Hutchinson (1591–1643) was born in Lincolnshire, England, into a heritage of religious individualism. Her father, Francis, a clergyman, went to prison three times for his unorthodox attitudes toward the Church of England. In 1578, John Aylmer, the bishop of London, ordered Marbury's arrest after the latter charged that Elizabethan bishops were ordaining ignorant ministers who could barely read. "Though I fear not you, I fear the Lord," Marbury told the Court of High Commission. When one of Aylmer's colleagues exclaimed in horrified tones, "This fellow would have a preacher in every parish church!" Marbury replied that the Bible required this. Asked by Bishop Aylmer where the money would come from to educate such learned preachers, Marbury replied, "A man might cut a good large tong out of *your* hide, and it would not be missed."[2]

As this exchange makes clear, Anne's astringent tongue and strong convictions were family as well as individual traits. In 1612, not long after her father's death, she married William Hutchinson, a merchant from a prosperous family, and they eventually had fifteen children. Hutchinson's maternal responsibilities did not, however, interfere with her growing commitment to the Puritan religion. She and her husband became close to Cotton, who immigrated to Massachusetts in 1633 because his teaching had been banned in England. In 1634, after Anne completed another pregnancy and gave birth, she and William followed Cotton to Massachusetts.

Known as a skilled midwife, Anne found her experience in great demand in her new home. It seems likely that her well-attended theological discussions "for women only" grew out of her midwifery practice. At a time when everything was infused with religion, midwives had a spiritual as well as practical importance. In England, Catholic midwives had been suspected of secretly baptizing infants into the Roman church. After Protestantism was established as the state church, English midwives frequently had to take an oath affirming that no child they delivered would be baptized "by any Mass-Latine, service or other prayers than such as are appointed by the laws of the church of England." Such an oath would not have been considered necessary in Massachusetts, where there were no Catholics in Hutchinson's time.[3] (This concern about baptism was not irrational for those who believed in the validity and permanence of infant christenings—regardless of the infant's inability to consent or the parent's wishes. In the nineteenth century, stealth baptisms of Jewish infants and small children by Catholic nurses—and even by other children—would be considered sufficient reason for authorities in the Papal States to remove "Catholic" children from their Jewish homes for instruction in the faith.)

Hutchinson's biblical discussions were eventually attended by men

as well as women—another factor that brought her to the attention
of the authorities. What threatened the Puritan theocracy in Massachusetts was not only the idea of a female preacher but Hutchinson's
belief in a personal relationship with God and in salvation by grace
alone. (Opponents labeled such beliefs antinomian—literally, "anti-
law.") Although Hutchinson remained a Puritan by her own lights,
her belief in the primacy of personal revelation was much closer to the
Baptist faith and became characteristic of born-again Christians in the
eighteenth and early nineteenth centuries, during the First and Second
Great Awakenings in America. Moreover, Hutchinson's views about
war were closer to Quakerism than to Puritanism, and her fate may
have been sealed by the opposition of some of her male supporters to
the colonists' armed conflict, beginning in 1637, with the Pequot Indians (many of whom were either killed or sold as slaves to other Indian
tribes that had backed the winning English side).

Hutchinson was brought to trial for her supposedly seditious
preaching in the same year as the outbreak of the Pequot War. Governor John Winthrop presided over the trial in his "city on a hill," and
the full record of the proceedings (Calvinists, in America as well as in
Europe, were meticulous record keepers) provides a fascinating insight
into the real American religious past. The discourse at the trial was
conducted at a high level, befitting a society that had made education
a priority even while settlers were still struggling to make their land
yield enough to feed their own families. As one historian puts it:

> Only six years after John Winthrop's arrival in Salem harbor,
> the people of Massachusetts took from their own treasury the fund
> from which to found a university; so that while the tree-stumps
> were as yet scarcely weather-browned in their earliest harvest fields,
> and before the nightly howl of the wolf had ceased from the out-
> skirts of their villages, they had made arrangements by which even
> in the wilderness their young men could at once enter upon the
> study of Aristotle and Thucydides, of Horace and Tacitus, and the
> Hebrew Bible. . . .[4]

But intellectualism and rationality are not identical, and the early
Puritan brand of the former coexisted with numerous irrational and
antirational beliefs—such as the convictions that witchcraft was both

real and threatening, and that heresy and witchcraft were identical. Moreover, the study of the ancients, from Aristotle to the Hebrew Bible, was not for young women but for young men.

Winthrop did not take long to get to the heart of the charges against Hutchinson—that she, a female, had dared to hold regular meetings in her home and had interpreted the Scriptures for a group that included both women and men. By what right, the governor asked, did Hutchinson "entertain" regular visitors for the purpose of theological discourse? Was she not breaking the commandment "Honor thy father and thy mother"? This question was based on the presumption that state and church authorities held the same moral and legal position in relation to citizens and congregants as a parent did to children.

> HUTCHINSON: But put the case, Sir, that I do fear the Lord and my parents. May not I entertain them that fear the Lord because my parents will not give me leave?
> WINTHROP: No but you by countenancing them above others put honor upon them.
> HUTCHINSON: I may put honor upon them as the children of God as they do honor the Lord.
> WINTHROP: We do not mean to discourse with those of your sex but only this: you so adhere unto them and do endeavor to set forth this faction and so you dishonour us. . . . By what warrant do you consider such a course?
> HUTCHINSON: I conceive there lies a clear rule in Titus that the elder women should instruct the younger and then I must have a time wherein I must do it.

The similarity, in tone, wit, and degree of certainty, between Hutchinson's testimony and that of her father in London nearly sixty years earlier, is unmistakable. Later in the trial, after a long examination about her beliefs regarding the role of grace and good works in salvation, Hutchinson replied unequivocally, "Now if you do condemn me for speaking what in my conscience I know to be truth I must commit myself unto the Lord." One of the examiners (all, of course, were men) asked her how she knew the true spirit of the Lord was speaking to her. "How," Hutchinson replied, "did Abraham know that it was God that bid him offer his son, being a breach of the sixth commandment?"[5]

This is the voice of a religious zealot—but a zealot who, like many other dissident Protestants, wished to create conversions or, as the Quakers put it, "convincements" through argument and persuasion rather than coercion. However, Hutchinson was certainly arrogant enough to think that anyone who had devoted sufficient time and thought to the study of the Scriptures could not fail to be convinced of her point of view. The only unusual aspect of this religious arrogance was that it emanated from a female. Hutchinson was convicted of heresy—an outcome that was never in doubt, given the biases of the judges—and sentenced to exile.

The final exchange between Winthrop and Hutchinson says it all. "I desire to know wherefore I am banished?" she asked Winthrop, whose closing peroration had simply ordered her expulsion because she was "a woman not fit for our society." Winthrop replied, "Say no more, the court knows and is satisfied."[6]

·

A year later, after being formally excommunicated by the church, Hutchinson moved to Rhode Island at the invitation of Williams, settling on land purchased from the Narragansett Indians. After her husband's death, in 1642, Hutchinson moved on, first to Long Island and then to the Dutch colony of New Netherland proper, in what is now the Bronx. (She may have left English territory because she feared that Massachusetts authorities might renew their pursuit of "heretics" who had fled their immediate domain.) Unfortunately, Hutchinson and her six youngest children, who had excellent relations with the Narragansett tribe in Rhode Island, walked straight into a conflict between the Siwanoy Indians and the Dutch. In August 1643, they were attacked and all were scalped, with the exception of the youngest daughter, Susanna, who was just nine years old. She was kidnapped but eventually ransomed by the Dutch. The fate of Hutchinson and her family was naturally greeted by many of her former judges in Massachusetts as God's verdict.

It has often been pointed out that it would be anachronistic to view Hutchinson (like Margaret Fell) by today's feminist standards, as a heroine fighting a male theocracy determined to crush her because, and only because, she was an uppity woman. Though it is certainly true that some of Hutchinson's theological views would have drawn negative attention from the rulers of the Massachusetts Bay Colony had she been a man, it is impossible to read the transcript of the civil trial, or of the church excommunication proceedings that followed, without seeing strong evidence that her offenses were compounded by her sex. "We do not mean to discourse with those of your sex," said Winthrop, who passed final judgment on Hutchinson as "a *woman* not fit for our society." Hugh Peter, a Salem minister who played an important role in the interrogation leading to her excommunication from the church, declared that Hutchinson "had rather bine a Husband than a Wife. And a Preacher than a Hearer; and a Magistrate than a Subject."[7] We have no evidence of whether Hutchinson would have preferred being a husband to being a wife (although even then there were ways to avoid having fifteen children if you were an unwilling wife), but it is probably quite true that she would rather have been a preacher than a hearer, since she was a preacher throughout much of her adult life. Precisely because Hutchinson was not a man eligible to be a civil magistrate, we can never know whether she would have been as devoted to liberty of conscience for others as she was to her own liberty. Certainly, if one reads only the Mayflower Compact and Winthrop's "city on a hill" speech (so beloved by recent American presidents), one would never suspect that the religious separatists who had settled Massachusetts turned out to be just as intolerant as the English rulers they left behind.

But Hutchinson's story resonates throughout American religious history precisely because of its highly individual character. Her reshaping of orthodox Puritanism to fit her own confident and, yes, abrasive intellect as well as her aggressive femininity was a precursor of the "religious marketplace" that would emerge in the United States. Long before Thomas Paine wrote, "My own mind is my own church," in *The Age of Reason,* Hutchinson was acting on that principle and insisting that it had a place on the continent to which she had immigrated.

I cannot remember from my school years whether I (or my teachers) had any idea of what Hutchinson actually did; I only remember that her name was always in the history texts. Hutchinson's importance was underlined, ironically, in an ideological battle over Texas textbooks in 2009, when right-wing religious leaders proposed that her name be removed from a fifth-grade history syllabus. Far-right academics conducting a curriculum review objected to a section in the syllabus asking students to "describe the accomplishments of significant colonial leaders such as Anne Hutchinson, William Penn, John Smith, and Roger Williams." The reviewers, who included the Reverend Peter Marshall, a right-wing evangelist who believes that Hurricane Katrina was the result of divine wrath against American liberalism, and David Barton, another minister, who asserts that the separation of church and state is a myth, stated that Hutchinson "does not belong in the company of these eminent gentlemen. She was certainly not a significant colonial leader, and didn't accomplish anything except getting herself exiled from the Massachusetts Bay Colony for making trouble."[8] *Making trouble.* It is certainly true that Hutchinson made trouble for Puritan theocrats, and that she did not, like Penn and Williams, found a colony. It probably would have been better to classify her as an important figure in the history of the battle for religious liberty. However, the people rewriting Texas's science and history curricula are interested not in religious liberty but in religious power, and they also object to the use of the word "theocracy" to describe Puritan Massachusetts—understandably so, since they want children to be taught that America actually was founded as a Christian nation. In any case, the Texas Board of Education decided to delete Hutchinson's name from the colonial section. The only mystery here is why Penn and Williams were not also deleted, since their views, by modern right-wing fundamentalist standards, were even more heretical than Hutchinson's. In any event, Hutchinson would surely have found herself in jail for a considerable amount of time, as Fell did, had she conducted her meetings in England. She would also have avoided being scalped.

The true importance of Hutchinson, Penn, and their kind lies in their contribution to the religious pluralism evident, before the outbreak of the Revolution, in colonies from New York to Virginia. The development of religious toleration during the colonial period was certainly uneven, for reasons that were in some respects similar to and in others very different from the progression of limited toleration in seventeenth-century Europe. The Salem witch trials, for example, took place more than a half-century after Hutchinson's trial and led to a fatal outcome for those accused of witchcraft. Yet the Salem hysteria, while often viewed as the epitome of conservative religious intolerance and superstition in American history, may be seen more accurately as the last gasp—or, at the very least, the onset of a final illness—of the theocracy that put Hutchinson on trial. The port town of Salem, like the colonial capital Boston, was increasingly cosmopolitan in its population, views, and diversions (including an array of decidedly non-religious entertainments characteristic of all ports). The hold of the church was slipping even though large numbers of people still believed in superstitions ranging from hellfire and damnation to witchcraft and demons. (Hellfire and damnation were regarded not as superstition but as Christian truth; the distinction between Christian "wonders" and non-Christian occultism or magic played an important role in Puritan thought.*) Yet severe criticism of the government's and church's role in the witchcraft trials, followed by official apologies, came within a decade—not a vast amount of time, as such controversies unfold, when one considers the centuries it took for the Catholic Church to apologize for its role in stimulating anti-Semitism, or the Lutheran Church to apologize for persecuting Anabaptists. Samuel Sewall, a Harvard graduate who wielded great power as the man in charge of the Governor's Council printing press for the colony, played an important role in bringing about the Salem convictions as a member of the court. Sewall's personal diaries reveal almost no regret about his role, but in December 1696, he publicly apologized for his part in obtaining the convictions. Every year until his death, he set aside a day of fasting and prayed for forgiveness for his sins in the conduct of the trials. John Calvin, by contrast, was proud of his role in helping to engineer the indictment and eventual execution of Servetus.

Both the persecution of Hutchinson and the Salem witch trials underline the diversity of doctrinal opinion *within* specific faiths that has marked American religious history as extensively as the existence of so many different denominations. Such intra-denominational conflicts existed in Europe, too, but they could not be resolved by the handy expedient of packing off a dissident or dissident group to unoccupied land.

·

A different route to the new, and often conflicting, models of religious expression in the colonies was emerging in what would become New

* For a discussion of how this distinction played out in New England, see Jon Butler's *Awash in a Sea of Faith* (Cambridge, Mass.: Harvard University Press, 1990), pp. 70–74.

York City—first settled by the Dutch in the 1620s as New Amsterdam, and taken over by the British in 1664. By the time the British arrived, the island of Manhattan was host to all the religious groups represented in the tolerationist city of Amsterdam, on the other side of the ocean. This was so in spite of the well-known prejudices of the Dutch director general, Peter Stuyvesant, who sought permission from authorities in the Netherlands to expel the first Jews arriving in New Amsterdam, from Brazil, in 1654. When Portugal had reconquered Brazil after a war with the Dutch, all Brazilian Jews were expelled— one of the many instances of the Inquisition's following Iberian Jews to the New World. Most returned to the Netherlands, but twenty-three decided to settle in the colony of New Amsterdam. For Stuyvesant, that number was twenty-three Jews too many. But the director general's request to expel the Jews from their new home was denied by the Dutch West India Company—bearing out Spinoza's observation about business and trade as the bases of Dutch religious toleration. Stuyvesant did not give up easily. He prohibited Jewish men from standing guard duty in the city and then tried to impose an extra tax on them for failing to fulfill the military obligations from which they had been barred by none other than the governor himself. Once again, the metaphor of a child who kills his parents and pleads for mercy on grounds that he is an orphan comes to mind. In any event, the Dutch West India Company and government overruled Stuyvesant again and the Jews were allowed to stand guard.

Stuyvesant loathed not only Jews but also nonconformist Protestants. His animus toward Quakers led to one of the most remarkable documents in American history, the Flushing Remonstrance, issued in 1657 by the leaders of the town of Flushing (in what is now the New York City borough of Queens). Stuyvesant had publicly tortured a twenty-three-year-old Quaker convert and pushed through a law making it a crime for anyone to harbor Quakers. No, said the citizens of Flushing, we will not obey this unjust law.

> The law of love, peace and liberty in the states extending to Jews, Turks, and Egyptians, as they are considered the sons of Adam, which is the glory of the outward state of Holland, so love peace and liberty, extending to all in Christ Jesus, condemns hatred, war and bondage. . . . Our desire is not to offend one of his little ones, in

whatsoever form, name or title he appears in, whether Presbyterian, Independent, Baptist or Quaker, but shall be glad to see anything of God in any of them, desireing to do unto all men as we desire all men should do unto us. . . . We cannot in conscience lay violent hands upon them, but give them free egresse and regresse unto our Town, and houses, as God shall persuade our consciences. And in this we are true subjects both of Church and State. . . .*

By 1663, the West India Company's directors had had enough of Stuyvesant's religious intolerance and sent him an irate letter. The directors said they wished that dissenting Protestant sects were not to be found in New Amsterdam, but they acknowledged, "Yet as the contrary seems to be the fact, we doubt very much if vigorous proceedings against them ought not to be discontinued, except you intend to check and destroy your population; which, however, in the youth of your existence ought rather to be encouraged by any possible means." Furthermore, the directors declared firmly, "the consciences of men, at least, ought ever to remain free and unshackled." Moderation had always guided the rulers of old Amsterdam, "and the consequence has been that, from every land, people have flocked to this asylum. Tread then in their steps, and, we doubt not, you will be blessed."[9] Tread not in their steps, the directors might as well have written, and you will be damned. Or you may at least lose your job, for you serve at our pleasure.

Since Stuyvesant had apparently acted imperiously in many matters having nothing to do with religion, he was unpopular enough by the time the British took over that his very absence eased the way for accommodation between the old Dutch and new English settlers. And although the Church of England became the established religion when the British assumed control of New York (and eventually all of the areas once occupied by the Dutch in the region), England's colonial governors were generally careful not to interfere with existing habits of religious toleration.

---

* This extraordinary document, long buried in the historical records of New York State, was discovered by the newspaper *Newsday* while its reporters were conducting research for a series of articles, published in 1997 and 1998, on the history of Long Island. I have, in some instances, replaced seventeenth-century spelling with modern usage.

In fact, British authorities generally maintained a hands-off policy toward both tolerant and intolerant religious practices in all of the colonies. In Massachusetts and Connecticut, where the Calvinist-influenced denominations had established Puritan theocracies, British colonial rulers did not attempt to impose Anglican ways on the populace. In Williams's Rhode Island and Penn's Pennsylvania, the authorities did not attempt to suppress nonconformist Protestantism, as bureaucrats devoted to the established Church of England did in the mother country. In Maryland, with a large Catholic population that would include the only Catholic signer of the Declaration of Independence, Charles Carroll, Roman Catholics practiced their religion with a freedom they had not been able to exercise in England since the early reign of Henry VIII. And they did so without (on the whole) suppressing the rights of Protestants.* This was true even though the one prejudice uniting all Protestant denominations, regardless of their degree of theological liberality or conservatism, was anti-Catholicism. (By the time of the Revolution, the question was largely moot in Maryland, since Protestant settlers had long outnumbered the founding Catholics. Although Maryland Catholics continued to exercise considerable financial and political influence, they did not control the exercise of religion in the colony.) American colonies were simply too far away for "established" religion to mean what it meant in both the seventeenth and eighteenth centuries in Britain, much less in France, which would contribute so many Americans of persecuted Huguenot ancestry to the revolutionary cause.

The mid-Atlantic colonies, notably Pennsylvania and New York (after Stuyvesant's desire to found a Calvinist theocracy was squelched, first by his countrymen and then by the British takeover), would serve as the real template for the American religious future. Especially in their largest cities, the mid-Atlantic colonies possessed a more ethnically and religiously diverse population than either New England or

---

* The possibility of equal rights for Jews, however, never occurred to Carroll—in sharp contrast to many of the other signers of the Declaration of Independence. In his old age, he wrote that when he signed the Declaration he "had in view not only our independence of England, but the toleration of all sects professing the Christian religion, and communicating to them all equal rights." This passage from Carroll's memoirs is quoted by Russell Nye in *The Cultural Life of the New Nation, 1776–1830* (New York: Harper & Row, 1960), p. 198.

the South, the latter with its great divide between white and black, between slaveholders and the enslaved. As the historian Jack Rakove notes, the mid-Atlantic area "was also a region where a modern vision of economic development was already taking hold."[10] In New England, the subdividing of limited land to provide farms for the sons of large families took place throughout the seventeenth century and, in the decades before the Revolution, was already producing migration westward. But New York, New Jersey, and Pennsylvania depended on the immigration of many groups—from Europe and the other American colonies—to build trade based not only on agricultural exports but on the products of skilled labor. The various groups in cities like New York and Philadelphia had to get along with one another for the economy to function (something the Dutch West India Company had tried, with little success, to impress on Stuyvesant).

Nothing would demonstrate the results of the English policies more vividly than a grand ecumenical event approximately a century after New Amsterdam became New York. In August 1763, His Britannic Majesty's colonial governor of New York proclaimed an official day of thanksgiving to express gratitude to God for England's victory in the French and Indian War. There is nothing extraordinary in the history of violent human conflict about the winning side's thanking a deity for a glorious victory. What was extraordinary, given the bitterness of the religious tensions still prevailing throughout much of Europe, was the degree of religious pluralism and civic harmony in evidence as church bells rang throughout lower Manhattan on that day. Thanksgiving services were held in Episcopal, Dutch Reformed, Presbyterian, French Huguenot, Baptist, and Moravian churches. More remarkable still, Congregation Shearith Israel, representing the city's small community of Jews, was also a full participant in the celebration. In Europe at that time, there was no country—however religiously tolerant or intolerant—in which a synagogue would have been placed on the same footing as a Christian church for purposes of an important civic event. The Jewish thanksgiving sermon was based on Zechariah 2:10, "Sing and rejoice, O daughter of Zion: for lo, I come, and I will dwell in the midst of thee, saith the Lord."[11] Roman Catholics were not represented in the official thanksgiving ceremonies; there were not yet enough Catholic immigrants to form an effective political pressure group in a city filled with religious denominations that hated the

Church of Rome. The first Catholic church in New York, Saint Peter's, was not completed until 1786.*

That the Catholic Church, where it possessed theocratic power, was still conducting persecutions for blasphemy, heresy, and witchcraft was very much a part of the consciousness of educated Protestants in the colonies. Less than three years after the church bells of different religions rang out in Manhattan, a nineteen-year-old French nobleman, Jean-François de la Barre, was beheaded in Abbeville for (according to the court's sentence) the crimes of singing impious and blasphemous songs against God; failing to bow to the Communion host being carried in a Corpus Christi procession; and possessing blasphemous books, most notably Voltaire's *Portable Philosophical Dictionary*. The sentence specified that Voltaire's work be burned, along with the Chevalier de la Barre's body, after the beheading.† Although more than two centuries had passed, there was no significant difference between this Catholic execution and the Protestant execution of Servetus engineered by Calvin. This internationally publicized execution took place on July 1, 1766—only a decade before the American revolutionaries were to put the finishing touches on the Declaration of Independence in Philadelphia. Such events, exemplifying the bloodshed that union between church and state had inflicted on the peoples of the Old World, were recent history, not a bad memory from a distant past, for the men who wrote the Declaration of Independence and the Constitution. Some of the founders were Christians and some were freethinkers, but when they sat down to write the nation's founding documents, nearly all of them had in mind the contrast between the religious pluralism expressed in the 1763 celebration in colonial New York and the European religious violence that had taken so many lives.

---

* Saint Peter's is the oldest Catholic parish in New York State. The current church, a historic landmark at the corner of Barclay and (what else?) Church Streets in the financial district, was completed in 1840, replacing the earlier structure.
† There are many different and sometimes conflicting versions of this affair, including those written by Voltaire and official Catholic Church historians, but there is no disagreement about the charges in the indictment or the sentence of the court. Catholic historians have often tried to minimize the role of the church, noting that the prosecution was carried out by secular authorities. That, of course, is exactly the point: the secular authorities were carrying out an old religion-based law rooted in the primacy of Catholicism and the assumption of the legal respect due religion.

The circumstances of Jews in colonies like New York—long before the federal Constitution gave them legal protection—offers what is arguably the most dramatic evidence of the differences between the New World and the Old. Five years after Congregation Shearith Israel participated in the celebration of the end of the French and Indian War, it appointed twenty-three-year-old Gershom Mendes Seixas (1745–1816) as its *hazzan,* or cantor. Seixas was the son of a Portuguese Converso whose family had fled to London in 1725, and then moved on to New Amsterdam, after being accused by the Inquisition of secretly continuing to practice Judaism. In the case of Seixas's father, who was responsible for his son's education in Hebrew and Judaism, the suspicion was obviously justified.* The younger Seixas would become a strong supporter of the American Revolution (though many members of his split congregation, like many other New Yorkers, bet on the wrong horse and backed the British). He believed that American independence, founded on the Enlightenment concept of natural rights, would establish the principle of religious liberty in ways that Jews had never before experienced in civil society. When Columbia College (founded in 1754 as King's College, now Columbia University) reopened after the Revolution, Seixas was appointed to the board of trustees. (By this time, Ashkenazi Jews, many refugees from the regions that now make up Germany, outnumbered Sephardim in Congregation Shearith Israel.) Seixas's appointment to the Columbia board of trustees was made at a time when Jews were barred from attending universities in all of the areas that constitute modern Germany. His stewardship at Columbia coincided with the period when Immanuel Kant, who taught at the University of Königsberg, permitted a small number of chosen Jews to audit (as the term is understood today) his philosophy seminars.[†] They could not receive any credit toward a degree, because they could graduate only if they converted to Christianity.[‡]

---

* Family histories of this sort, though they may not have been typical, strongly undercut generalizations like Benzion Netanyahu's regarding the disappearance of Judaism among Spanish and Portuguese Conversos.

† Königsberg, then a part of Prussia, was ceded to the Soviet Union by Germany at the end of World War II and is now Kaliningrad.

‡ The notorious Jewish "quotas" instituted by all Ivy League universities, including Columbia, in the early twentieth century were based not on religion but on ethnicity— something Seixas, as a descendant of Sephardic Jews, would have understood all too well. From around 1900 to the 1950s, Ivy League admissions officers were less interested in whether an applicant described himself as Protestant on his application than in his name

In the new American republic, there would be fierce social and economic discrimination, at different times and in different places, not only against Jews and Catholics but against many other old and new religious groups. These passions would occasionally turn violent. What would never happen, though, was the emergence of a national, government-supported system of legal religious persecution. Many members of minority religions would convert to the majority faith in America (as my father's family did) for social advantage, but conversion would never be a legal requirement for any form of advancement, as it was in many parts of Europe before the twentieth century. As far as the law was concerned, an American's choice of faith would always be a private, not a public matter.

•

There was, however, one glaring exception to the hands-off policy regarding religious choice and conversion on the part of colonial America's governing classes. As usual, the exception involved slavery and race. The mass conversion of slaves from paganism or Islam to Christianity, beginning in the late seventeenth century and proceeding as long as new slaves continued to arrive from Africa, is the single example of large-scale forced religious conversion in American history. (Although there were many missionary efforts among Indians, with varying degrees of success, there was no mandatory mass conversion.) The Christianization of African-born slaves and their descendants is not generally thought of as an example of forced conversion, because it took place within the context of the more overwhelming force that created slavery itself and because blacks by the end of the Civil War were—as they are today—overwhelmingly Christian by choice. How, exactly, African-born and African-descended slaves became Christians falls into the zone of the many largely unexamined consequences of slavery.

Initially, slaveholders in the seventeenth and early eighteenth centu-

---

and the country in which his parents were born—both giveaways of Jewishness. Both my grandfather Jacoby and my uncle, born in 1903, were graduates of Columbia College. My father, however, was born in 1914, and by the time he was ready to enter college, in 1931, Jewish "quotas" were firmly in place at Columbia. He went to Dartmouth College, which did institute its own quotas and kept them until the mid-1930s. There was also considerable discrimination against Catholic applicants by elite universities.

ries were far from convinced that their chattels should be encouraged
or even allowed to convert to Christianity. Assuming that they considered themselves good Christians, the owners could not fail to see a
certain contradiction between Jesus's teachings about the brotherhood
of man and their ownership of "brothers." But in the late seventeenth
century, when slavery began to expand dramatically in the American
colonies, none of the major Christian denominations were willing to
allow awareness of that contradiction to interfere with business. Penn,
to cite a particularly shameful example in view of his other beliefs about
human rights and justice, owned slaves himself and said unashamedly
that he preferred them to less reliable indentured servants. What master would feel otherwise? By definition, a term of indentured servitude
has a beginning and an end. It was not until the second half of the
eighteenth century that American Quakers, who were to play such an
important role in the nineteenth-century abolitionist movement, took
a firm stand against slavery. Not until 1774 did the American branch
of the Society of Friends state unequivocally that a Quaker could not
own slaves. Slavery was not, as is mistakenly thought by many today,
a strictly Southern institution. New York had the largest proportion of
slaves outside the South—between 12 and 18 percent of the population
in the eighteenth century, with an even larger percentage in New York
City. The religion of slaves was not, however, a major social issue in
the mid-Atlantic colonies, because slavery did not form the basis of the
entire economy.

In the South, where slavery *was* the economy and large numbers of
captives were concentrated on great plantations by the second quarter of
the eighteenth century, the question of slave religion was more urgent.
With blacks outnumbering whites in many areas of the South, the
African religious practices of many slaves could and did seem threatening to many masters. Should those in bondage be permitted to retain
their polytheistic African religious practices or be introduced to stories
from the Old and New Testaments? The problem—the intractable
problem—was that some Bible stories posed a moral challenge to what
was becoming the Southern Way of Life. That no major religion, while
claiming freedom for its own members, had hesitated to enslave others
was almost beside the point in the debate over whether slaves should
be subjected to Christian proselytizing. The Mosaic injunction "Let
my people go" should really have been written with the emphasis on

"my," but no matter. The Jewish Bible, and the story told in Exodus, were also integral to Christian teaching, and the willingness of the Israelites to make slaves of others was an inconvenient fact that neither Christians nor Jews wished to acknowledge. One need only recall the persistence of the phrase in Negro spirituals dating from slavery—"Go down, Moses, / Way down in Egypt's land; / Tell old Pharaoh / To let my people go!"—to understand that the Anglican planters were right to worry about the implications of conversion to a Christianity that also incorporated the Jewish biblical story. The planters were equally right, by their own lights, to worry about the consequences of teaching slaves to read.

In typical fashion, the planter class veered between fearing the effects of Christian proselytizing among slaves and claiming that slaves were too stupid to comprehend so complex a religion. In 1699, the Virginia General Assembly concluded that conversion to Christianity would be too arduous an undertaking for slaves because of the "Gros Barbarity and rudeness of their manners, the variety and Strangeness of their Languages and the weakness and Shallowness of their minds."[12]

At the same time, the Anglican clergy developed elaborate rationales and rituals to reassure planters that, should these weak and shallow minds prove, against all odds, capable of understanding Christianity, they would learn to understand their new religion as a yoke of obedience. Francis Le Jau, an Anglican minister (himself a convert from the Huguenot faith) in South Carolina, wrote a special oath in 1707 for slaves to take, in the presence of their masters, before being baptized. Each slave was required to swear "that you do not ask for the holy baptism out of any design to free your self from the Duty and Obedience you owe to your Master while you live."[13]

This oath was more than a formality (at least to the masters)— especially in South Carolina and Georgia, the colonies closest to Spanish-controlled Florida. The Spanish Crown had promised emancipation to any fugitive slave who converted to Catholicism after reaching its territory (although evidence about whether the Spanish colonial rulers actually delivered on this promise is thin). But authorities in the Southern colonies, if they were going to allow slaves to participate in the comforting rituals of Christianity, wanted no misunderstandings that equated religious conversion with a change in chattel status. It was up to the Anglican Church, which wanted to convert the slaves, to supply the planters with a rationale to reconcile Christianity with slavery. Of course, Paul's dictum that servants be subject to their masters was always extremely helpful.

Thomas Bacon, an Anglican minister from Maryland, in sermons delivered to mixed audiences of slaves and their masters, referred to slave owners as "God's overseers." Slaves were obliged to serve these overseers "as if . . . for God himself." Furthermore, they were bound to follow orders that were not only "peevish, and hard," but even those involving immoral acts.[14] So much for the rape of female slaves. In this world, slaves must not resist any command—however immoral the command might seem to a free person. Justice would wait for the next world. (Bacon's sermons were published in London and widely circulated among colonial planters as exemplars of how to teach slaves about Christianity in a way that provided religious sanction for them to stay in their proper, inferior place.)

The controversy over the meaning of conversion for slaves continued even as the colonies moved toward a revolution based on the philosophy of natural rights and the liberal ideals of the High Enlightenment. Colonial legislatures passed, and often redundantly reaffirmed, laws that explicitly denied emancipation to baptized slaves. These laws, as historian Winthrop Jordan points out in *White over Black* (1968), were specifically designed to reassure planters that the law did not countenance any idea that, although it might be morally sound for a Christian master to own a slave of another religion, it was wrong for the same master to own a Christian slave. Colonial legislatures reaffirmed the proposition that it was just fine for Christians to own other Christians (a position held by the church since late antiquity). The passage of such laws in all Southern and at least two Northern colonies by the second decade of the eighteenth century offers powerful evidence of the white ruling class's fear that even a supposedly weak-minded slave might be intelligent enough to perceive a conflict between a religion whose Lord, in his earthly incarnation, had proclaimed the dignity of all men, and a society that allowed slaves no dignity at all.

As late as the 1770s, both Anglican clergy and nonconformist Protestant leaders continued to reassure slave owners that Christianity did not mean freedom for human property. When the Second Great Awakening began, at the end of the century, moving many away from orthodox magisterial Protestantism and toward the fervor of born-again evangelicalism, the role of Christianity as a bulwark of slavery, and vice versa, only hardened. Conversion would admit slaves to the fellowship of Christian believers, but it would not admit them to the ranks of humans endowed by their Creator with the right to life, liberty, or the pursuit of happiness. No one has ever put it better than W. J. Cash in his classic *The Mind of the South* (1941). After 1800, the position of the Southern states—some, like Virginia, having been pioneers in institutionalizing the principle of the separation of church and state—moved toward that of the early Massachusetts Bay Colony. "Every man was in his place because He [God] had set him there," Cash concludes. "Everything was as it was because He had ordained it so. Hence slavery, and, indeed, everything that was, was His responsibility, not the South's. So far from being evil it was the very essence of Right. Wrong could consist only in rebellion against it. And change could come only as He himself produced it through His own direct acts, or—there was always room here for this—as He commanded it through the instruments of His will, the ministers."[15]

We have little access to what generations of slaves thought about Christian proselytizing in the late seventeenth and early eighteenth centuries, because there is almost no written record. On the subject of religion, the nineteenth century also yielded few testimonies. There are, however, several outstanding exceptions. One is Solomon Northrup's long-forgotten 1853 memoir, *Twelve Years a Slave,* restored to history by the Oscar-winning movie in 2013. Northrup, a free New York black man kidnapped into slavery, describes just the sort of sermon advocated by Reverend Bacon. The description is worth quoting in full precisely because it is so rare; Northrup, with his education and former life in freedom, was in a unique position to observe, as both an outsider and a slave, the conflict between slavery and Christian teaching.

Like William Ford, his brother-in-law, Tanner was in the habit of reading the Bible to his slaves on the Sabbath, but in a somewhat different spirit. He was an impressive commentator on the New Testament. The first Sunday after my coming to the plantation, he called them together, and began to read the twelfth chapter of Luke. When he came to the 47th verse, he looked deliberately around him, and continued—"And that servant which knew his lord's *will*,"—

here he paused, looking around more deliberately than before, and again proceeded—"which knew his lord's *will*, and *prepared* not himself"—here was another pause—"*prepared* not himself, neither did *according* to his will, shall be beaten with many *stripes*."

"D'ye hear that?:" demanded Peter [a slave] emphatically. "*Stripes*," he repeated, slowly and distinctly, taking off his spectacles, preparatory to making a few remarks.

"That nigger that don't take care—that don't obey his lord—that's his master—d'ye see?—that 'ere nigger shall be beaten with many stripes. Now, 'many' signifies a *great* many—forty, a hundred, a hundred and fifty lashes. That's *Scripter!*" and so Peter continued to elucidate the subject for a great length of time, much to the edification of his sable audience.[16]

Thus was conversion, originally feared by the planters, transformed into an instrument of subjection. One wonders what Robert Boyle, so dedicated to the conversion of non-Christians from Malaya to Turkey, would have thought of the dogma of absolute slave obedience as a condition for conversion. As Jon Butler, an eminent historian of early American religion, observes, "The advancing paternalism rooted in a doctrine of absolute obedience reinforced the growing violence of eighteenth-century slaveholding. . . . Blacks were not Sambo—the soft, docile, lethargic slave—but had become rebellion personified, and their 'insolence' was all but guaranteed by the doctrines that demanded absolute rather than conditional obedience, first rationalized by Anglican ministers in the colonies."[17] Moreover, non-Anglicans in slaveholding states in the seventeenth and eighteenth centuries—including nonconformist Protestants and Catholics in Maryland—raised no objections to the absolutist view of obedience promulgated by Bacon.

Northrup's memoir is a valuable commentary on slave conversion and religion not only because of its rarity but because it focuses, in almost journalistic fashion, on the actual religious practices encouraged and/or tolerated by masters. He is concerned with what people around him do and say, not with whatever inner spiritual experiences they might be having. Of great importance was the custom of allowing slaves to work *for pay* on the Sabbath, and this extra day of work on what was supposed to be the Christian day of rest was their only way of buying anything that the masters did not provide. Had these slaves been literate, they would surely have been as disinclined as fifteenth-century Spanish Conversos to leave a record of whatever their "true" religious feelings were. We know that, whatever form of Christianity was adopted by slaves, many traditional African religious practices—from circumcision to magic rituals—survived along with the religion fostered or permitted by individual masters. Like every mass conversion (as opposed to the individual, spiritualized conversions that occupy a disproportionate space in literature), the Christianization of America's slaves took place as a result of overwhelming economic and political forces. In the end, most masters concluded that it was better to live with slaves who professed a shared religion than with slaves who might adhere to demonic, unknown spiritual beliefs that promoted rebellion.

However, masters disapproved of—and often severely punished—slaves who organized their own, secret prayer meetings with slave preachers. The role of the slave preacher in this culture was tricky and dangerous, because he literally had to serve two masters. After the Civil War, one such preacher, Anderson Edwards, talked about his difficulties spreading the Gospel in Texas in the antebellum era. "When I starts preachin' I couldn't read or write and had to preach what massa told me and he say tell them niggers iffen they obeys the massa they goes to Heaven but I knowed there's something better for them, but daren't tell them 'cept on the sly. That I did lots. I tell 'em iffen they keeps prayin' the Lord will set 'em free."[18]

Another significant piece of autobiographical reflection by a literate slave dealing with the issue of conversion was written by Omar ibn Said (c. 1770–1864), an educated Muslim who was captured in his native Senegal near the end of the eighteenth century. Said's sketchy fifteen-page autobiography, written in Arabic, has not been made into a Hollywood movie, but its very existence provides a valuable reminder of the long-neglected historical fact that many Africans were not pagans or polytheists but monotheistic Muslims when they made the dreaded Middle Passage in slave ships. Estimates by various scholars of the proportion of Muslims among African-born slaves range from 10 to 20 percent.

The first slaves of Muslim background were brought to South America by the Spaniards in the early sixteenth century. By the time they arrived in the Americas, most had spent some time in Spain, where they were forced to convert to Christianity. One reason the Spanish did not want practicing Muslims as slaves was their fear that African Muslims might convert Indians to their faith. As one scholar notes, colonial rulers surmised that, "if Africans, who knew about horses, converted the Indians and then taught them equine skills, much of the Spaniards' military advantage would have been lost."[19] (There is something strange about this rationale, because Christianized African slaves would still have known about horses.) In any event, the English colonists who settled in North America a century later were not concerned about Islam and, as already noted, were ambivalent until well into the eighteenth century about whether slaves should be converted to Christianity at all. Muslims captured by slave traders in West Africa were more likely to be literate than other Africans, and Said belonged to this group. The literacy and education of slaves like Said (rooted in their culture's emphasis on the study of the Quran) often made them favored house slaves, but it was also important that they were literate in Arabic rather than English; Southern planters were as opposed to teaching slaves to read English as the Spanish had been to teaching equestrian warfare to Indians.

Said's autobiography was first set down in Arabic in 1831 and was translated into English many times. The original manuscript was thought to be lost but was found in a trunk on a plantation in Virginia and bought by a collector, who has displayed it both at Harvard's Houghton Library and at the International Museum of Muslim Cultures in Jackson, Mississippi.* The English translation used by scholars today was originally published in a 1925 issue of *The American Historical Review* and edited by J. Franklin Jameson (1859–1937), an important figure in American historiography. In the manuscript, Said describes his birth in the region of Futa Toro, near the Senegal River, but does not talk about his youth or explain how he obtained his education. He writes that he was captured by a large army (how large it was, and/or whether it was composed of European Christians or Muslim Arabs, is not apparent) and then describes the Middle Passage. He recalls his first master in Charleston as "a small, weak, and wicked man called Johnson, a complete infidel, who had no fear of God at all."[20] Then

---

* The history of the manuscript appears in an essay by Patrick E. Horn in *Documenting the American South,* a project of the University of North Carolina (http://docsouth.unc.edu/nc/omarsaid/summary.html).

Said escapes and is recaptured in Fayetteville, North Carolina, when he enters a Christian church, presumably to say his Muslim prayers in Arabic.

Said's jailers noticed that he was writing on the walls of his cell in Arabic (an offense for which he might have been killed had the writing been in English). He was then sold to a General James Owen, who recognized him as an educated man, and the educated man remained with the family for the rest of his life. (If he died in 1864—there are no details—he would technically have been freed by the Emancipation Proclamation.)

At some point after his purchase by Owen, Said converted to Christianity. Maybe. As one historian notes, "Tension between Said's critique of Christian slaveholders and his alleged conversion to Christianity runs throughout his autobiography, reflecting a critical dissonance that is missing from the celebratory tone of his [white Christian] biographers."[21] One account in a Christian publication actually describes Said's exposure to Christian Scripture (translated into Arabic) as a credit to the Christian God, who "causes good to come out of evil by making him [Said] a slave." Said, however, writes, "I reside in this our country by reason of great necessity. Wicked men took me by violence and sold me to the Christians."[22] Throughout, Said emphasizes the linguistic differences between his current Christian prayers and his old Muslim prayers. Two other surviving excerpts of Said's writing reveal the complexity of religious conversion under implicit, if not explicit, coercion. One is an Arabic transcription of Psalm 23. Said introduces the psalm with the preface "In the name of God, the merciful and gracious. May God have mercy on the prophet Mohammed." The second surviving piece of writing contains an English inscription on the back, "The Lord's Prayer written in Arabic by Uncle Moreau (Omar), a native African, now owned by General Owen of Wilmington, N.C. He is 88 years of age a devoted Christian." But the text is *not* the Lord's Prayer. It is actually a Quranic passage predicting a mass conversion of unbelievers to Islam, in which men will enter into "the region of Allah in companies."[23] The emotional conflict revealed in Said's brief memoir provides yet another piece of evidence that—at least at the outset—all conversions of slaves are in some sense forced, whether the slave was originally a polytheist or a monotheist, whether the master was cruel or lenient.

It is also vital to recall, as Americans were forcefully reminded in 2015 by the murders of nine Bible study group members at the historic African American church known as "Mother Emanuel," in Charleston, South Carolina, that independent black churches were never tolerated in the South under slavery. Mother Emanuel, originally called the Hampstead Church, was founded by freedmen in Charleston in 1818. The original church was burned down in 1822 after a plot by Denmark Vesey, one of its founders, to organize a slave uprising was discovered. In 1834, all black churches were outlawed in South Carolina, and free blacks, like many slaves, worshipped in secret until after the Civil War.

It could be argued that the tangled history of the conversion of slaves is a downbeat note—American exceptionalism in reverse—in what is essentially the story of a new society whose institutions would, however imperfectly, provide for freedom of conscience in a fashion that was still only a dream of certain philosophers in most of the Old World. However, the widespread neglect of the mass conversion of slaves to Christianity in standard nineteenth- and early-twentieth-century histories of American religion provides yet another example of the historical repression of race and racism as factors affecting every aspect of American culture. Far from being the exception that proves the rule of spiritual longing as the essence of all conversion, the Christianization of American slaves took place within a specific secular ideological context—in this instance, the South's need to justify treating people as property while exposing those same people to a prophet whose appeal, if the New Testament is to be believed, was based on his assertion that all human beings possess equal dignity. Slaves had none of the rights of a purely "spiritual" convert; in their outward religious behavior, as in all things, they could only follow their owners. What were the thoughts of slaves when they heard Jesus's promise, "I am come that they might have life, and that they might have it more abundantly" (John 10:10)? Northrup's sui generis memoir, which has a good deal to say about the uses of Christianity as an instrument of both control and consolation, has almost nothing to say about his own religious emotions (no doubt because his emotions about having been kidnapped from freedom into slavery were far more important to him than his religious feelings). Some of what we think we know today about slave religion comes from white abolitionists, like Harriet Beecher Stowe in *Uncle Tom's Cabin*, who made assumptions based on their own faith and on their desire to portray long-suffering, abused slaves as quasi-saints. The largest proportion of what we "know" about African American spirituality dates from after the Civil War, when the black church became the only American institution actually controlled by African Americans. But this fact of American history tells us nothing about the private, spiritual experience of conversion for slaves in the colonial and early republican, antebellum era—any more than Augustine's *Confessions* tells us anything about the experience of slaves in Hippo who, when a once-polytheistic master converted to Christianity in late antiquity, found that they, too, had been turned overnight from pagans into Christians.

Today, public opinion polls show that African Americans remain the most religiously devout group in the United States. For both black and white Americans, the historic importance of the black church in the civil rights movement has helped obscure the painful history of how slaves became Christians in the first place. The eventual relationship between the black church and the twentieth-century struggle for civil rights suggests that those seventeenth-century planters were absolutely correct to fear the unvarnished version of the Bible as a possible source of rebellion. That is why the conversion of slaves required that the Bible be mediated—as it never was for white American Protestants—by ecclesiastical and temporal overlords. And that is why generalizations about the spread of religious liberty in the colonial and early republican era must always be qualified by the realization that slaves never really had a choice, once their masters decided that the human beings they owned must adopt a bowdlerized form of Christianity.

•

Nevertheless, anyone who cherishes the secular side of America's heritage can only take pride in the American tapestry of religious pluralism that emerged during the colonial era. That the informal tapestry would be woven, in only 150 years, into the first government framework based not on the authority of God but on the rights of man, would seem nothing less than a miracle—or, at the very least, a Puritan "wonder"—to anyone with an inclination toward belief in the supernatural. The American colonists had—despite exceptions like the Salem trials, and often against the wishes of church leaders—used the seventeenth century to lay the foundation for a society in which freedom of religious choice (albeit only for the free) would be seen as a natural right rather than the gift of a benevolent ruler. The stage was then set for centuries of religious choice—including both religious proselytizing, conversion, and antireligious movements of all kinds. For once in Western history, these shifts of faith had nothing to do with political power or force. Freethinkers, Catholics, Protestants, Jews, who still lived in such danger in Europe: all were legally free to choose, even if those choices were inevitably affected by some of the same prejudices that had been a matter of law as well as faith in the Old World.

· **PART V** ·

THE JEWISH CONVERSION QUESTION:
WHERE CHRISTIANITY STUMPED ITS TOE

14

HEINRICH HEINE (1797–1856):
CONVICTIONLESS CONVERSION

PRESIDENT GEORGE WASHINGTON'S LETTER to the Jewish community of Newport, in which he emphasized that the new United States government required "only that they who live under its protection should demean themselves as good citizens," was written in the same decade of the eighteenth century as the birth of Heinrich Heine, who could never reconcile his attachment to German culture with having been born a Jew. Heine's life—whether he became a poet or not—would have unfolded in a very different fashion had he grown up in a society in which a Jew could claim full rights as a citizen without converting to Christianity. This baby, born at the height of the Enlightenment, did become the most beloved poet in Germany after Goethe—so beloved that the Nazis would have trouble expunging his verse, much of it set to music, from the national memory. All of the great composers of German Lieder—including Schubert, Brahms, Schumann, and Mendelssohn—drew on Heine's poems for their lyrics.

Pages of poetry, like prose, burn at 451 degrees Fahrenheit, but it is more difficult (as both Stalin and Hitler found) to wipe out the memory of lyric verse that resounds as a song, either figuratively or, as in Heine's case, literally, in the individual as well as collective cultural consciousness. His books were naturally among the thousands of volumes burned in Berlin by the Nazis in 1933, but the last words—

among the most quoted throughout the world since that time of horror—were his: "That was but a prelude; where they burn books, they will ultimately burn people also."* One can only wish that there was a monument, somewhere, coupling Heine's observation with Sebastian Castellio's encomium on the execution of Servetus: "Who burns a man does not defend a doctrine, but only burns a man."

Heine's life also offers an exemplary narrative of religious conversion undertaken for purely utilitarian, worldly purposes. His was a change of religious affiliation that could hardly be called a change of faith, since Heine made it clear in his writings that he had no more faith in any form of Christianity than in the Judaism of his birth. His decision to embrace nominal Lutheranism was informed by a tangled, tormented relationship with his own Jewish background and German culture—a defining conflict shared by many German Jews, and especially by intellectuals, from his generation through the pre-Nazi decades of the twentieth century. Had fifteenth-century Spanish Conversos been able to write about their conversions without fearing for their lives should they reveal any ambivalence, we might know how Paul of Burgos really felt about his change of faith. Instead, we know only how others viewed him. Conversions in Heine's culture, however, may be viewed both from the inside out and the outside in—although each vantage point seems lodged within a hall of mirrors rather than a stable landscape.

German Jews are often, and mistakenly, viewed as a "special case" in Jewish history—mainly because we know how the story ended. This awareness has produced a good deal of blame directed at both nineteenth- and twentieth-century German Jews for their failure to foresee a future that almost no one (despite the ex post facto prescience attached to Heine's words about book burning) imagined before it actually happened. The issues confronted by German Jews, including conversion and intermarriage, in their relationship with the larger culture have surfaced and resurfaced throughout modern Jewish history—from countries like Russia, where Jews were always profoundly oppressed, to the United States, where institutionalized legal equality overcame extralegal discrimination to produce the greatest success story of the Diaspora.

---

* The quotation is from Heine's 1821 play, *Almansor*.

Heine was born in Düsseldorf, where Jews were emancipated under Napoleon's occupation between 1806 and his defeat at Waterloo in 1815. The nine-year-old Heinrich watched French troops march into his town on the banks of the Rhine, and the municipality of some six thousand (fewer than 10 percent Jews) became a French arrondissement. The French occupation removed all legal, educational, professional, and political restrictions previously imposed on Jews by the Prussian state. As Amos Elon observes, Heine thus became part of the first, small generation of German Jews to "grow up as a free man."[1] His adult friend (and occasional intellectual antagonist) the liberal Jewish journalist Ludwig Börne was only eleven years older than Heine, but when Börne was born in Frankfurt, Jews were still locked into a ghetto at sunset and on Sundays. Like Heine, Börne converted to Lutheranism as an adult, and he, too, regretted having been baptized. (For many German-speaking Jewish converts to Christianity, this confused and ambivalent attitude toward their formal change of faith would manifest itself throughout the nineteenth and twentieth centuries, until the eve of the Holocaust. In his novel *The Conversion,* set in Austria before the First World War, the Israeli writer Aharon Appelfeld describes a civil servant, Karl, who converts—as Heine did—in order to secure a public job generally closed to Jews. After Karl and two other converted Jewish friends become involved in a bar fight with anti-Semitic peasants, the Jews argue about whether any convert from Judaism has the right to call their antagonists goyim because, as one of the converts argues, "we're *goyim* too." Karl replies, "I'm an apostate, not a *goy.*")[2]

When Heine was a young man, it seems unlikely (though not impossible) that a converted Jew would think that baptism had turned him into a *goy* rather than a nominal Christian. With Napoleon's defeat, which meant the end of the secular bedrock of the Napoleonic Code, all German Jews on formerly French-occupied territory were automatically returned to second- and third-class legal status.* Just four years after the withdrawal of Napoleon's armies, when Heine was twenty-one, violent anti-Jewish demonstrations known as the Hep! riots swept through cities along the Rhine. "Hep!," shouted by mobs

---

* Germany was not, of course, a united state until 1871. I am using the words "Germany" and "German"—to describe a cultural state of mind, not a state with defined borders—more loosely in this chapter, given that it deals with German-speaking Jews who considered the German language and German culture their true patrimony.

destroying and looting Jewish houses and businesses, was an acronym of the Latin *Hierosolyma est perdita* (Jerusalem is lost), attributed by legend to Roman soldiers during the siege of Jerusalem in 70, and to warriors of the First Crusade who stopped for recreational pogroms in the Rhineland on their way to liberate the Holy Land from Muslim infidels.

At the time of the Hep! riots, unconverted Jews were generally barred from state jobs, including employment at universities—the latter being a customary way for writers and artists to support themselves. At age twenty-seven, Heine was already a poet of some repute but remained financially dependent on his wealthy uncle, the Hamburg banker Salomon Heine. Heinrich was baptized into the Lutheran church on June 28, 1825, by a sympathetic pastor who apparently knew that the conversion was only a formality. To his friend Moses Moser, one of a circle of Berlin Jewish intellectuals who dreamed of uniting Judaism—or a Jewish educational background—with contemporary German culture, Heine wrote, "From my way of thinking, you can well imagine that baptism is an indifferent affair. I do not regard it as important even symbolically, and I shall devote myself all the more to the emancipation of the unhappy members of our race. Still I hold it as a disgrace and a stain upon my honor that in order to obtain an office in Prussia—in beloved Prussia—I should allow myself to be baptized."[3]

The plan was for Heine to support himself, and his writing, as a lawyer or teacher at a law school—both positions closed to unconverted Jews in Prussia. For many German Jews of his generation, conversion did open public jobs, including those in universities and government departments. Heine's and Moser's friend Eduard Gans, a protégé of Hegel at the University of Berlin and one of the first German Jews to earn a doctoral degree in jurisprudence and philosophy, finally converted to Protestantism (a few months after Heine) after having been denied any academic position. The magic baptismal waters soon landed him a job on the faculty of the University of Berlin. But that did not happen for Heine (possibly because of his openly expressed democratic political views). Heine was furious at Gans for converting, but he was too self-aware not to realize that his reaction was a projection of anger at himself for having done the same thing. Rarely has an opportunistic conversion produced so little for someone who considered baptism so great a stain upon his honor. "I think so often about Gans because I do not want to think about myself," he told Moser. "I get up at night and curse myself in front of the mirror."[4] Beloved Prussia. For Heine, as for so many other German Jews, the real beloved was the German language.* As Elon notes, Heine was the first German Jewish writer to assert (in 1820) that his true homeland, or fatherland, was the German language, "our most sacred possession, . . . a fatherland even for him who is denied one by malice and folly."[5]

•

If issues in intellectual and moral history could be settled by quantitative measures, the scholarly and religious attention devoted to Jewish conversions throughout the ages would have to be deemed disproportionate. During the past two thousand years of Western civilization, conversions from paganism to Christianity and from one branch of Christianity to another far outnumber any conversions from Judaism to Christianity (or vice versa). If we are considering secular influences on religious conversion, the Reformation alone changed many more people's lives than any attempt to convert Jews—by force, persuasion, or, most notably in Germany, the seductive promise of baptism as, in Heine's words, the "admission card to European culture." And yet the turning points and ultimate fates of civilizations are not determined by numbers alone. Judaism, to paraphrase Langston Hughes's famous line about slavery and blacks in white America, has always been the rock upon which Western Christianity stumped its toe.† Had the Moors, instead of moving east to Turkey (and beyond) and south to Africa, also dispersed themselves throughout Europe, as the Jews did after their expulsion from Spain, Western Christianity would have

---

* My great-grandfather, a German Jew who studied at the University of Breslau (now Wrocław, in Poland), immigrated to the United States in 1849, after taking part in the failed revolution of 1848. His continuing attachment to German culture was demonstrated in New York in the 1860s and 1870s, when he saw to it that both of his sons learned to read and write German. After my father's death, I found correspondence from the turn of the century in German between my grandfather and an unknown aunt in Berlin. Only with my father's generation, born in the twentieth century, did familiarity with the German language die out in the Jacoby family.

† In his poem "American Heartbreak," Hughes describes slavery as the "rock on which Freedom / Stumped its toe . . ."

had two damaged toes. There is no reason to think that the ghetto gates of the pre-emancipation era would not have locked in Muslims as well as Jews. But that would have been another story. The unconverted Jew and unconverted Muslim both posed a challenge to Christianity's absolute truth claim, and that is why the Convivencia collapsed with the Catholic rulers' reconquest of the Iberian Peninsula. In the end, though, only the Jews remained to pose the challenge by their unconverted presence in the heart of Europe.

Throughout Christianity's first millennium, literally millions of new believers were, had to be, the children, grandchildren, and great-grandchildren of pagans. Yet no one referred to these Christian converts as "assimilated pagans" or suggested that they were not to be trusted because their ancestors had once painted their skin and howled at celestial bodies as a form of worship. So it is impossible to write a secular history of religious conversion in the West without recognizing the special place of Jews, for many Christians of many eras, as a living rebuke to the majority religion. Judaism, like Christianity and Islam, is a historical religion but—even though Abraham is the biblical father of both Israel and Ishmael—Judaism has the first historical claim. The refusal of Jews to give up that prior claim made their conversion more important to Christians, at least until the recent modern era, than the conversion of any other people. (In my Catholic elementary school in the 1950s, our daily morning prayers still included a special plea for the conversion of the Jews as well as the conversion of Russia, thought to be lost to atheistic communism.)

Even converted Jews—assimilated into and in many instances making invaluable contributions to the cultures in which they lived—posed a challenge, because of the enduring suspicion that something about Jewishness adhered to a convert even after the ceremonial and theological rebirth of baptism. As Heine's comments about his conversion suggest, this Christian suspicion could in some instances be well founded—and not only because of the racialization of anti-Semitism that reached its apotheosis in Nazi Germany and had its closest antecedents in the Spanish cult and laws of *limpieza de sangre*. There was something about Jews themselves that prevented not their assimilation but their disappearance into Christian society, in a fashion that affected both the converted and the unconverted. And if Jews lived, as so many did in Europe, in societies that wanted them to disappear rather than assimilate, religious conversion did not, could not, accomplish that end.

For German Jews, the desire to be treated like everyone else—say, for purposes of getting an education or making a living—stood in delicate equipoise with a sense of specialness, of not merely having survived but of having contributed so much to their culture against such great odds. By the beginning of the nineteenth century, the tension between the Jews' sense of specialness and their knowledge of daily discrimination was heightened, and rendered more tragic, by their profound love for German culture and language. It is both the profundity of the love, and in some (though by no means all) respects the lack of reciprocity from German Christians—not that world's eventual ruination under Hitler—that gives the conversion experience of post-Enlightenment German Jews its particular poignancy.

Only fifty-four years separate Heine's birth from the arrival in Berlin of fourteen-year-old Moses Mendelssohn (1729–86), the father of the Jewish Enlightenment, known throughout Europe as the "German Socrates" and in Germany as "the Jewish Luther." (Given Luther's strongly expressed anti-Semitic views, the latter appellation is a stellar example of contemporary German intellectuals' misunderstanding of even the most respected Jews among them.) Mendelssohn was an observant Jew in the small-"r" reformed fashion, which would eventually turn into Reform Judaism with a capital "R." In spite of Mendelssohn's own religious devotion, four of his six children who lived to adulthood became converts to Lutheranism. His most famous grandchild, the composer Felix Mendelssohn-Bartholdy (1809–47), was an authentically devout Lutheran. The composer's father, Abraham, had changed his name to Bartholdy after converting to Christianity, but Felix always insisted on keeping the hyphenated "Mendelssohn." According to one account (possibly apocryphal), the young composer's father once presented him with business cards bearing the single surname "Bartholdy," and Felix threw them out.[6] But Mendelssohn's wife was the daughter of a Huguenot pastor, and the composer's deep interest in Christian music was a sore point with some of his Jewish contemporaries.* In 1846, the uncomfortable convert of convenience Heine wrote, with what can only be described as vulgar malice, to a

---

* To avoid confusion, I refer to the composer simply as Mendelssohn from this point.

friend, "If I had the good fortune to be Moses Mendelssohn's grandson, I would not use my talents to set the piss of the Lamb to music."[7] The composer's sincere Christianity, and his commitment to the revival of Bach's sacred music (which, astonishing as it seems today, went out of fashion for nearly seventy years after his death), did nothing to mitigate the taint of his Jewish lineage as far as Jew-haters were concerned.

Richard Wagner, in his notorious 1850 essay, *"Judentum in der Musik"* ("Jewishness in Music"), declared that Mendelssohn, as a Jewish composer, could never have achieved the profound musical understanding of a true German. This ex cathedra pronouncement was made even though Mendelssohn had become the key figure in the revival of interest in Bach's works in Germany. In 1829, at age twenty, Mendelssohn conducted a historic performance of Bach's long-forgotten *St. Matthew Passion.* The event marked the restoration of Bach's great liturgical composition to the most revered canon of German music. Based on Mendelssohn's own study of the score, the performance was the first to be widely reviewed by musical experts since Bach's death. While it would be foolish to suggest that Bach could ever have been totally forgotten, the renaissance of popular and critical acclaim for his body of work would surely have taken longer without Mendelssohn's intervention. The story of Felix Mendelssohn, never regarded as simply a German composer in his own time and of course reviled in the Nazi era, embodies, in the most sorrowful way, the limits of conversion as a transformative instrument for Jews in the country to which they were so deeply attached.

The end for the Mendelssohn line of German Jewish converts to Christianity is encompassed in the searing, ironic novel *Mendelssohn Is on the Roof,* by the Czech Jewish writer Jiři Weil. Prague, like Breslau, Danzig, Memel, and many other cities throughout the parts of Europe that once belonged to either the Austro-Hungarian or Prussian empire, had a large community of German-speaking Jews who identified themselves with German culture. In the novel, set in occupied Czechoslovakia (in Nazi-speak, the Protectorate of Bohemia and Moravia) during World War II and originally published in Czechoslovakia in 1960, SS General Reinhard Heydrich, a lover of music and—even for his breed—a notably virulent hater of Jews, has ordered his minions to remove a statue of the Jew Mendelssohn from the roof of a Prague concert hall. There is only one problem: the workers do not have the slightest idea of what the composer looked like, so they decide to tear down the statue with the biggest nose—which happens to be a bust of Wagner. The Nazis, worried that they may be making a mistake, then pick the wrong Jew to try to identify the real Mendelssohn. The SS commandeers, as an "expert" adviser, an ultra-Orthodox Talmudic scholar who does not listen to secular music or look at graven images, and to whom the name of the reformer and philosopher Moses Mendelssohn—forget about his grandson, the Christian composer—is anathema.

Ambitious Jews elsewhere, in continental Europe and in England, also faced the question of whether to convert in Christian societies that always perceived a conflict between being a Jew and being, say, a true Englishman or Frenchman. But it is difficult to imagine Heine's near contemporary Benjamin Disraeli (1804–81) writing about England with the double edge of Heine's famous opening lines from "Night Thoughts"—"Should I think of Germany at night / It puts all thought of sleep to flight." But, then, it is impossible to imagine a Jew, converted or unconverted, rising to the highest level of politics in nineteenth-century Germany, either before or after unification, as Disraeli did in Victorian England.

•

If there ever was a conversion of convenience, even though it turned out quite inconveniently, Heine's stealth baptism as a Lutheran certainly qualifies. His early life in French-occupied territory was not free of anti-Semitism, and his first mention of his Jewishness in his memoir, in a passage titled "My First Flogging," is infused with a characteristic ambiguity. Young Heinrich asked his father who his grandfather was, and his father replied, "Your grandfather was a little Jew, and had a long beard." For whatever reason, Heine repeated his father's comment to his classmates at school the next day and inadvertently started a commotion. "The boys jumped on to the benches and tables, pulled the blackboards down from the walls, threw them and the inkstands on to the floor," Heine recalled, "with shouts of laughter, bleatings, gruntings, yellings, and crowings—a fiendish concert, with one burden, 'His grandfather was a little Jew with a long beard.'" The class tutor, a Jesuit priest, blamed Heine for having aroused his schoolmates by talking about a grandfather who was a Jew with a beard. The miscreant was then "soundly flogged in consequence." Heine describes being beaten to the point where "the stripes left on my back were dark blue. I have never forgotten this."[8] He then provides a telling description of the ways in which such an experience affected his own imaginative picture of his Jewish family background.

> With the name of the man who gave me my first flogging, I recall the occasion of it, namely my unfortunate genealogical confession; and the association is still so strong that, whenever I hear of a little Jew with a long beard, I feel creeps down my back. . . . I never afterward felt any great desire to make a nearer acquaintance with such a doubtful grandfather, or to give a description of my family tree to a large audience, when it had been so badly received by a small one.
>
> I will not entirely pass by my paternal grandmother, though I have little to say of her. She was a remarkably handsome woman, and the only daughter of a Hamburg banker, known far and wide for his wealth; which leads me to suppose that the little Jew, who carried her off from her father's house to his humble home in Hanover, must have possessed some qualities besides his long beard, and been a worthy man.[9]

What this passage does not say is probably more important than what it does say. Why, if you were asking your father what his father was like, would his first response be that your grandfather was a little Jew with a beard? Why not say he was a butcher, a baker, a candlestick maker as well as a Jew? Why would a boy pass on such a provocative description to his (presumably Gentile) schoolmates? Why, exactly, does having married the daughter of a banker mean that the little Jew must have had some admirable qualities—especially since greed was a prominent feature of negative anti-Semitic stereotypes?

Heine remained financially dependent on his uncle Salomon, because his conversion, as already noted, failed to provide an admission ticket to a career in the Prussian bar after he received his law degree from the University of Göttingen. Writing poetry, then as now, was a financially insecure enterprise—even if the poetry of the *Book of Songs*, published in 1827, had already found a home in the hearts and minds of Germans who loved lyric verse. Heine is often considered one of the most easily translatable German poets into many languages, but all translations of lyric poetry into English are problematic, because of the relatively rigid English word order and absence of convenient case endings to facilitate rhyme. It is difficult to imagine, for example, that Heine's well-known (in Germany) poem, "The Home-Coming," written in 1823–24, resounds in this wooden fashion in German ears:

> *I ask'd for their aunts and their cousins,*
> *And many a tiresome friend;*
> *I ask'd for the little puppy*
> *Whose soft bark knew no end. . . .*
> *Then cried the little sister:*
> *"The small and gentle hound*
> *"Grew to be big and savage,*
> *"And in the Rhine was drown'd."*[10]

Yet there are other verses, in the same inevitably disappointing translations, that do convey the power of *The Book of Songs.*

> *I call'd the Devil, and he came,*
> *And with wonder his form did I closely scan;*
> *He is not ugly, and is not lame,*
> *But really a handsome and charming man.*
> *A man in the prime of life is the devil,*
> *Obliging, a man of the world and civil; . . .*
> *My juridical works did he kindly praise,*
> *His favourite hobby in former days.*
> *He said that my friendship was not too dear,*
> *And then he nodded, and look'd severe,*
> *And afterwards asked if it wasn't the case*
> *We had met at the Spanish ambassador's rout?*
> *And when I look'd him full in the face*
> *I saw him to be an old friend without doubt.*[11]

Heine's extensive body of prose is, not surprisingly, more accessible than his poetry to those who do not read German. His prose, including satirical essays, travel writing, letters, and clearly delineates his memoir, that his views on religion, Jewishness, Christianity, and his own conversion. In *Die Stadt Lucca,* based on his travels in Italy and completed after his return to Germany in 1830, Heine attacks all state-established religion—in part because he considered it the chief barrier to the unification of Germany. "Were there no state religion," he wrote, "no privileging of particular dogmas and rites, Germany would be united and strong and her sons would be glorious and free. But this way our poor fatherland is torn because of religious conflict, the people are split into hostile religious parties: Protestant subjects quarrel with their Catholic princes or vice versa. Everywhere there are suspicions of crypto-Catholicism or crypto-Protestantism, everywhere accusations of heresy, espionage of opinions."[12] (It is understandable that in 1830, with the sectarian religious wars of the seventeenth century in mind, Heine focused on denominational favoritism rather than on the larger issue of whether there should be any relationship at all between churches and state. He could not have anticipated the situation in modern, secular Germany, in which there is no established church but the state is involved in providing some financial support for many religious activities, including education. Nor could he have anticipated that Germany would have, as it does now, one of the largest Muslim populations in Western Europe—which has posed a challenge to the principle, first written into the Weimar Constitution, that church and state be separated but that the state hold a "cooperative" relationship with all faiths. During the past decade, for example, numerous court cases in Germany have involved the relationship between German laws protecting women's rights, and conservative Islamic religious practices that violate the secular statutes.)

In any case, Heine was being disingenuous, since he saw Catholicism as a far greater threat than Protestantism to both religious liberty and representative government. As a political liberal, he associated the Catholic Church with a wide variety of anti-modernist social positions, including support for an authoritarian monarchy and the divine right of kings. Most German Jewish intellectuals, who tended to be left of center politically, would never even have considered converting to Catholicism rather than Lutheranism. Heine, grappling with his own shame at having converted to Lutheranism for purely pragmatic reasons, wrote to Moser, "I really don't know how I can help myself in this bad situation. I might become Catholic and hang myself out of exasperation."[13]

It is impossible to exaggerate the pain and shame entangled with the conversions of many highly educated German Jews of this era. In 1842, while living in France, Heine wrote "The New Jewish Hospital in Hamburg." His uncle had endowed a hospital in Hamburg and was subsequently denied both local citizenship and admission to the city's Chamber of Commerce. Salomon Heine then decided that the hospital would be open to Gentiles only if and when full civil rights were conferred upon Hamburg's Jews. For Heine, this was an occasion to reflect on the misfortune of Jewish birth rather than on the evils of prejudice and discrimination.

> *A hospital for the poor and weary Jew,*
> *For sons of man that suffer three-fold ills;*
> *Burdened and baned with three infirmities;*
> *With poverty, disease, and Judaism!*
>
> *The worst of all has ever been the last,*
> *The Jewish sickness of the centuries,*
> *The plague caught in the Nile stream's slimy vale,*
> *The old unwholesome faith that Egypt knew.*
>
> *No healing for this sickness! All in vain*
> *The vapor-bath and douch, vain all the tricks*
> *Of surgery, vain all this house may bring*
> *. . . to its fever-tossing guests.*[14]

These lines were written in Paris, where Heine lived from 1831 (after the French revolt of 1830, which removed the Bourbons from the throne of France and replaced the reactionary Charles X with Louis-Philippe) until his death in 1856. He had left for Paris in early 1831, after witnessing another round of Hep! riots (partly in response to the turmoil in France) the previous fall. His last attempt to secure a state job with a steady income (as legal officer for the Hamburg Senate) was turned down. The liberal newspaper *Augsburger Allgemeine Zeitung* then offered Heine a job as its Paris correspondent, and he left Germany for good. (Although Heine never considered himself a permanent émigré, he returned to Germany just twice—to see his elderly mother—in the twenty-five years before his death.) From Paris, he continued to deliver sharp criticism of autocratic German politics and of the relationship between church and state in the various regions of Germany. Although he was not as dedicated a political liberal as his fellow émigré Börne, he was irritating enough to Prussian authorities that they made a formal request for Heine's expulsion to the French Foreign Ministry.* The French said no.

Heine, who spoke excellent French (though with a German accent) as a result of his schooling while Düsseldorf was occupied by Napoleon's troops, was highly regarded by leading contemporary French writers, including Victor Hugo, Honoré de Balzac, George Sand, and Alfred de Musset. In his mid-thirties, Heine cut a dashing, romantic figure. The writer Théophile Gautier would recall Heine as a "German Apollo" whose "blue eyes sparkled with light and inspiration; his round full cheeks, graceful in contour, were not of the tottering romantic lividness so fashionable at that date. On the contrary, ruddy roses bloomed, classically on them; a slight Hebraic curve interfered, without altering its purity, with the intention which his nose had had of being Greek; his harmonious lips, 'paired like two fine rhymes,' to use one of his phrases, had a charming expression when in repose; but when he spoke their red bow shot out sharp and barbed arrows, sarcastic darts which never failed in their aim; for no one was ever more cruel to stupidity. To the divine smile of Apollo succeeded the leer of the satyr."[15] In addition to the comment on a Hebraic curve that prevented Heine's nose from being Greek, Gautier alludes to the intellectual falseness of Heine's conversion: "If it was repugnant to him to believe that God made himself man, he had no difficulty in admitting that man had made himself god; and he conducted himself accordingly."[16]

Heine fell in love with a young Frenchwoman, Mathilde Mirat, and married her in a Catholic ceremony—though he did not convert to Catholicism—in the Church of Saint-Sulpice. The ease with which such a marriage, which contradicted just about every Roman Catholic regulation imaginable, could be arranged says much about the anti-clerical climate, at least among the educated upper classes, in early-nineteenth-century Paris. Heine and Börne were both witnesses at a

* One of Heine and Börne's many disagreements was about Napoleon, for whom Heine retained considerable admiration.

similar church wedding in Paris, about which Börne remarked, "Here a baptized Jew from Frankfurt is marrying a Christian woman from England—God only knows what her origins are. The wedding's in Paris and of the four witnesses, one is a Christian, one is a Jew, and two are converts who happen to be leading German writers and the pride of the German federation."[17]

The quarrels that did arise between Börne and Heine may have been due at least in part to the differences in temperament between a poet and a full-time political writer. Within a few years after their departure for France, both Heine's and Börne's works, defined as blasphemous, anti-Christian, and anti-German, were banned by the censors in a number of German states. Heine posed a problem for German readers (including censors) that someone like Börne did not, in that the former wrote poems touching deep feelings about the German land, landscape, and language—while at the same time writing prose that frequently excoriated the social, political, and religious foundation of German life. It was easier for nationalistic German readers (and censors) simply to hate Börne's works criticizing Germany, because he did not also write poetry that touched other, more emotional chords of attachment to his native land. In this respect, Heine presented much the same dilemma to the German censors of his day that the beloved Russian poet Boris Pasternak (1890–1960)—a Christian by conviction but a Jew by birth—was to pose in the twentieth century for Soviet censors. When, in his sixties, Pasternak wrote the novel *Doctor Zhivago*—published not in the Soviet Union but abroad—he questioned the very foundation of the Bolshevik Revolution in ways that were never addressed in his poems. How could the poet of Mother Russia be reconciled with the novelist describing the ruin of a world and the undermining of individual morality by the Leninist and Stalinist state? Such a man could not be allowed to leave the country to accept the 1958 Nobel Prize for Literature, even though—and because—copies of *Doctor Zhivago,* in samizdat as well as in editions issued by Russian émigré publishers, had by then been read by many Russian intellectuals.

In his preface to the epic poem *Germany: A Winter's Tale,* written in France and published in 1844, Heine described the dilemma posed by censorship with a candor that Pasternak, living inside a repressive police state, could not. Although Heine insisted that he had "hastened without fail to soften or cut out whatever seemed to be at odds with the German climate," he found that his Hamburg publisher wanted still more rewrites to evade the censors. "In my hasty-spirited annoyance," Heine acknowledged, "I have torn the fig leaves off some naked thoughts, and perhaps have given offense to ears of fastidious primness. . . . But what I foresee with even greater regret is the hue and cry that will be raised by those pharisees of nationalism whose antipathies coincide with those of the governments. . . . I can already hear their beery voices: 'You even slander our colors, you despiser of the fatherland, you friend of the French, to whom you want to surrender the free Rhine!' Calm yourselves. I shall respect and honor your colors when they deserve it, when they are no longer a pointless or servile triviality. Plant the black-red-gold flag on the heritage of German thought, make it the banner of a free humanity, and I will give my heart's blood for it."[18] Heine also declared that he would never surrender the Rhineland to the French, "for a very simple reason—because the Rhine belongs to me." He described himself as "the free Rhine's much freer son" and said he did not see why the area should belong to anyone but Germans.

Yet, in 1834, in his *On the History of Religion and Philosophy in Germany,* Heine had warned that a united Germany might be capable of enacting a bloody drama "compared to which the French Revolution will seem like a harmless idyll." It would be anachronistic to see this famous quotation as a prediction of what was to come in Nazi Germany, but it could certainly be seen as a harbinger of the brutality and crazed nationalistic militarism of the Franco-Prussian War. If it is difficult to reconcile the two Heines on display in these quotations, separated by only a decade, it is next to impossible to pass judgment on the multiple loyalties and layers of personality involved in his attitudes toward the religion of his birth; the nominal Protestantism of his conversion; and the "fatherland" he felt he could not inhabit without converting.

•

There are, however, a number of indisputable realities behind what one scholar calls Heine's "transparent masks."[19] He was an outsider many times over—an exile in France who never became a French citizen; a nominal Protestant; a German and a Jewish writer, considered both (or only one, depending on the reader's politics) by his countrymen. The German Lutheran theologian August Nodnagel bluntly made the case against any consideration of Heine as a purely German, Christian writer: "Indeed, one can see through him and not without reason he claims several times that he is a Protestant. He can say this a hundred times. We will continue to believe . . . that he is a Jew."[20] Heine spoke contemptuously of all religion, but his antipathy toward Catholicism, for political and theological reasons, was clearly stronger than his distaste for any other faith. In Germany (no wonder thoughts of that land kept him awake at night), his critiques of Catholicism were often dismissed on the grounds that, as a Jew by birth, he had no "standing" in disputes between the various branches of Christianity: only real Protestants had the right to attack the Roman Catholic Church. Heine had made himself a soft target for these essentially anti-Semitic arguments by his own denunciations of his conversion.

Heine's poem "Disputation," based on the many public disputations between rabbinical and Christian scholars in late medieval Spain, skewers both Catholic and Jewish teaching, but the choicest barbs are reserved for the Catholic side. The Franciscan debater begins by exorcising demons supposed to reside in his rabbinical opponent and moves on to the essential doctrine of Catholicism.

> *Having thus expell'd the devil*
> *By his mighty exorcism,*
> *Comes the monk, dogmatically,*
> *Quoting from the catechism.*

> *He recounts how in the Godhead*
> *Persons three are comprehended,*
> *Who, whenever so they will it,*
> *Into one are straightway blended.*

> *'Tis a mystery unfolded*
> *But to those who, in due season,*
> *Have escaped from out the prison*
> *And the chains of human reason.*[21]

The rabbi replies:

That three persons in your Godhead,
And no more, are comprehended,
Moderate appears; the ancients
On six thousand gods depended. . . .

That the Jews in truth destroy'd him
Rests upon your showing solely,
Seeing the delicti corpus
On the third day vanish'd wholly.[22]

This poem has often been criticized, especially by Orthodox Jews, as an example of Heine's "Jewish self-hatred," because the last verse quotes a Spanish noblewoman who says that both the rabbi and the Franciscan friar are in "stinking condition." Nevertheless, Heine definitely gives the rabbi the best and wittiest lines in this poem about the sort of disputation a Jew could never win, because, even if his arguments were deemed by the audience to be more clever than the Catholic case, the "winning" Jew would be either driven out of town or killed.

•

In February 1848, when the ultimately doomed democratic revolutions were springing up throughout Western and Central Europe, Heine suffered a seizure of some type that left him half paralyzed and half blind. He was largely confined to bed for the rest of his life, but his mental powers were unaffected (which suggests that the persistent gossip that he suffered and died from syphilis was unfounded). Heine wrote some of his most beautiful, witty, satirical, and politically powerful poems (including "Disputation") during the years of his drawn-out, painful dying. When he was physically unable to write, he dictated both prose and poetry. During these years, although Heine made it clear that he had no more use for Judaism as a religion than he did for Christianity, he wrote certain poems, notably "Princess Sabbath," that were not nostalgic but elegiac in their portrait of certain Jewish traditions. He envisions a prince named Israel, who has been transformed into a dog. And who, "As a dog, with dog's ideas, / All the week, a cur, he noses / Through life's filthy mire and sweepings, / Butt of mocking city Arabs." Once a week, though, the dog is transformed back into his real form.

> *But on every Friday evening,*
> *On a sudden, in the twilight,*
> *The enchantment weakens, ceases,*
> *And the dog once more is human.*

> *And his father's hall he enters*
> *As a man, with man's emotions,*
> *Head and heart alike uplifted,*
> *Clad in pure and festal raiment.*[23]

Needless to say, "Princess Sabbath," with its lovely echo of the traditional Jewish "Sabbath Queen," is the poem most quoted by observant but liberal Jews who wish to claim Heine as a Jewish poet and give him a pass on the conversion engendered by the German Jewish conundrum.

Many words, used more often than not as epithets, were employed by Heine's Jewish and Gentile contemporaries and by subsequent generations to describe his religious beliefs. They include "atheist," "pantheist," "apostate," "false convert," and just about every variant of "devious Jew" that can be imagined. He is probably best described by the Enlightenment term "freethinker," which leaves room for everyone from atheists to those who believe in a personal, albeit not an institutional, god. In the immense volumes of apocrypha concerning well-known antireligious figures, including Voltaire, Thomas Paine, and Robert Ingersoll, nothing is more persistent than the rumor that they recanted on their deathbeds and begged for God's forgiveness.* Although Heine did not alter any of his views about Catholicism, Protestantism, or Judaism, he did, as he stated unambiguously in the 1851

---

* Ingersoll's wife, Eva, who was present at his death in 1899, prepared notarized statements testifying that her husband had died as he had lived—as a nonbeliever in any deity or any form of the supernatural. Ingersoll had anticipated that clergymen would spread the same kinds of stories about his deathbed conversion as they had about Paine and Voltaire.

postscript to the volume *Romancero,* return to belief in some sort of personal god. There is no question that his physical agony played a role in this change of heart, because he explicitly states that he is not talking about a deist or pantheist god, who may have set the world in motion but subsequently plays no part in the affairs of men. "When one longs for a God who has the power to help," Heine acknowledges, "then one must also accept his persona, his otherworldliness, and his holy attributes as the all-bountiful, all-wise, all-just, etc. The immortality of the soul, our continuance after death, then becomes part of the package so to speak, just as a butcher gives a fine marrow-bone free to a good customer."[24] Eternal life as a succulent marrow bone is, it must be admitted, a more inviting prospect than a heaven with harps and winged creatures. Heine must, however, have wondered whether he had purchased enough ordinary stewing meat during his lifetime to merit the butcher's choicest offering. There is a pervasive sadness in Heine's religious journey, from his ambivalence about being a Jew, through a conversion motivated entirely by temporal, secular needs, to a death in which he—in contrast to more committed freethinkers, like Paine and Ingersoll—made a tentative attempt to hedge his bets as he neared the end. But, then, Paine and Ingersoll never had to live out their lives with the double message that filled the minds of so many German Jews: *You're better and smarter than your countrymen / You're worse because you're a Jew.*

Heine was well aware that many of his antireligious and anticlerical friends were dismayed by his new hope—however halfhearted it might be—of a personal god to help man in adversity. "Yes," he acknowledged, "I have made peace with the Creator, as well as the created, to the great indignation of my enlightened friends, who reproach me for thus falling back into the old superstition, as they like to call my coming home to God." But Heine also emphasized that his "homesickness for heaven" had never led him to embrace any religious creed—either the Judaism of his birth or the Christianity of his opportunistic conversion. "No," he said, "my religious views and persuasions have remained free from all connection with the Church; no bells allured, no candles blinded my eyes. I have not toyed with any symbols, nor renounced my right to reason. . . . No, my religious convictions and views have remained free from any attachment to a church. . . . I have not played with any symbolism, and my reason has not altogether been renounced. I have forsworn nothing, not even my old pagan gods: to be sure, I have turned away from them, but we parted with love and friendship."[25] He describes a visit to the Louvre in May 1848—the last day he ever left the house that contained what he called his "mattress-grave." When he gazed upon the statue of the Venus de Milo for the last time, Heine broke down.

"I lay a long time at her feet," he recalls, "and wept so bitterly that it would have moved a stone. The goddess looked kindly down on me, but hopelessly, as if she would have said, Dost thou not see I have no arms and cannot help thee?"[26]

15

THE VARIETIES OF COERCIVE EXPERIENCE

Perhaps the most widely held misconception about the history of Jews in the Western world is that forced conversion, embodied in the popular imagination by the Spanish Inquisition, belongs to a past so distant that it has no possible bearing on conversion in the modern era. This misapprehension is present whether physically coerced conversion is depicted and remembered with straightforward horror or with the ironic humor of Mel Brooks's Inquisition song in the movie *History of the World: Part I.*

The wide array of jokes about the Inquisition simultaneously offers evidence of and one explanation for the fact that forced conversion is lodged in much less accessible regions of modern memory than, say, slavery. The acceptability of jokes is one measure of the degree to which any society has relegated the memory of gross injustice to its dustbin of history: we do not make jokes about African American slavery in the United States (not, at least, in polite society)—an absence that indicates, at a minimum, a continuing sensitivity based on a bad conscience. The Inquisition (though not the Holocaust) is a source of endless comic exploitation everywhere in the Western world; no joke about Torquemada is considered too tasteless.* This dispar-

---

* This is true even in Spain, where the government has admitted ancestral responsibility for the expulsion of Jews in 1492 (though not precisely for the Inquisition).

ity in historical sensitivity persists even though the emergence of slavery coexisted with the re-establishment of the Inquisition in Spanish
and Portuguese New World colonies. Moreover, seventeenth-century
religious wars, aimed at imposing religious conformity within nation-
states in the Old World and imposing the choice of conversion or exile
on a mass scale, were contemporaneous with the arrival of slaves in
the English-dominated portion of North America. But those wars
were, for the most part, between different kinds of Christians and
therefore have somewhat less historical resonance in modern societies
whose Christian institutions have embraced ecumenicism as a necessary response to secularism. Thus, the medieval Jewish Converso,
stretched on the rack until he confessed to secret "Judaizing," remains
the classic image of the forced convert in the West. The persistence of
that image attests not only to the persistent power of anti-Judaism and
anti-Semitism in Western civilization but to general modern ignorance
about the frequency with which people of many beliefs used to find
themselves in torture chambers if they professed the wrong doctrine at
the wrong time in the wrong place. That free religious choice was the
exception, not the rule, for most of Western history—and the history
of monotheism—is uncomfortable to remember and useful to forget
for those who still detest secularism. Even if one leaves the Inquisition
aside, the Enlightenment and post-Enlightenment Jewish conversion
experience, especially in Europe and in Germany, provides a template
for religious switches based on many covert and overt social pressures.
Unlike the rack, these pressures are thoroughly compatible with modernism (a truth also applicable to evidence-proof secular ideologies
such as Stalinist Communism).

In the dominant social narrative about Jewish emancipation (though
not one shared by all Jews), progress and assimilation characterized the
lives of European Jews—at least in countries like Holland, Germany,
France, England, and those parts of Italy not subject to political control
by the Papal States. Notorious cases like the Dreyfus affair intruded
into this narrative and called it into question for both secular Zionists and devout Orthodox Jews but did not vitiate it entirely for either
Jews or Gentiles. Moreover, the new United States of America offered
unique civil protection for Jews and a haven for those who had given
up any hope of achieving equality or prosperity in Europe. If Jews did
not like the way they were treated in the Old World, they could leave
for a country where their legal emancipation had not been a question

since Day One of the nation's existence (whatever extralegal barriers might and did exist). With all of the new choices available to Jews on both sides of the Atlantic, why would truly voluntary conversion not be one of them? Why should anyone speak of forced conversion in a post-Enlightenment context? The two-hundred-year-old narrative of voluntary conversion of Jews as a long-term victory for religious freedom would be disrupted only by the Nazi death camps. That conversion had not saved those of Jewish "blood" from filling the trains rolling toward Auschwitz, Chelmno, Majdanek, and Treblinka was a reality that could not be denied by Jews or Christians—especially after the scandalous attempts by both the Catholic Church and some Protestant leaders to single out Christian converts from Judaism for protection from the Nazi assault on unconverted Jews.

·

In the nineteenth century, German Jews imagined that they were avoiding discrimination, not death, by converting. If one adopts the most optimistic narrative of progress in religious toleration, the conversions of Heine and his literary friends, or Moses Mendelssohn's children, cannot be considered "forced" simply because they chose to take advantage (or, in Heine's case, to *try* to take advantage) of the greater opportunities open to Christians. Furthermore, it was in one sense predictable that German Jews might be especially amenable to conversion, since Germany was the birthplace of a Reform Judaism that wished to fit into rather than stand out from Gentile culture. For Gentiles in many countries (at least for Protestants, who used the vernacular rather than Latin in their own services), a Judaism that was not couched entirely in an impenetrable—again, to Gentiles—ancient language seemed more open to each nation's culture. Whether Reform Jews might convert to Christianity was beside the point. Orthodox Jews have long maintained that Reform Judaism is only one step from a willingness to abandon Judaism altogether. The difference is in the perspective: For the Orthodox Jew, conversion to Christianity is seen as a cultural and religious catastrophe rather than a legitimate choice. Therefore, anything seen as a step on that road, such as the abandonment of the laws of family purity, or services in the vernacular rather than Hebrew in Reform synagogues, was a catastrophe in the making.

The holes—in some countries pinpricks, in others brutal gashes—in the toleration/progress story of modern Jewry become fully evident only when the general narrative is broken down into specifics. First, the situation of Jews varied so vastly from country to country in the nineteenth century, and from region to region within certain countries, that it is dangerous to talk about what conversion meant to all but the most religiously observant. Second, although the rack and pyre were no longer part of the repertoire of acceptable punishments for "false" religious beliefs in the industrializing, better-educated countries of the world, the idea that there were true and false religions was very much alive. Third, forced conversion, in the literal sense, was still a real possibility for Jews in some places, and that possibility not only called spiritually motivated, voluntary conversions of Jews into question (for Jews no less than for Gentiles) but thrust the worst of the bad old days into the somewhat more enlightened religious psyche of the nineteenth century. The world was growing smaller. Knowledge of what happened in places where the Inquisition, in the literal as well as metaphoric senses, was still active did not stay in those places.

•

The 1858 kidnapping of Edgardo Mortara, the six-year-old son of a Jewish family in Bologna (then part of the Papal States), on the orders of the local head of the Inquisition, was the most notorious case of forced conversion in nineteenth-century Europe. (And, no, the year 1858 is not a typo, as one of this manuscript's first readers, thinking that such an event could not have happened later than 1558, suggested.) Young Edgardo, it was alleged, had been secretly baptized by a Catholic servant of the Mortara family, and baptism—even though the boy had not yet reached what the church considered the age of reason—was irrevocable. Edgardo, now a Catholic, must be educated as a Catholic and by Catholics and could no longer live in a Jewish home. The abduction of the Mortara boy became an international *cause célèbre* at the time, but it—like many other cases of forced baptisms and conversions in the territory controlled (with occasional interruptions) by the Vatican until the unification of Italy in 1870—would be largely forgotten in the twentieth century. Only when a Brown University professor, David I. Kertzer, wrote a detailed account of the case (*The Kidnapping* *of Edgardo Mortara,* 1997) did the nineteenth-century Inquisition's activities in Italy re-enter the historical conversation about the special position of Jews in Western attitudes toward conversion.*

In 1998, the Vatican's Commission for Religious Relations with the Jews released a report, commissioned eleven years earlier by Pope John Paul II, titled, "We Remember: A Reflection on the Shoah." The report's conclusion—that Catholicism's historical religious anti-Judaism (Augustine's "harass, but do not destroy" ethic) bore no responsibility for modern political anti-Semitism—came as no surprise to anyone who understood the deep conservatism of a church hierarchy shaped over a long period by John Paul. In rejecting the idea that anti-Semitism was related to theological anti-Judaism, the report states:

> By the end of the 18th century and the beginning of the 19th century, Jews generally had achieved an equal standing with other citizens in most States and a certain number of them held influential positions in society. But in that same historical context, notably in the 19th century, a false and exacerbated nationalism took hold. In a climate of eventful social change, Jews were often accused of exercising an influence disproportionate to their numbers. Thus there began to spread in varying degrees throughout most of Europe an anti-Judaism that was essentially more sociological and political than religious.[1]

The most important sentence in this passage is the first one, which combines falsehood and fact in equal measure. Although some Jews (mainly "court Jews" and bankers) had achieved influential positions, the fantasy that by the beginning of the nineteenth century "Jews generally had achieved an equal standing with other citizens in most States" could not possibly have been approved with a straight face by

---

* In a subsequent book, *The Popes Against the Jews* (New York: Alfred A. Knopf, 2001), Kertzer recounts similar reactions to the ones I received from first readers of this manuscript. He recalls letters from readers asking, "You mean there was still an Inquisition in 1858? I thought the Inquisition was back in the 1400s or 1500s." Kertzer is the son of a rabbi, Morris Kertzer, who was director of interreligious affairs for the American Jewish Committee from 1949 until 1961. His particular mission, so soon after the Holocaust, was the improvement of relations between Christians and Jews.

the historically educated members of the Vatican commission—least of all by the erudite John Paul. The authors of "We Remember" knew perfectly well that the church had used all of its influence, wherever and whenever it could, to discourage political measures that eased civil restrictions on Jews whenever and wherever they were proposed. The fate of Jews under a regime directly controlled by the Vatican was most clearly demonstrated after 1814, when, with Napoleon's occupying army on the run, Pope Pius VII returned to Rome from exile. Napoleon's rule, as it had removed restrictions on Jews in French-occupied areas of Germany, took the same action in areas of Italy, including Rome, that were part of the Papal States. One of the pope's first edicts on his return to Rome restored the gated Roman ghetto and re-established the Inquisition, which had been abolished by the French during the Napoleonic era.

Thirty-four years later, Jews in Rome were treated once again to a brief period of emancipation. In 1848, with the Italian Risorgimento becoming a part of the democratic revolutions sweeping much of Europe, Pope Pius IX was exiled from Rome as the victorious troops headed by Giuseppe Garibaldi (soon to be joined by the other great leader of the Risorgimento, Giuseppe Mazzini) entered the ancient city. A secular Roman republic was proclaimed, and, yet again, the gates of the ghetto were opened and Jews were granted legal equality. This time, the papacy was rescued by a French government that did not share Napoleon's commitment to secularism, after Pius called on the Catholic states of Europe to come to his aid. Pius returned to Rome in April 1850, and one of his first acts—like that of his predecessor Pius VII—was the reinstitution of the ghetto. (One cannot accuse the nineteenth-century papacy of inconsistency.) His next move was to turn to the Rothschild bank for a loan. Originally, the Rothschilds said no deal unless Roman Jews were freed from the ghetto—the last in Western Europe by that time. Pius, in a private letter to James de Rothschild, head of the family bank in France, gave assurances that he would soon abolish the ghetto, while indicating that it would be unseemly to do so as a direct quid pro quo for the loan.

Needless to say, the Vatican got the loan but the edict ending the ghetto was never issued. Pius IX got the better of the Rothschilds through exactly the sort of sly double-dealing that was such a widely held Christian stereotype about Jewish financiers. Despite having been bailed out by the French Rothschilds, Pius was to play the critical role in the Mortara affair. None of this shady history is mentioned in the 1998 Vatican report claiming that the fortunate European Jews had already enjoyed equal civic status before those nasty nationalist movements of the nineteenth century came along to spoil things.

The word "conversion," and its special application to Jews, is never mentioned in the report. Nowhere do we see the ghosts of European Jews who had converted, for whatever reasons, to either Protestantism or Catholicism—of Ludwig Börne, born into a Frankfurt where he and his kind were, like Roman Jews, locked behind ghetto walls at night; of the Anglican-baptized Benjamin Disraeli, asking a stunned and bitterly divided House of Commons in an 1847 debate over the right of Jews to hold public office, "Where is your Christianity, if you do not believe in their Judaism?"; of Edgardo Mortara's heartbroken parents, Marianna and Momolo, whose son was spirited away to Rome and eventually became a priest. "We Remember" remembered only what the church wanted to remember.

The question is why it was so important to the Catholic Church, on the cusp of its third millennium, to pretend that civic equality had been established between Jews and Christians not only long before the Holocaust but before the civic emancipation of Jews in Italy and Germany; before the surge of late-nineteenth-century French anti-Semitism that produced the Dreyfus case; and before the increase in the number and destructiveness of pogroms in Eastern Europe and Russia, which drove millions of Jews to seek refuge in America after 1880. There is no single answer to this question, in part because of the church's desire, at the end of the twentieth century, to conflate fascism and communism as secular ideologies, having nothing to do with and antagonistic to all religion. In this scenario, secularism—not Nazism, or the silence and collaboration of many Christian bystanders—was the real villain in the murder of millions of Jews and also in the war that killed millions of others—many of them Christians. That vast subject has engaged scholars of widely varying political and religious views for decades, and it is beyond the scope of this book. But one part of the explanation for the church's position is its own historical attitudes and practices regarding the conversion of the Jews. In stating that by the beginning of the nineteenth century Jews had achieved equal standing in most states, the church makes no acknowledgment that, in the regions controlled by the Vatican itself, the Inquisition, directed by the pope himself, was still inflicting conversion on Jews. The conversions were forced by the same methods that French Catholics under Louis XIV had used on Huguenot children—dragging them from their homes. And what could be a better indicator of the lengths to which the church was prepared to go to gain even one soul for Catholicism than the behavior of its officials toward Jews in the only physical territory directly controlled by the pope?

The nineteenth-century Roman Inquisition did not steal thousands of children, as the persecutors of the Huguenots did; the toll probably amounted to no more than a few dozen. Most of these tragedies were instigated, as was the Mortara case, by the stealth baptism of a Jewish child by a Gentile servant or even a childhood friend. The baptism of Jewish children by Gentile servants occurred in many countries, but the ceremony had no civil consequences in most places. For cowed Jews living under the power of the Vatican in the Papal States, involuntary baptism had quite a different, practical significance. In some instances, a Jewish child was taken because his or her father had voluntarily presented himself for instruction in the Catholic faith. Under the law in the Papal States, the police—who fused civil and religious authority— were then permitted to remove the man's wife and minor children from the ghetto for instruction. A wife could leave if, after thirty-nine days of Catholic proselytizing, she was still not convinced of the truth of Catholicism, but she could not take her child with her. The child would have been baptized, thereby rendering him (like six-year-old Edgardo Mortara) a Catholic forever in the eyes of the church. Such a converted soul could never be returned to the pernicious influence of a Jewish mother or family. The Vatican's Inquisition archives, which were opened to scholars for the first time in 1998, reveal many earlier cases that, because they unfolded in a different political climate, never attracted the international attention that the Mortara case did. One of these was the experience of twenty-four-year-old Jeremiah Anticoli, who presented himself for instruction in 1815 and was told that his wife and seven-month-old baby must be "offered" Catholic instruction as well. That night, police entered the ghetto and took away nineteen-year-old Pazienza Anticoli and her baby, Lazzaro. Pazienza refused to convert and was released after the requisite thirty-nine days. Her husband, who lost his enthusiasm for becoming a Catholic when he found out that his wife refused to join him, returned to her in the ghetto a few days later. The real tragedy, as usual, was that they would never see their baby again. As Kertzer presents the account from the Inquisition archives, "Just a few days after Pazienza and Lazzaro had been brought to the House of the Catechumens, the boy had been baptized. . . . Lazzaro the baby Jew became a Christian and was given a new name that symbolized his new identity. He was now Bernardo Maria Fortunato Andrea Cardeli."[2] *Fortunato* indeed.

The House of the Catechumens, a dreary facility near the Church of Madonna dei Monti in Rome, was founded in 1543 by Pope Paul III and was intended to take in both Jewish and Muslim candidates for conversion. The building was always occupied mainly by Jews, since the Moorish presence in Rome was much smaller than the Jewish population. The House of the Catechumens had separate sections for men, women, and baptized Jewish men who wished to study for the priesthood. "As priests," Kertzer observes, "the former Jews were particularly valued by the Church for their ability to proselytize among their ex-brethren, familiar as they were with life in the ghetto and Jewish traditions. However, Jewish converts were considered to be unsuited for pastoral duties, and not permitted to become parish priests."[3]

This distinction between priests who were born Catholic and priests who were converted Jews is a telling indicator that conversion, however religiously sincere, was never quite enough to make a Jew equal to a Gentile in the eyes of the church. *Protestants* who converted to Roman Catholicism, as many notable Anglican clerics did in nineteenth-century England, were considered perfectly suitable for the usual priestly duties. That even the taking of Catholic Holy Orders did not expunge the taint of Jewish birth in the Papal States provides yet another piece of evidence for the connection between anti-Judaism, based on religion, and anti-Semitism, based on modern nationalism and racist ideology.

Those who voluntarily entered the House of the Catechumens— a place most Roman Jews would have gone to any lengths to avoid passing—were, overwhelmingly, men. Like Anticoli, most were in their twenties and came from poor families. Conversion to Catholicism offered poor Roman Jews a chance to make a living outside the ghetto, just as conversion to Protestantism offered wealthier, educated German Jews a chance to enter state and university jobs open only to Christians. The lure of improved economic circumstances was the common element in many "voluntary" conversions of Jews from such vastly different cultural backgrounds as those in Germany and the Roman ghetto. Most (though not all) Jewish women who converted did so because they lacked Pazienza's courage in standing up to her husband—and they did not have the heart to leave their forcibly baptized children behind in the House of the Catechumens.

That those children would live out their lives as Catholics—that many baptized as infants would know nothing about their origins as Jews—was a given. At age six, Edgardo Mortara would certainly have been in no position to resist round-the-clock religious indoctrination—even if he had initially been terrified by his removal from his parents' home. And Pius IX took a personal interest in the boy—an interest that, coupled with the pontiff's rigid and sincere concept of his religious duty, would make him impervious to international pressure. Not even the protests of the French government, whose troops had returned Pius to Rome and toppled the Roman Republic, would move the pope. The protests of liberal newspapers throughout Europe, and as far away as the United States, only stiffened his resolve. The Vatican countered with stories in the Catholic press, which was becoming a force in both European and American cities with growing Catholic populations. The articles painted a portrait of a joyful little Edgardo, now that he was removed from the malign influence of his Jewish parents and neighbors, who had fully absorbed the divine grace of baptism and wanted nothing so much as to remain a Catholic.

Edgardo was raised in a seminary and ordained in 1873, at age twenty-one. Pius IX, his surrogate father, established a lifetime trust to ensure Pio Edgardo Mortara's future support. He spent his life preaching throughout Europe, generally telling the story of how baptism by a servant girl had saved him from the error of life as a Jew. In Mortara's sermons, Pius IX was the saintly hero who stood up to the world—all of the secular, godless heretics who would have had him returned to his parents—and saved him for Christ. Pio Edgardo lived many more decades, spending most of his time after World War I in an abbey in Bouhay, Belgium. He died on March 11, 1940, at age eighty-eight, just two months before Nazi armies occupied Belgium. Had Pio Edgardo still been alive when the storm troopers marched in, he would likely have been torn from his monastery, as the German Catholic convert

Edith Stein was from her Dutch convent, and sent to his death as a Jew at Auschwitz.

The Mortara case is a milestone in the secular history of conversion not because it typifies the pressure on Jews and Judaism in the early modern era—the Papal States can hardly be viewed as typical—but because it embodies the persistence of political enforcement of religious faith in Western history. That this case also proved to be the beginning of the end for direct forced conversion underlines the length of time needed for societies to attain anything like true religious choice. Pius IX's obduracy even in the face of entreaties from the French government, which was still upholding the pope's anachronistic secular authority, helped lead, after Italian unification, to the shrinkage of temporal papal power to Vatican City. Moreover, the notion that a child could be supernaturally transformed, without his knowledge, by being sprinkled with water by a Catholic—any Catholic—exemplified the theological absolutism at the core of the church's teaching on conversion. Pius IX, in a meeting with the French ambassador, told the Duke de Gramont that Edgardo could never be returned to his parents, because the child himself had embraced Christianity. He declared, "It is impossible for the head of the Church, for the Representative of Jesus Christ on earth, to refuse this child, for he begged me with an almost supernatural faith to let him share in the benefit of the Blood that Our Lord shed for his Redemption." Adding that he had reflected on the case intensively, the pontiff declared, "My decision is irrevocable."[4] The idea that one man possesses the authority to decide what another can and should believe seems preposterous even in this formal diplomatic exchange: it was no longer palatable even to European monarchists. By overreaching, Pius IX sealed his fate with the secular governments of the West—whether monarchies or developing democracies.

That Edgardo Mortara's kidnapping was a forced conversion at the start is evident to anyone who does not share the belief that a sprinkling of baptismal water, wanted or unwanted, whatever the age of the baptized, is a binding religious contract. But there is also no doubt that Mortara, after years of being educated by Catholic priests, and becoming one himself, fully believed in the Catholic faith. Thus is an initially forced conversion transformed into the "voluntary" embrace of a new faith. The malleability of memory—the tendency of the human brain to absorb and accept the messages it receives over a long period of time—blurs the line between forced and voluntary conversion in every era; it fully justifies skepticism about apparent religious choices that may not have been "chosen" in the beginning.

Mortara's development into the devout Catholic priest Pio Edgardo is simply an extraordinary example of an ordinary phenomenon. It also explains, on more than one level, the disappearance of this important case, from both Italian secular and general Western history, for more than 125 years. It is understandable that the Catholic Church, in its more ecumenically inclined twentieth-century incarnation, would not have wanted to draw attention to a notorious intervention in a Jewish family—an intervention that strikes modern readers as belonging more to the Middle Ages than to the nineteenth century. Before the post-Holocaust era, when the church began to re-examine its historical behavior toward Jews, Pius IX's successors would have been reluctant to condemn their predecessor for the Mortara affair, out of a combination of embarrassment and agreement that the only good Jew was a converted Jew. These two conflicting points of view, if you believe that Catholicism is the only true religion, are not mutually exclusive. Moreover, it should not be forgotten that it was Pius IX who conferred the dubious gift of papal infallibility on his successors by pushing through the new dogma at the First Vatican Council in 1870.

For Italian Jews, as Kertzer suggests, the aftermath of the Mortara kidnapping raised different issues involving their image of themselves and their religion. The church's reports about the young boy's love of Catholicism, followed by the preachings of the obviously devout adult priest, may have turned the case from an insult into a source of deep shame. Kertzer argues that the controversy "became a kind of public test of the relative merits of the two religions. It was a test the Jews lost." It made no difference that "Italian Jews were well aware of the psychological pressures exerted on the small boy and had no trouble coming up with a secular explanation of his ultimate decision to abandon his family and Judaism. . . . This did not make the transformation any more palatable." The kidnapped child who had once been seen by Jews as an innocent victim "became a man who was disdained, whose character had to be discredited. He could not be happy, he could not even be fully sane, for were he happy and sane, it would reflect poorly on the religion of the Jews. It was best not to talk of him at all."[5]

There is no supernatural mystery about why a six-year-old boy— removed from home and his parents, placed under the tutelage and constant scrutiny of caretakers preaching another religion, and per-

sonally singled out by a protector of power and charisma, Pius IX—
would "choose" to embrace his new life as a Christian. Nor is there a
mystery about why the drama of socially—if not physically—forced
psychological conversion has played out so many times, on a larger
scale, in Western history. The common element in these dramas has
always been theocracy, whether Catholic or Protestant (Muslims having behaved in a more tolerant fashion than Catholics when they controlled much of Iberia). It made no difference whether the conversions
took place in Spain after the Reconquista; in regions of France or what
is now Germany as civil power alternated between Catholics and Protestants; in an England where, beginning with Elizabeth I, it was much
better to be a Protestant belonging to the state-established church; or,
on a vast scale, in tsarist Russia with the Russian Orthodox Church
as the state religion. In any of these places before the Enlightenment,
initially forced conversion could turn into real faith, especially after
enough generations passed for families to forget their heritage naturally. What is remarkable about the history of the forcibly converted
Jews in Spain and Portugal, including those who eventually settled in
the New World, is not that so many forgot all traces of their heritage
but that some retained remnants now being unearthed among people
whose Sephardic Jewish descent was a family secret for hundreds of
years.

If the history of the Roman Catholic initiation of forced conversion seems to occupy a disproportionate amount of space in this oft-
told tale, it is only because, since the early Christian era, the Catholic
Church was in charge of more land and people in the West for a longer
period of time than any other faith. Had John Calvin's theocrats been
in control of Europe from 400 to 1500, the horrors inflicted on individuals, and the repression of religious expression in large populations,
would tell us the same story about forced conversion—with different
actors. The Protestants had less time than the Catholics to try to control people's souls.

•

There is no doubt, however, of the special place still occupied by
Jews in the entire narrative of conversion in the Western world. Even
though conversions to gain social and professional advantages cannot

be described as "forced" in the same sense that conversions under the Inquisition were forced, such conversions certainly cannot be seen as unpressured. Spineless, perhaps. Disrespectful of their heritage, sometimes. Opportunistic, most of the time. But opportunistic abandonment of Judaism was not always accompanied by the deeply conflicted attitudes displayed by many German Jewish converts to Christianity over many generations.

Disraeli, for instance, always distinguished between religious Judaism, which he viewed (or said he viewed) in the conventional Christian way as the prelude to Jesus's fulfillment of Old Testament prophecy, and his Jewish ancestry. He saw his Jewish forebears with an esteem that can only be described as romantic (as evinced in several of his novels). It is impossible to imagine Disraeli writing something as contemptuous of Jews as Heine's poem "The New Jewish Hospital in Hamburg." It may well be more than a coincidence (a point overlooked by an extraordinary number of English biographers) that Disraeli's father had him baptized at the age when, had his son been preparing for life as a religious Jew, he would have been studying for his bar mitzvah. As described in many biographies of England's first (and only) prime minister of Jewish descent, Isaac D'Israeli's decision to baptize all of his children was partly the result of dissension within his synagogue, which was divided between followers of the Reform movement imported from Germany, and Orthodox Jews who resented the changes in traditional forms of worship. But D'Israeli (who always spelled his name with the apostrophe, clearly indicating "of Israel") was obviously aware that many avenues of achievement, most notably in public life, would be closed to his children if they did not convert to the Church of England. This is not to say that Benjamin Disraeli's father dreamed that his thirteen-year-old son might become prime minister, but he wanted his children to have more opportunities than they would have as Jews.* At age thirteen, Disraeli would have been fully aware of the secular implications of his baptism.

Exactly how sincere or devout a Christian Disraeli really was cannot

---

* Had Isaac D'Israeli been prescient enough to baptize his son because he expected him to become prime minister of England, it would have been a feat of clairvoyance on a par with American birthers' claim that Barack Obama's parents arranged to have his birth records transferred from Kenya to Hawaii because they knew their son was going to grow up to become president of the United States.

be determined from his life after he began his climb to the top of "the greasy pole." He presented himself, as anyone of his background would have had to do to pursue a successful career, as a committed Anglican, but always as one who acknowledged his origins, who believed that Jews and Christians should have equal legal rights, and who, in a celebrated 1847 debate in the House of Commons, enraged many members of his own party by suggesting that their opposition to Jewish emancipation on religious grounds was really a cover for anti-Semitism in the modern sense. "If one could suppose that the arguments which we have heard . . . are the only arguments that influence the decision of this question," a furious Disraeli argued, "it would be impossible to conceive what is the reason of the Jews not being admitted to a full participation. . . . But you are influenced by the darkest superstitions of the darkest ages that ever existed in this country. It is this feeling that has been kept out of this debate; indeed, that has been kept secret in yourselves. . . ."[6] Disraeli was confronting his good Christian colleagues with something that no one wants to hear if he considers himself a broad-minded, tolerant person—the possibility that, deep down, he is a bigot.

The history of the battle for emancipation of English Jews was no less drawn out and complicated than the same struggle in Germany—despite England's longer and stronger tradition of limitations on the power of monarchy and guarantees of some individual liberties. Thomas Paine, as an excise-tax collector for the Crown (among many jobs) before his immigration to America, wound up in trouble with his bosses when, in coffeehouse debates, he forcefully voiced his indignation that Jews were required to pay taxes but not allowed to vote in the mid-eighteenth century. Depriving Jews of legal rights, he declared in what was then, in nearly all Christian societies, a novel argument, was a violation of the natural rights of man. When reports of Paine's statements about Jews reached his superiors, he was ordered to cease involving himself in all religious and political controversy. He did not follow orders and was, predictably, fired. This no doubt made Paine more receptive than he would otherwise have been to the suggestion of Benjamin Franklin, then representing the colony of Pennsylvania in London, that a man of Paine's rebelliousness and passion for the rights of man would do better in the American colonies than in the mother country.

For Jews, the Test Acts of 1673 and 1678, which had actually been aimed at Catholics, required a Christian oath and public acceptance of the Eucharist from the Church of England before a man could hold public office. Obviously, the acts would prevent any unconverted Jew from entering Parliament (although restrictions on Catholics had been lifted in 1829, both nonconformist Protestants and Jews were still affected by the laws passed during the reign of Charles II). The 1847 debate in the House of Commons presaged repeated attempts to release Jews from the oath-taking requirement; such bills were passed many times in the Commons but were defeated in the House of Lords. The debate was especially bitter because Lionel de Rothschild had been elected to the House of Commons from the City of London but, as an unconverted Jew, could not take the oath. The legislative wrangling over the oath continued until 1858, with a compromise that enabled each House of Parliament to determine the qualifications for its members. This was a personal compromise, however, applying only to Rothschild. It was not until 1866, with a new Parliamentary Oaths Act for both Houses, that office, holding for English Jews became a right rather than a privilege.

It is true that no Jew born in London in the 1790s was locked into a ghetto at night, as Jews were in Frankfurt. It is equally true that Jewish children in mid-nineteenth-century England, France, Germany, and even retrograde Russia were not being taken from their parents after being baptized by rogue Christian servants. But it is not true, as the encyclical "We Remember" explicitly claims, that Jews had achieved "equal status" in most states—by either the beginning or the end of the nineteenth century.

One may dismiss a conversion like Heine's as a nasty, thoroughly self-interested business, undertaken by a man who disdained Judaism and Christianity equally and whose emotions about Germany were much more conflicted than, say, Disraeli's feelings about England. But there is no denying that the depth of Heine's cultural conflict was shared not only by many of his German Jewish contemporaries but by subsequent generations of converts from the ghetto to Auschwitz. Was Heine any more conflicted than Edith Stein, now a Catholic saint, canonized by Pope John Paul II in 1998? Leaving aside, for a moment, the bitter subsequent controversy over Stein's death as a Jew at Auschwitz and her canonization as a Catholic martyr, there is the Edith

Stein, a philosopher and religious scholar, who was baptized in 1922 and whose deeply spiritual writings leave no doubt of the depth of her Catholic devotion. And yet Stein, just a decade later, would try to convince her fellow Germans (she still considered them her fellows) of the rectitude of Jewish families. Less than a century separates the opportunistic conversion of Heine from the more spiritual conversion of Stein, and only twenty years separate the gates of Auschwitz from the conversions of the last generation of German Jews who thought they had a future, as Christian converts or as Jews, in Germany.

16

EDITH STEIN (1891–1942):
THE SAINTHOOD OF A CONVERTED JEW

I F SINCERITY OF RELIGIOUS BELIEF was the only criterion, there could be no comparison between the conversions of Heinrich Heine, in the early era of German Jewish assimilation, and Edith Stein, just a decade before the Nazi darkness began to obliterate that dream (or nightmare, depending on one's point of view). Stein's embrace of Catholicism and her later entry into the Discalced Carmelite Order emerged from the deep spiritual needs of a woman who was an intellectual, a philosopher, and something of a mystic, but who also respected her Jewish heritage in a way that Heine never respected his.

There was minimal opportunism in Stein's conversion to Catholicism, because converting to Protestantism would have furthered the same social objectives (such as obtaining access to better employment prospects in academia) while causing much less angst among her Jewish family members and friends. Catholicism, as in Heine's time, was regarded with much greater animus than Protestantism by German Jews, and a Jew who became a Lutheran was more acceptable—or less unacceptable—to observant Jews than one who became a Catholic. Despite Martin Luther's crude anti-Semitism, the Jewish experience of being persecuted by Catholics was much longer and more intense, and many of Stein's Jewish academic mentors and friends were themselves converts to Lutheranism.

Thus, there is a double irony to Stein's present status as a Catholic martyr. Had she been a Protestant, she would still have met her death in a concentration camp as a Jew, but her Catholicism had already created a barrier between her and many Jewish friends who had converted to Protestantism. Without the international furor over the Vatican's attempt to portray Stein not as a Jewish victim of the Holocaust but as a martyr for Catholicism under her religious name, Sister Teresa Benedicta of the Cross, she would likely be seen today primarily as a female scholar and religious thinker, ahead of her time in the complicated history of twentieth-century feminism's relationship with Western patriarchal faith.

Stein was a complex and somewhat opaque woman on both an emotional and an intellectual level. This reserve is more apparent in her unfinished autobiography, *Life in a Jewish Family*, than in her religious and philosophical writings—in part because one expects more intimate revelations in a memoir, and in part because she never really comes to grips with the connection between her theological and philosophical ideas and her personal life. Most of the autobiography was written in 1933, after Hitler's election as chancellor of Germany, and there is a sense of urgency, as Stein says explicitly, about her attempt to portray ordinary middle-class German Jewish life at a time when the Nazi demonization of Jews was in its early phase. And though the autobiography is packed with details about her family, Stein erects a perceptible shield between her feelings and the facts of her life. She tells us that she once dreamed of marriage and a great love, for example, but does not tell us why she abandoned that dream for a life as a Bride of Christ.

One of Stein's purposes in writing her autobiography—perhaps her main purpose, despite or because of her conversion to Catholicism in 1922—was to demonstrate that German Jews were loyal both to Germany and to their Jewish heritage. In her introduction, Stein states what must have been as obvious to her contemporaries as it is in retrospect—that the rise to power of the Nazis had "catapulted the German Jews out of the peaceful existence they had come to take for granted" and forced them "to reflect upon themselves, upon their being, and their destiny." She quotes a Jewish friend who lamented, "If only I knew how Hitler came by his terrible hatred of the Jews." Stein herself uses the phrase "the Jewish question" and claims that many Gentiles, including Catholic youth groups, "have been dealing with it in all seriousness and with a deep sense of responsibility." Then she poses a question that inadvertently demonstrates how deeply anti-Semitic stereotypes had penetrated the psyches of German Jews themselves. She asks, "Is Judaism represented only by, or even only genuinely by, powerful capitalists, insolent literati, or those restless heads who have led revolutionary movements in the past decades?"[1] Stein's answer—as a woman whose childhood was spent in a somewhat observant German Jewish family in Breslau, as a former volunteer nurse who loyally supported Germany during the First World War, and as a product of the German education system from grammar school through university—is an emphatic no. It is Stein's strong sense of Germanness, along with her indignation that some Germans might think of Jews only as "insolent" intellectuals, financiers, or revolutionaries, that links her to Heine and places her conversion in its social as well as spiritual context.

One telling anecdote about Stein's mother could easily be a coda to Heine's 1844 statement that "the Rhine belongs to me" and that he was "the free Rhine's much freer son." When Stein's parents were married in 1871, the words of their wedding song were set to the melody of a popular martial tune, titled "The Watch on the Rhine," which begins, *"Es braust ein Ruf wie Donnerhall"* ("Tumult and cry like thunder's roll"). The song was written around 1840 and refers to the French challenge to the boundaries of the Rhine—precisely the controversy that prompted Heine's comments.* Stein observed that her mother had chosen the melody for her wedding song because she had always been a "German patriot" and therefore, even after the rise of Hitler, found it "incomprehensible that anyone should dare to dispute her German identity."[2] (Stein's parents were married not long after the unification of Germany under Otto von Bismarck, the "Iron Chancellor," and this was a time of intense German patriotism, especially for Prussians. Incorporating the "Watch on the Rhine" melody into a wedding was the equivalent of playing "Dixie" in the South, or "The Battle Hymn

---

* The title turns up again in the 1941 Hollywood movie *Watch on the Rhine*, starring Bette Davis, written by Dashiell Hammett and released before America entered World War II. Here the context was quite different: the message was that the rest of the world should be paying more attention to the German threat to world peace.

of the Republic" in the North, at an American wedding reception during the Civil War.)

Edith, as she recounts in a later portion of her memoir, would become an admirer of Bismarck. One of her most distinguished teachers at the University of Göttingen was the historian Max Lehmann (1845–1929), who strongly opposed Prussian militarism and whose ideal was English liberalism. "This was obvious especially in his course on Bismarck," Stein would recall. "Since partiality always incited me to do justice to the opposite side, I became more conscious here than I had been at home [in her native Breslau] of the virtues of the Prussian character; and I was confirmed in my own Prussian allegiance."[3] In her autobiography, Stein never deals with the subject of exactly how those so-called virtues, whether attributed to Prussia in particular or to Germany in general, fitted into the nightmare the Jews were already beginning to live out under the Nazis (or into the different wartime nightmare of her youth).

•

I became aware of Edith Stein in the early 1980s, when few of her writings had been translated into English, because the feminist movement had raised the profile of women in religion, and scholars were beginning to re-examine the lost contributions of women to religious thought. I was also interested in her for eccentric personal reasons. She grew up in Breslau, where many of my Jacoby ancestors had lived, and she initially attended the University of Breslau, where my great-grandfather Maximilian Jacoby was a student before he immigrated to the United States in 1849. My aunt Edith, Maximilian's granddaughter, who was fifteen years younger than Edith Stein and was born in the United States, also became a devout Catholic convert from what was originally a highly assimilated German Jewish—and then American German Jewish—family. (When more of Stein's writing began to be translated into English, in the 1980s, my elderly aunt, who by then had become involved with the "charismatic Catholic" movement within the church, read them with great interest.) With a particular kind of soulful, dark-haired beauty that unmistakably suggested her Jewish descent, Aunt Edith also bore a striking physical resemblance to Stein, as the latter appears in photographs taken in her twenties and thirties.

Among the most peculiar observations in Stein's autobiography are references to her not looking Jewish—or, presumably, not looking like what Jews were thought to look like by anti-Semites. It is hard to know exactly what Stein was thinking when she wrote about her non-Jewish appearance in 1933. Perhaps she meant that she did not "look Jewish" in the sense that some Yiddish-speaking Eastern European Jews from shtetls "looked Jewish" by virtue of clothes, hairstyles, and manners connected with strict, old-fashioned religious observance. Or that she did not have the hooked nose and gross features portrayed in Nazi propaganda. But Edith Stein certainly did look Jewish, just as my aunt did, in a style, conveying adventurousness and braininess, evident in photographs of many intellectual American and European Jewish women in the first three decades of the twentieth century. Stein's autobiography displays keen powers of observation, so it is hard to figure out why she was such a poor observer of what her own appearance probably signified to Gentile Others. Certainly, her conviction that she looked like a Gentile did not flow from any desire to "pass." And yet she also makes a point of saying that she readily acknowledged her Jewishness before her conversion (and never denied her Jewish origins after her conversion) *even though she did not have to.*

Describing a friend—a convert to Lutheranism from Judaism—with whom she worked in a military hospital during World War I, Stein notes matter-of-factly, "Of course, in the lazaretto, anti-Semitic remarks were to be heard at times. On such occasions, Suse [the converted friend] forthrightly envied me the ability to come forward with a simple acknowledgment that I was Jewish. (By the way, this used to astound people since no one took me to be Jewish.)"[4] Even though "Stein" is one of many German names that can be either Jewish or non-Jewish, it is simply impossible, looking at snapshots of Edith in her late teens and twenties, to think that no one in a German work setting would have suspected or assumed that she was a Jew. Had she been one of the small number of Jews who tried to survive the Second World War within large cities in Nazi Germany by hiding in plain sight (especially in Berlin), her appearance would have offered her little protection.* In any case, Stein's views about the difficulty of a convert's coming forth and saying she was Jewish, or that she had been born into a Jewish family, reveal a deep confusion about the capacity

---

* See Leonard Gross, *The Last Jews in Berlin* (New York: Simon and Schuster, 1982).

of a formal religious conversion to wipe out one's cultural and ethnic background (and what many people in her time called "race"). And another premise underlies this story about responses to anti-Semitic remarks: Stein assumes that only a Jew (converted or not) would voice any objections. Her assumption, judging from many other contemporary memoirs, was undoubtedly correct.* Although garden-variety anti-Semitism certainly was not responsible for Stein's conversion to Catholicism, it was an important part of the cultural context in which her life and spiritual yearnings must be viewed.

Stein was born on October 12, 1891—as it happens, the date on which Yom Kippur, the Jewish Day of Atonement, fell that year. She was the youngest of eleven children (seven of whom lived to adulthood) of Siegfried and Auguste Courant Stein. In the curriculum vitae accompanying her doctoral dissertation, *On the Problem of Empathy,* in 1916, she wrote, "I am a Prussian citizen and a Jewess." Auguste Stein was a woman of formidable strength, which she needed: her husband died when Edith was only two years old, leaving his widow with substantial debts and seven children to educate. Although she had never worked outside her home, Auguste took over her husband's lumber business and made a success of it. "Supplying the bare essentials for our daily needs was not enough for my mother," Edith recalled. "To begin with, she set herself an enormous task: no one should be able to say that my deceased father's debts had gone unpaid; bit by bit, they were wiped out to the last *Pfennig.* Next, her children were all to have a good education."[5] That included the girls as well as the boys. Edith received what would today be called her elementary- and secondary-school education at a municipal girls' school in Breslau, from 1897 to 1906. Then she studied three more years at the *Realgymnasium* (the closest equivalent would be a liberal arts college) associated with her former school. After earning her certificate of graduation from a humanistic *Gymnasium*—a requirement for going on to a university at what would, in many other countries, be called the gradu-

---

* The whole question of whether "outsiders" should remain silent bystanders when they hear racial, ethnic, or religious slurs against another group is of course a perennial social and ethical issue in many societies. In multiethnic countries, this is often one of the first ethical questions children bring home from the schoolyard. What is striking about Stein's observation is the utter matter-of-factness of her idea, as a young woman, that only a Jew speaks out against anti-Semitic remarks.

ate level—Edith began to study psychology, philosophy, and German philology, among other subjects, at the University of Breslau. Then, in what would be a turning point in her life, she moved on to the University of Göttingen for another four semesters and met her future mentor, the philosopher Edmund Husserl (1859–1938). Husserl, a Jew who had converted to Protestantism (like so many of Edith's academic friends and teachers), is an important figure in twentieth-century philosophy as a founder of phenomenology, which, to simplify greatly, emphasizes the study of phenomena, or conscious experience, from the subjective first-person point of view.* The phenomenological school of philosophy, as has been pointed out by many scholars, was not based on any premises that opposed Catholicism (or, for that matter, orthodox Protestantism). Stein did not have to undergo a "conversion" from her philosophical beliefs to become a Catholic, as she would have if she had been—to cite just two examples—a Spinozan or a dialectical materialist.

Another important influence on Stein during her student years was the philosopher Max Scheler (1874–1928), one of her few Catholic professors. Scheler, the son of a Jewish mother and a Lutheran father, had converted to Catholicism as a young man but had left the church (perhaps as a result of a checkered marital history). Stein's dissertation on empathy was, in many respects, inspired by Scheler's *The Nature of Sympathy,* published in 1913. (Scheler's works would also have a powerful influence in the 1940s on a Polish seminary student, Karol Wojtyła, who would rise through the church hierarchy to become Pope John Paul II.)

At the time Scheler met Stein in Göttingen, he had recently returned to the practice of Catholicism. She recalls that he was "quite full of Catholic ideas at the time and employed all the brilliance of his spirit and eloquence to plead them. This was my first encounter with this hitherto totally unknown world. It did not lead me as yet to the Faith. But it did open for me a region of 'phenomena' which I could then no longer bypass blindly. . . . The barriers of rationalistic prejudices with which I had unwittingly grown up fell, and the world of faith unfolded

* This standard definition, which might be offered to students in Philosophy 101, would not be accepted—or would be greatly modified—by many disciples of the phenomenological movement.

before me."[6] (Stein does not mention that, in the years before his death in 1928, Scheler had once again distanced himself from the Catholic Church.)

This passage exemplifies Stein's unwillingness, for whatever reasons, to discuss the specifics of her own spiritual development in her autobiography. What "Catholic ideas" preoccupied Scheler at the time, and how did he present them to his pupils? It would certainly be interesting to know more about the "rationalistic prejudices" imbibed by Stein during her childhood—since she was to discard them so thoroughly not only by her conversion to Catholicism but by her attraction to the mystical writings of Teresa of Ávila (1515–82), who came from a Converso family on her father's side. Teresa's paternal ancestors, well-off merchants from Toledo, chose Catholicism over expulsion in 1492. Her grandfather was later convicted by the Inquisition of "Judaizing," but her father, Alonso Sánchez de Cepeda, bought a knighthood and tried his best to be accepted into Spanish Catholic society. At age twenty, Teresa entered the Carmelite Order, but, like Stein, she was never able to escape the taint of her Jewish origins in her own society. Her writings, which would one day place her among the small group of female saints of unquestioned high intellectual stature in the history of Catholicism, were always questioned and inspected by the Inquisition because of her Jewish origins—and because she was a woman.

Stein's "rationalistic prejudices" cannot have proceeded from Judaism itself, which Edith discarded as a personal religion when, at age fifteen, she stopped praying. Most summaries of Stein's life, including those disseminated at the time of her canonization, state that she became an atheist at fifteen, but if that is true, she does not (once again) say so explicitly. Certainly, there is a considerable gap between the abandonment of prayer and atheism. When Edith was growing up, her family was moderately but not extremely observant. The Steins were the kind of Jews who observed the High Holy Days and Passover but were just as or more likely to have a picnic in the countryside on an ordinary Sabbath as to spend the day in shul. The Stein boys would have studied to become bar mitzvah, but they were not systematically exposed to Jewish learning through years of religious schooling. The girls, as Edith's account of her secular education makes clear, were not exposed to any Jewish education beyond the basics of Sabbath and holiday observance, in which women, then as now, played an important role in the home. In this regard, acculturated, moderately observant German Jews were no different from more devout Orthodox Jews: sophisticated study of the Torah was not for women.

Most of Stein's reminiscences about her exposure to Jewish tradition within her family involve the celebration of special feasts. Her memories (again, in contrast to Heine) are fond and respectful of the "indomitable consistency that marks the Jewish spirit." Both as a Catholic thinker and as a German Jew in 1933, Stein was especially emphatic about the continuity between Judaism and Christianity. "Most Christians are unaware," she wrote, "that the 'Feast of Unleavened Bread,' in remembrance of the Exodus of the Children of Israel from Egypt, continues to be celebrated today in the identical manner in which it was celebrated by our Lord with his disciples when he instituted the Blessed Sacrament and took leave of his followers."[7] There is something unspeakably sad about this passage, by a devout philosopher-nun who has just realized her dream of becoming a Carmelite, as she writes on the edge of an abyss. She is trying, in a work intended not for philosophers or theologians but for a general German audience, to make her Christian compatriots see the continuity of the two religions. She is, in effect, raising the same question that Disraeli posed in the House of Commons in 1847: "Where is your Christianity, if you do not believe in their Judaism?" She is trying to hold back the oncoming barbarism and to correct the theological past, in which Jews in Germany, as in many parts of Europe, were in special peril during Christian Holy Week—when what mattered to the mobs was not that the Last Supper was a seder but that it was followed by the crucifixion. And the medieval German mobs blamed that crucifixion not on Romans but on Jews.

•

Stein completed her doctoral dissertation on empathy in 1916, at age twenty-four. A few lines from that paper illuminate the reasons why her philosophical bent would not pose a conflict with her later Catholicism. "To consider ourselves in inner perception," she asserts, "i.e., to consider our psychic 'I' and its attributes, means to see ourselves as we see another and he sees us. . . . It is possible for another to 'judge me more accurately' than I judge myself and give me clarity about myself.

For example, he notices that I look around me for approval as I show kindness, while I myself think I am acting out of pure generosity. This is how empathy and inner perception work hand in hand to give me myself to myself."[8] That we can only gain true self-knowledge through seeing ourselves as others see us and seeing others in a way that can comprehend their experience is a philosophy completely compatible with Christian (and many other religious) theologies. One wonders, had Stein survived the Holocaust, if she would have examined the loss of empathy, on a vast scale, that enabled ordinary men, in Christopher Browning's phrase, to treat Jews as members of another species.

It undoubtedly took Stein longer to complete her dissertation than it would have had she not worked as a medical assistant, nursing wounded soldiers (against her mother's wishes), during the First World War. Stein was no pacifist, and there is nothing in her autobiography to suggest that she had thought deeply about Germany's responsibility for the war. She considered caring for the wounded her patriotic duty, just as her military-age male university friends (Jewish and Gentile) considered it their patriotic duty to enlist.* Her account of those years is informed more by regret for lost security than by the moral indignation of an Erich Maria Remarque or of postwar British writers like Vera Brittain. "Our placid student life was blown to bits by the Serbian assassination of royalty," she recalls. "No one growing up during or since the war can possibly imagine the security in which we assumed ourselves to be living before 1914. Our life was built on an indestructible foundation of peace, stability of ownership of property, and on the permanence of circumstances to which we were accustomed."[9]

Throughout the war years, Stein's life was characterized by a combination of intellectual growth and professional frustration that may have had more to do with her being a woman, in a time and place where there was no socially recognized role for female intellectuals, than with her being a Jew. It is unlikely that Husserl, who had moved from Göttingen to the University of Freiburg, would ever have selected a woman as his assistant in 1916 if the brightest young men from the

---

* When the Nazis came to power, Jewish World War I veterans (especially those decorated for bravery) initially received a measure of protection from restrictions imposed on other Jews. Those preferences were revoked or ignored as the years passed, and in the end, Jewish veterans died in the concentration camps along with all other Jews.

universities had not been in the trenches. As Stein's perceptive translator, Sister Josephine Koeppel, O.C.D., notes, "One cannot be certain that she would have considered herself for that position."[10] While serving as Husserl's assistant, Stein not only received her doctorate in philosophy *summa cum laude,* but she began organizing Husserl's previous writings for a collected edition. However, Husserl, who was called "the Master" by his students, was not especially amenable to being organized; he even told Stein that his earlier work ought to be burned because it was outdated. (In Nazi Germany, his actual books would be burned, because of his Jewish origins.)

Meanwhile, Stein organized what she called a "Philosophical Kindergarten" to acquaint beginning students with phenomenology and the works of its founder. In 1918, Stein resigned from her job and began looking for a university-level teaching position. In a coincidence of history, Stein's replacement, in 1919, turned out to be her near contemporary Martin Heidegger (1889–1976), whose career as a German philosopher was not hampered by being a man, and who, after joining the Nazi Party in 1933, would became the rector of the University of Freiburg.

During the war years, Stein's search for an appointment as an entry-level professor turned out to be futile, in spite of the honors that accompanied her degree and a glowing recommendation from the Master. Throughout her unsuccessful search for a job that fit her credentials, Stein supported herself by giving private lessons to university-level students in Breslau. She also wrote essays and began to deliver lectures, in much the manner as adjuncts cobble together a living in the United States today. Because Stein was doubly marginalized as a Jew and a woman, it is impossible to know which disability played a larger role in her failure to find the academic job she craved. Even before the war, German women of Stein's generation were aware of and affected by the international woman suffragist movement and the general agitation for women's rights—more strongly developed in the United States and England than in much of Europe. Stein and her close female friends often discussed the problem of combining a career with marriage. "I was alone in maintaining, always, that I would not sacrifice my profession on any account," she recalled. "If one could have predicted the future for us then! The other three married, but, nevertheless, continued in their careers. I alone did not marry, but I alone have assumed an obligation [the life of a nun] for which, joyfully, I would willingly sacrifice any other career."[11]

Another unanswerable question is whether Stein would have been so preoccupied with religion in her twenties, or would have taken the enormous step of converting to Catholicism rather than Protestantism, had she been able to establish a more stable and promising (in conventional contemporary terms) academic career. That she had long been preoccupied with the meaning of suffering, and with the possibility of life after death, is as clear from her "secular" autobiography as it is from her writings on Catholic theology, particularly on the Christian meaning of Jesus's death on the cross. The Catholic belief in the intrinsic value of human suffering as an offering to God—as Christ suffered to redeem man—could not be further from commonplace Jewish teaching and belief. Emphasis on suffering as a positive force in human lives also differentiates Catholicism from many of the more liberal forms of Protestantism. Yet there are passages in Stein's writings that seem to bring the conventional Catholic view of suffering "down to earth" in a way that may have reflected, intentionally or unintentionally, the author's Jewish background. In one short essay, she writes:

> Thus, when someone desires to suffer, it is not merely a pious reminder of the suffering of the Lord. Voluntary expiatory suffering is what truly and really united one to the Lord intimately. When it arises, it comes from an already existing relationship with Christ. For, by nature, a person flees from suffering. And the mania for suffering caused by a perverse lust for pain differs completely from the desire to suffer in expiation. Such lust is not a spiritual striving, but a sensory longing, no better than other sensory desires, in fact worse, because it is contrary to nature. . . .
>
> . . . And so those who have a predilection for the way of the cross by no means deny that Good Friday is past and the work of salvation has been accomplished.[12]

In a 1930 letter to a friend and former student (who had become a Benedictine nun), Stein wrote that, whenever she had an encounter with another person that deepened her feeling "of our powerlessness to exert a direct influence, I have a deeper sense of the urgency of my own *holocaustum.*" Stein's use of the Latin *holocaustum* (notwithstanding the anachronistic fantasies of some of her biographers) had nothing to do with prescience about what is now called the Holocaust; she was talking about her offering of herself, as a person and a Catholic, in whatever capacity she was called to serve. As her doctoral dissertation states, she thought of giving herself to others—her *holocaustum*—as the way to give herself to herself.

In any case, Stein made the decision to convert to Catholicism after reading the autobiography of Teresa of Ávila, *The Book of Her Life,* in a friend's library in 1921. She also decided that she would, like Teresa, join the Discalced Carmelites. Stein was baptized on January 1, 1922, but her spiritual adviser, the Vicar General of the Diocese of Speyer (in which she was baptized), told her that she was not ready to enter the convent. This was an order, not a suggestion, in the days when nuns were not uppity and convent authorities would never have dreamed of admitting a postulant whose priest advised against such a move. There was, however, nothing unusual about advising a new convert against taking an immediate step to enter either the priesthood or a convent. Most priests, in every part of the world, would have told a recent convert to gain further experience in the Catholic faith before leaping into a religious vocation.

After her baptism, Stein took a job teaching at St. Magdalena's, a Dominican training institute in Speyer. During this period, she remained active as a lecturer on phenomenology and translated the letters and diaries of the famous nineteenth-century English cardinal (and convert from Anglicanism) John Henry Newman into German, as well as Thomas Aquinas's *Quaestiones* from the Latin.

Despite her absorption in her new religion, Stein had not given up her secular ambitions. In 1931, she made one last attempt to obtain a professorship at a German university—at Freiburg, where she had worked as Husserl's assistant. She spoke with Heidegger, the future Nazi and university rector, and he apparently received her politely but, not surprisingly, did nothing to help her get a job. Stein was also turned down by the University of Breslau, because, according to Josephine Koeppel, the university was unwilling to grant a professorship to a woman.* After that disappointment, she accepted a teaching job

---

* The Institute of Carmelite Studies, based in Washington, D.C., and staffed with outstanding translators and scholars of Catholicism like the late Sister Josephine Koeppel,

with the Catholic Pedagogical Institute of Münster, which was developing a curriculum for Catholic education. "Edith had never intended to teach," her translator observes. ". . . her career as a philosopher never became an actuality, and, therefore, teaching perforce took its place."[13]

In the spring of 1933, with Hitler in power, Stein's career as a teacher and an author came to an end in Germany. She was informed—as a Jew, not as a Catholic convert—that she could no longer teach in any German institution (including one run by the church itself). German Catholic leaders, despite their official position that converts from Judaism were no different from any other Catholics, accepted these new restrictions. That Edith Stein, Catholic convert, was immediately dismissed as a Jew from an insignificant job at an insignificant teacher training institute speaks volumes about the nonsensical idea that she was murdered at Auschwitz because she was a Catholic. In life as in death, she was treated as a Jew by the Nazis.

In April 1933—after her dismissal as a teacher but before she joined the Carmelites—Stein wrote a pleading letter directly to Pope Pius XI, whom she urged to speak out against the Nazi persecution of Jews, and against the use of traditional Christian justifications for the campaign. "For weeks," Stein said, "not only Jews but also thousands of faithful Catholics in Germany and, I believe, in the whole world, have been waiting and hoping for the Church of Christ to raise its voice to put a stop to this misuse of Christ's name. . . . All of us who are truthful children of the Church and who are observing conditions in Germany closely fear for the worst for the reputation of the Church if this silence goes on any longer." Pius XI's secretary of state, Cardinal Eugenio Pacelli, who would succeed him in 1939 as Pius XII, did not reply directly to this unknown German woman—how could such a person think she had the right to question church policy?—but instead wrote to a German arch-abbot who had forwarded her letter to the Vatican. Pacelli said only that he had shown Stein's letter to the pope and that he hoped Christ would protect his church in turbulent political times.[14] It is a measure of the power of Stein's conversion—and of her

---

is largely responsible for the preservation of Edith Stein's papers. Some of her letters and private writings were unquestionably lost during the war, when Carmelites feared that searches by the Gestapo might uncover communications that would endanger them as well as other people mentioned in the documents. But much of what she wrote, unpublished in her lifetime, was preserved by the nuns.

inability to contemplate the possibility that she might have made a mistake—that this indifferent response did not shake her determination to remain a Catholic or to become a nun.*

In October 1933, Stein's spiritual mentors finally agreed that she could join the Carmelite Order. Her mother, who had reluctantly accepted Stein's conversion to Catholicism, was even more upset by her decision to become a nun. Stein entered a Carmelite monastery in Cologne, and by the spring of 1934, she had become a novice, adopting the religious habit and the name Sister Teresa Benedicta of the Cross. Her brothers and sisters were beginning to find places of refuge around the world; Frau Auguste Stein fortunately died in 1936 and did not have to face the trauma of emigration or death in the concentration camps.

As a Carmelite, Stein was encouraged by her superiors to continue her philosophical writings. Her work, needless to say, could not be published in Germany. In 1938, she took her final vows of poverty, chastity, and obedience and became a full member of the Carmelite Order. However, the net was closing in on all Germans of Jewish descent, including those within the walls of convents and monasteries, and the sisters spirited Edith away to a convent in Echt, across the border in Holland, on December 31, 1938. Her older sister Rosa, who had stayed with their ailing mother until her death, wanted to join Edith and follow her in becoming a Catholic, and she was able to do so in early 1940. But all was lost, for both Stein sisters, when the Nazis occupied Holland in May of that year. In Echt, Edith and Rosa received the news that their older brother Paul, his wife, Trude, and their sister Frieda had been sent to Theresienstadt. Frieda died there in 1942, Paul and Trude in 1943. They died for the same reason that Edith and Rosa Stein, Catholic converts, died—because they were born Jews.

As Garry Wills observes in *Papal Sin,* the Vatican made the "ludicrous case" that Stein was killed for being a Catholic in a "tricky and roundabout way."[15] A joint statement in 1942 by Dutch Protestant ministers and Catholic bishops had condemned Nazi deportations of

---

* Both Stein's letter and the text of Pacelli's reply are contained in the once-secret Vatican archives covering the papacy of Pius XI, which were opened in 2006. The archives covering the even more controversial papacy of Pius XII, and his relations with Nazi Germany and Hitler, remain closed.

all Dutch Jews and had singled out Jews who had converted to Christianity, because "such measures would sever them from participation in the life of the Church." The Nazis then said they would make an exception for baptized Jews if the bishops would stop protesting. But the bishop of Utrecht (most other clergy backed down) issued a pastoral letter continuing to denounce the deportations, and the Nazis went after baptized Jews—even in convents. Nevertheless, the German occupiers' desire to silence Dutch Catholic and Protestant clergy does not mean that Edith and Rosa Stein were sent to Auschwitz because they were Catholics. On the contrary: if the Nazis had really wanted to get the bishops' attention, they would have deported all Catholic nuns or, for that matter, priests, not simply one nun and one refugee of Jewish descent. There was no roundup of Dutch Catholics (unless they had been born Jewish) after the bishops' letters.

Moreover, Stein's actions en route to Auschwitz demonstrate that she did not want to become a martyr or a victim. She tried to attract attention to her identity and her plight, leaving notes addressed to the Swiss Consulate at train stops along the way, and even offering to pay for help. Her faith was precious to her; had she imagined she was dying for it instead of for her Jewish birth, she would not have tried to escape. Because she had many international contacts, Stein—unlike many of her fellow Jewish deportees—knew what awaited them at the end of the journey.

According to an article published in a Cologne newspaper on August 9, 1982, the last time anyone on the "outside" saw Stein was when the deportation train stopped at Breslau Station in 1942. Johannes Wieners, a postal employee who had recently been drafted by the Wehrmacht, told the newspaper that a woman in a nun's habit stepped into the opening of the car and said, "This is my beloved hometown. I will never see it again. We are riding to our death." Wieners asked, "Do your companion prisoners believe that also?" She answered, "It is better that they do not know it." Wieners's fellow workers were annoyed at him for speaking to a Jew and told him so. He was eventually taken prisoner of war by the Red Army. Years later, after returning to Germany, he saw a picture of Stein in the newspaper and was sure that she was the nun with whom he had spoken when the train stopped in Breslau. Stein was gassed within the week.

A final report, dated June 2, 1958, by the Bureau of Information of the Netherlands Red Cross, confirms that Edith Teresa Hedwig Stein, whose last residence was the Monastery of the Carmelite Nuns, Bovenstestraat 48, Echt, Holland, was arrested on August 2, 1942, "FOR REASONS OF RACE, AND SPECIFICALLY BECAUSE OF JEWISH DESCENT." The capital letters are printed on the Red Cross document. The lie that Edith Stein, or any other Jewish convert to Christianity in Nazi-occupied Europe, died in a concentration camp not because she was a Jew but because she was a Christian, is imprinted on the history of modern Catholicism.

· PART VI ·

AMERICAN EXCEPTIONALISM:

TOWARD RELIGIOUS CHOICE

AS A NATURAL RIGHT

17

PETER CARTWRIGHT (1785–1872): ANTI-INTELLECTUALISM AND THE BATTLE FOR REASON

In 1801, when I was in my sixteenth year, my father, my eldest half brother, and myself, attend[ed] a wedding about five miles from home, where there was a great deal of drinking and dancing, which was very common at marriages those days. . . . After a late hour in the night, we mounted our horses and started for home. I was riding my race-horse.

A few minutes after we had put up the horses, and were sitting by the fire, I began to reflect on the manner in which I had spent the day and evening. I felt guilty and condemned. . . . All of a sudden, my blood rushed to my head, my heart palpitated, in a few minutes I turned blind; an awful impression rested on my mind that death had come and I was unprepared to die. I fell on my knees and began to ask God to have mercy on me.

—*Autobiography of Peter Cartwright, The Backwoods Preacher*, 1856

THUS DID PETER CARTWRIGHT, one of the most fiery evangelical Methodist preachers of America's first century as a nation, describe the beginning of his conversion experience at the Cane Ridge Communion, a famous 1801 revival meeting in southwestern Kentucky that eventually drew, according to some sources, tens of thousands of previously unchurched, or at least religiously lukewarm, souls. By other accounts, there may have been only thousands; perhaps the higher estimates were based on a symbolic usage of the number ten, resembling the use of forty in the Bible. Even allowing for the exaggeration of pious observers, the Cane Ridge gathering was one of the most significant (and widely reported, by recently established newspapers) religious events in American history. "Lord, make it like Cane Ridge" was a frequent prayer at American revival meetings for decades afterward.

The spiritual awakening of the young, largely unschooled (but not illiterate) Cartwright was, in many respects, typical of the evangelical conversions that would characterize American life throughout many cycles of religious fervor, exemplified in revival meetings in both the nineteenth and twentieth centuries. Born in Amherst County, Virginia, Cartwright grew up in a pioneer farm family that pulled up stakes two years after the end of the Revolutionary War (of which Peter's father was a veteran) and headed for Kentucky. Kentucky was the frontier, and the settlers were in danger from the lawless elements within their own communities as well as from Indians. What is now Logan County, where the family settled down, was known as "Rogues' Harbor." As Cartwright colorfully recounts:

> Here many refugees, from almost all parts of the Union, fled to escape justice or punishment; for although there was law, yet it could not be executed, and it was a desperate state of society. Murderers, horse thieves, highway robbers, and counterfeiters fled here until they combined and actually formed a majority. The honest and civil part of the citizens would prosecute these wretched banditti, but they would swear each other clear; and they really put all law at defiance, and carried on such desperate violence and outrage that the honest part of the citizens seemed to be driven to the necessity of uniting and combining together, and taking the law into their own hands, under the name of Regulators. This was a very desperate state of things.[1]

Gun battles and lynchings (the latter usually carried out by Regulators against criminals) were the stuff of daily life, and it was not easy to determine who was on the side of the law. Puritan hegemony, which had restrained ordinary criminal behavior as well as religious dissent in the early days of colonization in New England, did not exist on the frontier. Thus, the arrival of circuit-riding preachers, whose theological credentials came not from any Eastern divinity school but from their own conversion experiences, was greeted as a force for order in a society desperately in need of enforceable social norms. To churchgoing Americans in long-established small towns in New England or even in the large, less orderly cities of Boston, Philadelphia, and New York, revival meetings on the frontier looked like wild, disorderly melees bordering on the savage. To settlers on the frontier, the revivals could leave behind a new kind of security based on some sort of religious affiliation, which might also encourage the establishment of functional law enforcement institutions. As Richard Hofstadter observes in *Anti-Intellectualism in American Life,* "The style of a church or sect is to a great extent a function of social class, and the forms of worship and religious doctrine congenial to one social group may be uncongenial to another." The "possessing classes," Hofstadter argues, have generally shown more interest in reconciling religion with reason and with the observance of elaborate, traditional liturgical forms. The "disinherited classes," by contrast, have been moved more by emotional forms of religion and been hostile to ecclesiastical hierarchy associated with the upper classes.[2]

The one unusual aspect of Cartwright's upbringing on the frontier was that his father sent him, for a brief time, to a boarding school run by a traveling preacher for the Methodist Episcopal Church. There Cartwright learned to read and write—a capability that would greatly enhance his future prospects, in spite of his expressed disdain for higher education (at least insofar as it was considered a qualification for the ministries of upper-class denominations). Had he been illiterate, Cartwright would not have become one of the best-known Methodist ministers of his day. By the 1820s, frontier communities were beginning to regard the presence of a school as a necessary sign of civilization. Circuit-riding preachers on the frontier, at a time when many settlements in Indiana, Ohio, Tennessee, and Illinois lacked churches and ministers of their own, could enhance their influence through their own literacy. A Kentucky farmer might not have any use for a minister with a degree from the Yale Divinity School, but he did value a preacher who could actually read the Good Book.

Scholarly estimates indicate that 90 percent of the residents of the brand-new United States of America were "unchurched" when Cartwright was born in 1785, in the early years of the Second Great Awakening. "Unchurched" meant not that Americans were indifferent to religion but that they were in the process of moving to areas of the country beyond the reach of existing, formal religious institutions. Thus, a large proportion of the population was ripe for proselytizing, spread across the land at revival meetings over hundreds and eventually thousands of miles. Religious conversion, at least among Protestant denominations, became a feature of daily life in the formative decades of the republic. Furthermore—then as now—"born-again" experiences that took place without the exchange of one denomination for another were also considered forms of conversion. And—then as now—families whose faith was expressed mainly by saying grace before meals and going to church on Sunday could be irked and unsettled by a member who suddenly placed religion and Jesus at the center of every aspect of life. Cartwright does not tell us in his autobiography how his father and brother reacted to his sudden discovery that dancing and riding racehorses—which they enjoyed—not only wasted time but were sinful.

Cartwright's description of his own conversion moment at Cane Ridge, following several weeks of reflection upon the depravity of playing cards and betting on horses, is typical of many accounts by converts who were able to write about their experience.

> To this meeting I repaired, a guilty, wretched sinner. On the Saturday evening of said meeting, I went, with weeping multitudes, and bowed before the stand, and earnestly prayed for mercy. In the midst of a solemn struggle of soul, an impression was made on my mind, as though a voice said to me, "Thy sins are all forgiven thee." Divine light flashed all round me, and it really seemed as if I was in heaven; the trees, the leaves on them, and everything seemed, and I really thought were, praising God. My mother raised the shout, my Christian friends crowded around me and joined me in praising God; and though I have been since then, in many instances, unfaithful, yet I have never, for one moment, doubted that the Lord did, then and there, forgive my sins and give me religion.[3]

Many of these conversion accounts have an adolescent tone (whether or not they actually took place in adolescence). Nearly all such stories display an exaggerated consciousness of both sin and the possibility of redemption, a sense of being directly addressed by an otherworldly power, and supernatural manifestations within the natural world. Cartwright, like Saul on the road to Damascus, experiences a period of blindness. Flashing lights are as much a staple of conversion accounts from nineteenth-century revival meetings as a white light at the end of a tunnel is in every modern movie about near-death experiences. Unlike Augustine's *Confessions,* nineteenth-century American adolescent conversion stories generally skirt the subject of sexual sin: an excessive fondness for dancing is as close as Cartwright gets to the matter. But there is no doubt that these conversions were real, in the sense of being life-changing, to most of the people who experienced them, and that their very frequency, up to and after the closing of the frontier in the 1890s, shaped an American religious environment that would become more accustomed to and accepting of changes of faith than any country in Europe. It took time for existing religious institutions to catch up with the westward movement of settlers, and "backwoods" preachers, many self-appointed, would fill the gap.

.

Cartwright eventually settled in Illinois, where he mixed religion and politics with zest. Like most evangelicals, he was quick to denounce any hint of government interference with religion but was uninterested in the other side of the founding constitutional bargain, which restrains religious interference with government. In his first run for public office, in 1832, Reverend Cartwright, a Democrat, defeated a Whig, a young store clerk, for a seat in the Illinois state legislature. In 1846, however, Cartwright ran for Congress and was defeated by his former opponent, a lawyer named Abraham Lincoln. Lincoln shared Cartwright's lack of formal schooling but not his biblically literal (today they would be called fundamentalist) religious convictions and dismissal of Enlightenment thought. During the 1846 campaign, Cartwright charged Lincoln with deism and "infidelity"—an accusation based partly on the well-known fact that Lincoln did not belong to any church (an omission less acceptable socially in the 1840s than it had been when Cartwright was a young man). Moreover, Lincoln, who was born in 1809, was drawn to the books of Enlightenment thinkers ranging from the most liberal Protestants to outright atheists. Two of the books Lincoln was reading at the time of his first campaign against Cartwright were Enlightenment classics—Thomas Paine's *The Age of Reason* and Constantin Volney's *The Ruins.**

Cartwright's encounters with Lincoln (not altogether unfriendly, because they would come to agree about slavery) embodied a confrontation between two competing forces that have shaped American religious culture to this day. The first, exemplified by Cartwright's conversion, was a propensity for highly emotional, nonhierarchical, personal forms of religion associated with biblical literalism and revivalism. The second was a struggle—sometimes successful, sometimes not—within mainline American Protestantism to reconcile Christian faith with Enlightenment rationalism. Lincoln the freethinker— a man who, whatever his private beliefs were, would have nothing to do with organized religion—was shaped in part by the individualism of the frontier and in part by the mainstream religious split that encouraged not only the establishment of more liberal Protestant denominations but the rise of secular American freethought.

Between 1790 and 1830, roughly half of the Puritan-descended Congregationalist churches in Massachusetts (all of which were still tax-supported) had been transformed into Unitarian congregations.[4] The spread of less doctrinaire forms of Protestantism was closely related to the emergence in the early republic of leaders who eschewed traditional religious institutions. This split between the conventional Puritan-descended denominations and more liberal intellectual denominations was carried westward by settlers—first from New England to upstate New York, then to the Midwest, and finally to the Pacific Northwestern territories of Oregon and Washington.

The Unitarians, though not aggressive proselytizers in the fashion of evangelical revivalists, turned plenty of Puritans into converts to a personal form of religion that stressed reason and good works rather than blind faith, predestination, and divine fury. John Adams, for instance, belonged to this group—though he would never have called himself a "convert." He simply (and not so simply) opposed all forms of religion that involved intellectual or political coercion and did not

---

* Lincoln probably borrowed these books from a neighbor and Dartmouth College graduate, Dr. John Allen, who had moved west for health reasons and founded a debating society in New Salem for young men. At that point in Lincoln's life, he certainly could not have afforded to order costly books from eastern publishing centers.

make room for science and reason. It could not have been clearer from Adams's correspondence with Thomas Jefferson during the last fourteen years of their lives that the two men, despite their many political differences, were in fundamental agreement about religion. "We can never be so certain of any Prophecy," Adams wrote to Jefferson in 1813, "or the fulfilment of any Prophecy; or of any miracle, or the design of any miracle as We are, from the revelation of nature ie. Natures God that two and two are equal four. Miracles or Prophecies might frighten us out of our Witts; might scare us to death; might induce Us to lie, to say that We believe that 2 and 2 make 5. But We should not believe it. We should know the contrary."[5] A man like Adams, and thousands who moved from Puritan orthodoxy to liberal Protestantism or secular freethought (sometimes both) through rational re-evaluation rather than mystical revelation, would never have been found at a revival meeting, or trembling, like Robert Boyle, in fear for his immortal soul during a thunderstorm. Yet the split within the Puritan-descended churches that gave rise to Unitarianism and Universalism, in England as well as in the United States, was a conversion movement as surely as the revivalism that prompted farmers to pitch tents in muddy fields to hear preachers talk about salvation and damnation. The shift toward more liberal Protestantism was a long-term intellectual movement, not a sudden awakening—more like the modern transition to secularism from religious belief than the dramatic instantaneous religious conversions of the past.

The philosophy of Unitarianism and Universalism (if not the churches themselves) would prove well suited to the promotion of freethought on the frontier. The emotional revivalism personified by Cartwright found a larger and very different constituency in an antipodal position within the same unsettled society. What liberal Protestantism and evangelical fundamentalism had in common on the frontier was that they encouraged individualism in religious thinking—either the development of a personal relationship with God, or personal doubt about the existence of any divinity. Self-educated men like Lincoln learned to read with the Bible—usually the only book in their homes—as a text and needed years to find and absorb the thoughts of other, nonreligious authors and integrate them with earlier religious teachings. People who had to work hard to acquire the basic materials for learning could not cut the process short by embracing revelation while lightning flashed. Overnight conversions are so alien to the intellectual temperament that educated Americans (with some notable exceptions, such as William James) were inclined to dismiss even the most sincere accounts as inherently fraudulent.

·

Cartwright began his post-conversion preaching career during the same period in which Unitarianism was replacing the retrograde brand of Puritanism that had led, only 120 years earlier, to the Salem witch trials. While Cartwright was preaching his energetic new brand of biblical literalism on the frontier, Paine was penniless and scorned because of his antireligious beliefs. One Unitarian pastor, William Bentley of the East Church of Salem, was among the few clergymen to defend the great polemicist of the Revolution when he died in 1809. He praised Paine for his elevation of reason and said, "He was indeed a wonderful man, & he was the first to see in what part every System was most vulnerable. Even in his attacks on Christianity he felt without knowing it, the greatest difficulties which rational Christians have felt."[6]

Rational Christians. But the revivalist proselytizers on the frontier, in the South and the Middle West, were not in the business of promoting rational Christianity. Two and two could make five if God chose to suspend natural laws. The Cane Ridge meeting became the prototype of the emotional American revivals that would remain a powerful religious force well into the twentieth century, as Billy Graham would demonstrate in rural areas and in New York's Times Square. Thus, the confrontations between Cartwright and Lincoln in the 1830s and 1840s are not only curious footnotes in American history; they also exemplify the unending conflicts between supernatural belief and naturalistic reason that have characterized American religious life since the colonial era.

Yet serious anti-intellectual preachers like Cartwright took care to distance themselves from some of the symptoms of mass hysteria that broke out at revival meetings. Cartwright inveighed against the "running, jumping, barking exercise" of converts who then "professed to fall into trances and see visions . . . and when they came to, they professed to have seen heaven and hell, to have seen God, angels, the devil and the damned; they would prophesy, and, under the pretense of

Divine inspiration, predict the time of the end of the world, and the ushering in of the great millennium." (Flashing lights were all right.) These born-again Christians often claimed that they could heal all manner of illnesses in what Cartwright described as "an appeal to the ignorance, superstition, and credulity of the people, even saint as well as sinner."[7] Of course, it was a bad thing for evangelists who preached the truth of supernatural events said to have happened nearly two millennia earlier if their audiences should be swayed by converts who emerged from trances to preach the truth of supernatural events said to be happening at that very moment. What potential convert would not prefer a preacher who could make the blind see and the lame walk *right now* to a preacher who could only refer to miracles said to have been performed by a Galilean carpenter in ancient times?

Deliberate charlatanism was a serious problem for genuinely devout evangelists like Cartwright, not only because preachers who claimed to perform miracles would lure away converts but because deceiving the credulous in the manner of a magician was considered a sin by all religions. American intellectuals (including religious believers as well as nonbelievers) have often made the mistake of equating the emotionalism of all evangelical-revivalist conversions with the sort of outright fraud depicted in Sinclair Lewis's *Elmer Gantry*. But the most effective American proselytizers, from Cartwright through Graham—whether preaching in makeshift tents in the first three decades of the nineteenth century or in football stadiums and iconographic urban spaces during the 1950s—were always careful to distance themselves from frauds that, in a country with a free press, were bound to be uncovered at some point. Such caution was not only a matter of tactical prudence; evangelists sincerely believed that the meaning and purpose of conversion resided in forgiveness of sin and eternal salvation, not in improving one's temporal health or acquiring wealth. This is not to say that evangelists or their converts—like wealthy, more orthodox clergymen before them—had any objection to making money legitimately (Cartwright's autobiography was a best-seller in 1856) or to living well. But most of them were not, as some Unitarian intellectuals in Boston and New York would have liked to think, in the business of taking money from blind people who hoped to see or cripples who hoped to walk. Honest evangelical proselytizers were interested in miracles that took place within the heart and soul, and such spiritual transformations did not have to contradict the reason evident in inventions and medical advances that visibly improved the lot of human beings throughout their difficult lives on earth.

•

The highly emotional, often anti-intellectual revivalism of the Second Great Awakening was not only a function of geography but of the curious merger of spiritually hungry individuals with a competitive "religious marketplace"—a phrase that did not become fashionable until the late twentieth century but was always a fact of American religious life. There seems to have been no doubt in the minds of devout evangelicals that out-arguing and out-praying the competition was the best way to spread the news of the Gospel.

Cartwright describes an incident, not long after his own conversion, in which he and his fellow Methodists encountered a Jew who "was tolerably smart, and seemed to take great delight in opposing the Christian religion." At one of Cartwright's prayer meetings, "this Jew appeared" and told the Methodists that "it was idolatry to pray to Jesus Christ, and that God did not nor would he answer such prayers." Recognizing that the Jew's desire was to "get us into debate and break up our prayer-meeting," Cartwright asked him, "Do you really believe there is a God?" Yes, the Jew replied, he did believe in God. "Do you really believe that this work among us is wrong?" Cartwright asked. The Jew said he did believe that Christian proselytizing was wrong. One can only imagine what might have happened had such a comment been made at a prayer meeting in Geneva, Frankfurt, Lyon, or Edinburgh.

But Cartwright suggested a "test" resembling the one posed in the Bible by the prophet Elijah to the worshippers of Baal, who were asked to compete with the Israelites by offering the sacrifice of a bullock and waiting for the Lord to send fire from heaven to prove which religion was true. Elijah asked the Israelites and the Baal worshippers, "How long halt ye between two opinions? If the Lord be God, follow him: but if Baal, then follow him" (I Kings 18: 21).* Cartwright—who even

---

* Felix Mendelssohn used this scene, with lyrics drawn from the King James Bible, to powerful dramatic effect in his oratorio *Elijah*, which had its premiere in 1846 in Bir-

asked, as Elijah had, that God demonstrate his power by sending fire down to prove one side or the other right—told the Jew that if his God were the true God He would use the fire to put an end to Christian prayer.

> Our Jew began and said, tremblingly, "O Lord God Almighty," and coughed again, cleared his throat, and started again, repeating the same words. We saw his evident confusion, and we simultaneously prayed out aloud at the top of our voices. The Jew leaped up and started off, and we raised the shout and had a glorious time. Several of our mourners were converted, and we all rose and started into camp at the top of our speed, shouting, having, as we firmly believed, obtained a signal victory over the devil and the Jew.[8]

This story has several intriguing elements (apart from Cartwright casting himself in the role of a Jewish prophet to combat the beliefs of a Jew). First, a lone Jew appears in the backwoods of Kentucky to tell a group of Christian men that they are all wrong, and that by praying to Jesus they are worshipping an idol. Second, the Christian men don't beat up the Jew but try to show him the error of his ways with a biblically based test that both Christian and Jews, if they knew their Bible (as they certainly did in the early nineteenth century), would recognize. Third, the Jew probably runs off because he is scared, but nothing else happens to him in this primitive religious marketplace. Finally—and here is where American Christianity is already more lax than the Bible itself—Cartwright, unlike Elijah, has hedged his bets. For the God of Israel to triumph over Baal in the Bible, it was necessary not only that the Lord ignore the bullock offered for sacrifice by the priests of Baal but also that He send fire to signal His acceptance of the Israelites' bullock. Cartwright did not ask that his prayers be affirmed by fire from heaven; he asked only that the Lord *not* send down fire in answer to a Jew's prayer to end the Christian meeting. This was an impossible wager to lose (absent a lightning strike) and probably arose from the same caution that prompted Cartwright to oppose those who made faith healing a condition of and cause for conversion.

---

mingham, England. One can only wonder whether Heine, who mocked Mendelssohn for his role in the revival of Bach's Christian music, would have liked *Elijah* any better.

Judaism, as a religion, was not considered a particular threat in the antebellum republic—in part because there were so few Jewish immigrants at the time, and in part because Jews did not proselytize. Cartwright's story of his encounter with a Jew who challenged Christian proselytizing is so rare that I would be tempted to call it unique in the annals of the early republic if I were not certain that someone, from some distant niche on the Internet, would produce a letter about a great-great-great-grandparent's encounter with another wandering Jew who challenged Christianity as foolish idol worship.

•

The heterodox nature of American religious thought and practice, even among the least educated audiences at revival meetings, meant that proselytizing and conversion would become a permanent feature of life in the new land. Protestantism in general might be America's civil religion, but in fundamental matters involving the balance between faith and reason, Protestants were as divided among themselves as Protestants and Catholics had been during the battle over the Reformation in the Old World. These divisions created fertile soil not only for conversions but for the founding of entirely new religions—among them Mormonism, the Jehovah's Witnesses, and Christian Science.

It is tempting to conclude that the current liberal—some ardent believers would say promiscuous—American attitude toward conversion was an inevitable result of the presence of so many Protestant denominations, right from the start, in the new and spacious land—so spacious that a theocrat like John Cotton could call Roger Williams's expulsion from the Massachusetts Bay Colony not a banishment but an enlargement. However, religious pluralism and seemingly endless physical space to accommodate nonconformist believers were necessary but not sufficient for the formation of the laissez-faire American attitudes toward conversion that generally prevail today.

And not all conversions were equally acceptable. Anti-Catholicism was a prejudice that united American Protestants of otherwise feuding denominations and very different social classes. Elizabeth Ann Bayley Seton (1774–1821), like Peter Cartwright, came of age in the new American republic and was a religious convert—but that is all she had in common with the backwoods preacher. Seton, born into a prominent Episcopal family in New York City, would convert to Roman Catholicism, found the American Sisters of Charity, and eventually, in 1975, become a saint, canonized by Pope Paul VI. Everything about Seton's conversion—except that there was no way, in America, for her disapproving family to use the power of the state to stop her from changing faiths—was unusual for the early republican period.

For an Episcopalian in America, Catholicism was a huge step down on the social ladder and was seen in that light by nearly all within Seton's privileged circle of Episcopal friends and family in New York. Her grandparents settled in the New York area at the beginning of the eighteenth century; she was descended on her father's side from Huguenots who had fled France. By the time of the Revolution, though, everyone in the immediate family seems to have joined the Episcopal Church—the religion of choice for New York's social and economic upper class. When the nineteen-year-old Elizabeth married William Magee Seton, whose wealthy family owned an export-import firm, the ceremony was performed by the first Episcopal bishop of New York. The young Setons, like their entire family, were members of the fashionable Trinity Church on Wall Street. (Thanks to a 1705 land grant—now prime Manhattan real estate—from England's Queen Anne, the church possesses assets of more than two billion dollars, and its still-affluent congregation is embroiled in angry disputes over whether Trinity is doing enough for the poor.[9]) Seton, who had five children, was deeply involved in charitable work and seems to have taken her Episcopal faith as seriously as she would later take Catholicism. She and her sister-in-law Rebecca Seton were known as the "Protestant Sisters of Charity" for their efforts to help the poor in New York—much as Anne Hutchinson had been known for her activities as a midwife. In 1797, they helped found the Society for the Relief of Poor Widows with Small Children—a response to a desperate need that had been apparent since the end of the Revolution, when many young war widows were left with no means of support. Seton herself, who was not poor, would be left a widow in straitened circumstances when her husband died in 1803 of tuberculosis in Italy, to which the family had traveled in the futile hope that his health would be restored in a warmer climate. Seton's first serious encounter with Catholicism seems to have taken place during this trip, when the young couple stayed with a well-off Italian family with business interests in New York. The grieving young widow was apparently most impressed by the church's claim that, unlike the Church of England, it could trace its authority in an unbroken line to the apostles. When Seton returned to New York in 1804, she had five children under age eight and had already, according to her journals, decided to convert to Catholicism. Her family, however, was horrified—and Seton, although she had some money of her own, needed financial help. In any event, despite the family's opposition, Seton was received into the Catholic Church in March 1805 and made her First Communion two weeks later. Elizabeth's in-laws were particularly fearful that her proselytizing would influence younger members of the family, and her two youngest sisters-in-law did indeed convert to Catholicism—an astonishing and socially embarrassing development in such a prominent Protestant family. Salvation (presumably financial as well as spiritual) arrived in the form of a French émigré priest from Maryland, who invited Elizabeth to move to Baltimore and establish a Catholic school for the education of young children.

Seton then went on to found the American Daughters of Charity as, once again, the geography of America made room for religious change. A rich seminarian and another convert to Catholicism, Samuel Sutherland Cooper, purchased land for the sisters in Frederick County, in what is now the town of Emmitsburg, in 1809. Seton founded a tuition-free school for poor girls, and the institution is generally considered the beginning of Catholic education in the United States. Seton herself is now the patron saint of Catholic schools. Ironically—in view of Seton's descent from Huguenots—the rule for her new order was modeled after the rule for the seventeenth-century Daughters of Charity in France. Neither official biographies of Seton nor her own writings explain exactly how she reconciled motherhood with entering the convent and founding a new religious order, but most of her children would became devout Catholics. Two of her daughters, Annina and Rebecca, died young and were buried by their mother in Emmitsburg. Another daughter, Catherine, also converted to Catholicism, became a Sister of Mercy, and lived until 1891. Elizabeth's son William had seven children, one of whom became a nun and another an archbishop. The story of how this prominent Episcopal family became a prominent Catholic family at a time of immense prejudice against the Church of Rome sounds like a television miniseries, and it is clear that the first

American-born Catholic saint made as powerful an impression on her own children as she did on the religious and charitable institutions she founded.

America had come a long way in the 172 years separating Hutchinson's trial from Seton's founding of a new, important religious institution. Both were affluent (in relation to the societies in which they lived), strong-minded women with energy to spare. The circumstances of Seton's conversion were far from typically American; her immersion in a distant Italian and Catholic culture, at a time of immense emotional stress, unmoored her from the social constraints of her own society at a crucial point in her life. But even though Seton did lose her older family members and many friends as a result of her conversion, she—unlike Hutchinson—did not have to answer to any government body for her personal religious choice. She did not have to fear an inquisition or imprisonment, much less the stake. Seton's decisions would have been much more difficult had she not been a woman of high social status, but her life as a convert—however different from the American norm—could only have taken place as it did within the American legal context, which allowed her not only to choose a new religion but to develop a productive, much-admired (if only by her new Catholic friends) life after conversion. In another country, or a century earlier, she might have had to become a martyr in order to become a saint.

It is unlikely that Seton's relatives and friends would have reacted any more positively had she originally been a Baptist, a Congregationalist, or a Unitarian. Catholicism meant one thing to most American Protestants, regardless of their theological differences: Catholics believed in the infallibility of a foreign pope, and that idea was inimical to the professed ideals of a newly independent republic.

As the Catholic population began to grow in large cities in the 1820s and 1830s, anti-Catholic violence occasionally erupted and sometimes centered on suspicions of the church's proselytizing designs on Protestants. One of the most famous of these incidents took place in Boston on August 11, 1834, when a mob of working-class Protestants burned down an Ursuline convent school that had, ironically, been attended mainly by the daughters of upper-class Protestant Bostonians. (The kind of rigorous education, including classics, provided by the nuns was not readily available for girls in Boston at the time.) Rebecca Reed, an Episcopalian, had decided to convert and become an Ursuline nun in 1832 but had left after six months and written a pamphlet, titled *Six Months in a Convent,* accusing the Ursulines of forcing their students into Catholicism. The veracity of this accusation seems doubtful, in view of the ease with which the young woman left the convent, but it fed into the history of Old World forced conversion embedded in the minds of most American Protestants. Rumors that another woman was being held against her will led to the burning of the convent, an act condemned by the local (then Protestant-controlled) government. The event was denounced as a "horrible outrage" in the *Boston Evening Transcript* the next day, and the local government stationed troops and police around several Catholic sites, including the Cathedral of the Holy Cross. However, no troops were deployed on the grounds of the burned convent, and thugs returned to finish the work of destroying the institution's orchards, gardens, and fences.[10] These events, in a city that would, only a few decades later—after the great immigration triggered by the Irish Potato Famine of the 1840s—become a center of Irish Catholic population and political power, should be viewed against the social background of the first large-scale entry of Irish immigrants into the local labor market. Nevertheless, it is significant that the fuse was lit not by a dispute over jobs but by rumors that nuns were recruiting Protestant girls and coercing them into Catholicism.

•

Other forms of conversion drew social disapproval from a class perspective entwined with anti-intellectualism. Struggling settlers on the frontier, drawn to the emotional faith purveyed by revivalists, were as appalled by conversions to more intellectual faiths like Unitarianism and Universalism as they were by the overt anticlericalism beginning to be voiced by freethinkers. Cartwright tells the story of what he considered the disastrous conversion of the former Methodist preacher Dr. Beverly Allen, with whom he had boarded during the brief period of his childhood when he learned to read. It seems that Allen had abandoned Methodism for Universalism after shooting and killing a sheriff (for reasons Cartwright leaves unexplained), because Universalism promised that all could be saved. Lo and behold, Cartwright, having undergone his own conversion and become a Methodist minister, was called to the bed of the dying Universalist. "Just before he died I asked him if he was willing to die and meet his final Judge with his Universalist sentiments," Cartwright recounts. "He frankly said he was not. He said he could make the mercy of God cover every case in his mind but his own, but he thought there was no mercy for him; and in this state of mind he left the world, bidding his family and friends an eternal farewell, warning them not to come to that place of torment to which he felt himself eternally doomed."[11]

This story of a Universalist's deathbed abandonment of his belief in universal salvation is a reverse twist on the many tales of atheists and freethinkers who were said to have made deathbed conversions to the religion they rejected in life. Actually, the deathbed abandonment of Universalism makes a good deal less emotional sense, since the Universalist was condemning himself, whereas a dying freethinker embracing some undefined form of faith, like Heinrich Heine, was hedging his bets. To exclude *only* oneself from God's mercy is surely one of the stranger varieties of religious experience.

Finally, nineteenth-century American attitudes toward *new* religions, especially if they were successful and determined proselytizers like the Mormons and the Jehovah's Witnesses, ranged from suspicion to outright hostility and persecution. It is well known that Mormons, after Joseph Smith saw a vision in a glade in upstate New York in 1823 and received the golden plates with the Book of Mormon from the angel Moroni, were driven out of one place after another until they finally found a home in empty (except of Indians) Utah.* Proselytizing Jehovah's Witnesses—their religion founded by Charles Taze Russell in 1872—were and are considered pests because they still approach people in public places as well as by ringing doorbells. The negative public view of Witnesses turned into serious persecution at the beginning of the Second World War, when their refusal to salute the flag,

---

* The story of why no one but Smith ever actually saw Moroni's golden plates makes for hilarious reading. When Smith dug up the golden plates in 1827, he was supposedly warned by Moroni not to let anyone else see them. He did, however, allow his mother to look at a pair of glasses with precious gems where the lenses would normally be. The purpose of the gems was to help Smith translate the Book of Mormon into English from the "reformed Egyptian." Rumors about the golden plates made their way around the community of Palmyra, and Smith and his wife eventually fled to Harmony, Pennsylvania, supposedly hiding the plates in a barrel of beans. Even Smith's wife, Emma, never actually saw the plates—though she did take dictation of the text from her husband.

take oaths, or recite the Pledge of Allegiance would ultimately be vin-
dicated in one of the most important civil liberties cases in American
history, *West Virginia Board of Education v. Barnette.* This 1943 decision reversed a Supreme Court ruling issued only four years earlier, in
which the court had upheld the right of schools to expel children who
refused to recite the pledge. The earlier decision had led to the expulsion of more than two thousand Witness children from public schools
and was associated with mob violence in which Witnesses were tarred
and feathered and assaulted with weapons. In Nebraska, one Witness
was even castrated.

In the *Barnette* decision, Justice Robert H. Jackson, who later
became the lead American prosecutor at the Nuremberg war crimes
trials, declared that "if there is any fixed star in our constellation, it
is that no official, high or petty, can prescribe what shall be orthodox
in politics, nationalism, religion, or other matters of opinion or force
citizens to confess by word or act their faith therein."[12]

The long-term hostility to the Witnesses, dating from the nineteenth century, was also partly based on class. They drew many of
their converts from the poorer and less educated sectors of the population; in most communities, it was a social disgrace for a family from
an accepted religious denomination to lose a relative to what was perceived to be a weird religion operating at the margins of American
society. This was as true in the African American community as in
predominantly white religious denominations: black Baptists were
no more pleased than white Baptists when one of their own defected
to this strange new millenarian sect, which promised to save only
144,000 souls.

Mormonism seemed to be the marginalizing type of new religion at
first—particularly because of its practice of polygamy—but the church
showed its pragmatism by officially renouncing polygamy as a condition of Utah's admission to the Union in 1896. Moreover, Mormons—
with their American core population concentrated in Utah and
Nevada—would become wealthy and politically influential as a result
of generations of endogamous marriage and a culture that emphasized
the importance of supporting other Mormons financially as well as
socially. Although public opinion polls throughout the twentieth century showed continuing prejudice against Mormons—particularly
among evangelical Protestants—surveys taken during Mitt Romney's

unsuccessful presidential race in 2012 suggested that anti-Mormon sentiments had diminished considerably. No serious political analyst thought that Romney's religion played a significant role in his defeat by President Barack Obama.

Given that so many American religious prejudices are class-based, the financial success of the Mormon community may have played a more important role than any other factor in diminishing feelings against a religion that is still extraordinarily secretive about its practices. Today, the official Mormon Church has more than thirteen million members worldwide—with more outside than inside the United States. Missionary service, as many Americans learned for the first time from Romney's biography, remains part of every young Mormon man's religious obligation, but that service almost always takes place abroad. After their controversial beginnings, Mormons did not make the mistake of the Jehovah's Witnesses by practicing in-your-face proselytizing that offended Americans of other denominations.

Thus, the American majority's negative reaction to the three largest new religions founded in the nineteenth century was based not so much on arcane theological differences as on violations of widespread social norms. Regarding Mormons, the issue was polygamy. For the Witnesses, until their unwillingness to honor their country symbolically came to the fore, the issue was simply their refusal to mind their own business with regard to the religion of their neighbors. Christian Science, founded by Mary Baker Eddy in the 1870s, was something of a special case. When this religion—which rejected and still does reject contemporary science-based medicine—was founded, medicine had relatively little to offer in the way of cures. As the efficacy of medicine improved throughout the twentieth century, conversions to Christian Science began to fall. A religion that might have seemed reasonable to many people at a time when doctors knew little more than their patients about either the real causes of or remedies for disease began to look like fringe lunacy in a country and century that witnessed medical advances such as the near eradication of the scourge of polio.

The first commandment, which emerged in the early republican era, for exercising the Constitution's guarantee of religious liberty would seem to be: "Thou shalt not bug thy neighbors about adopting whatever loony theology thou art perfectly free to profess." This unwritten commandment was and is a source of persistent tension within American society, since proselytizing, for many believers, is an integral part of their practice of religion. But the tension did not negate the huge difference between the young American republic and the rest of the world—a founding document mandating that citizens of the United States be allowed to follow their consciences regardless of majority opinion. That this fundamental principle has been violated many times makes it more, not less, important. The legal underpinning for the right to choose one's faith, or no faith at all, continues to enable both the unusual American approval of religious conversion and the fierceness with which Americans sometimes turn against religions suspected of covertly or overtly undermining that freedom.

18

REMAKING THE PROTESTANT
AMERICAN COMPACT

I N THE EARLY REPUBLIC, the American religious marketplace consisted primarily of competitive proselytizing among various Protestant denominations—although the emporium was expanded by an infusion of Catholics after the Irish Potato Famine of the 1840s. But religious pluralism began to emerge on a much larger and more recognizably modern scale as a result of massive immigration from Europe between 1880 and 1924. During those transformative decades, the arrival of some twenty-four million immigrants—their ranks swelled by huge numbers of Slavic and southern Italian Catholics and Russian and Eastern European Jews—permanently altered the ethnic and religious composition of the United States. The American population more than doubled, from 50.1 million in the 1880 census to more than 106 million in 1920. The impact was felt most strongly in the nation's largest cities. In New York, sixty thousand Jews made up just 4 percent of the population in 1870. By 1920, 1.64 million Jews accounted for 29 percent of city residents in the five boroughs. One-third of the nation's Italian immigrants lived in the New York metropolitan area. The pattern was similar, in varying degrees, in all of the nation's large cities. In Chicago, for instance, the percentage of Polish-born immigrants—both Catholic and Jewish—increased nearly sixfold between 1890 and 1920.[1]

What was not understood or predicted at the time was the extent to which the new immigrants would transform the American religious landscape, not only by their sheer numbers but by the willingness of their children and grandchildren to cross religious and ethnic boundaries when they chose marriage partners. In their native lands, legally as well as culturally mandated boundaries had kept the future immigrants to America safely inside communities where, as the milkman Tevye says in *Fiddler on the Roof,* "everyone knows who he is and what God expects him to do." But these expectations, mandated by both God and God's presumed representatives on earth, would be much less clear on the other side of the ocean.

It is not that Americans in the early twentieth century—whether of recent immigrant stock or with roots dating from the colonial era—generally held positive views of religious conversion, or that they greeted marriages outside a family's traditional faith with anything approaching equanimity. A century earlier, the descendants of New England Puritans had been shaken when Congregationalists morphed into Unitarians—whether because of inward changes in belief, marriage to someone of a more liberal Protestant faith, or a combination of both. A Protestant family in cosmopolitan (by the standards of much of the rest of the country) New York, as can be seen from the reaction to Elizabeth Seton's conversion in the early nineteenth century, could be outraged by the transformation of a respectable Episcopal widow into a respectable Catholic nun. And the young nation's older, established Protestant denominations were always uneasy about the emotions unleashed by evangelical revivalism. But conversion in the decades before the great post–Civil War influx of immigrants nearly always took place within a Protestant and Anglo-Saxon context: even when a Protestant took the unusual step of converting to Catholicism, such conversions were not numerous enough to effect any basic change in the nation's religious and social framework. By the latter decades of the nineteenth century, however, the stage was set for conversions that would reshape the Protestant American compact.

Consider the home life of a Prussian-born Jewish immigrant couple, Gustav and Tina Ruben Gumpel, in Bridgeport, Connecticut, in the late nineteenth century. The Gumpels had lived on Manhattan's Lower East Side before moving to Bridgeport, where Gustav was a kosher butcher and (possibly) a rabbi.* Their youngest daughter, identi-

* Stories on the subject by the Catholic News Service, *The Jewish Week,* and *The New York Times* all referred to Gustav Gumpel as a "rabbi," but the Bridgeport congregation of

fied as Deborah on her 1887 birth certificate, converted to Catholicism in 1908 and then went on to marry a housepainter named Thomas O'Connor. The O'Connors were, by all accounts, devout Catholics, and their son, John, became a priest and, eventually, a bishop, and cardinal. When New York's Cardinal John Joseph O'Connor died in 2000, no one, including the cardinal himself (according to surviving family members) knew that his mother had been born Jewish. O'Connor apparently did know that his mother was a convert, but, according to a spokesman for the Archdiocese of New York, he assumed that she had converted from Lutheranism. "It wasn't a secret," said Joseph Zwilling, communications director for the archdiocese.[2] Actually, it was a secret—as much a secret as my father's Jewish background was throughout my childhood. (Cardinal O'Connor's idea that his mother had converted from Lutheranism is reminiscent of my father's tale of converting to Catholicism from Episcopalianism.) In any event, the story of O'Connor's Jewish heritage broke in the spring of 2014, when his eighty-seven-year-old sister, Mary O'Connor Ward-Donegan, wrote a personal essay for the publication *Catholic New York* about her mother's family. "The basic fact is, my mother was Jewish," she said. "That means my two brothers were Jewish, my sister was Jewish, and I am Jewish. Of that I am very proud." (She was referring not to her faith—she is a Catholic—but to the Jewish tradition that Judaism is matrilineally transmitted.)

The confusion and secrecy surrounding the conversion of O'Connor's mother was not atypical for conversions in either Jewish or non-Jewish immigrant families. What we don't know about this story is possibly more interesting than what we do know. How did the future cardinal's Jewish or Catholic relatives feel about religious intermarriage in the first decade of the twentieth century? Tina Gumpel died when her daughter was a toddler, but Gustav lived until 1914. (They are both buried in a Jewish cemetery near Bridgeport.) Did Gustav the kosher butcher have any contact with his daughter after she converted to Catholicism? Or would he have sat *shivah* when his daughter converted? How did the O'Connor side of the family feel about the Jewish convert in their midst? Did they even know that

---

which he was a member has no record of his having served as a rabbi there in any official capacity. This, perhaps, was more of a family legend or a wish, since being a butcher did not confer high status among Prussian Jews.

Dorothy Gumpel had been born into a Jewish family? (She did not marry the cardinal's father until nearly a year after her conversion.) If they knew, did the elder O'Connors embrace their Jewish-born daughter-in-law as they would have accepted a "cradle Catholic" of Irish heritage?

The historical importance of mixed marriages in the early twentieth century, whether they involved different sorts of Christians, Christians and Jews, or, for that matter, religious believers and atheists, lies not in how they were viewed by families or society at that time but in the stage they set for the pluralistic future in which we live now. There is no way to understand the exceptionalist American affinity for religious conversion without understanding the social consequences of the great immigration and its aftermath between the twentieth-century world wars. Only one generation separates O'Connor, one of the leading American Catholic clerics of the late twentieth century, from those Bridgeport grandparents buried beneath headstones carved in Hebrew letters. For that matter, only two generations separate Susan Jacoby, born in 1945 and raised a Catholic, from the young Jewish student Max Jacoby, who sought refuge in America in 1849 after participating in the unsuccessful democratic uprising of 1848 in Prussia.* If one measures history in generations rather than years, these are astonishingly short spans.

•

The era of unlimited mass immigration to America ended abruptly in 1924, when, in the wave of xenophobia and anti-Bolshevism that followed the First World War, Congress passed a restrictive law establishing a system of "national origins quotas" for would-be entrants to the United States. The legislation was basically an attempt to stop immigration of Jews and Catholics from the poorer regions of Europe. Chinese were already shut out by the Exclusion Act of 1882, and the 1924 law excluded other Asians as well.

The most tragic effect of the national-origins quota system would become apparent only in the late 1930s, when the Golden Door was

---

* All of the men in the Jacoby family married and had children relatively late in life, which explains why there were only two generations born in the United States between 1849 and 1945.

slammed shut to German and many prescient Polish and Russian Jews, desperate to leave what was becoming Hitler's Europe. From 1880 until the quota system was instituted, approximately one hundred thousand Jews a year had immigrated to the United States, reaching an estimated total of three million. In the first year after the 1924 law went into effect, only ten thousand Jews were able to enter the country—even though many already had relatives here. The impact on southern Italians was just as dramatic (though they would not wind up dead in Nazi gas chambers as a result). Under the old system, approximately two hundred thousand Italians came to the United States each year in the first decade of the twentieth century; the new quota was set at just four thousand. The blatant bigotry underlying the law was apparent in its statistical basis: annual quotas were set according to the proportion of a particular "nationality" in the American population in 1890—a time when white Americans were still, overwhelmingly, of Anglo-Saxon Protestant descent.[3]

None of this changed until the 1960s, when President Lyndon B. Johnson signed a signature piece of legislation, now largely forgotten, embedded in his vision of a "Great Society"—an act abolishing the quota system. As he signed the bill into law on October 3, 1965, Johnson described the immigration system imposed in the 1920s as "un-American in the highest sense."* In one of the near-poetic speeches for which the rough-hewn, controversial Johnson is almost never remembered, he declared, "Our beautiful America was built by a nation of strangers. From a hundred different places or more they have poured forth into an empty land, joining and blending in one mighty and irresistible tide. The land flourished because it was fed from so many sources—because it was nourished by so many different cultures and traditions and peoples."[4] And religions. That many of the strangers did not remain strangers became apparent as every sort of religious and ethnic intermarriage—still a relatively unusual phenomenon during the period when Cardinal O'Connor's parents began their life together—became increasingly common with each decade of the twentieth century.

Although the 1924 quota system did clamp down on what contemporary white Protestants considered the immigration of "undesirables," the closing of the door came too late to preserve the Protestant

---

* The provisions of the new immigration law went into effect in 1968.

domination of American religious life that had existed, in one form or another, since the beginning of the republic. Given that the main purpose of quotas was the preservation of white Anglo-Saxon Protestant power, the law became a failure in spite of itself. If the secular Constitution was the critical first element shaping American exceptionalist attitudes toward religious conversion, the great immigration to the United States in the four decades bracketing the turn of the twentieth century—the last period of essentially unlimited immigration in American history—was the second. Americans rarely consider the obvious fact that no other modern nation has been constructed entirely of people from elsewhere. Yet immigration remains a part of our national DNA, in spite of the ease with which we forget disgraceful policies like the quota system, and in spite of our ambivalence (to put it mildly) about both legal and illegal immigration today. No other country in modern history has ever voluntarily created a society in which people of very different faiths were placed, in large numbers, in close proximity to one another on an equal civil (albeit not social) footing. For people even to consider changing their religion, they must, at some point, become acquainted with people of other religions. And when they do develop relationships with people of other religions—in spite of the dire injunctions of small-"o" orthodox priests, ministers, rabbis, imams, and defenders of many other faiths—human beings display a maddening tendency to have sex with, fall in love with, and marry people outside their group. It happened in the late Roman Empire, as Christians, pagans, and Jews intermarried; it happened during the Iberian Convivencia, as both Muslims and Jews intermarried with Christians; and it began to happen in America, on a previously unimagined scale, when immigrants of different faiths and cultures began living near one another and often attending the same schools in poor and working-class neighborhoods from sea to shining sea.

Although the actual incidence of religious mixed marriage was undoubtedly much lower in the first three decades of the twentieth century than it is today, the best proof that intermarriage was a growing phenomenon lies in the documented efforts of American Catholic, Protestant, and Jewish authorities to discourage and, insofar as possible, anathematize the practice. At the heart of these ultimately unsuccessful efforts was the conviction that a mixed marriage would usually lead to the conversion of one spouse to another faith, or to a general attenuation of religious belief and practice on the part of both partners. In this gloomy analysis (from their point of view), the arbiters of faith were absolutely right—although attenuation of belief was probably a cause as well as a result of mixed marriage. However, laxity in religious practice and belief did not always ensue after a mixed marriage, especially if one partner converted to the religion of the other. During my years in parochial school, I often heard the nuns say that converts make the most devout Catholics—and this certainly must have been true when parents born into different religions, as Cardinal O'Connor's were, produced children who became nuns or priests. Yet it is a mistake to generalize about the religious outcome of intermarriage, regardless of whether one partner converts. My father, as a Catholic convert, was not especially devout—quite possibly because my mother, the "cradle Catholic," was downright subversive in her attitudes toward the church. "You don't have to believe what the nuns say; you can make up your own mind" was her standard comment whenever I would challenge something Sister Mary So-and-So had said about a theological question like the virginity of Christ's mother. It is now clear to me that attenuated religious belief long preceded my parents' marriage.

•

By the 1880s, the United States was not the only country whose government eschewed any interference with religious intermarriage. From the French Revolution through the unification of Germany—followed by Bismarck's 1875 law establishing civil marriage—one European country after another had disengaged the state from its long involvement with upholding and enforcing the laws of church and synagogue regarding marriage outside their faiths. The United States was, however, the only country in which the national government never backed up religious institutions in their efforts to discourage members from marrying outside the fold. You could be married by a minister, a priest, a rabbi, or a judge—all of whom were licensed to perform weddings in most states right from the start—and the government recognized you as husband and wife. The state did not care whether you were a Catholic marrying a Lutheran, a Baptist marrying a Methodist, or a

Jew marrying an Episcopalian: you were married in the eyes of the law, whatever your family or your church thought about the religious appropriateness of the match. You want to sit *shivah* for your son if he marries a *shiksa*? Fine. You want to welcome the new daughter-in-law, teach her to make latkes, and hope that she'll see the wisdom of converting? *Mazel tov.* Your government doesn't care. The same was (and is) true of divorce. Orthodox Jewish women, for example, are required by Jewish law to receive a *get*—a divorce decree allowing them to remarry in the faith—from their husbands. But the *get* has no standing in civil law: if an Orthodox Jewish wife receives a divorce decree from a civil court, she is legally, albeit not religiously, free to remarry. In similar fashion, American courts repeatedly refused to uphold prenuptial agreements, required before 1970 by the Roman Catholic Church, that children of a mixed marriage be raised in the Catholic faith. Catholic prenuptial agreements governed by Canon Law, like all religious contracts, were private affairs and no business of the state.

American public schools posed another problem for clerical authorities who wished to discourage, even though they could not legally prohibit, mixed marriage. As the new immigrants began arriving, local and state governments, particularly in the Northeastern, Middle Atlantic, and Midwestern states, began an unprecedented expansion of elementary and secondary school education. The new Jewish immigrants, so often shut out of the schools that existed in Russia and Poland, eagerly embraced American public education. Protestants, except for the small upper class that attended private schools, had always gone to public, called common, schools. The Catholic Church alone, after the Civil War, had begun to finance the only large, alternative religious school system in the United States. American Catholic leaders originally had hopes of arriving at some sort of arrangement with American states and localities, resembling a settlement that had emerged in Germany, in which parochial schools of all religions would receive taxpayer subsidies. Their hopes were stymied in the late 1870s and early 1880s, when sixteen states passed so-called Blaine Amendments, prohibiting taxation for any religious education.* In spite of the intense Catholic

---

* The amendments were named after Maine Representative James G. Blaine, who in 1875 had introduced a constitutional amendment that would have banned taxpayer sup-

emphasis on education—and this was still true at the high-water mark of parochial school attendance after the Second World War—only about half of Catholic children ever went to parochial schools. The rest either could not afford the tuition, or had parents who simply preferred public school. (The preference for public school was stronger among Italian Catholic immigrants, who often viewed the American church as "the Irish church.")

Jews, including many religiously observant immigrants from Russia and Poland, had very different attitudes from Catholics toward public schools. Jewish yeshivas enrolled only the most traditionally observant American Jews, regardless of whether they were first-generation immigrants, and were largely ignored by working-class immigrant parents, who saw their children as future clerk typists, bookkeepers, or business owners—and, by the second generation, teachers, doctors, and lawyers. For the most part, Jews were simply grateful for the opportunity to send their children to school, and they had no expectation of or desire for state support of religious education. If they wanted their children to go to a Jewish school, they would pay the tuition themselves. A state that left religion alone and allowed everyone to attend taxpayer-supported schools was the Jewish immigrant's dream.

Most significant from the standpoint of religious and ethnic intermarriage was the great expansion of high school enrollment that began shortly after the turn of the century. From 1900 to 1940, the population of high school graduates nationwide increased from 7 to 49 percent. The rise in high school attendance began well before the First World War and, in metropolitan areas, included many children of those who had immigrated in the preceding two decades. High school, for those generations, was a time when teenagers were not only "dating" in the modern sense but choosing marriage partners. Religious leaders would have been fools not to be fearful of the consequences, from the standpoint of keeping the faithful faithful, of having Jews, Catholics, and Protestants—the Big Three—go to school together at a time when hormonal urges are most powerful.

---

port for religious instruction nationwide. That amendment failed to obtain the necessary two-thirds majority in the Senate by just two votes. Had it passed and been ratified by the states at the time, tax vouchers for religious schools today would be clearly unconstitutional.

So it was that, in 1918, the Catholic Church revised Canon Law with its first explicit rules for priests confronted by lay Catholics who wished to marry someone of another faith. Pastors were urged to use every possible form of moral suasion to discourage mixed marriages, but the church recognized that, in countries like America, where individual rights were highly valued and a secular government prevailed, it was unrealistic to hope that all intermarriage could be prevented. Without the assistance of state coercion, priests would not be able to convince all young lovers that their desire to be together was unholy. In such instances, the priest was urged to treat the marriage as an opportunity to convert the non-Catholic. In a manual based on the 1918 Canon Law revisions that might well have been titled "Advice to Crafty Proselytizing Pastors" (its real title was "Pastoralia, Way of Approach"), priests were urged to conceal their displeasure when a "mixed" couple seemed bent on marrying.

> It will not help matters to visit our severest displeasure on the offenders, for such an attitude may only serve to force them into a more regrettable course of action. The non-Catholic party in particular should be treated with the utmost kindness and consideration. If this is done, a real opportunity may be created and a convert may be won to the Church. . . . If it is gently hinted that the prospects for future domestic happiness and peace will be brighter and that the necessary dispensation can be obtained more easily on condition that the non-Catholic consents to familiarize himself or herself with the doctrines of the Church, the latter rarely will manifest any reluctance to undergo the required instruction. . . . In this manner we may succeed in making a convert; but, whatever may be the outcome, nothing will be lost. For if the non-Catholic party does not enter the fold, at least he will gain a better appreciation of the Church, and the danger of perversion on the part of the Catholic will be lessened.[5]

If the non-Catholic, in spite of all this friendly persuasion, did not agree to convert before marriage, a special dispensation was required from diocesan authorities. A small local Catholic population, which might leave a Catholic woman an old maid if she insisted on a husband of her own faith, was one ground for such a dispensation. That a Catholic man in such a setting might be left a bachelor if he held out for a Catholic wife was *not* a cause for dispensation. One can only speculate about the reasons for this sex disparity in church recommendations. Perhaps it was assumed that a man was free to travel in search of a wife, but a good Catholic girl was not. Certainly, the status of a single woman in Catholic communities was much lower than that of an unmarried man. Becoming a nun was the only way to escape the stigma; in early twentieth-century Catholic America, there was no equivalent of the respectable New England Protestant spinster. Another cause for dispensation was unflinchingly realistic, in that it covered cases where there was "a strong suspicion that the two parties have had sexual relations," and that if they remained unmarried "worse things might happen." Another valid rationale kicked in when the worst had already happened and the woman was pregnant.

From these strictures, it could not be clearer that the process of obtaining permission for a mixed marriage from the Catholic Church was humiliating for both the Catholic and non-Catholic partners. That is one reason why any statistics about mixed marriages between, say, 1900 and 1940 seem to me inherently unreliable. Who knows how many independent-minded mixed couples never bothered to go through the rigmarole and simply took themselves off to a justice of the peace? It may be assumed that parish priests dealt with these instructions in varying ways, depending on their temperament and talent for diplomacy. My grandmother Minnie Broderick (née Rothen-hoefer), despite her complete willingness to convert from Lutheranism before she married my grandfather in 1919, remembered a particularly unpleasant parish priest who asked bluntly if she was "in the family way." Gran recalled, "I was shocked, because I would never let Jim do more than kiss me." My grandfather, who was not shocked, told the priest, "She's as innocent as the Virgin Mary, no thanks to me." Gramps was so angry at the priest that my grandmother had to persuade him, in deference to his mother's feelings, not to run off and get married by a judge. Some couples must have done exactly that, and they would not necessarily appear in parish records from which demographic statistics might be gleaned. Many of these couples, given the strong social pressure to display some religious affiliation during the first half of the twentieth century, probably went to *some* church— especially after they became parents. Thus, it is reasonable to assume that mixed marriages during, and for at least two decades after, the massive immigration of 1880 to 1924 were responsible for a considerable number of unrecorded "conversions of convenience" in the United States.

The church was concerned enough by 1932 to issue a special letter listing the ecclesiastical punishments for the Catholic spouse if prenuptial promises to raise children as Catholics were violated. Among these were religious annulment of the marriage, denial of the sacraments, and even public excommunication (if the partner in a mixed marriage was prominent enough to be seen as giving "public scandal"). "Perhaps the best indication of the continuing failure of the Catholic system to check what it has considered to be the undesirable results of religious intermarriage," the sociologist Milton L. Barron wrote in 1946, "is the fact that a large percentage of 'invalid' religious intermarriages have been noted in recent Catholic surveys. The term 'invalid mixed marriage' is defined by Catholics as marriage by a Catholic and a non-Catholic before a non-Catholic minister or civil official."[6]

Protestant authorities in America also disapproved of intermarriage, and their position stiffened considerably after the Catholics took a stronger stance in 1932. Soon after the Catholic declaration of penalties for violations of prenuptial agreements, the Committee on Marriage and Home of the Federal Council of Churches of Christ described the requirement of a promise to bring up children as Catholics as an "intolerable condition" that should be used by ministers to advise the Protestant partner against entering any such marriage. The committee also suggested that those of different *Protestant* denominations reach a prenuptial agreement to attend one church together—or to pick a third church agreeable to both. Exactly how this was to be accomplished was not specified. In the old days, when churches were listed in the Yellow Pages, there was no listing under "Third Churches" for, say, a Baptist and an Episcopalian looking for a religious compromise to avoid marital strife.

Intermarriage with Jews was a bridge much further for both Protestants and Catholics. Moreover, Jewish leaders in America were, for the most part, as opposed to intermarriage as the snide priest who asked my grandmother, in 1919, if she and my grandfather had to get married. Conservative and Orthodox rabbis had always refused to preside over marriage ceremonies unless the non-Jewish partner converted according to Jewish law (and according to whatever interpretation of the law was accepted by the particular rabbi). The stance of Reform rabbis was not as uniform, but there is considerable evidence that Reform Judaism in America grew more conservative on this issue as the number of mixed marriages increased in the first three decades of the twentieth century. As early as 1883, though, the prominent Reform leader Rabbi Isaac Mayer Wise delivered a public lecture with as negative a view of intermarriage as that promulgated in any Vatican declaration. Wise's remarks were specifically directed at those who believed it appropriate for Reform rabbis to officiate at mixed-marriage ceremonies in which both parties were relatively detached from religious belief and observance.

> It might be urged that there are thousands and tens of thousands of individuals in this country who profess no religion at all; hence they are free. . . . Why should any rabbi refuse to solemnize in behalf of Judaism the marriages of such irreligious parties whose parents happened to be Jewish on one side and Christian on the other, if no existing law restrains him? . . . To this might be replied: Because the parties are irreligious; or because such solemnization would be a mere mockery to persons who profess no religion . . . and no rabbi will abuse the authority vested in him to perform the task of a lower magistrate; no rabbi has the right to act the part of an ordinary stage actor—to go through a performance and pronounce formulas and benedictions to parties who believe in neither, and cannot consider themselves benefited by either, as the next justice of the peace can declare them man and wife without any performance or benediction.[7]

This position is certainly understandable, notwithstanding the possibility that the desire of the putative secular couple for a Jewish ceremony might indicate some degree of attachment to Jewish culture and a Jewish family. To a Catholic or Protestant clergyman, the loss of one of their faithful (and of potential children) to a mixed marriage might be regrettable and sinful, but the institutional faith would go on. For a long-embattled Jewish minority, the entry of one of its members into a mixed marriage (with or without actual conversion) meant a loss to a *people* as well as a faith.

In the twentieth century, especially as Hitler's threat began to loom in the 1930s, opposition to intermarriage grew stronger among American Reform rabbis. A survey in 1937 showed that more than 75 percent of Reform rabbis in the United States either refused to officiate at any mixed marriages or would perform the ceremony only if the non-Jewish partner had signed an agreement to raise the children as Jews.[8] Such an agreement was as unenforceable in a civil court as the prenuptial promises demanded by the Catholic Church.

·

And yet the rate of religious intermarriage continued to rise, first in the "greatest generation" and then, more dramatically, among the post–World War II baby boomers who came of age in the 1960s and 1970s. In the Catholic and Jewish communities whose authorities had opposed intermarriage most strongly, rabbis and priests had to cope with religious defection at a time when American public religiosity was at its zenith, in the 1950s. Indeed, the obligatory religiosity of American middle-class life—in contrast to the more comfortable secularism of Europeans in mixed marriages—may have produced more conversions here among intermarried couples. When the first question you are asked upon arriving in a new town is "What church do you go to?," it is natural to pick a church to go to.

The connection between the vast immigration of the late nineteenth and early twentieth centuries and the growing number of religious and ethnic intermarriages after the Second World War is more easily understood if social change is measured by the standard of generations rather than years. A considerable number of the American soldiers who fought what is remembered as the nation's "last good war" were the children of immigrants. A teenager who immigrated to America with his family in, say, 1915—before the quota system—would have been exactly the right age to marry and produce a son who would have served in the U.S. Army during the Second World War. And that son—unlike his parents from a Russian shtetl or an impoverished Sicilian hill town—would have a chance to go to college on the GI Bill. The immediate impact of the GI Bill is apparent in the numerical difference between the 160,000-member college graduating class of 1940 and the 500,000-member graduating class of 1950. Eventually,

2.2 million veterans would attend colleges (with another 3.5 million entering vocational institutions).[9]

The entry of so many more Americans into four-year colleges was the most important factor in the postwar rise in mixed marriages and conversions. Mario Puzo's novel *The Godfather,* followed by the 1972 blockbuster movie, offers a cameo of what was happening in families more ordinary than the Corleones. Michael, the youngest son of Don Vito Corleone (an immigrant from Sicily), is a war hero who attends an Ivy League school, where he falls in love with the New England Protestant Kay Adams. (Michael's father would presumably have been able to pay his tuition without the GI Bill.) When Michael and Kay finally marry, she is the one who converts—as one might expect when a nice girl from New England marries into a Mafia family. The movie doesn't make much of Kay's conversion, but Puzo uses it to set up the ending of the novel, when Michael has already engineered numerous murders and taken control of his father's Mafia empire. In the final scene: "As she had been taught to do, Kay struck her breast lightly with her clenched hand, the stroke of repentance. . . . She emptied her mind of all thought of herself, of her children, of all anger, of all rebellion, of all questions. Then with a profound and deeply willed desire to believe, to be heard . . . she said the necessary prayers for the soul of Michael Corleone."[10]

This kind of conversion story played out, on a less operatic scale, in ordinary families whose children had gone to college and met people from backgrounds unknown to their immigrant parents in insular communities. As the level of education rises, so has the incidence of religious intermarriage in every developed country in the modern era. Today, however, the proportion of interreligious couples is increasing at every educational level in the United States—a significant change since the middle of the twentieth century. The impact of higher education on religious intermarriage may have been more powerful in the past because less educated Americans, especially women, had fewer opportunities than they do today to meet anyone outside their immediate family and social group. Today, young women and men of different religions, ethnic groups, and races meet in the workplace—regardless of whether they are graduates of high schools, two-year community colleges, or the nation's most elite universities. They also communicate with one another on the Internet. The era when the social choices of teenagers and young adults could be circumscribed and controlled by family, neighborhood, and church is long gone. And, as can be seen from the lamentations about mixed marriages from priests, ministers, and rabbis in the 1930s, the breakdown of traditional mechanisms of social control had begun long before technology and expanded higher education accelerated the process.

The nuns of my childhood were not wrong in their conviction that many American conversions of the twentieth century would never have occurred without the impetus of mixed marriage. My father certainly would not have converted to Catholicism had he married a girl from a similar nonobservant Jewish background instead of my Catholic mother. That fact does not make his conversion insincere, but it does mean that he was more interested in family harmony—and in distancing himself from his Jewish origins—than in Catholic doctrine. In mid-century America, religion—especially when intertwined with tribal ethnic loyalties—was important enough to Americans that a marriage to a person of another faith was still considered somewhat *inconvenient.* Conversion, for many Americans of my father's generation, was a way to ameliorate the strain, rather than a profoundly felt spiritual or intellectual choice. These kinds of conversions would continue, in increasing numbers, in the next generation of baby boomers. The political scientists Robert D. Putnam and David E. Campbell, in *American Grace,* put together some of the best available studies and concluded that the rate of what they call "religious switching" rose steadily throughout the twentieth century, along with the rate of religious intermarriage.[11] There are, as I have already indicated, immense problems with all statistics about both conversion and intermarriage rates, because no one was keeping track of them in any systematic way before the Second World War. Astonishingly, the Gallup Poll began asking Americans about their attitude toward mixed marriages only in 1968, when nearly 60 percent of Americans already said they approved of marriages between Catholics and Protestants and Jews and non-Jews. By 1982, the approval figure had risen to 80 percent.[12]

If many American "conversions of convenience" were determined as much by social opportunism and intermarriage as by spiritual needs, and if they lacked an overwhelming intellectual or ideological component, that is not such a bad thing when one considers absolutist alternatives—both secular and traditionally religious. Conversions of convenience may have been the American norm for those who changed faiths from the 1920s to the 1950s, but the same decades of the twentieth century, on both sides of the Atlantic, saw ideologically driven conversions, especially by intellectuals, based entirely on an intense desire for certainty. Some converts embraced the faith of Stalinist Communism; others found solace in the most anti-modernist forms of traditional religion. Such conversions were never the norm, but because some involved famous literary intellectuals and scholars, they have exerted an outsize influence (especially in the United States and England) on our image of what it means to replace one faith with another. The normative American conversion experience undoubtedly had less to do with religious absolutism than with conventional social yearnings like those of my father. The pragmatic nature of so many American conversions from the 1920s to the 1950s presented a sharp contrast to the exemplars of absolutist conversions of intellectuals, on the left and right, clothed in traditional spiritual or modernist garb. Perhaps that very contrast accounts for both the romanticization and demonization that still surround the politically charged, impassioned conversions that took place at a time in the twentieth century when the world was locked in an epic battle between good and evil—whether those terms are defined in a secular or a religious sense.

INTERREGNUM

ABSOLUTISM AND ITS DISCONTENTS

19

TRUE BELIEVERS

From the psychologist's point of view, there is little difference
between a revolutionary and a traditionalist faith. All true faith is
uncompromising, radical, purist; hence the true traditionalist is
always a revolutionary zealot in conflict with pharisaian society,
with the lukewarm corrupters of the creed.

—ARTHUR KOESTLER, *The God That Failed*

I F I WERE TO BE GRANTED ONE WISH, in fairy-godmother fashion, it
would be that Arthur Koestler's analogy between secular and traditional faith-based absolutism, made at the midpoint of the twentieth century, remained true today only in a personal and psychological
sense. To put it another way, I wish that absolutist religion and absolutist conversion no longer possessed any public or political power anywhere in the world. As I have indicated in the introduction to this
book, I do not consider any form of secular thought a religion unless
the secular ideology possesses a civil enforcement mechanism (a critical qualification, to be sure). Nor do I believe that conversions to a
traditional religion pose anything but individual concerns as long as
they do not attempt to impose cultural hegemony (also a critical qualification). However, the new religio-political horrors that have marked
the opening decades of the twenty-first century, and their relationship
to the undead phenomena of absolute truth claims and forced conversion, have ensured the continuing relevance of Koestler's observation.

There have always been eras when it was particularly problematic
to separate individual conscience from the social causes and conse-

quences of religious choice. One of those periods extended from the beginning of the First World War until the end of the Second World War, when the clash between totalitarian and democratic values eventually engulfed most of the earth and its inhabitants. That organized secular totalitarianism was characterized by the same imperviousness to evidence as absolutist traditional religion was recognized by only a small minority of congenital skeptics.

Conversions by both American and European intellectuals to Stalinist Communism in the 1920s and 1930s were produced by a crisis of confidence in social institutions battered by a brutal war and then by a worldwide economic depression. But the same period also saw an extraordinary number of conversions by atheist intellectuals to Christianity—and the political implications of these contemporaneous leaps of faith have often been overlooked. Sometimes the converts to Communism were the same people who eventually turned to conservative forms of Christianity, and nowhere was this more true than in England and the United States.

It is one of the peculiarities of history and national character that some of the most famous absolutist conversions took place in two nations where absolutist politics never gained the upper hand at a dangerous time. For precisely that reason, certain Anglo-American conversions stand out as exemplary demonstrations of the intellectual and moral dangers of religious absolutism and of their persistent social influence in ways that sometimes outlast the original religious impulse. Whittaker Chambers (1901–61), known primarily in American history for his role as the accuser in the notorious Alger Hiss trial, comes to mind. So does his near contemporary C. S. Lewis (1898–1963), the English medieval and Renaissance scholar and author of the beloved *Chronicles of Narnia,* and the English journalist and critic G. K. Chesterton (1874–1936), whose *Father Brown* mystery series is one of the staple British imports that keep America's Public Broadcasting Service going year after year. There may be something to offend everyone in a comparison of the conversions of such seemingly disparate intellectual figures, but the common element is that they all, at one point or another, embodied the absolutist passions of their era. Chesterton (though he was of an older, Victorian-bred generation) converted to Roman Catholicism in the same decade when Chambers converted to Communism and Lewis converted from atheism to High Anglicanism. After leaving the faith of the Communist Party, Chambers and Koestler (1905–83), not surprisingly, came to know each other as anticommunist intellectuals.

•

It is arguably more difficult for Americans today to comprehend, in an imaginative sense, the political passions that produced both Nazism and Bolshevism than it would have been for an American patriot in revolutionary Boston to imagine that civil and religious authorities in his society had, less than a century earlier, executed people for witchcraft.

I must emphasize that I do not consider Nazism, or any other form of fascism, an alternative "religion" in the full sense that Stalinism was. In Spain, the Franco regime supported and was supported by the most conservative forces within the Catholic Church. In Germany, Nazi leaders realized that they would have had to pay too high a price in an attempt to wipe out traditional Christianity; Hitler's strategy was, instead, the attempted co-option of Christian institutions through such measures as his 1933 concordat with the Vatican and his appeal to the nationalism of both Lutheran and Catholic German clerics. It was entirely possible to consider oneself simultaneously a Nazi and a Christian, and millions of Germans did. German troops went into battle accompanied by both Lutheran and Catholic chaplains, and soldiers wore the traditional imperial belt buckle with the legend "*Gott mit uns.*" There were of course many instances of resistance to the Nazis—and their persecution of Jews—by individual Catholic and Protestant clergy, and by groups of lay Christians, throughout Europe, but the churches as institutions were concerned mainly with preserving their traditional sphere of authority.*

---

* The more widely publicized examples include the firm stance of the Lutheran Church in Denmark against the Nazi occupiers' attempt to deport all Danish Jews to Auschwitz; the help offered Jews by many bishops, priests, and nuns in northern Italy; the actions of historically Huguenot communities in Vichy France; and the resistance of the "Confessing Church" of dissident Lutherans in Germany. The Confessing Church in Germany, however—in contrast to the Danish Lutheran Church—was less helpful to unconverted Jews than to those who had converted to Protestantism and were nevertheless being persecuted.

Stalin's Soviet Union, by contrast, did attempt to root out traditional religion, and it was impossible, anywhere in the world, to be a committed Communist Party member and a religiously observant Jew or Christian. Koestler, who spent the last half of his adult life in England, viewed ideological conversions from the vantage point of an outsider and an insider. Born into a nonobservant Hungarian Jewish family, he joined the Party in Germany in 1931 and left, disillusioned with Stalinism, in 1938. In between, he spent a year in Stalin's Soviet Union and also fought against Franco in Spain, where he was captured and tortured by fascists. (His novel *Darkness at Noon,* first published in 1940 and never out of print since then, is set in the Soviet Union but also draws on his experiences as a political prisoner of Franco's forces.) Unlike many foreigners, Koestler understood Stalin's purges for what they were—the only way a ruthless and antirational secular religion could maintain its power to terrorize an entire people. In 1940, Koestler escaped from France to join the British Army, and he remained in England after the war. His voice has a particular resonance because, unlike many former Communists, he never joined the ranks of those who found a new home in a traditional religion that replaced one rigid set of irrational beliefs and rules with another.*

·

Koestler and Chambers, with their common history as apostate Party members, knew each other after the Second World War. Since the immense international publicity surrounding the 1940 publication of *Darkness at Noon,* Koestler may well have been the foreign ex-Communist best known to Americans. When Chambers died, Koestler wrote, "I always felt that Whittaker was the most misunderstood person of our time. . . . The witness is gone, the testimony will stand."[1]

---

* He was, however, deeply interested in the paranormal, and left the bulk of his estate to establish a chair for research in parapsychology at a university in Britain. Oxford and Cambridge turned down Koestler's bequest, which was finally accepted by the University of Edinburgh. Koestler's late-in-life enthusiasm for parapsychology had something in common with the interest of aging nineteenth-century freethinkers in spiritualism—a particularly common phenomenon among those whose children had died at an early age. In 1983, suffering from Parkinson's disease and terminal leukemia, Koestler committed suicide along with his wife.

Despite their immensely different cultural backgrounds, both men had spent their young adulthood searching for a secular creed that would provide the meaning and purpose of a traditional religion.

Chambers began his search for the One Big Truth as a Long Island teenager, influenced by a female mentor who was a Christian Scientist. He listed Christian Science as his "religion" on his 1920 application to Columbia University, but this seems to have been no more than a dalliance. When he joined the fledgling American communist movement in 1925, as his biographer Sam Tanenhaus observes, Chambers "had at last found his church."[2] His conversion took place while Koestler (who would not join the German Communist Party until 1931) was living on a kibbutz in Palestine and beginning to find that Zionism fell short (for him) as a guiding ideology.

Chambers's embrace of the Party also occurred in the same time frame as Chesterton's formal conversion to Roman Catholicism, which did not take place until 1922—even though the latter had long been an apologist for the most orthodox and traditional forms of Christianity. In 1926, Chesterton—who was raised a Unitarian—delivered himself of the astonishing pronouncement that the Roman Catholic Church was clearly "the only champion of reason in the twentieth century."[3] During the same period, Chesterton's argument played a role in the conversion of Lewis, who traveled intellectually and spiritually from atheism to Christian theism and finally to Anglicanism in 1931. Lewis did not make any assertions about the Church of England as a fount of reason, but instead offered a more general description of the pull of religion for the convert as "not even 'All or nothing' . . . Now [for the convert], the demand was simply, 'All.'"[4]

What all of these conversions in the 1920s and 1930s offered was authority and stability in a highly unstable time. Lewis, who is considered a much more modern and liberal religious thinker than converts to either Roman Catholicism or Communism of his era, nevertheless provides the most explicit description of the compulsive pull of faith and conversion in the autobiography of his early life, *Surprised by Joy*. The book was published in 1955, so it is informed by Lewis's knowledge of what both Nazism and Stalinism had wrought.

But who can duly adore that Love which will open the high gates to a prodigal who is brought in kicking, struggling, resentful, and darting his eyes in every direction for a chance of escape? The words *compelle intrare,* compel them to come in, have been so abused by wicked men that we shudder at them; but, properly understood, they plumb the depth of the Divine mercy. The hardness of God is kinder than the softness of men, and His compulsion is our liberation.[5]

Ah, that seductive *compelle intrare*! Lewis, a classics scholar, was being highly disingenuous in his suggestion that such an injunction was not to be feared unless it came from demonic secular leaders like Hitler and Stalin. As Lewis well knew, the phrase was first used in Christian apologetics by Augustine, who asserted that dissident Donatists must be compelled to attend Roman Catholic services. Upperclass Donatist leaders who refused were to be exiled, and servants and slaves beaten. (Augustine rationalized his *compelle intrare* from the parable of the great supper in chapter 14 of Luke, in which a lord of the manor is furious because invited guests use marriage or work as excuses not to come to dinner. "Go out into the highways and hedges," the master says to his servant, "and compel *them* to come in, so that my house may be filled.") How can any human being know what is on the other side of the door when he is told, *"Compelle intrare"*? And if the convert changes his mind, does the door swing both ways and allow an exit? These questions have no meaning in Dante's "Paradiso," that supernatural realm where the only answer can be *"La sua volontade è nostra pace"* ("His will is our peace")—a phrase echoed in Lewis's "His compulsion is our liberation." The door to paradise only swings one way, and what inhabitant of that divine kingdom would want it otherwise? In the natural realm, though, the assertion that "His compulsion is our liberation" is just that—an assertion based on faith rather than a conclusion rooted in evidence.

Compulsion as liberation is the theme that binds all of the converts who oscillated between secular and religious absolute truths during the years between the twentieth-century world wars. For the dazzled convert, Koestler observes, "There is now an answer to every question, doubts and conflicts are a matter of the tortured past—a past already remote, when one had lived in dismal ignorance in the tasteless, colorless world of those who *don't know.* Nothing henceforth can disturb the convert's inner peace and serenity—except the occasional fear of losing faith again, losing thereby what alone makes life worth living, and falling back into outer darkness, where there is wailing and gnashing of teeth."[6]

In contemplating the absolutist secular movements of the twentieth century, some secular humanists as well as many religious believers have propagated the mistaken notion that conversions to Stalinism in the 1920s and 1930s were a logical extension of nineteenth-century materialism and of modernism itself. If one digs deeper, to the notion of surrender that permeates all writings of ex-Communists who underwent two conversions in their lifetime, it is evident that the choice of twentieth-century Stalinism was a perversion of both modernism and nineteenth-century Marxism. The material misery of everyday life as it was experienced by Stalin's subjects (as well as by Soviet citizens in the less frightening post-Stalin era) demonstrates the fallacy of regarding statist Communism as "modern" in any sense other than its timing. Stalinism rejected not only the tender sentiments of "bourgeois humanism" that shaped the better angels of modernity but also the material science upon which the Soviet system claimed to be based. For me, the oxymoronic nature of the ubiquitous Soviet phrase "scientific communism" has always been demonstrated most clearly by the idiotic and tragic story of Stalin's rejection of Mendelian genetics and his embrace of the crackpot biologist Trofim D. Lysenko. Lysenko deemed it possible to build a *biologically* new Soviet man through socialist environmental manipulation, and he applied his beliefs to Soviet agriculture with disastrous results. Real scientists, who tried to fight Lysenkoism and predicted correctly that "socialist" biology would set back Soviet farming and biological research for at least a generation, were either fired or sent to perish in the Gulag.*

Thus, the fundamental mistake made by both Western converts to Communism and "reverse converts" who equated liberalism with Communism (as Chambers eventually did) was that they saw Stalin's Soviet Union as the culmination, not the negation, of all ideas of human progress since the beginning of the Enlightenment. A more accurate way of looking at such conversions is that they were permeated by antirationalism and intellectual submissiveness in modernist and rationalist packaging. The ideological packaging was so opaque

---

* For the most thorough examination of this subject, see *The Rise and Fall of T. D. Lysenko* (1969) and *A Question of Madness* (1971) by Zhores Medvedev, and *Let History Judge* (1971) by Roy Medvedev.

that it fooled both Western leftists and many traditionalist religious converts who, during the same period, considered their embrace of orthodox religion a blow against "scientific communism" and the exaltation of materialist technology. Little did most of them know, to paraphrase Clemenceau, that scientific communism was to science as Socialist Realist art was to both realism and art.

•

The tension between faith and real science (as distinct from bogus scientific communism) was, however, a serious issue in the conversions and reverse conversions of the first half of the twentieth century. The struggle against materialistic philosophy, which would produce many conversions to conservative Christianity, antedates Darwin and Marx as well as twentieth-century Soviet Communism. As demonstrated by Robert Boyle's and William Paley's arguments in the seventeenth and eighteenth centuries, religious concerns about intelligent design emerged as soon as more sophisticated microscopes, telescopes, and other scientific instruments began turning up all sorts of information conflicting with the Bible. Since that time, there has been no letup in the debates on this subject. In the twentieth century, the conclusion that design must imply an intelligent designer turns up over and over in Christian apologetics by ex-Communists like Chambers, as well as by converts to Christianity like Chesterton and Lewis. When it came to intelligent design, these very dissimilar men were all on the same page—a page that could not be turned and that signified the opposite of John Donne's glorious image of a transcendent "library where every book shall lie open to one another."

Chambers's account of the moment when he began to question atheism and, by extension, communism is almost comically reminiscent of Paley's analogy between the creation of the universe and the design of a watch—only, in Chambers's case, the source of illumination was his daughter's ear. In the foreword, written in the form of a letter to his children, to his 1952 autobiography, *Witness*, Chambers described "every sincere break with Communism" as "a religious experience." When anyone leaves the Communist Party, Chambers declared, the break occurs "because he must choose at last between irreconcilable opposites—God or Man, Soul or Mind, Freedom or Communism."[7]

Chambers was then famous and notorious as the essential prosecution witness in the perjury trial of the equally notorious Hiss, who was convicted of having lied to a congressional committee about having been a member of the Party. The "witness," who left the Party in 1938, testified that he and Hiss had been close friends as Communists in the 1930s, and had engaged in espionage for the Soviet Union. Chambers was led to repudiate Communism by a growing realization, beginning with his baby's ear, that the God of the Bible, not Stalin, was the arbiter of the universe.

> My daughter was in her high chair. I was watching her eat. She was the most miraculous thing that had ever happened in my life. I liked to watch her even when she smeared porridge on her forehead or dropped it meditatively on the floor. My eye came to rest on the delicate convolutions of her ear—those intricate, perfect ears. The thought passed through my mind: "No, those ears were not created by any chance coming together of atoms in nature (the Communist view). They could have been created only by immense design." The thought was involuntary and unwanted. I crowded it out of my mind. But I never wholly forgot it or the occasion. I had to crowd it out of my mind. If I had completed it, I should have to say: Design presupposes God. I did not then know that, at that moment, the finger of God was first laid upon my forehead.[8]

That parenthetical "the Communist view" is priceless. Chambers could just as easily have used the adjectives "evolutionist," "Spinozist," "atheist," "agnostic," or "humanist"—any word, really, that belongs to the vocabulary of Enlightenment reason, evolution by means of natural selection, or modernism in general. Chambers's overwrought absolutism comes through clearly in everything he has to say about the religious nature of both his embrace and his ultimate rejection of communism. I suspect that his tone had as much to do with the refusal of liberal intellectuals to believe his testimony against Hiss as with their own political views, which included an abhorrence of all informers of the McCarthy era.*

---

* Anyone who has read my book *Alger Hiss and the Battle for History* (2009) will know that I, like nearly everyone who has revisited this case during the past thirty years, am

Chesterton, who grew up and came of age during the late Victorian era, was still as flummoxed in the 1920s by Darwin's challenge to the concept of man as a special creation of God as Pope Pius IX had been in the 1860s. In 1864, Pius issued his *Syllabus of Errors,* which rejected just about everything that had taken place since the Reformation and said, in essence, "We do not seek or need an accommodation with science, with political systems that separate church and state, with societies where people believe that public schools should be free of church control. Like God, we will always remain the same." A major error of the modern world, the *Syllabus* declared, was the suggestion that the teachings of the church fathers "are no longer suitable to the demands of our times and the progress of the sciences."[9] This monolithic and confidently doctrinaire faith, as it remained throughout the first half of the twentieth century, would be a magnet and lodestar not only for disillusioned communists but for absolutist converts like Chesterton, with a psychological need to be, if not more Catholic than, at least as Catholic as the pope.

In 1916, Chesterton uncompromisingly described *The Descent of Man* as a vision that "really was a descent of man—[who] . . . had been kicked off his pedestal onto the floor."[10] Remove specific American place-names and dates: it becomes almost impossible, when evolution is the subject, to tell the difference between the English literary critic writing during the First World War and Chambers, the American Communist-turned-Christian writing in the 1950s. (In fairness to Chesterton, the unprecedented carnage of what was then called the "Great War"—even though the comment about Darwinian evolution appears in a book on Victorian literature—produced a new and heightened susceptibility to anti-evolutionism among many religiously inclined people, intellectuals and nonintellectuals alike, on both sides of the Atlantic. Social Darwinism had perverted Darwin's theory of evolution by extending the notion of the "survival of the fittest" from man in a state of nature to man in a state of civilization—an idea that was explicitly rejected by Darwin himself.* As religious traditionalists

---

convinced that Chambers told the truth and Hiss lied in his testimony before the House Un-American Activities Committee in 1948 and his two trials in 1949 (the first ending in a hung jury and the second with a conviction). For several decades, however, a majority of liberal intellectuals thought Chambers was the liar.

* In *The Descent of Man,* Darwin argued that natural selection becomes subordinate to environmental factors—which include the moral evolution of man—as soon as humans

saw it, the world's most recent war owed a good deal to secular rejection of the biblical concept of man as "a little less than the angels." In America, the three-time presidential candidate and Woodrow Wilson's secretary of state, William Jennings Bryan, would become the leading exponent of postwar anti-evolutionism.)

Lewis's thinking was much deeper than Chesterton's and as far removed in tone from the spottily educated Chambers's as could be imagined. Yet Lewis, notwithstanding his less hectoring and absolutist *tone,* shared Chambers's and Chesterton's preoccupation with evidence for a plan in creation, and he offered one of the more novel variations on the argument for a divine and intelligent designer. What is unusual about Lewis's argument for design is that he combines it, in *Mere Christianity,* with his answer to the unanswerable theodicy question. And this book is based on a series of lectures delivered by Lewis and broadcast by the BBC during the Second World War—a time when, as was the case during the First World War, the question of how a loving God could allow such evil in the world loomed particularly large for religious believers. By the time the lectures were first published as a book in 1952, the theodicy question had become even more unavoidable in light of postwar revelations about the full horrors of the Nazi concentration camps. Lewis struggles, like all Christian philosophers, to reconcile evil with divine design.

> My argument against God was that the universe seemed so cruel and unjust. But how had I got this idea of *just* and *unjust*? A man does not call a line crooked unless he has some idea of a straight line. What was I comparing this universe with when I called it unjust? . . . A man feels wet when he falls into water, because man is not a water animal: a fish would not feel wet. Of course I could have given up my idea of justice by saying it was nothing but a private idea of my own. But if I did that, then my argument against God collapsed too—for the argument depended on saying that the world

---

enter into a state of civilization. "The aid which we feel impelled to give to the helpless is mainly an incidental result of the instinct of sympathy," he said, "which was originally acquired as part of the social instincts, but subsequently rendered . . . more tender and widely diffused. Nor could we check our sympathy, even at the urging of hard reason, without deterioration in the noblest part of our nature. . . . If we were intentionally to neglect the weak and the helpless, it could only be for a contingent benefit, with an overwhelming present evil."

was really unjust, not simply that it did not happen to please my private fancies. . . . Consequently atheism turns out to be too simple. If
the whole universe has no meaning, we should never have found out
that it has no meaning: just as, if there were no light in the universe
and therefore no creatures with eyes, we should never know it was
dark. *Dark* would be a word without meaning.[11]

Justice cannot possibly be a concept invented by human reason,
any more than an ear as an instrument for perceiving sound can be
the product of eons of evolution by means of natural selection. This
argument is, in its emphasis on an intellectual rather than a physical
design, more subtle than that of Chambers (or Boyle or Paley). But it
is really the same naked argument dressed in donnish clothes, with the
addition of the essential charge made by all of the religiously orthodox against atheism: *There can be no morality without religion.* Justice,
compassion, forgiveness cannot possibly be ethical concepts that arise
from the concern of human beings for one another but must be the
overarching, implanted work of a divine creator. The human brain, by
itself, cannot conceive of either absolute or relative justice. And if evil
and injustice exist, then the imperfect understanding and nature of
man must be the reason. In this discussion linking divine design and
human concepts of justice and injustice, belief in free will (including
the freedom to think) lurks, as it always does, as the escape clause.
But Lewis does not say any of this in an authoritarian tone; there are
a good many ifs along the way to obscure, for a modern reader, the
Augustinian and Thomist origins and destination.

·

The relationship between politics and conversion to a traditional religion is neither as clear nor as linear as the relationship between politics
and a conversion to a rigid secular ideology. Chesterton and his friend
and contemporary Hillaire Belloc (1870–1953), also a devout Catholic
(though he was raised in the faith), formulated a distinctly odd, now
largely forgotten political philosophy know as "Distributism." Belloc
and Chesterton (often joined in the portmanteau "Chesterbelloc,"
coined by George Bernard Shaw) promoted their philosophy, until
Chesterton's death in 1936, in the contrarian magazine *G.K.'s Weekly.*

The publication was founded in 1925, and Chesterton explained that his magazine would fight for Catholic "ethics and economics," just as a magazine like the *New Statesman* did for "Socialist ethics and economics." The connection between Chesterton's religious views and his politics, once he converted to Catholicism from Anglicanism in 1922, was clear. He had dabbled in spiritualism in his youth—a commonplace among lapsed Protestants in the late nineteenth century—and returned to Anglicanism when, in 1901, he married a woman who took the Church of England seriously. His conversion was prompted by the conviction, held by all English intellectuals who followed the path from Anglicanism to Roman Catholicism, that the English church was a wobbly imitation of the "real thing"—the One True Church that Henry VIII had forsaken for Anne Boleyn. There is no doubt that Chesterton thoroughly approved of the stand against modernism and materialism embodied in the *Syllabus* of Pius IX. In a 1926 book dealing specifically with conversion to Catholicism, Chesterton declared that there was no other institution "to say a single word for the family, or the true case for property, or the proper understanding of the religious peasantries, while the whole press is full of every sort of sophistry to smooth the way of divorce, of birth control, of mere State expediency and all the rest."[12] The Distributists called for a dismantling of industrial capitalism, a return to a romanticized Catholic tradition dating from the Middle Ages, and the re-establishment of medieval guilds to provide a more humane life for ordinary workers. That life wasn't actually so great for those "religious peasantries" or for medieval stonecutters seems not to have occurred to Chesterton. His late-twentieth-century reputation as a clever but essentially minor literary figure has been re-evaluated and upgraded in recent years, partly as the result of a major biography, by the Roman Catholic priest and Oxford theological scholar Ian Ker, published in 2011. Ker is considered the world's pre-eminent living authority on the works of the nineteenth-century Catholic Cardinal John Henry Newman (1801–90), who converted from Anglicanism to Roman Catholicism literally midway in his life's journey, in 1845.

Newman's works remained an important influence, well into the twentieth century, on Catholicism—and particularly on Catholic converts—in both the United States and Europe. Edith Stein—who, coincidentally, converted to Catholicism in the same year as

Chesterton—began translating Newman's diaries and letters into German shortly after her baptism. But there is little evidence in Chesterton's dogmatic pronouncements to support Ker's view of him as a worthy descendant of Newman. Chesterton's apologetics, with their romanticized view of the medieval world, seem much less modern than Newman's nineteenth-century works, which cannot easily be classified as theologically conservative or liberal (though both factions within Catholicism have tried to lay claim to him). In general, Newman is regarded as a man ahead of his time in Catholic history. His writings exerted much more influence on participants in the Second Vatican Council, in the 1960s, than on the First Vatican Council, in the late 1860s.

For Chesterton, even men of deep faith—if it is a *liberal* faith—are killjoys guilty of undermining belief in the miraculous. As early as 1908, he dismissed any "liberal" clergyman as a bogeyman "who wishes at least to diminish the number of miracles; it never means a man who wishes to increase that number. It always means a man who is free to disbelieve that Christ came out of His grave; it never means a man who is free to believe that his own aunt came out of her grave."[13] There is a legion of famous Anglo-American cultural figures (not all of them conservatives), from Shaw to William F. Buckley, Jr., who considered Chesterton an impressive intellectual because he could always produce a well-turned English phrase. But a sentence may give off verbal sparks and still amount to utter nonsense. Actually, in societies infected by reason, libertarianism, and liberalism, any man is perfectly free to believe that his aunt rose from her grave. However, there is a word, used by rational conservatives as well as liberals, for such a person, and the word is "delusional." It is only when the resurrection is said to have taken place thousands of years ago, and faith in the miracle has been codified in a powerful religion, that we shrink from applying the pejorative "delusion" to the belief that anyone has ever walked out of a tomb on his or her own two feet.

But, then, Chesterton was the author of a good many witty putdowns of reason and rationality. "When learned men begin to use their reason," he said, "I generally discover they haven't got any."[14] He also placed his wit at the service of the most predictable prejudices of the British upper classes of his time, including anti-Semitism. He opposed closer relations between the British government and the United States on general principle (who knew that *Father Brown* would become such a big hit on American educational television long after his death?) and remarked, "We have dipped the Union Jack in surrender to the Stars and Stripes, out of respect for the sort of Jew who cannot get into any club in New York."[15] Come to think of it, there isn't anything witty in this passage. It is simply unvarnished anti-Semitism, and Chesterton's embrace of one of the most vulgar prejudices of his British contemporaries further undermines attempts to portray him as a distinguished figure in Anglo-American intellectual history.

•

Lewis, by contrast, did not try to substitute wit for reason, and was one of the least overtly political converts, in either the religious or the secular direction, of his time. Although he is best known today as the author of *The Chronicles of Narnia,* Lewis became, in his long life, one of the leading apologists for Christianity in the twentieth century. The absence of in-your-face politics may explain why a number of his books on religion are still read. The U.S. National Institutes of Health director, Dr. Francis Collins, cited *Mere Christianity* and Lewis as important influences on his own conversion from atheism to evangelical Christianity in the late 1970s.

The disproportionate influence exerted in America by the conversion stories of both Chesterton and Lewis (especially Lewis, who possessed a gift for presenting abstruse theological argument in popular form) has been compounded in recent decades by the cultural distance that makes it even more difficult now than it was in the mid-twentieth century for Americans to view lionized English writers as men of their own troubled era rather than as superior beings with some sort of special insight into rarified matters of the soul. A particular element in Lewis's influence is the popularity of the *Narnia* fantasies and their preservation in the mass entertainment media. Lewis's conversion to Anglicanism rather than Roman Catholicism was a disappointment to his close Catholic friend Tolkien (1892–1973).* But the melding of

* Tolkien's mother was a convert to Catholicism from the Baptist faith. Her conversion in 1900 led to a permanent break with her Baptist family, which cut her off from all financial support (she was a widow) after she became a Catholic. Tolkien's mother died

religious symbolism with pagan fantasy that characterizes both the *Narnia* series and Tolkien's *The Hobbit* and *Lord of the Rings* indicates their commonality of devotion. Oh, all right, so Lewis in particular could never have predicted what modern marketing would do with his Jesus symbol, the virtuous and adorable lion Aslan. And neither Tolkien nor Lewis could have imagined that their works would beget the phenomenon of Harry Potter and that, yea, verily, alleged grown-ups would line up by the thousands every few years for premieres of the latest movie featuring the supernatural. But the fantasy worlds of both writers do intersect with their intellectual and theological worlds, in that they are permeated by contempt for modernism and materialism.

·

For all of the converts between the wars—whatever direction or directions they took—the changes of faith were central to their lives. "The mark of the Faith is not tradition; it is conversion," Chesterton asserts. "It is the miracle by which men find truth in spite of tradition and often with the rending of all the roots of humanity."[16] Chambers describes his conversion *to* communism, which occurred in 1925, in much the same terms. Embracing communism in what Chambers called the "dying world" of bourgeois humanism after the First World War was as much a religious experience as leaving the Party would be for him in late 1938. For Chambers, the Party alone offered "faith and a vision, something for which to live and something for which to die. It demanded of me those things which have always stirred what is best in men—courage, poverty, self-sacrifice, discipline, intelligence, my life, and, at need, my death."[17]

In view of the parallels between the centralized authority of the Catholic Church and the Communist Party, it is not surprising that scholars and journalists have focused so much attention on ex-Communists who converted to Catholicism. I was surprised, for example, to learn that Chambers, after leaving the Party, had chosen first Episcopalianism and then Quakerism, with its central tenet of an Inner Light that can never be dictated from any outside force, rather than Catholicism.

---

of diabetes when he was twelve, and she named a Catholic priest as his legal guardian so that he would be raised in her faith.

Chambers had his problems with Quakerism, too—probably because Quakers tend to be political liberals, for whom Chambers had nothing but contempt. Much of this contempt was rooted in his belief that liberals had swallowed many of the arguments of Marxism (and Chambers made no real distinction between Marxism and the twentieth-century Bolshevism he had embraced). But if Chambers's view of liberalism and democratic socialism was distorted, that is understandable in light of the widespread belief of American liberals, well into the 1990s, that Hiss was the victim and Chambers the villain. If a man is telling the truth, as I believe Chambers did, and is not believed by a large group of people, the witness would have to be a secular saint to judge that group with any objectivity. I have often wondered whether Chambers would have turned to Catholicism had he lived longer.

There is no question that Roman Catholicism, with its centralized authority, was in a better position than other religions to provide a haven for homeless Communists longing for direction. In America, Bishop Fulton J. Sheen specialized in celebrities and in former Communists.* Among his decidedly non-Communist celebrity converts were Clare Boothe Luce, the renowned violinist Fritz Kreisler, and Henry Ford II. Two of his most prized converts, forgotten now but well known at the time, were Louis Budenz, former editor of the American Communist Party newspaper *The Daily Worker,* and his wife, Margaret. My favorite story demonstrating the wholeheartedness of conversions to and from Communism appeared in a 1980 profile of Margaret Budenz, then seventy-one, in *People* magazine. The author interviewed Budenz, who had converted to Catholicism, along with her husband (who had been raised a Catholic before he became a Communist and an atheist), by Sheen in 1945. The couple already had three children born out of wedlock; Bishop Sheen married Margaret and Louis in Saint Patrick's Cathedral shortly after Margaret

---

* Bishop Sheen was named "Venerable"—a first step on the road to sainthood—in 2012 by Pope Benedict XVI. He was supposed to be on the fast track toward beatification—the penultimate step in the march toward sainthood—when his corpse became the subject of an unseemly battle between the Archdiocese of New York, where he spent most of his career and died, and the Diocese of Peoria, Illinois, where he was born. Sheen is buried in the crypt beneath Saint Patrick's Cathedral on Fifth Avenue, and New York is not about to give up his body to be the centerpiece of a new shrine in Peoria. Pope Francis will presumably have to referee this embarrassing turf war.

was baptized and Louis confessed his sins and returned to the church. The *People* story reports that Margaret, to underline her "wholehearted commitment to Catholic doctrine, tossed her diaphragm into a trashcan at Grand Central Terminal."[18] A fourth daughter was born to the born-again Budenzes thirteen months later.* This seems to me a quintessentially American story, if only because it is hard to imagine a European Catholic convert—from communism or from one traditional religion to another—talking to a celebrity magazine about having thrown away her contraceptive device as a demonstration of her new Catholic loyalties.

Still, Americans tend to be too fond of claiming that something is specifically an American phenomenon. (We can't seem to get over John Winthrop's idea of ourselves as inhabitants of "a city on a hill" that cannot be hid.) Tanenhaus, in his definitive 1997 biography of Chambers, describes *Witness* as "a uniquely American book, for only in America do religious and political ideals become interchangeable, even indistinguishable."[19] This evaluation misses the mark. Even though religion does play a larger role in American politics today than it does in any Western European country, there is nothing uniquely American about the attraction of early-twentieth-century leftist intellectuals to communism, as attested to by the memoirs and letters of Koestler and numerous other European political activists. Tanenhaus is right to point out that Chambers's religio-political absolutism does indeed have American antecedents in the Puritan jeremiads of Jonathan Edwards and Cotton Mather, with their vision of human beings as inherently fallen creatures, and of worldly affairs as a titanic battle between those who would elevate man beyond his station and those who know we are only saved or damned by the grace of God. But this theology—like the anger at social and economic injustice that drew so many intellectuals to communism—flourished on both sides of the Atlantic.

The voice whispering *compelle intrare* is most seductive when it is articulated and heard not by the wicked but by the good, and when it seems to come from deep inside rather than from the outside. The

---

* Margaret Budenz, who died in 2002, was a teacher at a Catholic girls' school for many years. One of her former students, *People* reported in its dutiful pursuit of celebrity, was Jane Curtin, then appearing on *Saturday Night Live*.

religious imperative is at its most powerful when explained with words of beauty and emotion by converts who, like Lewis and Stein, could never be imagined as tyrants imposing their beliefs on others. Such words make it easy to forget that compulsion, in the emotional, psychological, political, and religious realms, often presents itself in the first instance in the attractive guise of voluntary surrender to an overwhelming good. Yet, as the Russian poet Joseph Brodsky once observed, the worst ideas in human history rarely announce themselves by walking through the door and declaring, "Hi, I'm Evil" to the ready supplicant.[20] On the corporal plane, we speak of "falling in love"—not of choosing to love (not, at least, until the first overwhelming enchantment has diminished enough to allow a return of the material world to the consciousness of the lovers). Christian mystics speak of the love of God in precisely the same fashion—in lyrical, besotted terms whose only mortal equivalent is the early throes of passionate sexual love. Communism, too, was a love affair, for those who saw the compulsion of the Party not only as a personal liberation but as the liberation of the human race. "Arise ye prisoners of starvation / Arise ye wretched of the earth / For justice thunders condemnation / A better world's in birth." No one converted to Bolshevism in its early years because he or she thought a *worse* world was in birth. However, opportunistic conversions would become much more common in the Soviet Union by the late 1920s, as Stalin solidified his control of the state bureaucracy and punishment for resisting Stalinist ideology grew more stringent. As in the early Christian era, the spread of a new empire gave rise to a new faith.

It seems to me entirely understandable that, at a time when many intellectuals were attracted to Communism, many others were attracted to the more structured, authoritarian forms of Christianity. It is equally understandable that, although there were many instances of prominent ex-Communists embracing Catholicism, very few Party members (including those raised as Jews) showed any interest in observant Judaism after leaving their secular religion. Judaism differs from Christianity in that the former has not compelled anyone to come in since the nasty conquests of pagans described in the early books of the Bible. Judaism, for more than two millennia, has said "you may" rather than "you must" to potential converts.

Koestler beautifully described the combination of seduction and hope involved in all conversions when he wondered about his eventual fate after communism. He noted that he had been a Party member for seven years—the same amount of time that Jacob worked for Laban in order to receive permission to marry his daughter, Rachel. When Jacob's time was up, his bride was led into a dark tent, and he discovered the next morning that he had slept not with Rachel but with her ugly sister, Leah.

I wonder whether he ever recovered from the shock of having slept with an illusion. I wonder whether afterwards he believed that he had ever believed in it. I wonder whether the happy end of the legend will be repeated; for at the price of another seven years of labor, Jacob was given Rachel too, and the illusion became flesh.

And the seven years seemed unto him but a few days, for the love he had for her.[21]

PART VII

THE WAY WE LIVE NOW

20

"THE GREATEST": MUHAMMAD ALI AND THE
DEMYTHOLOGIZING DECADE

O N APRIL 8, 1966, *Time* magazine published a cover story with the stark interrogatory headline "Is God Dead?" The article, which brought *Time* its largest newsstand sales in two decades, was a response to the secularization (real and perceived) of American society in what Philip Roth has called "the demythologizing decade." It was also an effort to come to grips, through a year's worth of interviews with theologians and religious leaders, with the future of religion at a time when fewer and fewer people believed in the literal God of the Bible, that all-powerful being who dispenses rewards and punishments from a vantage point that humans cannot hope to know or judge. The lengthy analysis—a departure from the terse style that defined the magazine—was concerned almost entirely with the challenge to traditional Judaism and Christianity posed by secularism, atheism, and science. Islam, despite the highly publicized conversion of heavyweight champion Muhammad Ali, was never mentioned. The author had nothing to say about any form of religious conversions—a peculiar omission at a time when the baby boomers were exploring both liberal and conservative religious ideas unimaginable to earlier generations during which even conversions from one mainstream Protestant denomination to another could become cause for soul-searching and social scandal. As we know, God turned out to be very much alive for a majority of Americans (though His health was much poorer in Europe). But many of the young would choose to worship a divinity who looked quite different from the white-bearded celestial God of their fathers.

The widespread religious experimentation of the late 1960s and early 1970s seemed (to some of the young as well as to members of older generations) to be one part of a rebellion against every cultural force, including traditional faith, that had shaped the parents of the boomers. Nice middle-class American boys and girls returned, intoning Vedic chants, from trips to India. Children of observant but non-Orthodox Jews suddenly discovered religious "roots" dating from eighteenth-century Poland rather than from New York's cosmopolitan Upper West Side (or, for that matter, from the Lower East Side of the first-generation immigrants, who had seized eagerly on the secular public education denied them in Eastern Europe and Russia). Protestants brought up in families whose idea of religion had been getting baptized, married, and buried by a minister (and attending services on Christmas and Easter) suddenly discovered as personal and demanding a relationship with God as Peter Cartwright did in the early nineteenth century. Some of these "converts" of the sixties did not stay converted after they had managed to irritate their parents sufficiently and thumb their noses at the bourgeois American social order. For others, however, there were deeper and more lasting religious, cultural, and political motivations, and their attitudes would eventually lay the foundation for a more widespread American acceptance of all types of conversions, as well as for the right to reject religion altogether.

No one personified this transition with greater controversy and clarity than Ali. If you were young when Ali was young and believed that it was possible to make the world over again, he resides somewhere in the region of the brain reserved for the incomparable, the unbroken, the unintimidatable ones who stand up to their society and say, "No." If you hated the social instability of the period (whether you were young, middle-aged, or old), you considered Ali a traitor. From either perspective, Ali was no more a "typical" convert of the American sixties than Augustine was a typical convert to Christianity in the fourth century, or Edith Stein was a typical German Jewish convert to Catholicism in the third decade of the twentieth century. However, his conversion was—like those of Augustine, Stein, and many other well-known people described in this book—inseparable from the contemporary social upheaval that was producing a widespread re-examination of the accepted truths of dominant and respected religions.

Nothing could have been more inconvenient for Muhammad Ali, born Cassius Marcellus Clay and raised a Baptist in Louisville, than his conversion to Islam in 1964 and his attempt, three years later, to claim conscientious-objector status when he was about to be drafted during the Vietnam War. Since I was already an atheist, I had no more admiration for Islam than for any other religion when Ali announced his conversion; indeed, I wondered at the time whether he knew anything about the historical role of slavery in the Muslim as well as the Christian world. What impressed me about Ali was not his substitution of one proselytizing, truth-monopolizing religion for another but his willingness, as a famous athlete, to place his career on the line for what was bound to be a wildly unpopular exercise of personal conscience. I thought at the time that Ali was likely to be assassinated. Looking back on that decade—bloodily punctuated by the murders of little girls attending church, civil rights workers and demonstrators in Mississippi and Alabama, the president of the United States, a presidential candidate, and the nation's most important black leader—I still find it surprising that Ali was not gunned down in his twenties.

These days, the mortality of the seventy-four-year-old former heavyweight champion is all too evident. The young boxer whose wits and tongue were once as quick as his fists and feints, as he effortlessly came up with unforgettable phrases, from "Float like a butterfly, sting like a bee" to "I'm so fast that last night I turned off the light switch in my hotel room and was in bed before the room was dark," has fallen silent. Ali, who once estimated that he had taken twenty-nine thousand punches to the head in his long athletic career, suffers from advanced Parkinson's disease, which has destroyed his speech.[1] I remember that his words already sounded mildly slurred when he was in the late stages of his boxing career, as the 1970s drew to a close. Another of his sayings was "I am the greatest. I said that before I even knew I was." But "the greatest" knew no more at that time than the rest of society or the medical establishment about the long-term effects of repeated concussions. (It was well known, though, that many aging boxers suffered from what was called "punch-drunk syndrome.")

I was working on the college newspaper at Michigan State University on the day in 1964 when the twenty-two-year-old Ali, the seven-to-one underdog who had just become heavyweight champion of the world by defeating Sonny Liston, announced that he was joining the Nation of Islam and changing his birth name of Cassius Clay. I have never had any use for boxing (in spite of all the great sportswriting it has produced), but, as a reporter, I immediately recognized the importance of his conversion, not only as the individual statement of a lionized black athlete but as a leading indicator of social changes that would become more pronounced in the second half of the 1960s.

Islam, as one of the world's three historical monotheistic faiths, did not mean to Americans then what it means now. Islamic extremism was not associated with international terrorism—a concern that scarcely existed in the American consciousness before the Palestinian terrorist group Black September murdered eleven Israeli athletes at the 1972 Olympics in Munich. Even after Munich, even after the first attempt to bomb the World Trade Center, in 1993, American concern about terrorism did not reach anything like the levels it did after the 9/11 attacks in the United States or the November 13, 2015, assaults that left 129 dead in Paris—a city shaken ten months earlier by murderous ISIS attacks on a kosher supermarket and the satirical magazine *Charlie Hebdo*. There were many fewer Muslim immigrants in the United States of the 1960s than there are today, and Americans were not so much hostile to as ignorant about the varieties of Islam practiced around the world. But Americans *were* aware of one form of the Muslim faith—the Nation of Islam, headed by Elijah Muhammad and known, to most whites, as the "Black Muslims." That was the group Ali had joined, and the majority of white Americans considered it to be both anti-white and anti-Semitic (not without reason, based on Elijah Muhammad's rhetoric). Ali's conversion was not sudden, and his interest in the Nation was of some years' standing; he had first learned about the organization in 1959, when he fought in a Golden Gloves tournament in Chicago, Elijah Muhammad's home.

What apparently impressed the teenager about Elijah Muhammad's organization was its emphasis on the need for black self-sufficiency—at a time when the slogan "Black Power" had not yet been used publicly and the civil rights movement emphasized racial integration. When Ali proposed to his English teacher at Louisville's Central High that he write a term paper on Black Muslims in America, she became nervous and refused to approve the subject. "Something had resonated in his mind," writes David Remnick, the *New Yorker* editor who began his journalistic career as a sportswriter for *The Washington Post,* "something about the discipline and bearing of the Muslims, their sense of hierarchy, manhood, and self-respect, the way they refused to smoke or drink or carouse, their racial pride."[2] (The group's emphasis on self-discipline also accounted for its appeal to young black prison inmates who were trying to turn their lives around.)

The Nation of Islam was founded in 1930 in Detroit by Wallace D. Fard Muhammad, a somewhat mysterious figure who disappeared in 1934, when the leadership of the group was assumed by Elijah Muhammad (no relation). In the theology preached by both Fard and his successor, a single atom began to spin, about seventy-six trillion years ago, and that atom produced the earth and then the first man—a black man—now known as Allah. Allah, in turn, created the rest of the universe and the entire black race. Those who consider the story of Allah as the first black man inherently less plausible than the story of Adam and Eve in the Garden of Eden, or, for that matter, than the stories of the Quran revealed to *the* Muhammad in the seventh century, may dismiss the Nation of Islam as a cult. For me, the Nation's beliefs add up to just one more entry in the catalogue of goofy religious myths, enabling specific groups of people to single themselves out as special in the eyes of the creator of their world. In any case, and whatever one thinks of any religion, it is safe to say that most white Americans had never heard of the Nation before the early 1960s. They were also unaware of a history, which antedated the sixties, of Islam's attraction for black American artists and intellectuals.

An astonishing number of well-known jazz musicians, for example, became Muslims in the late 1940s and early 1950s. These included, among many others, the pianist Ahmad Jamal (born Fritz Jones), the singer Aliyah Rabia (Dakota Staton), and the tenor saxophonists Musa Kaleem (Orlando Wright) and El Hajj Abdullah Rasheed Ahmad (Lynn Hope). All of these musicians had many white fans, and their conversions did not attract anything like the attention or hostility that Ali's would in the sixties. As Hisham D. Aidi observes in *Rebel Music: Race, Empire, and the New Muslim Youth Culture,* many journalists, including members of the black press, thought "that Muslim identity helped blacks in America sidestep (legal) racial barriers, especially down South."[3] That might have been true, at least for the few who talked publicly about being Muslims and actually performed in exotic-looking garb that might be associated, rightly or wrongly, with Islam. But it seems doubtful that most whites who liked jazz knew anything about the relationship between Islam and their favorite musicians. I was a huge fan of Ahmad Jamal and heard his trio perform in a Chicago nightclub in 1961, when I was fifteen. It never occurred to me that the name of the handsome black pianist had anything to do with his religion. If I had thought about it at all (which I did not, in my ignorance and starstruck awe), I would have assumed that "Ahmad Jamal" was a stage name.* Artists have always received a pass for somewhat unconventional behavior, and black musicians could practice their faith, whatever it might be, without drawing much antagonism from white or conventional middle-class black America. (Oh, those crazy bohemians!) Ali, far more famous than any musician, would receive no such pass.

One might think that African American interest in Islam in the twentieth century was derived from knowledge passed on from generation to generation by the descendants of educated Muslim slaves like Omar ibn Said. However, scholars who have explored the long-neglected subject of enslaved African Muslims in the United States can establish no such connection. Sylviane A. Diouf, whose *Servants of Allah: African Muslims Enslaved in the Americas* is a scrupulously researched account of both the efforts and the failure of literate Muslim slaves to pass on their religion, points out that Elijah Muhammad, despite the Islamish trappings of many of his followers, never claimed to be descended from Muslims. His father was in fact a Baptist minister.[4] The last black Americans born to slaves who had any knowledge of their Muslim origins would have died by the 1920s. And

---

* Ahmad Jamal also shook my hand, along with the hands of the other audacious fifteen-year-olds from an Okemos, Michigan, high school who had sneaked out of their Chicago hotel at night, during a class trip, to hear jazz. I had called the club and explained that, although we were not old enough to drink alcohol, we understood that we would have to pay the cover charge and that I would pay in advance. (I knew that a nightclub manager would not be thrilled to see a large party of people who weren't old enough to drink legally and might therefore take up a table for the price of Coca-Cola.) Apparently, the manager told the musicians, because we were given a prize table at the front of the club, and the trio took our special requests. Did these Muslim musicians hate white people? I don't think so, given the trouble they took to make a special experience even more unforgettable for a bunch of very white teenagers.

the hostility toward—often outright prohibition of—slave literacy in the United States provided a particular obstacle to the passing on of knowledge about a faith that depended on a book and, unlike Christianity, forbade visual representation. As Diouf observes, "It is one thing to maintain one's literacy in Arabic, but it is quite another to acquire it from scratch in the absence of time, adequate structures, and tools. . . . Even if a book or Koran in Arabic was available, doubtless a slave child could not have found the amount of time necessary to learn how to read it."[5]

Thus, African Americans were on their own when they developed a unique—for once, that description is an understatement—quasi-Islamic faith in the twentieth century. As a matter of fact, nothing could be more blasphemous to traditional Muslims than Elijah Muhammad's notion of Allah as a man—black or otherwise, whether created by a single spinning atom or a shooting star. That would be a form of one of the greatest Muslim sins, *shirk,* which means the association of anything or anyone with Allah. In Islam, a man cannot be God.

When Ali joined the Nation in 1964, the organization was locked in a bitter rivalry between Elijah Muhammad and Malcolm X, who had been censured by the Nation for his comments describing the assassination of President John F. Kennedy as a case of "chickens coming home to roost." In 1965, the charismatic Malcolm—who was moving toward a more racially inclusive view and expressed a desire to work with other, non-Muslim civil rights leaders—left the Nation. Another reason for Malcolm's split with Elijah Muhammad was the latter's propensity for violating his own precepts about sexual morality and engaging in affairs with women—several of whom he impregnated—on his staff. Malcolm was assassinated on February 21, 1965, and three members of the Nation were convicted of his murder. But the young Ali, who had once admired Malcolm greatly and would come to admire him again as the years passed, sided with the Nation in the 1960s.* This decision did not necessarily do Ali any good with many black Americans. At the time he became a Muslim, many blacks (most of

---

* The best account of Ali's complicated relationship with Malcolm X appears in David Remnick's *King of the World.* Written in 1998, when Ali was still able to express himself in private interviews, the book traces the evolution of Ali's views about race and religion. He told Remnick that one of his greatest regrets in life was his break with Malcolm.

whom, if they were over thirty, still called themselves and wanted to be called Negroes) joined their white contemporaries in rejecting the Nation as a bona fide religion. Overwhelmingly Christian and Baptist in their religious orientation, middle-class black Americans were frequently baffled, embarrassed, and worried that the Black Muslims would incite white hostility at a time when the civil rights movement needed more white support. As Ali notes in his 1975 autobiography, *The Greatest* (written with Richard Durham), professional backers and friends of both races warned him that he would ruin his career and reputation by acknowledging his conversion to Islam. "When I finally made it known that I was a Muslim," Ali recalls, "almost every educated friend, associate and prominent person I knew, black as well as white, was horrified. Sugar Ray Robinson warned me that my career would be wrecked if I became a 'Black Muslim.' Jackie Gleason urged me to 'reconsider the step' he heard I was about to take. 'Don't let yourself be used,' he said. I thanked him for his advice, but I told him the main ones I didn't want to be used by were the enemies of black people, those who help oppress and subordinate them."[6]

No group was more convinced that Ali was being "used" than the nation's sportswriters, almost all of whom were white. In 1965, after I graduated from college and became a reporter for *The Washington Post*, I heard a veteran sports columnist—a man whose writing I admired greatly—call the heavyweight champion "a jock so dumb he believes in voodoo." That comment was mild compared with what actually appeared in many mainstream publications. Myron Cope, in a 1964 article titled "Muslim Champ" in *The Saturday Evening Post*, described "Clay" as "fighting a socio-religious battle with the Christian world." (Most sportswriters and publications refused, for years, to call the fighter Muhammad Ali and continued to use the name Cassius Clay.) Cope claimed that Ali had "completely severed communication with whites" and "still acts the clown for TV cameras but only to sell fight tickets." Jeff Nilsson, director of the *Saturday Evening Post* online archives, points out in an analysis of the 1964 coverage that Ali had hardly cut off all communication with whites, given that he agreed to speak extensively for the article with Cope himself (even though he was well aware of the sportswriter's hostility toward him). The political opinions expressed by Ali in the interview were anything but extreme. Discussing Nation of Islam rhetoric calling whites "devils," Ali explained, "I'm stressing just the works that the whites generally have been doing. They blow up all these little colored people in church, wash people down the street with water hoses. It's not the color that makes you a devil, just the deeds that you do. . . . If you be a blue race, and you do the works of the devil, then we can call you a devil. You got white people who dies under demonstrations, died under tractor wheels for colored people. I wouldn't call them no devil."[7]

Reading these words, which might just as easily have been "by their fruits ye shall know them," many twenty-first-century Americans—especially the young—will find it hard to understand what so enraged middle-aged, mid-twentieth-century white sportswriters about Ali's conversion. Ali sounds like exactly what he was—a highly intelligent but poorly educated (by his own account) young black man who was trying out a new way of thinking that differed not only from his upbringing as a black American Baptist but from the shiny, contented image that white America wanted to see in people of color who had achieved worldly success. In 1965, another antagonistic *Saturday Evening Post* writer, Bill Bridges (in a story that was never published), argued that an upcoming bout between Ali and the former heavyweight boxing champion Floyd Patterson was being considered a battle between the Christian and Muslim religions. "After Patterson was defeated, however," Nilsson observes tartly, "there was no more talk about the match proving which was the superior faith."[8] But the extreme disrespect manifested by most older sportswriters toward Ali in the 1960s was likely motivated less by real knowledge about or hatred for Islam in any form than by a combination of racism and the envy-distorted psychological relationship that existed (and still does) between those who can only write about the sport they love and those who can actually play the game. The unwritten clause in the contract between most sportswriters and the athletes they cover (and this contract was much more powerful fifty years ago than it is today) was: "You do these splendid things with your body, but I write about them as I see fit, because I've got the brains."* An athlete who said, "I'm not who you think I am or want me to be," was breaking the agreement.

---

* One important reason the contract is less binding today is the presence of women sportswriters on every major beat. Female sportswriters who cover Major League baseball, for instance, do not labor under the delusion that, were it not for some fickle twist of fate, they might have made it to the big leagues. Looking at male athletes without the lens of envy, they are less disappointed and angry when the sports "heroes" turn out to be merely human.

•

It is impossible to separate the antagonistic reaction to Ali's conversion from the rage that greeted his refusal, in 1967, to be drafted. After stating bluntly that he had no quarrel with the Viet Cong because none of them "ever called me nigger," Ali was immediately stripped of his boxing license in the state of New York. In June 1967, an all-white jury promptly sentenced him to five years in jail for draft evasion. Ali never went to prison, because he posted bond while his case was being appealed. His claim to conscientious-objector status was denied by every lower appeals court, and it took four years for the case to make its way to the Supreme Court. In 1967, although there was a growing antiwar movement on college campuses, the American public at large had not yet turned decisively against the Vietnam War. Although the armed services, in the era of the draft, were much more representative of the general population than is today's volunteer military, the war in Vietnam (unlike the Second World War) was being fought disproportionately by both poor blacks and poor whites. Deferments were available for college students, so the middle and upper-middle classes had many more opportunities to avoid being drafted. Athletes and entertainers also frequently received deferments. Joining the National Guard and staying at home, as the future president George W. Bush did, was another option widely used by the sons of the upper-middle class and by celebrities who wanted to avoid actual combat in Southeast Asia. Had Ali not become a Muslim and then taken a public antiwar position, he could probably, like so many athletes, have kept his deferment and never been required to serve. Or, for that matter, he could have served his time in the military by engaging in bouts staged for the entertainment of the troops. But that was not for the proud champion of a sport that had always been tainted by racism, when blacks who beat whites, like the storied heavyweight Jack Johnson in 1910, were punished for their success.

By the time Ali came along, boxing at the highest level had become an all-black sport. As Remnick notes, the history of black boxing in America, like everything to do with race, goes back to slavery, as "plantation owners amused themselves by putting together their strongest slaves and letting them fight it out for sport and gambling."[9] Slaves wore iron collars and were required, like their forebears in the ancient world, to fight nearly to the point of death. Ali, who obviously loved boxing in his youth, was nevertheless well aware of this history. "They don't look at fighters to have brains," he said in 1970. "They don't look at fighters to be businessmen, or human, or intelligent. Fighters are just brutes that come to entertain the rich white people. Beat up on each other and break each other's noses, and bleed, and show off like two little monkeys for the crowd. We're just like two slaves in that ring. The masters get two of us big old black slaves and let us fight it out while they bet: 'My slave can whup your slave.' That's what I see when I see two black people fighting."[10] And yet Ali did fight other black men, and he fought for and was paid millions. It does not take a psychoanalyst to figure out that Ali's religious conversion might have been part of an effort to cope with his ambivalence about the sport that had brought him riches and fame but could not be separated from the humiliation of black men in the American past (and, as Ali saw it, in his own life).

In his autobiography, Ali provides a small sampling of the phone calls he received after his announcement that he would not serve in the Vietnam-era army. Most of the callers were anonymous, but a deputy sheriff who had escorted the boxing champion many times in Miami was an exception. "He had a soft drawl, like a fatherly bigot," Ali recalls. "'Now Cassius, you just done gone too far now. Somebody's telling you wrong. Them Jews and Dagos you got around you. Now, some of my boys want to come down and talk to you, for your own good.' Another caller simply said, 'You gonna die, nigger, die before the night's out!'"[11] Ali chose to base his antiwar position on selective, peace-loving passages from the Quran, which—like the Christian and Jewish Bibles—can offer something to rationalize just about any belief.

One of the most touching aspects of *The Greatest* is Ali's growing wonderment that there were very different phone calls—from people uninterested in sports or in Ali's achievements as a boxer—congratulating him on his stand. Students called, asking Ali to speak on college campuses, and he experienced the "strange new feeling . . . without planning or even wanting it, [that] I was an important part of a movement I hardly knew existed."[12]

Ali, known generally for his brashness, was always humble when it came to his own lack of intellectual credentials and educational background. His reflections revealed the pain of an intelligent man who understood that he had never been offered or obtained an education commensurate with his potential. One day, Ali received an overseas phone call—still a rarity in the 1960s—from an old man he had never heard of. The man, a British antiwar activist, asked Ali if he had been quoted accurately in the press and said, "I suppose the world has more than incidental curiosity about what the World Champion thinks. Usually he goes with the tide. You surprised them." Ali told the man he might soon be coming to England, to fight the European heavyweight champion, Henry Cooper. He then asked his caller which fighter he would bet on. The caller laughed, "Henry's capable, you know, but I would pick you." Ali gave what he described as his stock, flip answer to such responses: "You're not as dumb as you look." Ali and his caller would frequently exchange cards and notes, but it wasn't until two years later, as Ali was browsing through a volume of the *World Book Encyclopedia*, that he learned that his correspondent, Bertrand Russell, was a famous philosopher and mathematician who had gone to jail in England for his antiwar writings during the First World War. Ali immediately typed a letter of apology to Russell for his offhand remark, "You're not as dumb as you look," and Russell replied that he had enjoyed the joke. Ali hoped to visit Russell in England, but his passport was confiscated after his conviction for draft evasion. By the time it was returned, four years later, after the Supreme Court overturned the conviction, Russell had died in 1970, at the age of ninety-seven. "I thought of him whenever I visited England," Ali said, "and for years I kept a picture of his warm face and wide eyes. 'Not as dumb as he looks.'"[13]

Because Ali's boxing license was revoked in every state after his conviction for draft evasion, he did not fight from March 1967 until October 1970, in what would have been the prime of any athlete's career—his late twenties. Ali's ultimate legal fate, and the slow change in public attitudes toward his decision to convert and oppose the war, also offer striking examples of the possibilities of toleration in a society weighed down by racial injustice but lifted up by the separation of church and state and a strong tradition—however frequently it has been honored in the breach instead of in reality—of respect for freedom of conscience. Both the better and the worse angels of the American nature were at work in the life of this extraordinary man.

The Department of Justice, under Presidents Johnson and Richard

Nixon, had opposed Ali's claim of conscientious-objector status. When the case reached the Supreme Court in the spring of 1971, Associate Justice Thurgood Marshall recused himself because he had been Johnson's solicitor general. (Marshall, the first African American Supreme Court justice, was appointed to the high court by Johnson in 1967.) The court in 1971 was closely divided, a hybrid of aging New Deal liberals and appointees from the Eisenhower, Kennedy, and Johnson administrations. Nixon had already begun to reshape the court by appointing Warren Burger to succeed Earl Warren as chief justice. In addition to Marshall and the recently appointed Burger, the court included Justices Hugo L. Black, William O. Douglas, John Marshall Harlan II, William Brennan, Jr., Potter Stewart, Byron White, and Harry Blackmun. The key justice in this decision was Harlan, appointed by Eisenhower in 1955. (He was the grandson and namesake of the nineteenth-century Supreme Court justice who was called "the great dissenter" and is best known for his stellar, lone dissent in the 1893 case *Plessy v. Ferguson.* This notorious case established the "separate but equal" doctrine of segregation, which lasted until 1954, when the high court declared segregated schools inherently unequal in *Brown v. Board of Education.*) With Marshall having recused himself, the decision in Ali's case might well have gone against the plaintiff. However, Harlan, an old-fashioned moderate Republican and a judicial conservative, became convinced over time of the sincerity of Ali's personal, religiously based antiwar views (even though Islam is obviously not a pacifist religion). He set about persuading the other justices, including his friend Burger, to reconsider the constitutional questions that had been overwhelmed, four years earlier, by racial and pro-war passions. In the end, the vote to strike down the lower-court rulings denying Ali conscientious-objector status was eight to zero. The decision, constructed on narrow grounds, says not that Ali qualified as a conscientious objector but that the Department of Justice had failed to prove its case. The Justice Department and the lower courts had erred, the Supreme Court stated, in asserting, with no proof, that Ali's views were based entirely on his racial and political beliefs and not on his religious views. The court's decision rendered the issue of military service essentially moot for Ali, who, at twenty-eight and as a father, was not likely to be drafted in ordinary circumstances.

After his victory in the nation's highest court, Ali returned to the boxing ring. He suffered the first defeat of his professional career at the hands of Joe Frazier in 1971. On October 30, 1974, Ali regained the world heavyweight championship by defeating George Foreman (after beating Frazier in a rematch). His last meeting with Frazier in the Philippines, dubbed, "The Thrilla in Manila," in 1975, was one of the most brutal fights in boxing history. The fight finally ended when Frazier's trainer, over the boxer's protests, refused to let him answer the bell for the fifteenth round. Both men had taken relentless punishment, and Ali was declared the winner on a technical knockout.

In the late 1970s, observers noticed that Ali was beginning to stutter and that his hands sometimes trembled. He retired from boxing in 1981 and was diagnosed with Parkinson's in 1984, at age forty-two.

·

In his life after boxing, Ali has, improbably, been transformed from the black nemesis hated by many whites into a revered figure—revered for the moral stand he took against the war and not for his boxing titles. "Who could have predicted in the late 1960's," asked Budd Shulberg in 1998, "when Muhammad Ali was reviled by the sporting press and most of white America as a black racist, a mouthy troublemaker, that he would be the obvious choice to light the torch at the 1996 Olympic Games in Atlanta, as a symbol of international understanding, peace, and love?"[14] Though he remained an observant Muslim, Ali's religious views shifted in his thirties, away from the Nation to mainstream Sunni Islam. It seems likely, had Malcolm X lived and continued on his path of interracial and interreligious cooperation, that he and Ali would have been reconciled. In his last interview with Remnick, in the late 1990s, Ali said, "I'll tell you how I'd like to be remembered: as a black man who won the heavyweight title and who was humorous and who treated everyone right. As a man who never looked down on those who looked up to him and who helped as many of his people as he could—financial and also in their fight for freedom, justice, and equality. As a man who wouldn't embarrass them. As a man who tried to unite his people through the faith of Islam that he found when he listened to the Honorable Elijah Muhammad. And if all that's asking too much, then I guess I'd settle for being remembered as a great boxing champion who became a preacher and a champion of his people. And I wouldn't even mind if folks forgot how pretty I was."[15]

As long as he was physically able, Ali participated in the kind of civic events that would have been unimaginable venues for him in the charged political climate of the sixties. In 1988, the two hundredth anniversary of the ratification of the Constitution, Ali was selected by the California Bicentennial Foundation to ride in the Tournament of Roses Parade as a symbol of the enduring and ever-evolving meaning of the Constitution and the Bill of Rights. Two years later, he traveled to Iraq a few months before the first Gulf War in a successful attempt to persuade Saddam Hussein to release fifteen American hostages being held as "human shields" in the event of a Western attack. At the time, many Europeans and Americans—from former government officials to ordinary citizens with trapped relatives—were visiting Iraq in attempts to get their citizens or loved ones released. The correspondent of *The New York Times,* in one of the snottier articles about this understandable human phenomenon, took a special slap at Ali. "Surely the strangest hostage-release campaign of recent days has been the 'good-will tour' of Muhammad Ali, the former heavyweight boxing champion," wrote the correspondent, Philip Shenon. "Mr. Ali, who became a hero in the Muslim world after he converted to Islam in the 1960s and changed his name from Cassius Clay, suffers from the impaired muscular control of Parkinson's syndrome, and he has attended meeting after meeting in Baghdad despite his frequent inability to speak clearly."[16] Shenon, with a talent for turning the word "hero" into a slur, was not a medical expert, since he seemed unable to recognize the difference between impaired muscular control—which affects speech as well as other physical actions—and an inability to think.* And he could not resist slipping the name Cassius Clay into the story. What many found more improbable than Ali's trip to Iraq was his being awarded, in 2005, the Medal of Freedom, the nation's highest civilian honor, by President George W. Bush. But Bush's motivation could not have been more obvious: he wanted to honor a Muslim American in an effort to discourage domestic bigotry in the post-9/11 era, and who better than a man who was now, in an unpredictable turn of history, a heroic figure to many? Unable to speak, Ali attended the White House dinner, though he could only accept with gestures.

---

* One wonders whether the writer would consider it equally strange that the actor Michael J. Fox, also afflicted with Parkinson's, attends many meetings concerned with the rights of the disabled.

But his remarks to Remnick had been those of a man at peace with being both a Muslim and an American—not the words of a man who would refuse an invitation to the White House. Moreover, his 1990 trip to Iraq, in view of his status as the most famous American Muslim in the world, also made perfect sense in terms of his relationship to both his faith and his country. Why wouldn't "The Greatest" use his publicity value to shine a light on the plight of American hostages held by a Middle Eastern Muslim dictator? The mature Muhammad Ali certainly wasn't as dumb as he had looked, as a young man, to a great many white Americans.

Because of Ali's difficulty in articulating his thoughts in recent years (actually, decades), it is impossible to trace the evolution of his religious beliefs except by inferences drawn from his actions. By all accounts (including those of journalists, family, and friends), he remains a devout and observant Muslim, according to his personal understanding of what Islam means. His daughter Hana Yasmeen Ali said in 2005 that her father always prayed five times a day until advanced Parkinson's made it too difficult for him to kneel. It is Ms. Ali who told an interviewer that her father had embraced Sufism—a kind of mysticism that exists within every branch of Islam—and become "very spiritual—more spiritual now than he is religious."[17] Who knows? Ali's daughter was twenty-eight when she was interviewed in 2005. The squishy phrase "spiritual but not religious" has only become common during the past twenty years, as the number of Americans who want to claim some connection with a deity but do not want the obligations of traditional religion has grown. "Spiritual but not religious" sounds like an American in her twenties or thirties. This phrase, perfectly designed to avoid taking a stand, certainly doesn't sound anything like Muhammad Ali in the days when he was able to speak for himself. In his daughter's book about him, Ali is quoted as saying that he thought he would be the Muslim Billy Graham until he got Parkinson's. Now, that *does* sound like the brash young Ali.

•

The change in Ali's public reputation has not occurred because a majority of Americans necessarily agree with the charges he leveled against his country in the 1960s and 1970s. I doubt that Bush had read

The Greatest when he decided to award Ali the Medal of Freedom. Ali's recollections about his feelings when he was asked by a lieutenant to step forward and be drafted would certainly have made a unique citation to go with the medal:

> But who is this white man, no older than me, appointed by another white man, all the way to the white man in the White House? Who is he to tell me to go to Asia, Africa, or anywhere else in the world to fight people who never threw a rock at me or America? Who is this descendant of slave masters to order a descendant of slaves to fight other people in their own country?[18]

Part of the explanation for the honors showered on Ali surely lies in the infinite American capacity for historical amnesia. To most Americans born after 1970, who know next to nothing about the Vietnam War or the Nation of Islam—and are taught next to nothing about the controversies of the sixties in public school history classes—Ali is a black man who once stood up for, well, *something*. He is not seen today as the dangerous (to received opinion), challenging figure he really was. He is also one of the last living, larger-than-life figures from that era—despite the illness-induced diminution of his powers. And let us not underestimate the sentimentality associated with the severe disability of someone who was once an athletic giant. Even if Ali made a mistake in initially swallowing the more peculiar teachings of Elijah Muhammad, he has paid his debt to society! If America can forgive Bill Clinton for having oral sex in the Oval Office, they can certainly forgive a man who said some intemperate words about the souls of white folk when he was in his twenties.

And, oh yes—Ali has a Jewish grandson. In accepting children and grandchildren who have made their own religious choices, he is behaving exactly like a majority of his generation of Americans. One of the last times Ali was spotted in public was in the spring of 2012, when he attended the bar mitzvah of his grandson Jacob Wertheimer at a Philadelphia synagogue. His daughter Khaliah Ali-Wertheimer, who was raised a Muslim and who, like much of the family, seems to have a laissez-faire attitude about religious choice, is married to a Jew. The couple allowed their son to choose his own religion. Congregation Rodeph Shalom, where the bar mitzvah ceremony was held, is a Reform synagogue. In Reform Judaism, the child of a non-Jewish mother and a Jewish father is accepted as Jewish if he performs acts—obviously, a bar mitzvah qualifies—that publicly identify him with Judaism. Conservative and Orthodox Jews would require a formal conversion for the child of a non-Jewish mother to be considered a Jew.

•

There is also little doubt that one factor in the change of public attitudes toward Ali has been the growing acceptance of religious conversions of all kinds during the past four decades. His conversion—controversial though it was at the time—was consistent with a period of immense religious change unparalleled since the Second Great Awakening. Liberalizing religious trends ranged from a new interest in Eastern faiths, especially Buddhism and Hinduism, to a diminution, triggered by the Second Vatican Council, of fidelity to traditional Roman Catholic dogma among American Catholics. But conservative trends were equally important, and the resurgence of right-wing evangelical Christianity was the most important story missed by the media until the movement could no longer be ignored, after the Supreme Court's 1973 *Roe v. Wade* abortion decision. Albert Mohler, head of the Southern Baptist Theological Seminary, points out that, although the 1966 "Is God Dead?" cover story in *Time* completely ignored the new evangelicalism, the phenomenon "would produce a memorable cover story for *Newsweek,* exactly ten years later."[19] During the demythologizing decade, a little-known group called the Campus Crusade for Christ began organizing at colleges across the nation—an effort that would produce a new generation of energetic, effective, well-educated evangelical leaders. In 1967, in a location of great symbolic importance, the Crusade held its national convention on the campus of the University of California at Berkeley. A key event took place on the steps of Sproul Hall—the site where thousands of students had gathered in 1964 to protest campus restrictions on free speech, setting the pattern for subsequent protests on other campuses throughout the nation. A young evangelist named Jon Braun stood on the steps and praised Jesus as the "world's greatest revolutionary." The Crusade, which had only 109 employees in 1960, grew into a national organization with sixty-five hundred paid staff members by the mid-1970s. Today, the group proselytizes around the world.

But the rise of right-wing Christian evangelicalism was not the only conservative religious movement of the sixties. The attraction of many children of nonobservant secular or conventionally observant mainstream Jews to Hasidic sects caused as much angst in many Jewish families as a conversion to Catholicism would have fifty years earlier. Known as the Baal Teshuva movement, after a Talmudic term that literally means "master of repentance," the attraction of some young Jews to a form of Judaism based on practices dating from seventeenth- and eighteenth-century Eastern Europe and Russia involved a rejection of cultural assimilation and a return to an ethos that abhorred both the Jewish Enlightenment of Moses Mendelssohn and secularism. I well remember how my husband's aunt, an observant Conservative Jew, wept when her son, who had changed his name from Joseph to Elijah, refused to visit her home with his children because she did not keep kosher. Exactly why the new convert to Satmar Hasidism considered "Elijah" a more authentically Jewish name than "Joseph" was, like so much about his new religious enthusiasms, a mystery.

In certain respects—although this was covered up by the American obsession with the "black" in "Black Muslims"—Islam in the United States also expressed socially conservative instincts in the 1960s and 1970s. Young African American women who covered their heads with the hijab and wore long, flowing dresses that concealed their bodies were just as culturally out of step with the sexual revolution of the sixties as young Hasidic women who donned sheitls (wigs) to cover their hair (thought to be unbearably provocative to men) and wore opaque stockings and long skirts to conceal the shape of their legs. Some of these converts to conservative religion in the seventies were motivated by a deep disgust with the drugs and sexual promiscuity that had once pervaded their young lives. (My husband's cousin Joseph a.k.a. Elijah married a woman who was so ashamed of having had many lovers while she was taking the Pill that she not only stopped using contraception but also dyed her abundant, gorgeous red hair a dull brown, so that, even when she removed her sheitl, her erotic luster would be dimmed.) Many of the new young right-wing Christian evangelicals shared the same disillusionment as Hasidic Jews and Black Muslims with the sexual and pharmacological experimentation of the counterculture.

The writer Adam Hochschild, in a memoir of his complicated relationship with his father—who at the time disapproved of many of his life choices—captures the spirit of the era nicely. Hochschild notes that his own career and marital choices began to seem far less unconventional to his father as he saw the children of his many friends become "followers of various messiahs, Oriental and otherwise. So you say young Johnny's at . . . Cartwright College? And doing . . . Christian work? I welcomed all these departures from familiar paths. The more divorces, the more gurus, the better! It made my own life's course look quite reasonable by comparison, and much of Father's disapproval gradually evaporated. At least I wasn't in an ashram."[20]

It is impossible to determine how many of the religious changes of the sixties—whether they could be described as liberal or conservative, as a departure from or a return to tradition—turned out to be lifelong, life-changing conversions. There are no good studies about how many of the "returned" young Jews stuck with the kosher kitchens and itchy wigs; how many members of the Nation of Islam remained Muslims, much less respectful of Elijah Muhammad; how many who began studying Buddhism or Hinduism in their youth went on to become more than dabblers in the Eastern cultures they originally knew nothing about. We know more about Catholics. Reliable research shows that more than 20 percent of Americans born in the United States who were raised as Roman Catholics no longer consider themselves Catholics.[21] Many of these ex-Catholics are children of the sixties, disappointed by the failure of the church to follow through on hopes for reform (particularly in teachings about contraception, divorce, and maintaining an all-male priesthood) engendered by the Second Vatican Council.

Because a propensity for reinvention has always been a part of the American story, the religious experiments and realignments of the sixties made conversion seem more respectable and much more normative than it had been in the past. Eventually, that aura and assumption of respectability extended even to such a controversial figure as Ali. What once seemed like a radical religious and political decision by an anti-white athletic champion now seems inseparable from a time when many Americans were questioning their most cherished values as part of our most cherished traditions exalting freedom of conscience. Muhammad Ali said: No, I am not a Christian. And, no, I am not someone who will fight this war. But he, too, sang America. And America eventually listened to the song.

21

AMERICAN DREAMING

A FEW YEARS AGO, I was browsing in a Judaica store on Manhattan's Upper West Side when I noticed a greeting card in the shape of a menorah proclaiming, "Congratulations on Your Conversion." On the inside, the new convert was saluted with a "Mazel Tov." Despite the ambivalent attitudes that have always characterized the unique American experiment in religious pluralism, a greeting card celebrating someone's change of faith probably does reflect the current positive stance of most members of the American public toward conversion (as well as the greeting card industry's determination to profit from every conceivable life milestone). A religious phenomenon that has been the cause of so much bloodshed throughout history has been transformed, in American society, into a cheerful slogan affirming tolerance and the right to choose. Tell an Italian or a Norwegian friend, as I have, about this card, and she assumes that you are making some sort of joke—one that does not translate well. It is not that Europeans disapprove of conversion but that they simply do not share the American penchant for treating religious choices as a smorgasbord of free second (and sometimes third) helpings.

We do not know whether the (probably) Christian relatives of the new convert to Judaism were as pleased as the Jewish side of the family and as willing to offer their support and felicitations. But it can be predicted, with a fair degree of certitude, that the Christian parents are unlikely to disinherit their converted child or cut themselves off from their future grandchildren. There may be a good deal of angst when Christmas and Hanukkah arrive every year, but the families will likely find ways to cope. It is now the American Way. It is even the way for the minority of Americans who are, as I am, committed atheists and secular humanists. I would not be thrilled if a child of mine became a religious believer and raised my grandchildren as believers. But I cannot imagine banishing a child or grandchildren from my life, as Westerners did for centuries and people still do in many cultures and areas of the world, because of religious differences. I, too, sing America—in a secular voice.

One may laugh—as I did—at a greeting card slogan summing up a transformation that, however it begins, involves some of the deepest and most intense human feelings about our relationship to time and eternity. But it is doubtful that anyone who truly believes in her own religion, or who feels a strong connection to the ethnic and social history entwined with that religion, is entirely happy about a close relative's (especially a child's) conversion to another faith.

In the 1960s, even though the baby boomers had begun to enter mixed marriages in sharply rising numbers, it was more socially acceptable than it is today to express ambivalence about the conversions that often followed. This was true not only of conversions to unpopular religions like the Nation of Islam or the Jehovah's Witnesses but of conversions to faiths that enjoyed wide social acceptance. Many who, in theory, think that one religion is as good as another believe deep down that their own religion—or what it signifies culturally—is better than others. In 1961, Philip Roth remarked:

> The fact is that, if one is committed to being a Jew, then he believes that on the most serious questions pertaining to man's survival—understanding the past, imagining the future, discovering the relation between God and humanity—that he is right and the Christians are wrong. As a believing Jew, he must certainly view the breakdown in this century of moral order and the erosion of spiritual values in terms of the inadequacy of Christianity as a sustaining force for the good. However, who would care to say such things to his neighbor?[1]

This statement could be paraphrased and applied to people of many religions, as well as to atheists and secular humanists. As an atheist, I do view religion in general as an inadequate force for sustaining the good, and some religions as forces for promoting outright evil. However, who would care to say such things to her neighbor?

One may concede the tone-deafness to painful history that characterizes much American discourse about faith, but it cannot be emphasized enough that there have, from time immemorial, been much, much worse ways to deal with the fact that people do—for whatever reasons and with varying degrees of conviction—change their religious beliefs and practices. Since these worse ways—ranging from censorship to mass murder—have hardly disappeared from the world, it is important to consider the positive as well as the negative aspects of the simplistic, comical, yet weirdly reassuring American greeting-card message that a conversion is an occasion for congratulations.

First, this is a country in which fewer than one-third of Americans agree with the proposition that has always been the rationale for religious violence and forced conversion: "My religion is the one, true faith leading to eternal life."[2] An American may secretly consider her religion the best path to salvation without considering it the *only* path.

Religious dogmas, as well as religious prejudices, that were taken for granted a century ago have lost their power and social respectability for huge numbers of Americans. Of the overwhelming majority who identify as Christians, more than two-thirds believe that Judaism can also lead to eternal life—even though eternal life is a concept central to Christian, not Jewish, thought. Americans who believe this most strongly are Catholics, of whom 77 percent say Jews can attain eternal life.[3] (Remembering the daily prayers for the conversion of the Jews in my parochial school, I could hardly believe this statistic when the ever-reliable Pew Research Center reported it in 2008.) A majority of Americans believe that even Muslims—and Islam was the least popular religion in the Pew poll—can go to heaven. And 56 percent of American Muslims (compared with only 18 percent of Muslims worldwide) believe that people of other religions can go to heaven.[4]

Atheists are the only group considered unfit for eternal life by a majority of Americans. Only 42 percent of all Americans—and just one out of four white evangelical Protestants—believe that atheists can hope for eternal bliss in heaven if they lead good lives on earth. This belief is of no practical importance to atheists, who of course do not believe in an afterlife, but it is a measure of the social disapproval that American atheists encounter in this life if they admit that they do not believe in any god. That the word "atheist" has a special pejorative connotation in the United States is apparent in another finding of the Pew survey. Although a majority of Americans think that heaven will be free of atheists, 56 percent (and two-thirds of Catholics) believe that "people with no religious faith" can merit eternal life.[5] If you want your fellow Americans to approve, you are much better off saying that you are "spiritual but not religious" (a phrase I have never heard in Europe) or even that you are "nothing in particular"—as a vast majority of those unaffiliated with any church told the Pew researchers. Nevertheless, a survey conducted by the Pew researchers in 2014 indicated that the proportion of Americans who are willing to call themselves atheists or agnostics, while still small in absolute numbers, has increased significantly in just seven years. Those identifying themselves as atheists jumped from 1.6 percent in a survey published in 2007 to 3.1 percent in 2014. During the same period, those who call themselves Christians declined by more than eight percentage points—with most of the losses among Roman Catholics and mainline Protestant denominations.[6]

There is a paradoxical relationship between the unique (in the West) American antagonism to atheism and the unique American enthusiasm for religious conversion. If you believe, as so many Americans do, that there can be no morality without religion—but you also believe, as so many Americans do, in freedom of religious choice—it follows that almost any religion is better than none, and even "nothing in particular" is better than affirmative, unashamed atheism. Atheists believe in ethics grounded in the natural world, whereas all forms of Christianity (still and for the foreseeable future the dominant religion of the West, however spottily practiced it may be) ground their ethical imperatives in the expectation of supernatural rewards or punishments.

•

Statistics bear out the exceptionalism of American attitudes toward conversion. Approximately half of Americans report that they have changed religions at least once in their adult lives, and many have done so more than once.[7] According to a study of religious patterns in forty countries, the conversion rate in the United States is more than five times that in Norway and nearly six times that in Italy. There are similar disparities between the United States and nearly every other developed country studied in both Europe and Asia.[8] (A notable exception is Canada—the only country with a higher conversion rate than the United States. Immigration, with its tendency to lead to mixed marriages that also foster conversions over generations, has played as critical a role in Canadian society as it has in the United States.)*

Individual religious conversions take place in every democratic society for a wide variety of reasons, but they are woven into the fabric of American society in a way considered odd in most other prosperous parts of the modern world. I would be willing to bet that no one among former British Prime Minister Tony Blair's English friends sent him a "congratulations on your conversion" card when, in 2007, he switched from Anglicanism to Catholicism (although Pope Benedict XVI, whom Blair had met while both were in office, might well have privately communicated sentiments along those lines). Aggressive professions of religious devotion, as embodied in public recognition and celebration of conversion, are so very . . . well, *American.*

The low rate of European conversion is attributable not to deep faith in traditional religion but, as several recent popes have noted, to the displacement of religion by secularism. That one no longer attends the church in which one was baptized—whether the default religion is Protestantism in Northern Europe or Catholicism in Southern Europe—is not considered a reason to begin searching for another faith. Many European atheists get married in church to please the older members of their families but then have nothing more to do with religion. "My wife and I were married by a priest to please our mothers," a Florentine friend told me, "but we drew the line when it came to religious education for our children. We don't believe in any of that, and we don't want our children to be taught by priests and nuns."

---

* A caveat: This study's last conversion statistics date from 2001. It is entirely possible that conversion rates have increased in some developed countries, particularly in the nations of Eastern Europe where restrictions on freedom of religion were eased with the end of the Soviet empire, during the past fifteen years. It is also likely that a new generation of Muslim immigrants has had an impact—however one views that impact—on second- and third-generation Muslims, particularly in Europe, whose religious observance had lapsed.

In most of the historically Christian countries of Europe, it is no liability if a political candidate is known to be an atheist, and voters would find it perfectly normal if their nation's president or prime minister had never been known to attend a church service in his or her adult life. What Europeans would find strange is a religious odyssey like that of Nevada's Democratic Senator Harry Reid, a lukewarm Protestant who married a Jew and, after their wedding, converted to Mormonism along with his wife. French voters may tolerate an unmarried president who leaves his longtime mistress for another mistress, but they might not be as accepting of a once-Catholic prime minister who, having married a Jew, decided that he and his new wife would take the "mixed" out of mixed marriage by becoming Huguenots. Or Mormons, for that matter.*

The parents of Reid's future wife, Landra Gould, had wanted their daughter to marry a Jew and would tear up Harry's letters before she could read them. Reid even knocked his future father-in-law to the ground in his front yard as they battled over the prospective mixed marriage. (It is tempting to see this as a bad omen for a man who eventually became a leader in the Senate, where literally punching out your opponent is a poor way to make a political deal.) In an interview in *The New Yorker,* Mrs. Reid said, "Before we got married, we had talked about it and decided we were not going to let religion divide us after what we'd been through. If we were going to find something, we were going to find it together."[9] The Reids' assumption that they must "find something" is what makes this a quintessentially American story, even though the religion they found had almost nothing to do with either of their backgrounds.† A cynic might suspect that, even as a young man, Reid had political ambitions, and the religion to which he and his wife converted just happened to be the faith of the most powerful voting bloc in the state of Nevada. But Reid said he was most

* We have known that Mormons do send missionaries to France since Mitt Romney's 2012 presidential campaign revealed that he had performed his compulsory missionary service in that skeptical society. I have always felt sorry for Romney on this score: imagine what it must be like to spend a year in France, proselytizing for a religion that forbids the consumption of both coffee and wine.

† The Church of Jesus Christ of Latter-day Saints does consider its founding members to have been descended from the "lost tribes of Israel," but this is, needless to say, a doctrine rejected by all branches of Judaism.

impressed by Mormonism's emphasis on family. (Apparently, Judaism did not take enough of an interest in family for the Reids—especially since Jews do not constitute a large proportion of voters in Nevada.) In any event, Landra's parents, like so many Americans who would have preferred that their children marry within their faith, eventually reconciled with the couple. Until his wife's parents died, Reid said, his family observed the Jewish holidays. The Mormon Reids had a traditional Jewish mezuzah at the entrance to their longtime house in the serendipitously named town of Searchlight, Nevada (they have since moved to Las Vegas).

In the United States, the Reids' decision to switch to a third religion after a mixed marriage is actually the choice of a surprisingly robust minority. The authors of *American Grace* suggest that 15 percent of religious switches involve mixed couples who choose a third faith rather than pick a religion already observed by one of the partners.[10] That this practice should be so prevalent strikes me as much more peculiar than the high rate of conversion in the United States. I cannot imagine, for instance, that I might marry an observant Jew and that we would decide to become Unitarians as a compromise between my atheism and his Judaism. I know a Unitarian couple who made just such a decision, but the husband was not a devout Jew; he celebrated Passover, Rosh Hashanah, and Yom Kippur (though he almost never got through the entire fast day without a forbidden snack) and rarely observed Shabbos. And the woman was not seriously committed to her atheism; she was content to avail herself of the "spiritual but not religious" escape hatch. A couple's selection of a third religion may have little to do with spiritual conviction, but it fits perfectly into the "religious marketplace" model. He wants to live in an apartment in Manhattan, she wants to live in the suburbs, so they settle on a townhouse in Brooklyn (before townhouses in Brooklyn moved into New York City's fashionable and unaffordable real-estate stratosphere).

The option of picking a third religion may seem bizarre to anyone who takes either religion or atheism seriously, but it probably makes more sense than a choice made by some naïve members of my generation, who actually thought they could raise children in two faiths. The idea was that children could hear Jesus hailed as the Messiah by a Christian priest, and a rabbi would tell them the Messiah had not yet arrived. Then, when the time came, the lucky kids (*Free to*

Be . . . You and Me) could simply choose their own religion, after they had sorted out the dual messages.* That seems to be what happened after Muhammad Ali's daughter married a Jew and their son chose to become bar mitzvah. The adoption (and adaptation) of a third religion and the decision to raise children in two religions have one thing in common: they regard faith as a commodity.

Thus, the American tolerance for politicians who change faiths for whatever reason is perfectly consistent with the high incidence of conversion among the population as a whole. Several years ago, an essay by the perceptive religion writer Mark Oppenheimer appeared in the *New Republic* with the interrogatory headline "Why Are American Politicians Always Switching Religions?" The answer—which the headline writer obviously did not know—is that politicians *don't* switch religions more frequently than other Americans, and that explains why conversion is rarely a negative and often a positive factor in campaigns. Just as voters no longer penalize candidates for being divorced (if the divorces have been conducted with a modicum of discretion), they are not about to penalize a candidate for religious behavior similar to their own.†

Former Republican Speaker of the House Newt Gingrich is on his third wife and his third religion, although he is (probably) never going to run for office again. Why would he, when he is now aboard the pundit-consultant gravy train reserved for ex-politicians who can still speak fluently and show up on time in one television studio after another? Gingrich was baptized a Lutheran and later became a Southern Baptist (an advantageous, whether adventitious or not, step for a politician from Georgia). His religious odyssey ended (probably) in 2009, when, married to a new Catholic wife, he converted to Catholicism. In an essay for the *National Catholic Register*, Gingrich explained that, although he was a Baptist when he met Callista

---

* *Free to Be . . . You and Me* was a 1974 book, conceived by the actress Marlo Thomas with the support of the Ms. Foundation, designed to break down gender stereotypes and emphasizing that both boys and girls can grow up to do anything they want to do.
† Actually, many voters no longer seem to care even if divorce is conducted with the utmost indiscretion. Former South Carolina Governor Mark Sanford was elected to Congress after a marital split characterized by the maximum indiscretion of having ignored state business and lied about taking a hike on the Appalachian Trail when he was actually in Argentina with his mistress. Newt Gingrich's checkered marital history begins with his divorce from his first wife, who was suffering from breast cancer at the time.

Bisek, a congressional staffer, he attended Mass with her every Sunday and listened to her sing in the choir of the Basilica of the Shrine of the Immaculate Conception in Washington, D.C. (The essay does not tell readers whether Gingrich was attending Mass with Callista while they were having the six-year affair that ended his second marriage.) "Throughout our travels," he recalled, "whether Callista and I were in Costa Rica or Africa, she was adamant about finding a local Mass on Sunday. Listening to 'Amazing Grace' being sung in Chinese at Mass in Beijing was a beautiful experience, and worshipping with believers across the world opened my eyes to the diversity and richness of the Catholic Church."[11] (The song "Amazing Grace" cannot have been new to Gingrich, since the lyrics were written by an evangelically inclined Anglican minister—a reformed slave trader—around 1772. It is one of the most famous Protestant hymns in history and could never have been sung at a Catholic Mass before the Second Vatican Council of the 1960s, when restrictions on the inclusion of "Protestant" music at Catholic services were eased. But it would certainly have been sung in the Lutheran and Baptist churches of Gingrich's previous incarnations.)

•

The doubling of "nones"—Americans unaffiliated with any religion—since the turn of the millennium deserves special attention, because it is likely to have a significant impact on conversions and mixed marriages. Two-thirds of Americans who were raised as Catholic or Protestant but now say they are religiously unaffiliated, have changed faiths more than once in their adult lives.[12] Exactly how many of these leaps of faith are thoroughly considered intellectual and spiritual shifts—comparable, say, to the conversions of G. K. Chesterton and C. S. Lewis—is unclear. Those who converted to another faith, as opposed to becoming unaffiliated and more secular, were much more likely to say that their spiritual needs were not being met in their former religion. Thus, the changing American religious landscape of the twenty-first century combines a lapse into secularism more characteristic of European countries with a search for another religion that is uniquely American. The Pew pollsters found that the "unaffiliated" do not necessarily "lack spiritual beliefs or religious behaviors; in fact, roughly four-in-ten unaffiliated individuals say religion is at least somewhat important in their lives."[13]

I am skeptical about the validity of this conclusion—though I do not doubt that it is based on what the Pew researchers were told. The main caveat about the purported importance of religion to "nones" is the existence of strong pro-religious pressure in American society. Who but a committed atheist is going to tell a pollster, "Not only do I not belong to a church, but I have no intention of ever joining"? After I wrote an op-ed column for *The New York Times,* urging atheists to come out and not hide behind the "spiritual but not religious" label, I received a sobering letter from a mother in a suburb of Dallas.[14] She said, "I am an atheist, but I pretend to be a Unitarian because I'm afraid my kids would be bullied at school if I were known as an atheist. So we say we're Unitarians because it's closer to what my husband and I really believe than most religions. Would you be willing to sacrifice your kids for your convictions?" This is an excellent question—one I am ashamed to admit that I never considered as a resident of New York City, where atheism is not stigmatized as it is in many parts of the country.

Among the 22.8 percent of Americans who call themselves unaffiliated in the 2014 Pew poll, 15.8 percent describe themselves as "nothing in particular," with the rest split between atheists and agnostics.[15] The popularity of the "nothing in particular" category is another reason for doubting that religion has any serious significance to those who do not practice their faith in a visible (to themselves as well as others) way. Some of the unaffiliated could also be described as confused or flat-out lazy. There are, without question, many Americans who want to keep some religious option open—in theory—without assuming the practical duties of anyone who actually belongs to a church, temple, or mosque. This insurance-policy religiosity hardly qualifies as the kind of faith that is even somewhat important in a person's life, although it may be more comfortable for the "nones" to keep up the pretense for a pollster. There may also be sincere people who place themselves in the "spiritual but not religious" category because to them, spirituality means concern for truths that transcend the material and the physical. By this definition, everyone—from atheists to religious fundamentalists—is spiritual. One might as well call oneself "philosophical, but not religious."

   That the United States remains an overwhelmingly Christian society—albeit one composed of many different types of Christians—is often forgotten in the nation's larger, more cosmopolitan cities. Even now, more than 70 percent of Americans still identify themselves as Christians (either Protestant or Catholic).[16] Jews make up only about 1.9 percent of the total American population, Muslims 0.9 percent, Buddhists and Hindus 0.7 percent apiece.* The overestimation of America as a society in which pluralism nearly always promotes tolerance—and where we all get along if only we believe in God—has fueled many of the religion-centered culture wars of the past thirty years. We all get along until some public issue like abortion or assisted suicide, which reveals deep fault lines between and within religions, comes up for a vote.

   Nor do religious identification statistics reveal what it means to individuals when they describe themselves as Protestants, Catholics, Jews, or members of any other religion. This is particularly true of Jews, many of whom consider themselves Jews—and are considered Jews by others—regardless of whether they practice any form of religious Judaism. "Catholic," too, no longer has an agreed-upon meaning. Are you a Catholic who believes and follows the teachings of the church hierarchy forbidding contraception, abortion, and remarriage after divorce, or do you, like the majority of American Catholics, disagree with these precepts and live by your own conscience?

   As for "Protestants," are you a Protestant who goes to church every Sunday or once a year? If you are an evangelical Protestant, are you theologically and politically liberal or conservative? Evangelicalism is often thought to be synonymous with political conservatism—the mass media are particularly prone to this generalization—but there are liberal as well as conservative evangelicals. Former President Jimmy Carter, for instance, is a liberal evangelical Baptist who left the South-

---

* These figures, derived from Pew research surveys and other, less comprehensive sociological studies, are not and cannot be exact—although they are a fair reflection of the statistical relationship between minority and majority religions in the United States. The U.S. Census Bureau is prevented by law from asking questions about religion. The difficulty of reaching an accurate count is well illustrated by the American Jewish community. There are many more Americans who consider themselves Jewish in an ethnic and cultural sense than there are Americans who practice religious Judaism. My guess—and it is only a guess—is that all of the small minority religious groups are slightly larger than data from surveys suggest at this time.

ern Baptist Convention because he disagrees with its stance on many
social and economic issues—but especially on equality for women.
Carter is still a Baptist; he is simply a different kind of Baptist from
many Southerners of his generation. Even when people stay within the
boundaries of the religion in which they were brought up, they may
undergo changes of belief as profound as those associated with any
traditional conversion.

·

A new and critical factor has entered the American religious mix—
growing public ignorance, particularly among the young, about religion itself. Since the beginning of the 1990s, studies have shown that a
majority of American adults—in what is supposedly the most religious
nation in the developed world—do not know such basic facts of religious history as the names of the four Gospels.[17] This decline in what
the historian Stephen Prothero calls religious literacy is part of the more
general decline in education (and therefore knowledge) in the humanities, and it has serious cultural implications that extend beyond religion.
The answers to a 2010 Pew poll about religious knowledge make one
wonder not about the teaching of religion in homes and church schools
but about the teaching of history in public elementary and secondary
schools over the past fifty years. Only 46 percent of Americans know
that Martin Luther began the Reformation, and just 45 percent know
that the Jewish Sabbath begins on Friday. Fewer than a third know that
the Puritan Jonathan Edwards, author of that immortal sermon "Sin-
ners in the Hands of an Angry God," was a key figure in the First Great
Awakening. (Presumably, most of these people do not know what the
First Great Awakening was.) How do you teach world history in high
school without mentioning Luther? Or the history of colonial America
without talking about fire-and-brimstone Puritans? Many Americans
know as little about their own religions as they do about other people's
religions. Roughly 45 percent of Catholics, for example, do not know
that their church teaches that the bread and wine in the sacrament of
the Eucharist have been transformed into the actual body and blood of
Jesus (a dogma that was involved in many conversions to Protestantism during the Reformation and, like the Trinity, was a cause of great
bloodshed). Information about religions other than Christianity and

Judaism is in even scarcer supply, with the exception of obvious references to religion-related political developments that appear regularly in the news. Slightly more than half of Americans can name the Quran as Islam's holy book, and 62 percent have somehow managed to learn that Hinduism is the majority religion in India. Fewer than half, however, know that the Dalai Lama is a Buddhist.[18]

Self-identified atheists and agnostics scored highest on the test, followed by Jews, Mormons, white evangelical Protestants, white Catholics, and white "mainline" Protestants. The three lowest-scoring groups were Hispanic Catholics, black Protestants, and those who identified themselves as "nothing in particular." For anyone interested in the future of religious belief or nonbelief (or both), it is significant that, among the unaffiliated, those who think of themselves as "nothing in particular" are so ignorant about all religion. That the largest group among the unaffiliated knows less about religion than most other Americans—and much less than committed atheists—does not lend support to the wishful thinking of some secularists that the growth of the "nones" is likely to produce a more coherent and socially powerful secular movement in the United States. Atheism, because of its strong pejorative connotation in the United States, cannot easily be accepted by Americans unless they have educated themselves about the history of both belief and doubt. Until recently, most atheists grew up in nonatheist homes, so the starting point for their journey was some form of religious education. Adult atheists over age forty today are likely to have read both the Bible and Thomas Paine (which was also true of freethinkers in the nineteenth century). But those content to be and think of themselves as "nones" are unlikely to have read even the most basic works about either religion or atheism. What cannot be foretold from these studies is whether children who have been raised by atheist parents—there will be many more in twenty years—will have as much religious knowledge as older, self-educated atheists do today.

One reason I place so much emphasis on the relatively high level of religious knowledge among American atheists is that the findings contradict the contention of many anti-secularist scholars and theologians that religious ignorance is the real driver of secularism in Europe. The French sociologist Danièle Hervieu-Léger, for example, has described the secularism of once-Christian Europe as a form of cultural amnesia rather than as an intellectual choice—the product of a broken chain of memory rather than of doubt about the truth of traditional religion. If that were true, atheists ought to know less, not more, about traditional religions than the religious. I have no doubt that Europeans, like Americans, are more ignorant about religion and the history of Western civilization today than they were even a decade or two ago (although the religion polls offer more data on the United States). But committed atheism—in the United States and nations where atheism is more acceptable than it is here—develops more frequently as the result of extensive rather than deficient religious education.

It is often seen as a paradox that Americans, who are much more religious than Europeans if religious commitment is measured by formally expressed belief in a traditional God, eternal life, and miracles, know so little about the religions that most claim to practice. I am not so certain that there is an inherent contradiction between a high level of faith and ignorance about the teachings and history of that faith. It may even be easier to consider religion important in your life if you do not know exactly what that religion traditionally teaches and demands. (After all, opposition to reading the Bible in the vernacular was always based on ecclesiastical authorities' entirely reasonable fear that a little knowledge was a dangerous thing when it came to acceptance of dogma.) However, religious conversions, or switches of faith, that take place in the absence of knowledge are very different from the examined conversions of Muhammad Ali or the Baal Teshuva of the 1960s and 1970s. Regardless of what one thinks about those conversions—shaped by an era of social rebellion, and disturbing to individual families as well as the larger society—or of the religions themselves, they were not undertaken lightly but, to borrow from the Book of Common Prayer, reverently, soberly, and in the fear of God. They fit my definition of conversion because they required a major change in the convert's way of life.

God is not dead, but many of the institutions purporting to represent Him on earth are on life support (as is the weekly news magazine that posed the question more than half a century ago). My best guess—and it is only an educated guess—is that both the rate of religious conversion and the European-style shift to secularism will continue to rise over the next thirty years in the United States, as children born in the first decade of the twenty-first century begin to marry and have children of their own. For the majority of Americans, who still do identify—however tenuously—with a religion, conversions as a result of interfaith marriage are likely to become even more common. If I were a gambler, I would bet that young atheists today will raise their children as atheists but that those who call themselves "nothing in particular" will not be anxious to pass that label on to their offspring. It would not be entirely surprising if children of the "nones"—raised neither in a serious religious nor in a thoughtful atheist and humanist tradition—provided fertile recruiting ground for a new generation of religious converts. The unanswerable question is whether more secular Americans will realize that nothing has never proved to be a very good substitute for something, will stop fearing social censure, will openly identify themselves as atheists or humanists, and will establish institutions that provide yet another choice within the American religious marketplace. We can be sure of one thing: the marketplace, in contrast to areas of the world still cursed by religious coercion, will remain open for business.

DARKNESS VISIBLE

I F IT WERE POSSIBLE to divide our planet into impermeable compart-
ments, it would also be possible to end this secular history of religious
conversion on a more optimistic or, at the very least, a less anxious
note. Forced conversion would no longer be an issue worth talking
about if the Enlightenment concept of natural rights, which gave birth
to secular law that forbids the slaughter of people for choosing one
supernatural philosophy over another, had taken root throughout the
world. But, as everyone who eschews weak-minded religious and political correctness knows, religious persecution and coerced conversion
remain realities, not half-forgotten nightmares from the distant past,
for millions around our uncompartmentalized and uncompartmen-
talizable globe.

When I began the research for this book a decade ago, I never imagined that I would be writing the conclusion at a time when there was
actually a real controversy about the question of whether a conversion
to Islam by a Christian hostage held by ISIS (a.k.a. ISIL, a.k.a. the
Islamic State) could be considered "voluntary." James Foley, an American journalist beheaded in Syria by ISIS in 2014, was by all accounts a
devout Catholic before being taken hostage (for a second time) in the
Middle East. After the gruesome video of his execution was released,
some of his former fellow captives, released for ransom, said that Foley

had converted to Islam during his imprisonment and that his conversion appeared to be a genuine change of faith. But his mother, Diane Foley—a Eucharistic minister* at the family's parish church in New Hampshire—was told a different story by other released French and Spanish captives who knew her son. "What the hostages had told me was that by saying that he had converted to Islam, he would be left alone five times a day, without being beaten, so that he could pray," said Ms. Foley. Pope Francis, according to the Foley family, had called their son a martyr in a phone call of condolence. After the dispute about the possible conversion to Islam surfaced, Cardinal Angelo Amato, prefect of the Vatican's Congregation for the Causes of Saints, said that any discussion about declaring Foley a martyr would be premature but that a change of faith "not done freely does not indicate a conversion."[1] That such a subject is even being discussed in the second decade of the twenty-first century is a measure of the darkness that has reached out from a medieval past to involve otherwise sensible people in a nonsensical argument about whether there can be such a phenomenon as voluntary conversion when the "convert" in question has been starved, tortured, and threatened with execution. There cannot be. There never could be, at any point in history.

The issues raised today by either the frequency or the scarcity of religious conversions in the United States and Europe may be of critical concern to religious institutions, but they are luxury problems insofar as the progress of human liberty is concerned. Even from a devoutly religious standpoint, does it really matter if God appears dead to some, as long as others are perfectly free to reach a different conclusion? Are conversions of convenience—motivated more by some social need, including the desire for community, than by any deep spiritual conviction—harmful to either society or individuals? Can conscious and conscientious secular humanism offer coherent moral precepts that will be recognized in the public square by those who insist that only religion can serve as a basis for both private and public morality? How are we to educate children about the historical role of religion when fewer and fewer people are being exposed to a

---

* Eucharistic ministers in the church are lay Catholics, both men and women, chosen to aid in the distribution of Holy Communion if not enough priests or official deacons—who must be male—are available.

serious education in their own faith—much less any other? None of these questions, debated with varying degrees of respect and rancor by theologians, politicians, and academics, mean as much to people's daily lives as persecution for choosing the wrong faith once did in the West, and still does in societies where people must continue to live with the knowledge that they may be thrown out of their homes, imprisoned, tortured, raped, or murdered for what they believe—or do not believe—about God.

Although knowledge about religion, encompassing differences as well as commonalities among faiths, is essential from a cultural stand-point, concentration on the fine points of dogma does little to shed light on more important issues involving ethical values. I doubt that anyone other than a practicing Catholic needs to know the particulars of the doctrine of transubstantiation, or that anyone but an Ortho-dox Jew needs to understand the laws of family purity, which (among other requirements and prohibitions) regulate sexual relations between husbands and wives to avoid the "uncleanness" associated with men-strual periods. I am certain, though, that responsible citizenship in every democracy, on every continent, requires knowledge and under-standing of the long, tortuous battle for the liberation of men and women from religious compulsion. Both the modern American dream of absolute religious tolerance and the more limited ideal of toleration that emerged from the carnage of seventeenth-century Europe remain just that—dreams—in societies blind to the vision of a free conscience as a human right.

From the Middle East and Africa to Southeast Asia, fear is an omnipresent reality for countless numbers of Christians; atheists and freethinkers; practitioners of ancient Middle Eastern creeds that incor-porate elements of many religions; and Muslims whose beliefs differ from those of Islamic theocrats. The terrorist theocrats—possessors of twenty-first-century technology with minds stuck in the eighth century—defy any concept of predictable human progress with the violence they have inflicted on religious dissidents (many of them dissidents only vis-à-vis the warped religio-political ideology of their captors).*

* I wish, instead of calling the victims dissenters or dissidents, that I could use the won-derful word once used by Russians to describe those who were skeptical about the Soviet

Fear of religious persecution is not confined to those menaced by Islamic terrorist groups. The status of Christians and practicing Buddhists—ranging from second-class to persecuted—in China remains an unresolved human rights issue. In many areas of India, mixed couples (usually a Hindu woman and a Muslim man) now live in fear of physical attacks from right-wing Hindu nationalists who consider such unions an abomination and a plot to convert Hindu women to Islam.[2] The same people are also opposed to intermarriage with Christians and have attacked Christian churches and businesses. The Hindu extremists, like the nuns who taught me in the 1950s (but reserved their predictions of punishment for the afterlife), are right in terms of their own narrowly defined religious interests: when someone marries a person of another faith, the union often results in the conversion of one partner. So what?, says the post-Enlightenment society. Never, says the pre-Enlightenment theocratic mentality.

The most extreme and widespread acts of violence today are committed mainly by radical Muslim men. These thugs believe that they are entitled to impose their absolute truth claims on Muslims who do not agree with their brand of Islam as well as on those who dare to practice another faith or to abjure belief in any god. Yet many in the Western world, for a variety of reasons, refuse to see that such truth claims and forced conversion are central to the terrorist enterprise— that religious domination is not only a means to a political end but an end in itself. There are secular as well as religious liberals who simply cannot comprehend the kind of blind faith that makes vicious young men believe they are doing God's work when they cut off the heads of people who do not agree with them.

Some religious believers do not wish to acknowledge the violence inflicted in the name of God by their ancestors (in a metaphoric and sometimes literal sense), before secular law stopped privileging one form of faith over others. This is a peculiar form of thin-skinned religious sensibility, since modern Christians do not in fact bear any more responsibility for atrocities committed by medieval crusaders than, say,

---

regime. The term was *inakomysliashchii;* literally, "one who thinks differently." This locution nicely captures the wide variety of people, with a wide variety of beliefs, who may be trapped in the nets of absolutist enforcers. It is a more elastic and inclusive term than the English "dissenter" or, in religious terms, "heretic."

modern Egyptians do for their ancient forebears' charming religious custom of entombing living slaves along with their dead noble masters. They do, however, bear responsibility for trying to sanitize their own history in order to pretend that "true" religion never has, never can instigate violence.

Secular liberals, by contrast, tend to emphasize "tolerance." Because freedom of conscience is such a deeply held secular value, some well-meaning but intellectually confused secular thinkers have trouble separating legitimate criticism of fanatical religion from "hate speech." The easiest course for anyone—religious or secular—who is uncomfortable criticizing any aspect of religion is to avoid making careful distinctions, pretend that this violence has a purely political or economic explanation, and deny that crazed faith—perish the thought—has anything to do with such terrible acts. It is undeniable that extreme fundamentalist forms of religion, with their emphasis on martyrdom and rewards in the afterlife, tend to flourish in societies affording little opportunity in this life, but it is equally undeniable that retrograde religion itself fosters social, educational, and economic deprivation in a vicious cycle.

The most disgusting statement after the terrorist attacks of September 11, 2001, was made by Osama bin Laden himself, who, in a video-taped message, declared, "Let the whole world know that we shall never accept that the tragedy of al-Andalus should be repeated." But the best of al-Andalus, stripped of hagiography, represented exactly the sort of society hated by Bin Laden and his ilk—hated for its promiscuous mingling of cultural customs, its exchange of ideas, its emphasis on secular as well as religious knowledge. The medieval Muslim translators of Greek classics into Arabic, who played a critical role in making the Renaissance possible, would have been slaughtered by men like Bin Laden. What the violent religious lunatics hate most of all, as they always have, is the idea that human beings have the right to use their own minds to determine their own beliefs. For Bin Laden to talk about the Convivencia as if he were its heir was a genuine sacrilege (as opposed to the promiscuous use of the adjective "sacrilegious" to describe any belief with which a fanatic disagrees). The Christian Bin Ladens of the late Middle Ages destroyed al-Andalus, as the Muslim Bin Ladens today wish to destroy any fruitful, free intermingling of Islam with modernity.

Permit me, for the special benefit of those—including President Barack Obama and former President George W. Bush—who maintain that "terrorism has nothing to do with Islam," to restate my position on this matter. Bush and Obama have understandable political reasons for their position—they do not want American action against a terrorist minority to be seen as a war on an entire faith—but they are wrong to pretend that the terrorists' behavior has nothing to do with their idea of the Muslim religion. It is as ridiculous to say that modern terrorism has nothing to do with Islam as it would be to say that the murder of Hypatia in the fifth century had nothing to do with the violent side of early Christianity, that the Crusades and the Inquisition had nothing to do with Roman Catholicism, or that the executions of Michael Servetus and countless Anabaptists had nothing to do with John Calvin and Calvinism or with Martin Luther and early Lutheranism.

Some apologists for religious correctness argue that the very phrase "religious violence" is at best a misnomer, at worst a libel, because religion has always been entangled with politics—and politics is the real driver of what is called religious violence. The works of Karen Armstrong, a former Catholic nun who passed through a brief period of atheism and now writes immensely popular books stressing the good in all religions, epitomize the view of faith as a largely innocent actor in tribal and nationalist violence. In an interview filled with wishful rewriting of just about every religion's history as well as comical errors of fact, she declares:

> The prophets of Israel, for example, were deeply political people. They castigated their rulers for not looking after the poor; they cried out against the system of agrarian injustice. Jesus did the same, Mohammed and the Quran do the same. Sometimes, religion permeates the violence of the state, but it also offers the consistent critique of that structural and martial violence.[3]

Of course, a case can be made for just about everything from the Bible and the Quran—as long as one disregards contradictory passages in the same books. As the Duchess says to Alice in Wonderland, "Tut, tut, child! Everything's got a moral, if only you can find it." I suppose, if the term is used somewhat loosely, "agrarian justice" might be seen as one concern of certain Hebrew prophets. Moses, after all, began demonstrating the Lord's power after the pharaoh ordered the Hebrews to make bricks without straw—which could be considered an example of not only agrarian but workplace injustice. And Elijah vanquished the worshippers of Baal and ended the agrarian injustice of a long drought, though it is true that this particular injustice was initiated by God Himself. (For a genuine economic critique, one would do better to fast-forward to 1797 and the decidedly secular Thomas Paine's influential pamphlet, straightforwardly titled *Agrarian Justice,* which advocated an estate tax on land to finance old-age pensions.) Somewhat less comical than the vision of Israel's prophets as advocates for agrarian reform is the assertion that religion offers a consistent critique of state-sponsored martial violence. If there is one challenge that has never been offered by politically dominant religions, it is a critique, consistent or otherwise, of militarism—in ancient or modern states. Whenever and wherever pacifist religions emerged, they were always persecuted minority faiths. Only modern, secular governments recognize the rights of conscientious objectors. But even if one is not a pacifist and accepts the idea that there are some "just wars" (as I do), religions in the pre-modern era opposed militarism only when it threatened believers in their own faith.

In twentieth-century Europe, in both Hitler's Germany and Mussolini's Italy, priests who spoke out and worked against fascist militarism (and the persecution of Jews) were often the objects of ecclesiastical censure emanating from the Vatican, under Popes Pius XI and XII.* Heroic anti-fascist, anti-militarist clergy—only some of their names known to history—represented a dissident, not a dominant, strain within both Roman Catholicism and German Protestantism. Both the righteous Gentiles who did everything they could to save Jews, and the clerics, including two popes, who concerned themselves only with

---

* For a devastating account of the Vatican's refusal to criticize Italian and German militarism in the dangerous run-up to World War II in the 1930s, see David I. Kertzer's *The Pope and Mussolini: The Secret History of Pius XI and the Rise of Fascism in Europe* (New York: Random House, 2014). Kertzer notes that on Hitler's April 20 birthday in 1939—little more than a month after Nazi troops gobbled up what was left of Czechoslovakia—Pope Pius XII's papal nuncio in Berlin offered the Führer the pope's congratulations, and church bells throughout Germany were rung in celebration of the blessed event.

the fate of Jews who had converted to Christianity, were part of the "real" Christianity. Or, to be more exact, *Christianities*. When people say that some atrocity has nothing to do with "real" religion, what they usually mean is that they want to remember only religious good and consign religious evil to a memory hole. Sometimes they also mean that evil committed in the name of God has nothing to do with their own interpretation of a particular religion. The obvious shortcoming of such rationalizations is that real religion is and always has been in the eye of the beholder.

Those who wish to absolve Islamic ideologues of responsibility for terrorism will not even take terrorists at their own word when they use their faith as justification for their acts. Bin Laden, according to Armstrong, "talks about God and Allah and Islam and the infidels and all that, but he had very clear political aims and attitudes towards Saudi Arabia, towards Western involvement in Middle Eastern affairs. The way he talked always about Zionists and crusaders rather than Jews and Christians—these are political terms."[4] First, Zionists and crusaders are not only political (and sometimes neutral historical) terms but can be, and often are, used as code words for anti-Jewish and anti-Christian views. More important, the inseparability of religious from political ideology is precisely what makes extremist religion such a dangerous force in any era. "Thus sayeth the Lord" has always been the most powerful justification offered by conquerors; the melding of religion with nationalism and/or anti-colonialism reinforces rather than reduces the importance of the religious part of the equation. But why take Bin Laden at his word? We Westerners know he didn't mean all that stuff about infidels and was only speaking politically in his rantings about Zionists.

The religiously correct also equate Christendom's crimes in the Middle Ages with the crimes of radical Islamists today—as if today's Islamic terrorists somehow deserve a pass because Christians once engaged in similar behavior.* The heart of true liberalism is belief in

---

* There is also a mirror-image conservative Christian response to any mention of the Crusades, as I discovered when I wrote an op-ed piece for *The New York Times* titled "The First Victims of the First Crusade" (February 15, 2015). This essay dealt with the massacres of Jews in the Rhineland by Crusaders en route to Jerusalem in 1096, and my author Web site crashed with e-mails from far-right Christians who objected to any negative talk about the Crusades and to any mention of Jewish victims. These correspon-

the possibility (if not always the attainment) of progress; there is nothing liberal about suggesting that anyone, anywhere in the world, of whatever religious or nonreligious persuasion, should be forced to live in the twenty-first century by the standards of medieval theocracy, for as long as it takes their captors to catch up with the last millennium, give or take a few centuries, of history.

This does not—I repeat, *not*—mean that all or most Muslims are terrorists or sympathize with terrorists. But it is a fact that most (though by no means all) terrorists in the world today are Muslims. That the terrorists are Muslims who have been condemned by many other Muslims, and that they have killed and persecuted more Muslims who disagree with them than they have anyone else, is also a fact—and an overwhelmingly important one. The British journalist Sunny Hundal, in an essay published by *Al Jazeera,* describes the rise of ISIS as "probably the worst event in recent Muslim history since 9/11." With a bluntness and candor not displayed by enough Western journalists, Hundal—the son of Sikh Indian parents—observes that ISIS has taken aim first at moderate and modernist Muslims. "The Islamic State (ISIS) is a direct descendant of al-Qaeda," he argues, "but there is one key difference: Its leaders believe fighting 'apostates' is more important than fighting non-Muslims for now. . . . The caliphate, say its fighters, will never be truly powerful unless apostates and 'fake' Muslims are first weeded out—and their definition of 'apostate' expands to include anyone who stands against them."[5] Apostasy is part of the language and history of monotheism and involves—at a minimum—forbidding anyone born into the faith to leave it. In its maximalist form, as Hundal suggests, the definition of apostasy encompasses anyone—of whatever faith—who is so foolish as to oppose those who would control thoughts as well as deeds. This concept remains a philosophical tenet of ultra-conservative factions within Christianity, Judaism, and Islam—but it no longer has any secular force except in Islamic societies (whether established states or the spoils of temporary conquest) ruled by Shariah.

---

dents ignored the fact that the piece compared Hebrew and Christian chronicles of the Crusaders' behavior with newspaper accounts of the terror imposed by ISIS. My favorite example of the genre was one e-mail from a man who said I was obviously "obsessed" with Jews because I had inherited my Semitic ancestors' "frog-like" facial features. His views may not represent the "real" Christianity but they certainly represent real anti-Semitism.

Some on the religious and secular left are perfectly happy to call violence "religious" as long as the term is applied only to non-Muslims. Dean Obeidallah, a political comedian and contributor to *The Daily Beast* and MSNBC, excoriates the media for calling Islamic terrorists "Islamic" but failing to call the murderers of abortion doctors "Christian terrorists."[6] I don't know about anyone else in the media, but I am perfectly comfortable applying the label "Christian terrorists" to the clinic bombers and the killers of doctors who perform abortions, and I have done so many times in speeches. Moreover, to say that they are motivated by *their* brand of Christianity, as the murderous Muslim fighters are motivated by *their* brand of Islam, is not to say that the majority of Christians agree with them. The difference is that these Christian terrorists go to jail in the United States, under secular law, for their crimes; American juries have proved completely unsympathetic to the attempts of clinic bombers and assassins of doctors to rationalize their actions on religious grounds. Who will obtain justice for the girls kidnapped from their schools, raped, and sold into slavery in Nigeria by Boko Haram (the group to which Obeidallah referred when he chastised the press for calling Islamic terrorists "Islamic")?

Furthermore, it is patronizing to Muslims to suggest that they are too undiscriminating to tolerate the proper identification of terrorists who want to force all Muslims within reach of their violence into the same demented mind-set. Malala Yousafzai, the co-recipient of the 2014 Nobel Peace Prize, is a Muslim, too, and she nearly died when a member of the Taliban—the Islamic terrorist Taliban—tried to kill her because of her advocacy of education for women. She shared the prize with Kailash Satyarthi, an Indian and a Hindu who has campaigned against child labor and child slavery. Would it surprise you to know that the Hindu wing nuts, intent on protecting their women from falling in love with Muslim or Christian men, are uninterested in Satyarthi's campaign against child trafficking? Who cares if boys and girls are routinely sold into sexual slavery, as long as grown women are forbidden to fall in love with a man of another faith and convert to his religion? Should we not call Malala a Muslim? Or should we simply reserve religious identification for *good* Muslims and pretend that there are no evil Muslims who want to wipe out the very memory of the cultural cross-fertilization that characterized the best of the Convivencia?

The Enlightenment bashers on the religious and political right deserve as much contempt for their exploitation of this issue as the religiously correct hypocrites on the left. Suddenly these people—from the textbook censors in Texas to the Fox News pundits—have discovered that Islamic terrorists hate "our" values—secular values such as the separation of church and state, which the political right has persistently tried to eviscerate and write out of American history. And they have discovered that Muslims—all Muslims, not just right-wing terrorists and theocrats—lack respect for women's rights. Yes, the world would certainly be a paradise for women who want to control their own minds and bodies if the Christian right were in charge and those pesky Muslims would just disappear.

In much of Europe, reluctance to address forthrightly the religious aspect of terrorism comes from two other sources—guilt about the history of European colonialism in many parts of the Muslim world, and anxiety about the presence of such a large Muslim immigrant population.* One favorite way around the juxtaposition of fear created by terrorist acts in Europe and the presence of a significant Muslim population is the contention that terrorism is essentially a political problem created by the Israeli-Palestinian conflict. (And, yes, there are also Jewish terrorists. One of them, a law student associated with a far-right, ultra-Orthodox group in Israel, assassinated Israeli Prime Minister Yitzhak Rabin in 1995.) The use of Israel to "explain" Muslim terrorism is much less common across the political spectrum in the United States than in Europe, but the argument is advanced on both continents. For the hard right, tarring most Muslims with the terrorist brush is justified by the contention that Muslims hate Israel because they hate Jews. Love for Jews, like concern for women's rights, is also a recent discovery—roughly forty years old—for the American religious right. It was in the 1970s that right-wing evangelicals discovered common ground with Jewish neoconservatives on the subject of

---

* In 2010, Muslims made up 7.5 percent of the population in France, 5 percent in Germany, and 4.6 percent in the United Kingdom, but only 0.8 percent in the United States. Projections for 2030 are that Muslims will make up 11.3 percent of the French population, 7.1 percent of Germans, 8.2 percent of U.K. residents, and 1.7 percent of Americans. Such demographic projections by the Pew Research Center are based on current birthrates and rates of immigration—both of which could, of course, change in two decades. Birthrates, in particular, frequently defy demographic projections based on present trends. The huge influx of refugees fleeing war in Syria could also have a major impact.

Israel. The Jewish neocons, in embracing the conservative evangeli-cals on this issue, have simply decided to ignore the main reason why right-wing Christians value the State of Israel so highly. For those who believe in the book of Revelation, modern Israel will be the site of the battle of Armageddon, when every last non-Christian on earth will be left to perish (the ultimate penalty in the fundamentalist fantasy world for refusing to convert). At the same time, fundamentalist believers will be whisked up to heaven to "rapture"—a word used as both a verb and a noun in the far-out precincts of the Christian right. For the hard political left, by contrast—especially in Europe—the trouble is Israel itself, always seen as a guilty, illegitimate wolf attacking Palestinian lambs.

But let us suppose, for a moment, that a miracle far more marvelous than the parting of the Red Sea has occurred. Israel has withdrawn from the occupied territories and dismantled the settlements; Hamas and all other Palestinian combatants have recognized the right of Israel to exist; and a secure Palestinian state has been established. And, oh yes, the Israeli government has persuaded its own zealots to give peace a chance and clamped down hard on those who would use violence to nullify any agreement. Education is flourishing in the new Palestine, and skilled advisers from both Israel and the Palestinian diaspora are pouring across the peaceful border to help rebuild a ravaged land. Even in this fairy-tale scenario, I would bet that Islamic—yes, Islamic; yes, Muslim—terrorists would continue to pose a threat to the physical and mental peace of the world. The new target might be anywhere. It could certainly be the new Palestine, which would be a living reproach to those who wish to isolate Muslims and feed the grievances of the dispossessed. I do not expect, however, that I will have to make good on this bet (which would give me no pleasure), because the toxic mixture of religion and politics among both Israelis and Palestinians means that a miracle of Biblical and Quranic proportions would be needed to produce a real peace settlement.

.

Anyone who thinks that forced conversion is irrelevant to the aims of Islamic terrorists today would do well to read medieval accounts of the First Crusade, which began in 1096, after Pope Urban II issued a call for Christian knights to liberate the "Holy Land" from Muslim control. The parallels between the religiously driven behavior of today's jihadists and that of the good eleventh-century Christian soldiers—as described by both Hebrew and Christian chroniclers—are startling. When Pope Urban issued his call for the First Crusade, he did not suggest that the crusaders massacre Jews during the long trek to Jerusalem. But that is what happened, and one might well wonder exactly what the pope thought thousands of young men, unmoored from their homes and charged with a religious mission to capture and murder "infidels" in a faraway land, were going to do on the long journey from Northern Europe to Jerusalem. Why not practice on that other, older group of infidels—the Jews? Ironically, the crusaders en route to Jerusalem through Europe offered Jews the same choice—convert, leave, or die—offered by ISIS to Christians and other religious minorities in Iraq and Syria.

Accounts by medieval chroniclers of the destruction of Jewish communities on the crusaders' route south resemble newspaper accounts in 2014 of the ISIS occupation of cities in Iraq and Syria. The town of Trier, on the Moselle River, was an early stop for the crusaders. A Hebrew chronicler reported that, after the Jewish community had made an unsuccessful attempt, by paying off a bishop, to persuade the crusaders to bypass their community, the trapped Jews sought refuge in the bishop's palace. Fearful that he, too, would be murdered by the crusaders, the bishop told the Jews, "The emperor himself could not save you. . . . Be converted or accept upon yourselves the judgment of heaven." The chronicler describes the bishop's final abandonment of the Jews. "In the gateway there was a door like the grate of a furnace. The enemy stood around the palace by the hundreds and thousands, grasping sharp swords. They stood ready to swallow them alive, body and flesh. Then the bishop's military officer and ministers entered the palace and said to them: 'Thus said our lord the bishop: Convert or leave his place. I do not wish to preserve you any longer, . . . You cannot be saved—your God does not wish to save you as in earlier days.'"[7] Albert of Aix, a Christian, described a similar slaughter in Mainz at the hands of a band of crusaders headed by one Count Emico. Again, there is a bishop who promises the Jews protection for money but is unable to deliver. "Then the excellent Bishop of the city cautiously set aside the incredible amount of money received from them [the Jews].

He placed the Jews in the very spacious hall of his own house, away from the sight of Emico and his followers, that they might remain safe and sound in a very secure and strong place." The Jews were anything but safe, as Albert goes on to explain:

> But Emico and the rest of his band held a council and, after sunrise, attacked the Jews in the hall with arrows and lances. Breaking the bolts and doors, they killed the Jews, about seven hundred in number, who in vain resisted the force and attack of so many thousands. They killed the women, also, and with their swords pierced tender children of whatever age and sex. . . . Horrible to say, mothers cut the throats of nursing children with knives and stabbed others, preferring them to perish thus by their own hand rather than to be killed by the weapons of the uncircumcised.
>
> From this cruel slaughter of the Jews a few escaped; and a few because of fear, rather than because of love of the Christian faith, were baptized. With very great spoils taken from this people, Count Emico, Clarebol, Thomas, and all that intolerable company of men and women then continued on their way to Jerusalem. . . .[8]

There are so many common elements in the behavior of the crusaders en route to recapture Christian shrines from Muslims and the terror inflicted by groups like ISIS that, were it not for photographs of weapons that did not exist in the eleventh century, a Martian might assume that these were contemporaneous events. They include the choice between conversion and exile or death; the murders of women and children as well as of men who take up arms against the marauders; the destruction of cultural artifacts that offend the beliefs of the terrorists; and the imposition of financial penalties for anyone—"convert" or not—who tries to stay.

In June 2014, ISIS occupied the Iraqi city of Mosul, where Christians had coexisted for more than a millennium with Muslims. The city was also home to the Yazidis, a tiny religious sect whose theology includes elements of Zoroastrianism as well as Islam and Christianity, and the Mandeans, an ancient non-Christian Gnostic faith whose prophet is not Jesus but John the Baptist. And there were at least two sects of Shiite Muslims, whose interpretation of Islam ran counter to whatever medieval concepts ISIS professes to represent. After blowing up a thirteenth-century Muslim shrine that had survived the Mongol invasion and possessed a fabled vaulted honeycomb ceiling—the terrorists have made a concerted effort to destroy any Muslim, Christian, or ancient pagan art objects they consider idolatrous—ISIS fighters then turned to the people of Mosul. According to CNN, whose team of reporters included many Arabic-speakers, ISIS ordered the Christians trapped in Mosul to convert to Islam, pay extra taxes to Islamic Shariah courts, or face "death by the sword." Christians who did not agree to convert and pay extra taxes were given a deadline to leave the city before they would be put to death.[9] Sound familiar?

Another terrible similarity between the plight of the Rhineland's Jews during the First Crusade and the situation of all religious groups targeted by terrorists in the Middle East is the uncertainty about whether even an agreement to convert would help a person avoid execution—at least long enough to flee. Forced converts in the Middle East today (including Western hostages), like Conversos and Moriscos in Spain during the Inquisition, can never really win. Who would not suspect a Christian (or Muslim) in territory controlled by ISIS of concealing his true beliefs in order to save his life by embracing the terrorists' brand of Islam?

•

The horrors now being perpetrated in the name of a particular form of Islam provide yet another demonstration of what most religions, unmediated and unchecked by secular law, have been capable of doing throughout history. It took European Christendom more than six centuries to move from the mind-set that produced the Crusades to the *beginnings* of the concept of freedom of religion as a human right. For reasons that are beyond the scope of this book, and are political as well as religious, only a small proportion of the world's largest Muslim communities have extensive experience with the long battle for freedom of conscience that is one of the greatest achievements of secular democracy. A widely publicized Pew poll of Muslims in Southern Europe, Russia, the Middle East, and Asia shows a close correlation between the absence of experience under secular government and support for strict Shariah penalties. Only 15 percent of Muslims in Bosnia, for example, and only 20 percent in Kosovo, support making Shariah the law of their lands. (Before the massacres of Muslims by Serbian Christians in the 1990s, Bosnia—especially in cities like Sarajevo—was a cosmopolitan society in which religious intermarriage was common.) In Turkey, where traditional Shariah courts were eliminated in the 1920s, only 12 percent of Muslims support government by Islamic law. But in Afghanistan and Pakistan, 99 percent and 84 percent, respectively, want rule by Shariah. In Egypt, where there has always been a huge gap between a secularized, educated elite and the poor—under British colonial rule, as well as since independence in 1953—74 percent of Muslims favor religious justice over secular courts and laws.[10]

·

The relationship between shaky (or nonexistent) secular governing traditions and repression of overall religious freedom is also evident in the persecution of atheists and others who question theocratic practices in the Muslim world. In 2013, a Shariah court in Saudi Arabia—where no religion but Islam is permitted—sentenced the human rights activist Raif Badawi to the ancient penalty of a thousand lashes for "insulting Islam" by establishing a Web site to promote respect for freedom of religion, free speech, and women's rights. The first flogging, which specified lashes to be administered fifty at a time on successive Fridays (the Muslim Sabbath)—took place, in all its medieval glory, in January 2015. By then, the court had actually increased the defendant's original sentence. Saudi officials kindly postponed the second lashing after doctors examined Badawi and found that his wounds had not healed sufficiently for him to be flogged again without dying. The practice of letting torture victims heal just enough so that they can live to be tortured another time is also an ancient one.

Indonesia, by contrast, has a "religious freedom" law that does guarantee freedom—but only for believers in Islam, Catholicism, Protestantism, Buddhism, Confucianism, and Hinduism. Approximately 88 percent of Indonesians are Muslim. Any Indonesian citizen who criticizes *any* of these faiths can be sentenced to up to five years in prison for "insulting a major religion." (Presumably, it is all right to insult the "minor religions" not specified in the law.) If the Internet is used as a forum for negative comments about religion, an additional six-year sentence may be imposed for blasphemy. Indonesia's constitution, based on a political philosophy called Pancasila, criminalizes blasphemy at the same time that it "guarantees" freedom of religion and speech. Alexander Aan, a government data analyst and an atheist raised in a traditionalist Muslim family, was convicted in 2012 of "inciting religious hatred" for posting commentaries explaining his nonbelief in the existence of God on an atheist Facebook site established by Indonesians living in the Netherlands. When Aan's Facebook postings became public knowledge in January 2012 (none of the articles about his case explained exactly how that happened), a mob showed up at his government office. "They wanted me to stop saying there is no God," he explained. "I told them it was my right to express my beliefs."[11] Police officers stepped in, supposedly to prevent violence, and Aan was taken to the local police station and charged with inciting religious hatred. Having been sentenced to two and a half years in prison in June 2012, he was paroled after nineteen months. Before his trial, police had to transfer Aan from his local prison in West Sumatra's capital, Padang, because he was badly beaten by a group of inmates who knew that he was an atheist. There were also public calls for his beheading.

While he was awaiting his sentence in 2012, Aan told a correspondent for *The Guardian* that he considered himself an atheist from an early age but hid his beliefs from his family and participated in all Muslim rituals. "From 11, I thought, 'if God exists, why is there suffering? Why is there war, poverty, hell. My family would ask me my thoughts but I knew my answers would cause problems, so I kept quiet." When he was twenty-six, in 2008, he finally told his family that he was an atheist, and his parents and siblings responded with disappointment and pleas for him to return to Islam.[12]

According to international human rights organizations, persecution of all religious minorities—including those protected by Indonesia's constitution—has increased in Indonesia during the past ten years. Although both Catholicism and Protestantism are supposedly protected religions, the Indonesian Communion of Churches has reported that at least eighty churches have been closed each year since 2004. Other unprotected groups, such as the Baha'i and Shia and Ahmadiyah Muslims—just as in the Middle East—have faced mob violence, sometimes leading to death, from terrorists. But atheists occupy a special place in the psyches of those who want to see Indonesia turn in a more radical and theocratic Islamist direction. "If you are not a religious person, you might be dangerous to others, behaving without control and doing anything you like," said the Muslim Padang clan chief, Zainuddin Datuk Rajo Lenggang. "Religion brings order. You cannot be an individualist."[13]

•

What Indonesia demonstrates, above all, is the impossibility of true freedom of conscience under any legal system based on favoritism for particular religions or for religion in general. Many Americans, including supposedly sophisticated members of the national media, just don't get it. In *The Wall Street Journal*, Benedict Rogers reports:

> According to the guiding political philosophy, Pancasila, Indonesia is a land of religious tolerance. The country's six recognized religions . . . supposedly enjoy equal protection under the law in the Muslim-majority nation. Pancasila is Indonesia's official ideology. Children nationwide have been taught to believe it since the country's independence in 1945. Pancasila is also a myth.[14]

Of course Pancasila is a myth. And even if it were everything it claimed to be, religious "tolerance" cannot exist under a government that officially favors six hundred religions, six religions, or one religion. Unless people are free to convert to any religion or to reject religious belief altogether, there is no such thing as true liberty of conscience.

Wherever there is endemic confusion between religious and secular law, religious dissent and religious dissenters, of every ilk, are treated as the Other, the enemy. Vaguely expressed ideals of religious tolerance are no substitute for written guarantees. In Indonesia's neighbor Malaysia, the government prohibits the use of the Malay word for God—which just happens to be "Allah"—by non-Muslims. (About 60 percent of Malaysians are Muslim, but the country has substantial Buddhist, Christian, and Hindu minorities.) The ruling is posted on the government's "e-fatwa" Web site. Since 1981, the printing, publication, and possession of Malay-language Bibles has been against the law, on the grounds that vernacular Bibles could be used to proselytize Muslims (an illegal act in Malaysia) and seduce them into converting to another religion. The backstory to this Malaysian law's concern about proselytizing is the seventeenth-century translation of the King James Bible into Malay, financed by Robert Boyle for the explicit purpose of promoting conversions to Christianity among indigenous peoples in an area where the English were establishing a naval and trading presence. In today's Muslim-majority Malaysia, it is emphatically *not* illegal for Muslims to proselytize citizens of other religions. Again, fear and loathing of conversion to the "wrong" religion emerge as central concerns of theocracies—in this case, of a government that presents itself to the West as the very model of a modern, tolerant Muslim state where minorities may practice their religions (as long as they don't flash vernacular Bibles around on the bus).

Limited religious toleration was a huge step forward in seventeenth-century Europe; in the twenty-first century, grudging toleration shows only that much of the world is far behind on the road illuminated by ideas of human rights that emerged from the Enlightenment and nineteenth-century secular liberalism. Moreover, many people in many parts of the world do not want to go down that road at all.

Some years ago, in a review of my book *Freethinkers,* an American religious conservative criticized me for my positive view of the "so-called" Enlightenment. Since he was a Protestant, he presumably did not object to my unmodified use of the term "Reformation." The Enlightenment bashers like to focus on the Jacobin terror in France and ignore the Scottish, British, and American Enlightenments—as well as the Enlightenment-steeped framers of the Constitution, who brought the United States into being without the internal revolutionary terror that occurred in countries, such as France, with a long history of a state-established church tied to the monarchy and aristocracy. Most "what if?" questions cannot be answered with any degree of certitude. We do know, however, what societies look like today if they have *not* gone through the tortuous, centuries-long journey from medieval theocracy through an Enlightenment that—however flawed and still a work in progress—recognizes the right of all human beings to believe exactly what they want, to change their religious beliefs as often as they want, or to believe in no religion at all. We can answer the question of what the Western world would have been like without the Enlightenment because we can see what other human beings are enduring now for holding the wrong beliefs in the wrong place at the wrong time, in societies where so-called secular law is subordinate to the laws and lawlessness of self-appointed spokesmen for God.

The great irony inherent in attempts to suppress both religious proselytizing and religious conversion (unless the convert chooses the faith favored by a state or a would-be state run by terrorists) is that they ignore not only the villain of modern secularism but the older historical experience and beliefs that absolutists claim to revere.

The history of all religions suggests that the human desire to explore new forms of belief is unstoppable, and that coercion, for whatever length of time it may succeed, produces a false uniformity that collapses as swiftly or slowly as social conditions permit. In his Edinburgh lectures, William James argued that all religions develop as a solution to a profound uneasiness. He described the uneasiness, "reduced to its simplest terms," as "a sense that there is *something wrong about us* as we naturally stand," whereas the solution "is a sense that *we are saved from the wrongness* by making proper connection with the higher powers."[15] That the "proper connection" can never be permanently imposed through exemplary beheadings or the banning of "sacred" texts in the vernacular is a lesson that has been administered repeatedly to various groups of coercive True Believers (including secularist totalitarians). James was talking about being saved from a sense of wrongness in a psychological and/or spiritual sense; this liberal thinker of the nineteenth century was, after all, a descendant of Calvinists. If the religious impulse is indeed rooted in a profound sense of unworthiness and the need for rescue from a fallen state, the inability of humans to agree on one "proper connection" to a greater power—regardless of external pressure—is the most persistent feature of religious history.

When the Cathars were annihilated in the early fourteenth century, any monarch or bishop in Western Europe would have assumed that Roman Catholicism had been established, for all time, as the only proper route to Christian salvation. Yet, it took less than two centuries for Martin Luther to usher in the Reformation by nailing his theses to the door of the church in Wittenberg (or, at least, to be credited with nailing his theses to the door). After then, it became a matter of decades, not centuries, before one new form of Christianity after another appeared—and before all of the dissident denominations began seeking converts in spite of extreme persecution. James argues that one of the most "curious peculiarities" of human beings is their susceptibility to sudden and complete conversion, but it is even more peculiar that people have shown themselves willing to die for their choice of one faith over another when both are rooted in the unseen and unprovable. That many people—not necessarily a majority, but enough—are willing to make the ultimate sacrifice is undeniable. Thus, belief in the effectiveness of forced conversion, whether politically or spiritually motivated (usually both), is always a demonstration of evidence-proof faith taken to an extreme. It is proof of a religion's weakness, not strength—of a lack of confidence in a particular faith's persuasive spiritual powers, even when it possesses the temporal power of a theocracy. As the well-educated liar Bin Laden certainly knew, the early Muslim rulers of al-Andalus did not force Christians or Jews to convert to Islam, but many did in fact convert—whether for social advantage, because they fell in love with a Muslim, or, who knows, maybe because the newer faith seemed to offer a more proper connection, in the Jamesian sense, to a higher power. And it couldn't have hurt that the Muslim invaders—unlike the Visigoths and the Christians—were introducing new crops, restoring aqueducts, and disposing of sewage in ways unknown since Roman times.

The United States—the only nation in which it has been against the law, right from the start, for the government to interfere with freedom of religion—offers further proof, if more is needed, of the appeal of voluntary conversion. As an atheist, I take no pleasure in the fact that so many Americans are so eager to connect with a higher power that they would rather embrace not one but two or three faiths in a lifetime than entertain the possibility that there may be no power greater than our own. Furthermore, the American separation between church and state—which the leaders of the religious Right have tried so tenaciously to deny and demolish—is a historical tradition and a legal fact for which they should fall on their knees and thank their god. The United States is not a Christian nation, but Americans are, as Supreme Court Justice William O. Douglas observed, "a religious people." We may be a more religious people than the inhabitants of secular Europe precisely because we are not a Christian nation with a Christian government. American civil society might well be as secular as France or Spain today if we, too, had encoded in our national DNA the memory of having been imprisoned, tortured, or murdered by the state for our choice of the wrong religion.

The catch is that government noninterference with the demonstrably strong human impulse toward voluntary conversion does not serve the goals of only one religion; if the heritage of persecution is strong, it may not even serve the purposes of religion in general. Yes, if you allow the distribution of Malay-language Bibles in Malaysia, some Muslims will probably decide that they prefer Jesus to Muhammad. And, yes, if Saudi Arabia stops whipping human rights activists until their backs are too bloody to be whipped any more, some Saudis will doubtless decide that they do not want any part of any god—and embrace Paine's credo, "My own mind is my own church." That is the nightmare of the modern inquisitors who threaten the peace and security of the world. That would be the glory of a world in which the liberty to choose any religion or no religion is recognized as a universal human right, and forced conversion becomes, finally, nothing more than a hideous oxymoron from the past.

ACKNOWLEDGMENTS

The idea for this book was first suggested to me fifteen years ago by my dear friend and onetime editor Aaron Asher, who died in 2008. I discussed many of the premises of *Strange Gods* with Aaron during the years before I actually started writing.

This is my third book published by Pantheon, and I cannot say enough in praise of Editor in Chief Dan Frank's meticulous attention to every detail involved in looking after a book that takes years to research and write. The broad knowledge Dan brings to the whole process was always more rare than sentimentalists about the "good old days" of book publishing like to think, but his qualities are even rarer today.

Betsy Sallee, editorial assistant *extraordinaire,* made everything work more smoothly and displayed seemingly inexhaustible patience with an author who is digitally challenged when confronted by electronic copy editing. Kelly Blair (along with Caravaggio) designed the spectacular cover. Jane Hardick and Maralee Youngs are the best proofreaders I have encountered in my career.

I especially want to thank Hank Burchard, who was one of my first copy editors at *The Washington Post* when we were kids in the newspaper business, for reading the entire manuscript and, once more, applying his pencil to my copy. Mark Lee, Angeline Goreau, and Johanna Kaplan made valuable suggestions along the way. Philip Roth read the last chapter and provided a word of encouragement at the moment that comes to nearly every writer—the spasm of fear, when you are nearing the end of years of work on a book, that makes you think you will never finish.

Bob and Blaikie Worth, whose interest in anything to do with secularism never seems to run dry, provided their usual supportive attention.

Most of this book was written in the Frederick Lewis Allen Room of The New York Public Library, where I spent years reading real, physical books—the kind that make you think of other scholars and authors who held the same copies in their hands more than a century ago. I am especially indebted to Jay Barksdale and Carolyn Broomhead, who were in charge of the research rooms for writers while I was working on *Strange Gods*.

As always, I owe much to my agents and friends, Georges and Anne Borchardt.

NOTES

Author's Note: When a printed work is easily accessible online from a reliable source, I have indicated this with a parenthetical (W) after the endnote. In most cases, the work can be accessed by typing the precise title into a search engine. Because Web addresses change so frequently, I have provided them only when the page has been maintained continuously for several years by an established institution.

1 AUGUSTINE OF HIPPO (354–430)

1. Saint Augustine, *Confessions,* trans. R. S. Pine-Coffin (New York, 1961), p. 59.
2. Ibid., p. 32.
3. Peter Brown, *Augustine of Hippo: A Biography* (Berkeley, 1967), p. 160.
4. Christopher Hitchens, "When the King Saved God," *Vanity Fair,* May 2011. (W)
5. Benzion Netanyahu, *The Origins of the Inquisition in Fifteenth Century Spain* (New York, 1995), p. 14.
6. Saint Augustine, *The City of God,* trans. John Healey (Edinburgh, 1909), vol. 2, pp. 200–201.
7. James Carroll, *Constantine's Sword: The Church and the Jews* (New York, 2001), p. 218.
8. Ibid., p. 219.
9. Cited in Marc Saperstein, *Moments of Crisis in Jewish-Christian Relations* (Philadelphia, 1989), p. 11.
10. Saint Augustine, *Confessions of St. Augustine,* trans. Rev. Dr. E. B. Pusey (1838; London, 1909), p. 37.
11. C. R. C. Alberry, *A Manichean Psalmbook,* cited in Brown, *Augustine of Hippo,* p. 49.
12. Pine-Coffin, Introduction, in Augustine, *Confessions,* p. 24.
13. Cited in Brown, *Augustine of Hippo,* p. 48.
14. Augustine, *Confessions,* Pusey trans., pp. 100–101.
15. Ibid., pp. 9–10.
16. Ibid., pp. 33–34.
17. Ibid., p. 34.
18. Garry Wills, *Augustine's Confessions* (Princeton, 2011), p. 23.

19. Augustine, *Confessions,* Pusey trans., p. 34.
20. St. Augustine, *Soliloquies,* book I, p. 17, trans. C. C. Starbuck, rev. and ed. by Keven Knight as originally published in English in *From Nicene and Post-Nicene Fathers,* 1st ser., vol. 7, ed. Philip Schaff (Buffalo, N.Y., 1888), http://www.newadvent.org/fathers/1703.htm. (W)
21. Saint Augustine, *On the Sermon on the Mount,* book I, p. 41, trans. William Findlay, rev. and ed. by Keven Knight as originally published in English in *From Nicene and Post-Nicene Fathers,* 1st ser., vol. 6, ed. Philip Schaff (Buffalo, N.Y., 1888), www.newadvent.org/fathers/16011.htm. (W)
22. Marcus Aurelius, *Meditations,* trans. Christopher Gill (Oxford, Eng., 2013), book 6, p. 41.
23. *Confessions,* Pine-Coffin trans., p. 178.
24. Saint Augustine, *The Confessions of St. Augustine,* trans. J. G. Pilkington (New York, 1963), p. 173.
25. Ibid., pp. 177–78.
26. Augustine, *Confessions,* Pusey trans., p. 297.
27. Ibid., pp. 296–97.
28. Ibid., pp. 299–300.

2 THE WAY, THE TRUTH, THE LIFE, THE EMPIRE

1. Edward Gibbon, *The Decline and Fall of the Roman Empire* (New York, 1954), vol. 2, p. 816.
2. Cited in Sarah Zielinski, "Hypatia, Ancient Alexandria's Great Female Scholar," Smithsonian.com, March 14, 2010. (W)
3. Charles Freeman, *The Closing of the Western Mind* (New York, 2005), p. xix.
4. Augustine, Letter 125.2, cited in Peter Brown, *Through the Eye of a Needle: Wealth, the Fall of Rome, and the Making of Christianity in the West, 350–550 AD* (Princeton, 2012), p. 324.
5. Freeman, *Closing,* p. 84.
6. Ibid., p. 85.
7. Lactantius, "On the Deaths of Persecutors," p. 33. (W)
8. Cited in Rod Nordland, "Persecution Defines Yemen's Remaining Jews," *New York Times,* Feb. 18, 2015.
9. Robin Lane Fox, *Pagans and Christians* (New York, 1986), p. 17.
10. Brown, *Through the Eye of a Needle,* p. xxiv.
11. Ibid., p. xxvii.
12. Cited in Jonathan Kirsch, *God Against the Gods* (New York, 2004), p. 247.
13. Rosemary Radford Ruether, *Faith and Fratricide: The Theological Roots of Anti-Semitism* (New York, 1974), p. 193.
14. Cited in John Holland Smith, *The Death of Classical Paganism* (New York, 1976), pp. 169–70.
15. Benzion Netanyahu, *The Origins of the Inquisition in Fifteenth Century Spain* (New York, 1995), p. 14.
16. N. McLynn, *Ambrose of Milan: Church and Count in a Christian Capital* (Berkeley, 1994), pp. 181–95, cited in Freeman, *Closing,* p. 225.
17. Morris Kline, *Mathematical Thought from Ancient to Modern Times* (Oxford and New York, 1990), vol. 1, p. 181.

18. Peter Brown, *The World of Late Antiquity* (New York, 1989), p. 104.
19. Ibid., p. 33.
20. Socrates Scholasticus, "Of Hypatia the Female Philosopher," cited in Michael A. B. Deakin, *Hypatia of Alexandria: Mathematician and Martyr* (Buffalo, 2007), pp. 147–48. (W)
21. John of Nikiu, *The Chronicle of John of Nikiu,* chapter LXXXIV, cited in ibid, pp. 148–49. (W)
22. Cited in Pierre Chuvin, *A Chronicle of the Last Pagans,* trans. B. A. Archer (Cambridge, Mass., 1990), p. 86.
23. Larry Rohter, "Science vs. Zealots, 1500 Years Ago," *New York Times,* May 23, 2010. (W)
24. Chap. XVI, "The Temple of Serapis (AD 391)," *Sketches of Church History.* (W)
25. Ibid.

3 COERCION, CONVERSION, AND HERESY

1. Saint Augustine, "On Catechizing the Uninstructed," chap. 6, rev. and ed. by Kevin Knight as originally published in English in *From Nicene and Post-Nicene Fathers,* 1st ser., vol. 3, ed. Philip Schaff (Buffalo, N.Y., 1887), http://www.newadvent.org/fathers/1303.htm. (W)
2. Saint Augustine, *Confessions,* trans. R. S. Pine-Coffin (New York, 1961), pp. 75–76.
3. Michael S. Horton, "Pelagianism: The Religion of the Natural Man." (W)
4. Pelagius, "To Demetrias," in Peter Brown, *Augustine of Hippo: A Biography* (Berkeley, 1967), p. 343.
5. In John Ferguson, *Pelagius: A Historical and Theological Study* (Cambridge, Eng., 1956), p. 60.
6. In ibid.
7. Ibid., p. 160.

4 BISHOP PAUL OF BURGOS (c. 1352–1435)

1. Yitzhak Baer, *A History of the Jews in Christian Spain,* trans. Louis Schoffman (Philadelphia, 1961), vol. 1, p. 141.
2. Joseph Pérez, *The Spanish Inquisition: A History,* trans. Janet Lloyd (New Haven, 2005), p. 12.
3. Benzion Netanyahu, *The Origins of the Inquisition in Fifteenth Century Spain* (New York, 1995), p. 168.
4. Cited in ibid., p. 140.
5. Judith Gale Krieger, "Pablo de Santa Maria, the Purim Letter and *Siete Edades del Mundo,*" *Mester,* vol. 17, no. 2 (Fall 1988). (W)
6. Baer, *History of the Jews,* p. 141.
7. Netanyahu, *Origins of the Inquisition,* pp. 170–71.
8. Ibid., p. 171.
9. Baer, *History of the Jews,* p. 141.
10. Cited in ibid., pp. 143–44.
11. Cited in ibid., pp. 147–48.
12. Ibid., p. 148.

13. Cited in ibid., p. 149.

14. Krieger, "Pablo de Santa Maria." (W)

5 *IMPUREZA DE SANGRE:* THE CRUMBLING OF THE CONVIVENCIA

1. S. M. Adams et al., "The Genetic Legacy of Religious Diversity and Intolerance: Paternal Lineages of Christians, Jews, and Muslims in the Iberian Peninsula," *American Journal of Human Genetics,* vol. 83, no. 6 (Dec. 12, 2008), pp. 725–36. (W)

2. Roger Collins, *The Arab Conquest of Spain, 710–797* (Cambridge, Mass., 1989), pp. 720–97.

3. María Rosa Menocal, *The Ornament of the World: How Muslims, Jews, and Christians Created a Culture of Tolerance in Medieval Spain* (Boston, 2002), p. 25.

4. Matthew Carr, *Blood and Faith: The Purging of Muslim Spain* (New York, 2009), p. 17.

5. Menocal, *Ornament of the World,* p. 28.

6. Carr, *Blood and Faith,* p. 3.

7. Menocal, *Ornament of the World,* p. 135.

8. Joseph Pérez, *The Spanish Inquisition,* trans. Janet Lloyd (New Haven, Conn., 2005), p. 2.

9. Cited in Robert Pasnau, "The Islamic Scholar Who Gave Us Modern Philosophy," National Endowment for the Humanities, Nov.–Dec. 2011, http://www.neh.gov/humanities/2011/novemberdecember/feature/the-islamic-scholar-who-gave-us-modern-philosophy. (W)

10. Cited in Rabbi Michael Leo Samuel, "Maimonides' Practical Advice: On Feigning Apostasy . . . ," Nov. 2009, http://rabbimichaelsamuel.com.

11. Shaul Magid, "The Great Islamic Rabbi," *Washington Post,* Dec. 30, 2008. (W)

12. David Shasha, "Moses Maimonides: Arab Jew, Religious Humanist," *Huffington Post,* March 9, 2010. (W)

6 THE INQUISITION AND THE END

1. Joseph Pérez, *The Spanish Inquisition,* trans. Janet Lloyd (New Haven, Conn., 2005), p. 27.

2. Ibid., p. 34.

3. Howard M. Sachar, *Farewell España: The World of the Sephardim Remembered* (New York, 1994), p. 73, cited in Cullen Murphy, *God's Jury: The Inquisition and the Making of the Modern World* (Boston, 2012), p. 102.

4. Pérez, *Spanish Inquisition,* pp. 24–25.

5. Caesarius of Heisterbach, "Dialogue on Miracles V," *Medieval Sourcebook,* www.fordham.edu.

6. Kevin Ingram, ed., *The Conversos and Moriscos in Late Medieval Spain and Beyond* (Boston, 2009), vol. 1, p. 12.

7. Pérez, *Spanish Inquisition,* p. 49.

8. Ibid., p. 50.

9. Cited in ibid., p. 185.

10. Cited in Peter Godman, *The Saint as Censor: Robert Bellarmine Between Inquisition and Index* (Boston, 2000), p. 3.

7 JOHN DONNE (1572–1631)

1. Cited in Christopher Hibbert, *The Virgin Queen: Elizabeth I, Genius of the Golden Age* (Reading, Mass., 1991), p. 89.
2. John Stubbs, *John Donne: The Reformed Soul* (New York, 2007), p. viii.
3. "Thirty-nine Articles of Religion," Church of England, 1562. (W)
4. King James to the Papal Nuncio, Nov. 1603, cited in Stubbs, *John Donne*, p. 180.
5. John Donne, *Pseudo-Martyr*, ed. Anthony Raspa (London, 1993), chap. 6, pp. 143–44.
6. Ibid., "The Preface," p. 13.
7. Ibid., chap. 3, p. 37.
8. John Donne, *The Sermons of John Donne*, ed. George R. Potter and Evelyn M. Simpson (1953–62), vol. 4, pp. 106–7.
9. Donne, "Divine Meditations," 8, lines 1–2.
10. Donne, *Devotions upon Emergent Occasions* (Ann Arbor, 1959), pp. 23–24.
11. Ibid., Meditation XVII, pp. 107–8.
12. Isaak Walton, *The Lives of John Donne, Sir Henry Wotton, Richard Hooker, and Robert Sanderson* (London, 1670, reprinted 1927), p. 75.
13. Donne, "Death's Duel," in *Devotions*, p. 171.

8 "NOT WITH SWORD . . . BUT WITH PRINTING"

1. Thomas Foxe, *Acts and Monuments*, ed. S. J. Cattley and J. Pratt (London, 1877), p. 720.
2. Kenneth G. Appold, *The Reformation: A Brief History* (London, 2011), p. 59.
3. Ibid., p. 69.
4. Miriam Usher Chrisman, "Lay Response to the Protestant Reformation in Germany: 1520–1528," in *Reformation Principle and Practice*, ed. Peter N. Brooks (London, 1980), p. 36.
5. Ibid., p. 41.
6. Ibid., pp. 38–39.
7. Ibid., p. 43.
8. Ibid., p. 46.
9. Appold, *Reformation*, p. 94.

9 PERSECUTION IN AN AGE OF RELIGIOUS CONVERSION

1. Kenneth G. Appold, *The Reformation: A Brief History* (London, 2011), p. 169.
2. Stefan Zweig, *The Right to Heresy: Castellio Against Calvin*, trans. Eden and Cedar Paul (New York, 1936), pp. 43, 55.
3. Lawrence and Nancy Goldstone, *Out of the Flames* (New York, 2002), p. 32.
4. Robert Ingersoll to Philip G. Peabody, May 27, 1890. Cited in Susan Jacoby, *The Great Agnostic: Robert Ingersoll and American Freethought* (New Haven, 2012), pp. 203–5.
5. William Osler. "Michael Servetus," *Johns Hopkins Hospital Bulletin*, vol. XXI, no. 226 (Jan. 1910).
6. Cited in Roland H. Bainton, *Hunted Heretic: The Life and Death of Michael Servetus, 1511–1553* (Providence, 2011), pp. 144–46.

7. Cited in Zweig, *Right to Heresy,* p. 156.

8. Rev. Frank J. Schulman, "Unitarianism Begins: Sebastian Castellio," Unitarian Universalist Fellowship of Fairbanks, Alas., 2003. (W)

9. "The Servetus Controversy," H. Henry Van Meeter Center for Calvin Studies, Calvin College. (W)

10. Benjamin J. Kaplan, *Divided by Faith: Religious Conflict and the Practice of Toleration in Early Modern Europe* (Cambridge, Mass., 2007), p. 85.

11. Pierre Jurieu, *Last Efforts of Afflicted Innocence,* cited in John Marshall, *John Locke: Toleration and Early Enlightenment Culture* (Cambridge, Eng., 2006), p. 19.

10 MARGARET FELL (1614–1702): WOMAN'S MIND, WOMAN'S VOICE

1. Charles James Spence Manuscript, chap. III, p. 135, cited in Isabel Ross, *Margaret Fell: Mother of Quakerism* (York, Eng., 1984), p. 11.

2. Cited in George Fox, *A Journal or Historical Account of the Life, Travels, Sufferings, Christian Experiences, and Labour of Love in the Work of the Ministry, of That Ancient, Eminent, and Faithful Servant of Jesus Christ, George Fox, with Contributions by Margaret Fox and William Penn,* vol. 1, p. 62 (orig. published 1694). The full text, scanned from an 1831 edition, is available online at www.hallvworthington.com. (W)

3. Cited in Ross, *Margaret Fell,* p. 11.

4. Ibid.

5. Jan de Hartog, *The Peaceable Kingdom* (New York, 1972), p. 38.

6. Testimony to George Fox by Margaret Fell, in Ross, *Margaret Fell,* p. 15.

7. Margaret Fell, *A brief collection of remarkable passages and occurences relating to the birth, education, life, conversion, travels, services, and deep sufferings of that ancient, eminent, and faithful servant of the Lord, Margaret Fell, by her second marriage, Margaret Fox* (London, 1710), cited in *Autobiographical Writings by Early Quaker Women,* ed. David Booy (Hampshire, Eng., 2004), pp. 151–52.

8. Bonnelyn Young Kunze, *Margaret Fell and the Rise of Quakerism* (London, 1994), p. 137.

9. Margaret Fell, *Works,* pp. 202–10, cited in ibid.

10. John Marshall, *John Locke, Toleration and Early Enlightenment Culture* (Cambridge, Eng., 2006), p. 112.

11. Cited in Ross, *Margaret Fell,* p. 211.

12. Cited in ibid., p. 218.

13. Cited in Richard H. Popkin, "Spinoza's Relations with the Quakers in Amsterdam," *Quaker History,* vol. 73, no. 1 (Spring 1984), pp. 14–28. (W)

14. Kunze, *Margaret Fell,* p. 230.

15. Bonnelyn Young Kunze, "An Unpublished Work of Margaret Fell," *Proceedings of the American Philosophical Society,* vol. 130, no. 2 (Dec. 1986), pp. 424–52. (W)

16. Margaret Fell, Final Letter to the Assemblies of Quakers, April 1700, in *Margaret Fell's Letters—The Way to Righteousness,* www.hallvworthington.com. (W)

11 RELIGIOUS CHOICE AND EARLY ENLIGHTENMENT THOUGHT

1. Papers of George Washington, Library of Congress, vol. 325, pp. 19–20. A facsimile is available online at www.tourosynagogue.org. (W)

2. John Marshall, *John Locke, Toleration and Early Enlightenment Culture* (Cambridge, Eng., 2006), p. 18.

3. Cited in Andrew Hill, "Thomas Aikenhead," Dictionary of Unitarian and Universalist Biography. (W)

4. "Last Heretic—Edward Wightman," Burton-on-Trent Local History Archive, http://www.burton-on-trent.org.uk/1612-last-heretic. (W)

5. Cited in Marshall, *John Locke*, p. 107.

6. Cited in Paul Mark Sandler, "The Trial of William Penn," *Daily Record*, Feb. 9, 2007. (W)

7. Ibid.

8. E. Benoit, *Histoire de l'édit*, vol. 3, pp. 445–58, cited in ibid., p. 20.

9. Baruch Spinoza, *A Theologico-Political Tract*, in *The Chief Works of Benedict de Spinoza*, trans. R. H. M. Elwes (London, 1900), vol. 1, p. 27. (Hereafter *Tractatus*.)

10. Cited in Marshall, *John Locke*, p. 156.

11. Spinoza, *Tractatus*, vol. 3, p. 246.

12. Cited in Isabel Ross, *Margaret Fell: Mother of Quakerism* (York, Eng., 1984), p. 91.

13. Rebecca Newberger Goldstein, *Betraying Spinoza* (New York, 2006), p. 4.

14. Ibid., p. 43.

15. Spinoza, *Tractatus*, frontispiece.

16. Spinoza, Letter XLIX, cited in ibid., p. xxxi.

17. Ibid., p. 261.

18. Rebecca Newberger Goldstein, "Reasonable Doubt," *New York Times*, July 29, 2006.

19. John Locke, *An Essay Concerning Toleration* (London, 1667), in John Locke, *A Letter Concerning Toleration and Other Writings*, ed. Mark Goldie (Indianapolis, 2010), pp. 127–28, http://oll.libertyfund.org/titles/2375. (W)

20. Ibid., p. 123. (W)

21. John Locke, "Amendment I (Petition and Assembly)," in *Letter Concerning Toleration*. (W)

12 MIRACLES VERSUS EVIDENCE:
CONVERSION AND SCIENCE

1. Baruch Spinoza, *The Letters*, trans. S. Shirley (Indianapolis, 1995), p. 124, cited in Jonathan I. Israel, *Radical Enlightenment: Philosophy and the Making of Modernity, 1650–1750* (Oxford, Eng., 2001), p. 242.

2. A. R. Hall and M. B. Hall, "Why Blame Oldenburg?," *Isis*, no. 53 (1962), pp. 482–91.

3. Cited in "Robert Boyle," Stanford Encyclopedia of Philosophy, July 6, 2010. (W)

4. Diana Severance, "Robert Boyle Converted in a Thunderstorm," www.Christianity Today.com. (W)

5. Ibid., p. 5.

6. Robert Boyle, *Boyle on Atheism*, ed. J. J. MacIntosh (Toronto, 2005), pp. 301–2.

7. Ibid., p. 275.

8. Francis Collins, "The Question of God," *Other Voices*, Public Broadcasting Service, 2004. (W)

9. Spinoza, "Of Miracles," in *Tractatus*, chap. 6, p. 81.

10. Robert Boyle, *Selected Philosophical Papers of Robert Boyle*, ed. M. A. Stewart (New York, 1979), sect. II, p. 179.

11. Cited in Michael Hunter, "Aikenhead the Atheist," in *Atheism from the Reformation to the Enlightenment,* ed. Michael Hunter and David Wootton (Oxford, Eng., 1992), p. 227.

12. Boyle, *Selected Philosophical Papers of Robert Boyle,* sect. II, p. 183.

13. Israel, *Radical Enlightenment,* p. 247.

14. Ibid., pp. 248–49.

13 PRELUDE: O MY AMERICA!

1. "A Reply to Mr. Williams His Examination: and Answer of the Letters Sent to Him by John Cotton," in *Publications of the Narragansett Club* (Providence, 1862), 1st ser., vol. II, p. 19, cited in Sidney E. Mead, *The Lively Experiment: The Shaping of Christianity in America* (New York, 1963), p. 13.

2. Cited in Timothy D. Hall, *Anne Hutchinson: Puritan Prophet* (Boston, 2010), p. 9.

3. Ibid., p. 56.

4. Moses Tyler Coit, *A History of American Literature, 1607–1765* (Ithaca, N.Y., 1949), pp. 85–86.

5. Transcript, Trial at the Court at Newton, 1637, of Anne Hutchinson. (W)

6. Ibid.

7. Cited in Hall, *Anne Hutchinson,* p. 147.

8. Cited in Lauri Lebo, "Texas Board of Education Wants to Change History," *Religion Dispatches,* Annenberg Center at the University of Southern California, Aug. 12, 2009. (W)

9. Cited in W. W. Sweet, *Religion in Colonial America* (New York, 1942), pp. 151–52.

10. Jack Rakove, *Revolutionaries* (New York, 2011), p. 77.

11. John A. Dix, *History of the Parish of Trinity Church in the City of New York* (New York, 1889–1950), vol. 1, p. 304, cited in Jon Butler, *Awash in a Sea of Faith* (Cambridge, Mass., 1990), p. 177.

12. Cited in Winthrop Jordan, *White Over Black: American Attitudes Toward the Negro, 1550–1812* (Chapel Hill, N.C., 1968), p. 184.

13. Cited in Butler, *Awash in a Sea of Faith,* p. 140.

14. Thomas Bacon, *Four Sermons Preached at the Parish Church of St. Peter, in Talbot County, . . .* (London, 1753), pp. 30, 31, 34.

15. W. J. Cash, *The Mind of the South* (New York, 1941), p. 81.

16. Solomon Northrup, *Twelve Years a Slave* (New York, 2014), pp. 82–83.

17. Butler, *Awash in a Sea of Faith,* p. 146.

18. Quoted in Albert J. Raboteau, "The Secret Religion of Slaves," *Christianity Today,* http://www.christianitytoday.com/ch/1992/issue33/3342.html.

19. Daniel Pipes, "Servants of Allah: African Muslims Enslaved in the Americas," *Middle East Quarterly,* Dec. 2000. (W)

20. Omar ibn Said, "Autobiography of Omar ibn Said, Slave in North Carolina," 1831, ed. J. Franklin Jameson, *American Historical Review,* vol. 30, no. 4 (July 1925), pp. 787–95. (W)

21. Patrick J. Horn, *Summary of Autobiography of Omar ibn Said, Slave in North Carolina, 1831* (Washington, D.C., 1925), in *Documenting the American South,* University Library of the University of North Carolina at Chapel Hill. (W)

22. Cited in ibid.

23. Cited in ibid.

14 HEINRICH HEINE (1797–1856): CONVICTIONLESS CONVERSION

1. Amos Elon, *The Pity of It All: A Portrait of the German-Jewish Epoch, 1743–1933* (New York, 2002), p. 92.
2. Aharon Appelfeld, *The Conversion,* translated from the Hebrew by Jeffrey M. Green (New York, 1998), pp. 98–101.
3. Cited in "Heinrich Heine," *The Jewish Encyclopedia.* (W)
4. Letter to Moses Moser. April 23, 1826, in Heinrich Heine, *Confessio Judaica* (Berlin, 1925), p. 64, cited in Elon, *Pity of It All.*
5. Heinrich Heine, *Sämtliche Schriften* (Munich, 1975–85), vol. 2, p. 7, cited in ibid., p. 118.
6. Jessica Duchen, "Mendelssohn the Misunderstood," *Jewish Chronicle,* Jan. 22, 2009. (W)
7. Cited in Elon, *Pity of It All,* p. 145.
8. Heinrich Heine, *Heinrich Heine's Life Told in His Own Words,* trans. Arthur Dexter (New York, 1893), pp. 28–29.
9. Ibid., p. 29.
10. Heinrich Heine, "The Home-Coming," in *The Poems of Heine: Complete,* trans. Edgar Alfred Bowring, C.B. (London, 1889), p. 198.
11. Ibid., p. 211.
12. Cited in Ari Joscowicz, "Heinrich Heine's Transparent Masks: Denominational Politics and the Poetics of Emancipation in Nineteenth-Century Germany and France," *German Studies Review,* vol. 32, no. 1 (2011), p. 74. (W)
13. Cited in ibid., p. 71.
14. Heinrich Heine, "The New Jewish Hospital at Hamburg," in *The Standard Book of Jewish Verse,* compiled by Joseph Friedlander, ed. Alexander Kohut (New York, 1917).
15. Heine, Heinrich, Foreword, *The Book of Songs* (East Aurora, N.Y., 1903), pp. ii–iii.
16. Ibid., p. iv.
17. Cited in Elon, *Pity of It All,* p. 142.
18. Heinrich Heine, Preface, *Germany: A Winter's Tale,* 1844, in *The Complete Poems of Heinrich Heine: A Modern English Version,* trans. Hal Draper (Boston, 1982) pp. 481–82.
19. Joscowicz, "Heinrich Heine's Transparent Masks." (W)
20. Cited in ibid. (W)
21. Heinrich Heine, "The Disputation," *Poems of Heine: Complete,* p. 495.
22. Ibid., pp. 498–99.
23. Heine, "Princess Sabbath," trans. Margaret Armour, in *Standard Book of Jewish Verse.*
24. Heine, "Postscript to Romancero," in *Complete Poems,* trans. Draper, p. 695.
25. Heine, "The 'Romancero,'" in *Heinrich Heine's Life,* p. 345.
26. Ibid., p. 346.

15 THE VARIETIES OF COERCIVE EXPERIENCE

1. "We Remember: A Reflection on the Shoah," pt. III, March 16, 1998. (W)
2. David I. Kertzer, *The Popes Against the Jews* (New York, 2001), p. 41.
3. Ibid., p. 43.
4. Correspondance Politique Rome, vol. 1009, pp. 18–19, Archives, Ministères des Affaires Étrangères, cited in ibid., p. 122.

5. David I. Kertzer, *The Kidnapping of Edgardo Mortara* (New York, 1997), p. 302.
6. Hansard Archive of Parliamentary Debates, 3rd ser., vol. xcv, pp. 1323–31. (W)

16 EDITH STEIN (1891–1942): THE SAINTHOOD OF A CONVERTED JEW

1. Edith Stein, *Life in a Jewish Family: Her Unfinished Autobiographical Account,* trans. Josephine Koeppel, O.C.D. (Washington, D.C., 1986), p. 23.
2. Ibid., p. 47.
3. Ibid., p. 266.
4. Ibid., p. 343.
5. Ibid., p. 43.
6. Ibid., p. 260.
7. Ibid., pp. 68–69.
8. Edith Stein, *On the Problem of Empathy,* trans. Waltraut Stein (Washington, D.C., 1989), pp. 88–89.
9. Stein, *Life in a Jewish Family,* p. 293.
10. Ibid., p. 416.
11. Ibid., p. 123.
12. Edith Stein, "Love of the Cross," 1934, http://essays.quotidiana.org/stein/love_of_the_cross/. (W)
13. Josephine Koeppel, O.C.D., in Stein, *Life in a Jewish Family,* p. 425.
14. Segretaria di Stato, Affair Ecclesiastici Straordinari, Germania, Archivio Segreto Vaticano, Vatican City, in David I. Kertzer, *The Pope and Mussolini: The Secret History of Pius XI and the Rise of Fascism in Europe* (New York, 2014), p. 208.
15. Garry Wills, *Papal Sin: Structures of Deceit* (New York, 2000), p. 54.

17 PETER CARTWRIGHT (1785–1872): ANTI-INTELLECTUALISM AND THE BATTLE FOR REASON

1. Peter Cartwright, *Autobiography of Peter Cartwright* (Nashville, 1856), p. 30.
2. Richard Hofstadter, *Anti-Intellectualism in American Life* (New York, 1963), p. 56.
3. Cartwright, *Autobiography,* pp. 37–38.
4. Jon Butler, *Awash in a Sea of Faith* (Cambridge, Mass., 1990), p. 220.
5. *The Adams-Jefferson Letters,* ed. Lester J. Cappon (Chapel Hill, 1959), vol. 2, p. 373.
6. William Bentley, *The Diary of William Bentley* (Salem, Mass., 1905), vol. 3, p. 442.
7. Cartwright, *Autobiography,* pp. 46–47.
8. Ibid., pp. 50–51.
9. Sharon Otterman, "Trinity Church Split on How to Manage $2 Billion Legacy of a Queen," *New York Times,* April 24, 2013. (W)
10. "Burning of the Charlestown Convent," *Boston Evening Transcript,* Aug. 12, 1834, http://www.yale.edu/glc/archive/949.htm. (W)
11. Cartwright, *Autobiography,* p. 28.
12. 319 US 624. (W)

18 REMAKING THE PROTESTANT AMERICAN COMPACT

1. These figures are based on U.S. Census Bureau records from 1870 to 1930.
2. In Alison Leight Cowan, "The Rabbi Cardinal O'Connor Never Knew: His Grandfather," *New York Times,* June 10, 2014. (W)

3. All figures on immigration are extrapolated from U.S. Census records from 1890 to 1940 and from the specifications of the federal Immigration Act of 1924, which established the system of "national origins quotas." A breakdown of quotas for specific countries is available at http://historymatters.gmu.edu/d/5078. (W)

4. President Lyndon B. Johnson's Remarks at the Signing of the Immigration Bill, Liberty Island, NY, Oct. 3, 1965, www.lbjlib.utexas.edu. (W)

5. Charles Bruehl, "Pastoralia, Way of Approach," *Homiletic and Pastoral Review,* vol. XXX (May 1930), pp. 798–801, cited in Milton L. Barron, *People Who Intermarry* (Syracuse, N.Y., 1946), pp. 21–59. Reprinted and revised as "The Church, The State, and Intermarriage," in *The Blending American,* ed. Milton L. Barron (Chicago, 1972), pp. 66–67.

6. Barron, ed., *Blending American,* p. 68.

7. Cited in ibid., p. 59.

8. Ibid., p. 60.

9. Milton Greenberg, "The GI Bill of Rights: Changing the Social, Economic Landscape of the United States," in *Historians on America,* ed. George Clack (Washington, D.C., 2007). (W)

10. Mario Puzo, *The Godfather* (New York, 1972), p. 448.

11. Robert D. Putnam and David E. Campbell, *American Grace: How Religion Divides and Unites Us* (New York, 2010), p. 138.

12. Gallup Polls, cited in ibid., pp. 151–52.

19 TRUE BELIEVERS

1. Cited in Hilton Kramer, "Whittaker Chambers and the Judgment of History," *New Criterion,* Feb. 1997.

2. Sam Tanenhaus, *Whittaker Chambers: A Biography* (New York, 1997), p. 46.

3. G. K. Chesterton, *The Catholic Church and Conversion* (London, 1926), p. 21.

4. C. S. Lewis, *Surprised by Joy: The Shape of My Early Life* (New York, 1955), p. 218.

5. Ibid., p. 219.

6. Arthur Koestler, in *The God That Failed,* ed. Richard Crossman (New York, 2001), p. 23.

7. Whittaker Chambers, *Witness* (New York, 1952), p. 16.

8. Ibid.

9. *The Syllabus of Errors Condemned by Pope Pius IX,* Papal Encyclicals Online. (W)

10. G. K. Chesterton, *The Victorian Age in Literature* (London, 1916), p. 111.

11. C. S. Lewis, *Mere Christianity* (New York, 1956), pp. 31–32.

12. Chesterton, *Catholic Church and Conversion,* cited in Dudley Barker, *G. K. Chesterton* (London, 1973), p. 261, cited in Jay P. Corrin, *G. K. Chesterton & Hillaire Belloc: The Battle Against Modernity* (London, 1981), p. 104.

13. G. K. Chesterton, *Orthodoxy* (London, 1909), p. 232.

14. G. K. Chesterton, in *Illustrated London News,* Nov. 7, 1908.

15. G. K. Chesterton, "Straws in the Winds: Exodus from Europe," *G.K.'s Weekly,* Dec. 28, 1929.

16. Chesterton, *Catholic Church and Conversion,* p. 22.

17. Chambers, *Witness,* p. 196.

18. Jane Reiker, "No Longer Red and Far from Dead, Ex-Communist Margaret Budenz, 71, Enthralls Her Catholic Students," *People,* May 5, 1980. (W)

19. Tanenhaus, *Whittaker Chambers,* p. 468.

20. Joseph Brodsky, "A Commencement Address," *New York Review of Books,* Aug. 16, 1984.
21. Koestler, *God That Failed,* p. 75.

20 "THE GREATEST": MUHAMMAD ALI AND THE DEMYTHOLOGIZING DECADE

1. Tim Dahlberg, "Muhammad Ali, 70, Remains Upbeat in Fight Against Parkinson's Disease," *Seattle Times,* Jan. 16, 2012.
2. David Remnick, *King of the World* (New York, 1998), p. 127.
3. Hisham D. Aidi, *Rebel Music: Race, Empire, and the New Muslim Youth Culture* (New York, 2014), p. 100.
4. Sylviane A. Diouf, *Servants of Allah: African Muslims Enslaved in the Americas* (New York, 1998), p. 207.
5. Ibid., p. 181.
6. Muhammad Ali with Richard Durham, *The Greatest* (New York, 1975), p. 245.
7. Jeff Nilsson, "Religion Steps into the Boxing Ring: Ali in '64," Jan. 21, 2012, *Saturday Evening Post* archives, http://www.saturdayeveningpost.com/2012/01/21/archives. (W)
8. Cited in ibid.
9. Remnick, *King of the World,* p. 221.
10. Cited in ibid.
11. Ali with Durham, *The Greatest,* p. 139.
12. Ibid.
13. Ibid., pp. 140–41.
14. Budd Schulberg, "The Champ," *New York Times Book Review,* Oct. 25, 1998.
15. Cited in Remnick, *King of the World,* pp. 305–6.
16. Philip Shenon, "Mideast Tensions: At Baghdad's Bazaar, Everyone Wants Hostages," *New York Times,* Nov. 26, 1990.
17. In Deborah Caldwell, "Muhammad Ali's New Spiritual Quest," interview with Hana Ali, 2005, www.beliefnet.com. (W)
18. Ali with Durham, *The Greatest,* p. 202.
19. Albert Mohler, "Looking Back: TIME Asks, 'Is God Dead?,'" Sept. 21, 2009. (W)
20. Adam Hochschild, *Half the Way Home: A Memoir of Father and Son* (Boston, 2005), pp. 195–96.
21. *Religious Landscape Survey,* Pew Research Center, Sept. 15, 2014. (W)

21 AMERICAN DREAMING

1. Philip Roth, "Some New Jewish Stereotypes," in Philip Roth, *Reading Myself and Others* (New York, 1985), p. 200. Originally a speech delivered at Loyola University, 1961.
2. *Many Americans Say Other Faiths Can Lead to Eternal Life,* Pew Research Center, Dec. 18, 2008, p. 1. (W)
3. "Which Religions Can Lead to Eternal Life?," table in ibid.
4. "How U.S. Muslims Are Different," Pew Research Center, April 2013. (W)
5. Ibid.

6. "America's Changing Religious Landscape," Pew Research Center, May 5, 2015, http://www.pewforum.org/2015/05/12/americas-changing-religious-landscape/.

7. "Faith in Flux," Pew Research Center, April 27, 2009, rev. Feb. 2011, p. 3. (W)

8. Robert J. Barro, Jason Hwang, and Rachel M. McCleary, *Religious Conversion in 40 Countries,* Harvard University, Cornerstone Research, March 2010. (W)

9. Cited in Elsa Walsh, "Minority Report," *New Yorker,* Aug. 8, 2005.

10. Robert D. Putnam and David E. Campbell, *American Grace: How Religion Divides and Unites Us* (New York, 2010), p. 143.

11. Newt Gingrich, "Why I Became a Catholic," *National Catholic Register,* April 2011.

12. "Faith in Flux," p. 3.

13. Ibid.

14. Susan Jacoby, "The Blessings of Atheism," *New York Times,* Jan. 5, 2013. (W)

15. "America's Changing Religious Landscape," Pew Research Center, May 5, 2015.

16. Ibid.

17. George Gallup, *The Role of the Bible in American Society* (Princeton, N.J., 1990), p. 17.

18. "U.S. Religious Knowledge Survey," Pew Research Center, Sept. 28, 2010. (W)

DARKNESS VISIBLE

1. Cited in Jim Yardley, "A Test of Faith in Brutal Captivity," *New York Times,* Feb. 22, 2015.

2. Sonia Faleiro, "An Attack on Love," *New York Times,* Nov. 2, 2014.

3. Michael Schulson, "Karen Armstrong on Sam Harris and Bill Maher: 'It fills me with despair, because this is the sort of talk that led to the concentration camps,'" Nov. 23, 2014, Salon.com. (W)

4. Ibid.

5. Sunny Hundal, "The Real Threat from the Islamic State Is to Muslims, Not the West," *Al Jazeera,* Aug. 26, 2014. (W)

6. Dean Obeidallah, "The Boko Haram Terrorists Are Not 'Islamic,'" *Daily Beast,* May 12, 2014. (W)

7. "The Hebrew First-Crusade Chronicles: I," in Robert Chazan, *European Jewry and the First Crusade* (Berkeley, 1987), pp. 290–91.

8. "Albert of Aix and Ekkehard of Aura: Emico and the Slaughter of the Rhineland Jews," *Internet Medieval Sourcebook,* ed. Paul Halsall, Fordham University, http://www.fordham.edu/halsall/source/1096jews.asp. (W)

9. Shelby Lin Erdman, Mohammed Tawfeq, and Hamdi Alkshali, "Islamic Extremists Kill 270 in Attack on a Gas Field in Central Syria, Report Says," CNN, July 28, 2014. (W)

10. "Beliefs About Shariah," *The World's Muslims: Religion, Politics and Society,* Pew Research Center, April 30, 2013. (W)

11. Kate Hodal, "Indonesian Atheists Face Battle for Religious Freedom, *Guardian,* May 3, 2012. (W)

12. Joe Cochrane, "Embrace of Atheism Put an Indonesian in Prison," *New York Times,* May 4, 2014. (W)

13. In ibid. (W)

14. Benedict Rogers, "Indonesia's Religious Repression," *Wall Street Journal,* April 7, 2013.

15. William James, *The Varieties of Religious Experience: A Study in Human Nature* (1902), p. 508.

SELECTED BIBLIOGRAPHY

Adams, John, and Thomas Jefferson. *The Adams-Jefferson Letters.* Vols. 1–2. Edited by Lester J. Cappon. Chapel Hill: University of North Carolina Press, 1959.

Aidi, Hisham. *Rebel Music: Race, Empire, and the New Muslim Youth Culture.* New York: Pantheon, 2014.

Ali, Muhammad, with Richard Durham. *The Greatest: My Own Story.* New York: Random House, 1975.

Alighieri, Dante. *La Divina Commedia,* Vol. I, *Inferno.* Edited by Natalino Sapegno. Florence, Italy: *La Nuova Italia Editrice,* 1968.

Appold, Kenneth G. *The Reformation: A Brief History.* London: Wiley-Blackwell, 2011.

Augustine, Saint. *The City of God.* Translated by John Healey. Edinburgh: John Grant, 1909.

———. *Confessions of St. Augustine.* Translated by J. G. Pilkington. New York: Heritage Press. 1963.

———. *Confessions of St. Augustine.* Translated by R. S. Pine-Coffin. New York: Dorset Press, 1961.

———. *Confessions of St. Augustine.* Translated by E. B. Pusey in 1838. London: Chatto & Windus, 1909.

Baer, Yitzhak. *A History of the Jews in Christian Spain.* Vols. 1–2. Translated from the Hebrew by Lewis Schoffman. Philadelphia: Jewish Publication Society of America, 1961.

Bainton, Roland H. *Hunted Heretic: The Life and Death of Michael Servetus, 1511–1553.* Boston: Beacon Press, 1953. Revised edition, Providence: Blackstone Editions, 2011.

Baird, Robert. *Religion in America, or an Account of the Origin, Relation to the State, and Present Condition of the Evangelical Churches in the United States with Notices of Unevangelical Denominations.* New York: Harper & Brothers, 1845.

Barron, Milton L., ed. *The Blending American: Patterns of Intermarriage.* Chicago: Quadrangle Books, 1972.

Bentley, William. *The Diary of William Bentley.* Vols. 3–4. Salem, Mass.: Essex Institute, 1905.

Bethencourt, Francisco. *The Inquisition: A Global History, 1478–1834.* Cambridge, Eng.: Cambridge University Press, 2009.

Bilde, Per. *Flavius Josephus Between Jerusalem and Rome.* Sheffield, Eng.: JSOT Press, 1988.

Booy, David, ed. *Autobiographical Writings by Early Quaker Women.* Hampshire, Eng.: Ashgate Publishing, 2004.

Boyle, Robert. *Selected Philosophical Papers of Robert Boyle.* Edited by M. A. Stewart. New York: Harper & Row, 1979.

Brooks, Peter N., ed. *Reformation Principle and Practice: Essays in Honour of A. G. Dickens.* London: Scolar Press, 1980.

Brown, Peter. *Augustine of Hippo: A Biography.* Berkeley: University of California Press, 1967.

————. *Through the Eye of a Needle: Wealth, the Fall of Rome, and the Making of Christianity in the West, 350–550 AD.* Princeton: Princeton University Press, 2012.

————. *The World of Classical Antiquity.* New York: W. W. Norton, 1989.

Browning, Robert. *The Emperor Julian.* London: Weidenfeld & Nicolson, 1975.

Burckhardt, Jacob. *The Age of Constantine.* Translated by Moses Hadas. London: Routledge & Kegan Paul, 1949.

Butler, Jon. *Awash in a Sea of Faith.* Cambridge, Mass.: Harvard University Press, 1990.

Calcagno, Antonio. *The Philosophy of Edith Stein.* Duquesne, Pa.: Duquesne University Press, 2007.

Carr, Matthew. *Blood and Faith: The Purging of Muslim Spain.* New York: The New Press, 2009.

Carroll, James. *Constantine's Sword: The Church and the Jews.* Boston: Houghton Mifflin, 2001.

Cartwright, Peter. *Autobiography of Peter Cartwright.* Nashville: Abingdon Press. Original edition, Nashville: Pierce & Washabaugh, 1856.

Chambers, Whittaker. *Witness.* New York: Random House, 1952.

Chazan, Robert. *European Jewry and the First Crusade.* Berkeley: University of California Press, 1987.

Chesterton, G. K. *The Catholic Church and Conversion.* New York: Macmillan, 1926.

————. *Orthodoxy.* London: John Lane, Bodley Head, 1909.

Chisnall, Peter. *John Henry Cardinal Newman: A Man of Courage, Conflict, and Conviction.* London: St. Paul's Publishing, 2001.

Chrisman, Miriam Usher. *Conflicting Visions of Reform: German Lay Propaganda Pamphlets, 1519–1530.* Atlantic Highlands, N.J.: Humanities Press International, 1996.

Collins, Roger. *The Arab Conquest of Spain, 710–797.* Oxford, Eng., and Cambridge, Mass.: B. Blackwell, 1989.

Corrin, Jay P. *G. K. Chesterton and Hillaire Belloc: The Battle Against Modernity.* Athens, Ohio: Ohio University Press, 1981.

Crossman, Richard, ed. *The God That Failed.* With a new foreword by David G. Engerman. New York: Columbia University Press, 2001. Original edition, London: Hamilton, 1950.

Curtis, Edith. *Anne Hutchinson: A Biography.* Cambridge, Mass.: Washburn & Thomas, 1930.

Davidson, Ian. *Voltaire in Exile.* New York: Grove Press, 2004.

De Hartog, Jan. *The Peaceable Kingdom.* New York: Atheneum, 1972.

Deakin, Michael A. B. *Hypatia of Alexandria: Mathematician and Martyr.* Buffalo: Prometheus Books, 2007.

Diouf, Sylviane A. *Servants of Allah: African Muslims Enslaved in the Americas.* New York: New York University Press, 1998.

Donne, John. *The Collected English Poems.* Edited by A. J. Smith. New York: Penguin Classics, 1996.

———. *Devotions upon Emergent Occasions, Together with Death's Duel.* Ann Arbor: Ann Arbor Paperbacks, University of Michigan Press, 1959.

———. *Pseudo-Martyr.* Edited by Anthony Raspa. London: McGill-Queen's University Press, 1993.

The Sermons of John Donne. Edited by George R. Potter and Evelyn Simpson. Berkeley: University of California Press, 1962.

Elon, Amos. *The Pity of It All: A Portrait of the German-Jewish Epoch, 1743–1933.* New York: Picador, 2002.

Fell, Margaret. *A declaration and information from us the people of God called Quakers, to the present governors . . .* London: Printed for T. Simmons and R. Wilson, 1660.

———. *For Manasseth ben Israel: The call of the Jewes out of Babylon. . . .* London: Printed for Giles Calvert, 1656.

Ferguson, John. *Pelagius: A Historical and Theological Study.* Cambridge, Eng.: Heffer & Sons, 1956.

Fox, Robin Lane. *Pagans and Christians.* New York: Alfred A. Knopf, 1986.

Freeman, Charles. *The Closing of the Western Mind.* New York: Random House, 2005.

Friedlander, Joseph, compiler, and Alexander Kohut, ed. *The Standard Book of Jewish Verse.* New York: Dodd, 1917.

Gaboriau, Florence. *The Conversion of Edith Stein.* Translated by Ralph McInerney. South Bend, Ind.: St. Augustine's Press, 2002.

Gibbon, Edward. *The Decline and Fall of the Roman Empire.* Vols. 1–3. New York: Random House, Modern Library, 1954.

Ginzburg, Carlo. *The Cheese and the Worms: The Cosmos of a Sixteenth-Century Miller.* Translated from the Italian by John and Anne Tedeschi. Baltimore: Johns Hopkins University Press, 1980.

Godman, Peter. *The Saint as Censor: Robert Bellarmine Between Inquisition and Index.* Boston: Brill, 2000.

Goldstein, Rebecca Newberger. *Betraying Spinoza.* New York: Schocken Books, 2006.

Goldstone, Lawrence and Nancy. *Out of the Flames.* New York: Broadway Books, 2002.

Goodman, Martin. *Mission and Conversion: Proselytizing in the Religious History of the Roman Empire.* Oxford, Eng.: Clarendon Press, 1994.

Hall, Timothy D. *Anne Hutchinson: Puritan Prophet.* Boston: Longman, 2010.

Heine, Heinrich. *The Book of Songs.* East Aurora, N.Y.: Roycrafters, 1903.

———. *The Complete Poems of Heinrich Heine: A Modern English Version.* Translated by Hal Draper. Cambridge, Mass.: Suhrkamp/Insel, Boston, 1982.

———. *Heinrich Heine's Life Told in His Own Words.* Edited by Gustav Karpeles. Translated from the German by Arthur Dexter. New York: Henry Holt, 1893.

———. *The Poems of Heine: Complete.* Translated by Edgar Alfred Bowring, C.B. London: George Bell & Sons, 1889.

Hibbert, Christopher. *The Virgin Queen: Elizabeth I, Genius of the Golden Age.* Reading, Mass.: Perseus Books, 1991.

Hochschild, Adam. *Half the Way Home: A Memoir of Father and Son.* Boston: Mariner Books, 2005.

Hofstadter, Richard. *Anti-Intellectualism in American Life.* New York: Alfred A. Knopf, 1963.

Hunter, Michael, and Daniel Wootton, eds. *Atheism from the Reformation to the Enlightenment.* Oxford, Eng.: Clarendon Press, 1992.

Ingram, Kevin, ed. *The Conversos and Moriscos in Late Medieval Spain and Beyond.* Vol. 1. Boston: Brill, 2009.

Israel, Jonathan I. *Radical Enlightenment: Philosophy and the Making of Modernity, 1650–1750.* Oxford, Eng.: Oxford University Press, 2001.

James, William. *The Varieties of Religious Experience.* New Hyde Park, N.Y.: University Books, 1963.

Jordan, Winthrop. *White Over Black: American Attitudes Toward the Negro, 1550–1812.* Chapel Hill: University of North Carolina Press, 1968.

Kamen, Henry. *The Disinherited: The Exiles Who Created Spanish Culture.* London: Allen Lane, 2007.

———. *Inquisition and Society in Spain in the Sixteenth and Seventeenth Centuries.* London: Weidenfeld & Nicolson, 1985.

Kaplan, Benjamin J. *Divided by Faith: Religions Conflict and the Practice of Toleration in Early Modern Europe.* Cambridge, Mass,: Belknap Press, Harvard University Press, 2007.

Kertzer, David I. *The Kidnapping of Edgardo Mortara.* New York: Alfred A. Knopf, 1997.

———. *The Pope and Mussolini: The Secret History of Pius XI and the Rise of Fascism in Europe.* New York: Random House, 2014.

———. *The Popes Against the Jews.* New York: Alfred A. Knopf, 2001.

Kirsch, Jonathan. *God Against the Gods.* New York: Viking Compass, 2004.

Kunze, Bonnelyn Young. *Margaret Fell and the Rise of Quakerism.* London: Macmillan, 1994.

Lea, Henry Charles. *A History of the Inquisition of the Middle Ages.* Vols. 1–3. New York: Harbor Press, 1955.

———. *A History of the Inquisition of Spain.* Vols. 1–4. New York: AMS Press, 1988.

Lewis, C. S. *Mere Christianity.* New York: Macmillan, 1956.

———. *Surprised by Joy: The Shape of My Early Life.* New York: Harcourt, Brace, 1955.

Lippy, Charles H. *Pluralism Comes of Age: American Religious Culture in the Twentieth Century.* Armonk, N.Y.: M. E. Sharpe, 2000.

Locke, John. *A Letter Concerning Toleration and Other Writings.* Edited by Mark Goldie. Indianapolis: Liberty Fund, 2010.

Marcus Aurelius. *Meditations.* Translated by Christopher Gill. Oxford, Eng.: Oxford University Press, 2013.

Marshall, John. *John Locke, Toleration and Early Enlightenment Culture.* Cambridge, Eng.: Cambridge University Press, 2006.

Mead, Sidney E. *The Lively Experiment: The Shaping of Christianity in America.* New York: Harper & Row, 1963.

Meeks, Wayne A. *The First Urban Christians: The Social World of the Apostle Paul.* New Haven: Yale University Press, 1983.

Monter, William. *Frontiers of Heresy: The Spanish Inquisition from the Basque Lands to Sicily.* Cambridge, Eng.: Cambridge University Press, 1990.

Murphy, Cullen. *God's Jury: The Inquisition and the Making of the Modern World.* Boston: Mariner Books, 2012.

Netanyahu, Benzion. *The Marranos of Spain.* New York: New York Academy for Jewish Research, 1966.

———. *The Origins of the Inquisition in Fifteenth-Century Spain.* New York: Random House, 1995.

Nock, A. D. *Conversion: The Old and the New in Religion from Alexander the Great to Augustine of Hippo.* Oxford, Eng.: Clarendon Press, 1933.

Northrup, Solomon. *Twelve Years a Slave.* New York: Penguin, 2014.

Osler, William. *Michael Servetus.* Baltimore: Lord Baltimore Press, 1909.

Paine, Thomas. *The Thomas Paine Reader.* Edited by Michael Foot and Isaac Kramnick. London: Penguin, 1987.

Parkes, James. *The Conflict of the Church and the Synagogue.* New York: Hermon Press, 1974.

Pérez, Joseph. *The Spanish Inquisition: A History.* Translated by Janet Lloyd. New Haven: Yale University Press, 2005.

Perry, Mary Elizabeth, and Anne J. Cruz, eds. *Cultural Encounters: The Impact of the Inquisition in Spain and the New World.* Berkeley: University of California Press, 1991.

Popkin, Richard H. *Disputing Christianity.* Amherst, N.Y.: Humanity Books, 2007.

Putnam, Robert D., and David E. Campbell. *American Grace: How Religion Divides Us and Unites Us.* New York: Simon & Schuster, 2010.

Raphael, David, ed. *The Expulsion 1492 Chronicles: An Anthology of Medieval Chronicles Relating to the Expulsion of the Jews from Spain and Portugal.* North Hollywood, Calif.: Carmi House Press, 1992.

Remnick, David. *King of the World.* New York: Random House, 1998.

Ross, Isabel. *Margaret Fell: Mother of Quakerism.* London: Longman's, Green, 1949.

Roth, Norman. *Conversos, Inquisitors, and the Expulsion of the Jews from Spain.* Madison: University of Wisconsin Press, 1995.

Roth, Philip. *Reading Myself and Others.* New York: Penguin, 1985.

Ruether, Rosemary. *Faith and Fratricide: The Theological Roots of Anti-Semitism.* New York: Seabury Press, 1974.

Sconza, M. Jean. *History and Literature in Fifteenth-Century Spain: An Edition and Study of Pablo de Santa Maria's* Siete Edades del Mundo. Madison: University of Wisconsin Press, 1991.

Segal, Alan F. *Paul the Convert.* New Haven: Yale University Press, 1990.

Shapiro, Michael. *The Jewish 100: A Ranking of the Most Influential Jews of All Time.* New York: Citadel Press, 1994.

Smith, John Holland. *The Death of Classical Paganism.* New York: Charles Scribner's Sons, 1976.

Spector, Sheila A. *Byron and the Jews.* Detroit: Wayne State University Press, 2010.

Spinoza, Baruch. *The Chief Works of Benedict de Spinoza.* Vols. 1–2. Translated from the Latin by R. H. M. Elwes. London: George Bell & Sons, 1900.

Stein, Edith. *Life in a Jewish Family: Her Unfinished Autobiographical Account.* Translated by Josephine Koeppel, O.C.D. Washington, D.C.: ICS Publications, 1986.

———. *On the Problem of Empathy.* Translated by Waltraut Stein. Washington, D.C.: ICS Publications, 1989.

———. *Woman.* Translated by Freda Mary Oben. Washington, D.C.: ICS Publications, 1996.

Stubbs, John. *John Donne: The Reformed Soul.* New York: Norton, 2007.

Sweet, W. W. *Religion in Colonial America.* New York: Charles Scribner and Sons, 1942.

Tanenhaus, Sam. *Whittaker Chambers: A Biography.* New York: Random House, 1997.

Weil, Jiří. *Mendelssohn Is on the Roof.* New York: Penguin, 1992.

Wickersham, Jane K. *Rituals of Prosecution and the Roman Inquisition of Philo-Protestants in Sixteenth-Century Italy.* Toronto: University of Toronto Press, 2012.

Wills, Garry. *Augustine's Confessions.* Princeton: Princeton University Press, 2011.

———. *Papal Sin: Structures of Deceit.* New York: Doubleday, 2000.

Wilson, A. N. *Paul: The Mind of an Apostle.* London: Sinclair-Stevenson, 1997.

Yerushalmi, Yosef Hayim. *From Spanish Court to Italian Ghetto: Isaac Cardoso, a Study in Seventeenth-Century Marranism and Jewish Apologetics.* New York: Columbia University Press, 1971.

Zweig, Stefan. *The Right to Heresy: Castellio Against Calvin.* Translated by Eden and Cedar Paul. New York: Viking, 1936.

INDEX

A NOTE ABOUT THE AUTHOR

Susan Jacoby is the author of eleven previous books, including *Never Say Die, The Age of American Unreason, The Great Agnostic: Robert Ingersoll and American Freethought,* and *Freethinkers: A History of American Secularism.* She began her career as a reporter for *The Washington Post* and is now an independent scholar specializing in the history of secularism and religious liberty. She lives in New York City. For more information, visit www.susanjacoby.com.

A NOTE ON THE TYPE

This book was set in Adobe Garamond. Designed for the Adobe Corporation by Robert Slimbach (b. 1956), the fonts are based on types first cut by Claude Garamond (ca. 1480–1561). Garamond was a pupil of Geoffroy Tory and is believed to have followed the Venetian models, and it is to him that we owe the letter we now know as "old style."

Typeset by North Market Street Graphics, Lancaster, Pennsylvania
Printed and bound by Berryville Graphics, Berryville, Virginia
Designed by Maggie Hinders

Crowfoot Library
Self Checkout

04:32 PM   2016/06/29

Aug. 8

1. Strange gods : a secular history of conversion
3906514 7637571   Due: 7/20/2016,23:59

Total 1 item(s).

To check your card and renew items
go to www.calgarylibrary.ca
or call 262-2928